SPACE
HAS NO
FRONTIER

To my darling wife Judy

SPACE HAS NO FRONTIER

The terrestrial life and times of Sir Bernard Lovell

John Bromley-Davenport

BENE FACTUM PUBLISHING

Space Has No Frontier

First published in 2013 by
Bene Factum Publishing Ltd
PO Box 58122
London
SW8 5WZ
Email: inquiries@bene-factum.co.uk
www.bene-factum.co.uk

ISBN: 978-1-903071-98-4

Text © John Bromley-Davenport

The rights of John Bromley-Davenport to be identified as the Author of this Work have
been asserted by him in accordance with the Copyright, Designs and Patents Act, 1988.

All rights reserved. This book is sold under the condition that no part of it may be
reproduced, copied, stored in a retrieval system or transmitted in any form or by any
means, electronic, mechanical, photocopying, recording or otherwise without prior
permission in writing of the publisher.

A CIP catalogue record of this is available from the British Library

Cover and text design: www.mousematdesign.com

Print edition printed and bound in Malta on behalf of Latitude Press

Picture credits:
Text photographs: The Royal Society, Punch Limited, Rhod Taylor and the Lovell family.
Picture sections: The Royal Society, Rogers Photo Archive / Argenta Images, Mark
Postlethwaite, Adam Block, Jodrell Bank, Wayne Young, Press Association Images, Vladimir
Kurt, John C. McConnell, Andrea Dale, the Congleton Chronicle, John Bromley-
Davenport and the Lovell family.
Author photograph: Charlotte Bromley-Davenport.

Every effort was made to find the appropriate copyright holder of the pictures in this book. In
some cases this has not been possible and no infringement is intended.

Contents

Acknowledgements

During the two and a half years of research and writing for this book I have received an enormous amount of help from people across the world, without which I could not have written it. My profound thanks to all of them and apologies if I have left anyone out of this array.

Members of the Lovell family, including Bryan Lovell, Judy Spence and Philippa Holmes have been most generous in providing information and photographs. Irene Lamb's memories and photographs have been an invaluable resource and I am very grateful for her constant support. My thanks also go to Janet Eaton, Anthea Hollinshead, Christine Bibby, Raymond and Anne Lowe and Rhod Taylor for a fund of anecdotes and recollections. Michael Ashbrook, Billy and Lizzie Bromley-Davenport, Lavinia and Rose Cholmondeley, Canon Peter Hunt, Anita and Jeffrey Lockett, Brendan Rosse, Geoffrey and Betts Sparrow, Alex, John and Lala Wilbraham have all given liberally of their time to help me.

Francis Graham Smith has been of great assistance with the science, reading the chapters on astronomy and allowing me to raid the glossary of *Pathways To the Universe,* the book he wrote with Bernard Lovell. I hasten to add that any errors on matters scientific are mine alone. At Jodrell Bank Tim O'Brien and Theresa Anderson have been of great assistance. Special thanks are due to three Russian scientists, Vladimir Kurt and Leonid Matveenko of the Russian Academy of Sciences, and Roald Sagdeev, now at the University of Maryland, USA. I am very grateful to Baron Martin Rees of Ludlow and Professor Brian Cox for allowing me to quote from their own tributes to Bernard Lovell's memory. My thanks, too, to Eliza Manningham-Buller for her insight into the stresses of being a Reith Lecturer.

Without the help of professional archivists the task of sifting through the mass of material would have been impossible; in this connection I have been greatly assisted by James Peters, at the John Ryland's Library, Manchester, Keith Moore, Jennifer Kren and the staff of the Royal Society, Paul Stevenson, Assistant Head of the DBI KI Records at the Ministry of

Defence, and numerous others at the Imperial War Museum, the National Archive at Kew and the British Library (amusingly situated opposite O'Neill's Irish Pub in the Euston Road).

I am also extremely grateful to my agent, Michael Sissons, whose encouragement has been unfailing, Fiona Petheram, Tim Binding and all at Peters Fraser and Dunlop and Tim Guinness, and Auriol Griffith-Jones for her superb and meticulous indexing. I must also acknowledge with gratitude my publisher Anthony Weldon for having faith in the project and Dominic Horsfall whose help as editor has been invaluable.

None of this would have been possible without the friendship, the extraordinary memory, the prolific writing and documenting and the sheer wit and interest of the subject himself, Sir Bernard Lovell. I hope that my efforts provide a fitting memorial for a remarkable man.

Finally I must thank my wife, Judy, for her constant support, and constructive analysis and all the members of my family for their help and encouragement.

John Bromley-Davenport
4th October 2013

CHAPTER ONE

The Ages of Man

"They said we could stay for two weeks and sixty-five years later we are still here!" Sir Bernard Lovell is ninety-seven years old; on a glorious spring morning, warmly blanketed and muffled, he is being pushed across the lawn at Jodrell Bank, a frail figure in his wheelchair; his eyes are dim and, against the radiant blue of the sky, he can see only the outline of the great Radio Telescope, which he created and which bears his name; but his demeanour is sprightly, his mind is sharp and his conversation is full of wit and interest. For more than half a century the instrument has soared majestically above the Cheshire plain; the intricate structure, the delicately woven web of girders, the gigantic paraboloid with its reflecting surface of sheet steel and the massive supporting towers, rotating on railway tracks, combine to endow it with an ethereal beauty. 20 miles away to the south-west, visitors teeming up the steep slopes of a rocky outcrop, crowned by the ancient monument of Beeston Castle, gaze down in wonder upon this modern monument to scientific enterprise, transfixed by the sight of the great white bowl as it tilts towards them, gleaming in the sun.

The gentle hum of motors and the grinding of wheels on tracks disturb the stillness of the air at Jodrell. It is 8th April 2011. Elaborate preparations have been made for Sir Bernard's first visit to the newly opened Discovery Centre, which, before long, will also be teeming with visitors. The observatory he founded with Manchester University has been at the hub of his life; it has made him famous throughout the world; his enthusiasm for the Telescope and its work has never waned; his desire to share and disseminate his knowledge and beliefs is as keen as ever; and the contribution which his creation has made to man's understanding of the Universe is immense.

The occasion is one for rejoicing. It has just been announced that, in the face of fierce competition from at home and abroad, this centre of research has been chosen to lead a multinational project, to construct the largest and most powerful observatory in the world. The Square Kilometre Array of three thousand radio telescopes will be built in the Australian and

South African deserts; it will have the power to explore the deepest mysteries of the Universe; it will greatly increase the ability of scientists to probe the first moments of time. Only three years ago Jodrell Bank was under threat from government cuts; today, the future of the facility is secure. The opening of the Discovery Centre provides the perfect opportunity to celebrate the institution and the drive and energy of the man who gave it life.

Generations of Lovells are buried in the village churchyards of Oldland Common, Bitton and Kingswood, situated between the cities of Bristol and Bath, whose inhabitants were described in less than flattering terms by John Wesley in a letter to Mr. D in 1738:

> Few persons have lived long in the West of England who have not heard of the colliers of Kingswood; a people famous, from the beginning hitherto, for neither fearing God nor regarding man; so ignorant of the things of God that they seemed but one remove from the beasts that perish; and therefore utterly without desire of instruction, as well as without the means of it.[1]

History does not relate whether any Lovells were numbered amongst the ungodly; but the moral tone of the village was greatly improved a year later as a result of Wesley's interventions and the foundation of a school:

> The scene is already changed. Kingswood does not now, as a year ago, resound with cursing and blasphemy. It is no more filled with drunkenness and uncleanness and the idle diversions that naturally lead thereto. It is no longer full of wars and fightings, of clamour and bitterness, of wrath and envyings. Peace and love are there. Great numbers of the people are mild, gentle, and easy to be entreated. They 'do not cry, neither strive'; and hardly is their 'voice heard in the streets'; or, indeed, in their own wood; unless when they are at their usual evening diversion – singing praise unto God their saviour.[2]

At the beginning of the twentieth century Kingswood and Oldland Common were still isolated settlements, untouched by the sprawling growth of the city which was to swallow their identities and to replace their rural charms with the urban dormitories of today.

Bernard's maternal grandmother, Emily Adams, was born at Oldland, in 1851. She and her husband Alfred kept the village grocery shop and Bernard's mother, Emily Laura, was the youngest of their four children.

Following the premature death of Alfred, his widow continued to run the business, with a benevolence towards her impoverished customers which shocked her children when they examined the books after her death, in 1931, and saw, with incredulity, the extensive list of outstanding debtors. Many years later, Emily's unsophisticated attitude to financial control was to find an echo in the approach of her grandson to such matters.

The Lovell and Adams families were preeminent in Oldland and played a central role in the activities of the village. They shared interests in music and sport, singing together in operettas, performing the Messiah each Christmas and displaying athletic prowess on the cricket field. So numerous were the Adams sportsmen that they were able to form their own cricket team and to take on all comers in an annual match. Nor did Laura Adams let the family down; wearing voluminous skirts, she captained the Kingsland women's team; perhaps the Lovell family brass band trumpeted her successes on the field, in those pre-Great War days, when female participation in sport was a rarity.

Barely a stone's throw from the Adams store, Gilbert Lovell ran a small trading business specializing in the supply of accessories for horse-drawn vehicles and in the sale of a new fangled form of transport, the bicycle. He was four years older than Laura, who was born in 1885; in that closely interwoven society he must have known her from infancy and no doubt observed her with increasing interest as she grew into womanhood. They married in 1910 and lived at first with Mrs. Adams, above the shop. It was here that their only son was born on 31st August 1913.

The child was named Alfred Charles Bernard. The first two names were selected in honour of members of the family. Bernard, the name by which he was always known, had been chosen a few weeks before his birth, during a chapel service in which his parents sang *Jesus thou joy of loving hearts*, Ray Palmer's translation of a twelfth-century hymn; so enchanted were they by its sentiments that they determined to name any boy child after the original author, the French Abbott Bernard de Clairvaux. No doubt it was the Gallic connection which gave rise to Bernard Lovell's habitual pronunciation of his name in the French manner, emphasising a flat 'aa' in the second syllable.

Gilbert Lovell was a man of uncompromising faith and values. He was largely self-educated and supplemented the rather basic schooling of the 1890s by his voracious appetite for reading. He could quote long tracts from the King James Bible, which provided sure foundations both for his beliefs and for his considerable abilities as an orator. He was a prolific lay preacher, much in demand at Methodist chapels in the district; he delivered three or four sermons every Sunday, cycling or driving his pony and trap in all weathers from one venue to the next. One of Bernard's fondest childhood memories was the sound of his father's voice, reciting lengthy passages of scripture and rehearsing his sermons as he paced up and down the garden in the early morning.

Although Gilbert was generally a very kind and an indulgent father, transgressions could induce less than happy moments, when quotations from holy writ were used to rebuke the boy in stern biblical tones, with frequent invocations of damnation and deliverance from the fires of eternity. In spite of these sometimes terrifying injunctions, the influence of a strict religious upbringing and the joys of regular Sunday worship were always remembered with affection and gratitude by his son, whose love of the Church and especially of its music endured throughout his life, even though his father's literal acceptance of concepts such as hellfire and the Creation were ultimately rejected.

Bernard's childhood experience of religion was the foundation of a faith in the spiritual nature of man and existence, which was not to be dimmed, in later life, by his voyages into scientific discovery. As his awareness of the physical properties of the Universe and its origins grew, he developed an understanding which suggested to him that there is no frontier to existence and that no final resolution to the mysteries of time and space can be arrived at. As he grew older, his consciousness of man's inability to plumb the ultimate depths of knowledge confirmed him in the view that the issues of faith and the existence of a 'Great Architect' could never be discounted or disproved.

Soon after their son was born, Gilbert and Laura moved from the shop to a small single-storey house nearby. It was surrounded by fields; the village was exactly 7 miles from both Bath and Bristol, but the roads and lanes were quiet, motor cars were rarely seen, and the traffic, consisting almost entirely of bicycles and horse-drawn vehicles, presented few dangers to Bernard and his playmates. It was a peaceful place; there was no public transport and nothing in the way of organised entertainment, so parents allowed their children out from dawn to dusk; they could wander about the lanes and into the fields and woods enjoying the simple pleasures of childhood; bowling hoops, kicking a football, flying kites or climbing trees, before returning home late in the day with bouquets of wild flowers for their mothers and the fruits of the hedgerows in their season, to adorn their tea tables.

There was nothing in this existence or in the histories of the Lovell or Adams families to suggest that the latest addition to their ranks was destined for anything more in life than the peaceful tenor of the ways of his forefathers. Neither an aptitude for science nor indications of great scholarship were readily apparent in the parents, their relations or their ancestors; nothing in their background suggested that their boy's intellect or ambitions would differ from theirs in any way; and when his school days began no one was in the least surprised or concerned that he showed scant interest in the lessons. Yet today, on the fields behind their little house, is a great seat of learning which bears his name: across a time span which connects two centuries, the Sir Bernard Lovell School, provides a link between his early education in a tiny village school and the extremities of mankind's scientific endeavour, epitomised by his life's work and the Lovell Telescope.

Back at Jodrell, as Bernard and his companions make their way to lunch in the new restaurant, the Telescope, mirrored in the glass doors of the Discovery Centre, provides a magnificent and appropriate backdrop to the scene. After lunch he will be driven home to The Quinta, where they are expecting a visit from a dear friend, the pianist Rose Cholmondeley, who will play Chopin while he recovers from the exertions of the morning. Perhaps for a moment, as the music wafts through the house, his mind will cast back ninety years to just such a spring morning in Gloucestershire; perhaps for a moment, he will picture a seven-year-old child closing the wicket gate of the cottage garden; perhaps for a moment he will contemplate the astonishment which a glimpse of the future would have brought to the little boy as he walked along the lane, "with his satchel and shining morning face, creeping like snail unwillingly to school".

CHAPTER TWO

Unwillingly to School

The teachers at the village school might have been forgiven for concluding that the Lovell boy's lack of attention to his studies indicated a slothful and lethargic nature. But the sharpest of schoolmasters may be deceived by appearances and nothing could have been further from the truth. At a young age, Bernard was capable of assiduous application to those activities which stimulated his imagination. Once his interest was aroused, he devoted himself to the mastery of whatever took his fancy with diligence and determination; whether it was music, cricket or the study of the natural world and the countryside, he worked tenaciously to perfect his knowledge and skill to the summit of his ability. In later life, this single-minded approach was to see him through many apparently intractable difficulties, even if those around him sometimes felt that his fortitude amounted to stubbornness, as he would have been the first to concede.

Gilbert and Laura were born into families consumed by the love of music and cricket and, from his earliest youth, their son was imbued with their enthusiasm. A piano teacher was engaged and Bernard learned quickly, so that, before long, he was able to play for the family, when they gathered for Sunday prayers, and to take a leading role in morning assembly at the village school. His keenness for the piano continued until the age of ten, but at that stage constant practice and the laborious scales became a drudge and he neglected the music lessons. His Uncle Alfred Adams was an accomplished musician and the regular organist in Chapel. When he heard that his nephew had given up the piano, he suggested that he might enjoy playing the organ and offered to teach him. Bernard was an enthusiastic pupil and Uncle Alfred proved to be an inspired instructor; soon he played well enough to deputise at divine service and his love of the instrument was further enhanced by visits to Bristol with another uncle, who took him to organ recitals in the Colston Hall.

For most small boys, the pleasure of kicking or hitting a ball is irresistible and Bernard was no exception. In this his father offered every encouragement and when the business of the day was done he would never tire of bowling at him and passing on his skill and knowledge. His mother continued to play cricket for Kingsland Ladies and Gilbert and many members of the family on both sides would turn out for the men of Oldland. Watching the grown-ups at play in the cricket field further kindled his love affair with the game and on one memorable occasion, when still a small boy, he was commandeered into playing for the Adams family team on the grounds that he qualified because his mother was born an Adams. History does not relate how he fared, but it was an experience which he treasured in his memory.

Bernard's parents, Gilbert and Laura, in later life, outside their home at Oldland Common.

It was during these years of primary school that the seed of another lifelong passion was sown; it was a seed which was to grow into a plant of great significance. On 14th November 1922 the voice of Arthur Burrows was heard broadcasting the recently formed BBC's very first news bulletin from Marconi House in the Strand. Shortly afterwards, a teacher at the school told her young charges about an extraordinary new invention, 'the wireless', which enabled someone speaking in London to be heard 120 miles away in Bristol. Bernard was intrigued and began to ask questions. Before long, his parents were persuaded to install aerials and rudimentary receiving equipment at home and, with a pair of bulky headphones clamped to his ears, he heard the crackly broadcasts for himself. The excitement of listening to music or the spoken word over the airwaves spurred him into further investigation and with the help of a journal on the new science, he taught himself how to build a small receiver with a piece of wire and a crystal. The sounds emanating from this little contraption were intermittent and barely audible, but the thrill of achievement which he derived was immense. These first efforts were soon followed by further study and the development of a much more sophisticated system. By the time he reached his eleventh birthday he had built a set which was able both to receive and to transmit signals. This third great enthusiasm did nothing to improve his academic performance as he transferred from primary to secondary school.

Kingswood School was founded in 1921 and was conveniently situated not far from Oldland Common. Quite where Bernard would have completed his education had it not been for the timely opening of this establishment, is unclear; probably he would have remained at the village school until he reached the age of fourteen;[3] he would then have gone in to trade with his father and one of the great minds of the twentieth century would have been lost to the world. He left the village school and moved to Kingswood at the beginning of 1924, when he was aged ten and a half. The new school was only 2 miles away and all the year round, and in all weathers, he would bicycle there, often in the company of his cousin Jack, who was in the same class. In the summer they would ride with their cricket equipment strapped onto their backs and every hour not taken up by lessons would be filled with games and practice.

When it became too dark to play Bernard cycled home and hurried to his room to work on his latest radio project. Gilbert had recently installed a generator which drove a dynamo and provided the house with electricity, a welcome improvement on the candles and oil lamps of earlier years. The machinery enraptured his son and, when he could tear himself away from his wireless, there was nothing he enjoyed more than tinkering with the motor and the switches, constantly endeavouring to improve the performance and flexibility of the supply. From his intricate work on these machines he learned a great deal about improvisation and making do with whatever materials were to hand and his knowledge about electricity grew in parallel with his increasing understanding of the mysteries of radio. School homework was not high on the agenda.

A major fire at Kingswood School in the 1960s destroyed all their records. Fortunately we can gain some insight into the progress of A.C.B. Lovell from his reports, some of which were kept by his parents and are now to be found in the Lovell archives at the Royal Society. The comments were cryptic, but informative. Spring term, 1924, Arithmetic: 'Weak'; Summer 1924, Arithmetic: 'Needs to try harder'; Autumn 1925, Physics: 'Capable of doing much better'; Spring 1926, Arithmetic: 'Weak'; but his physics had improved, if only to the modest extent of being described: 'Fair'. From being thirty-second out of thirty-four in the class during his first term, he continued to bump along the bottom for several years.

Not that his parents were greatly concerned by his lack of scholastic ability. They took the enlightened view that, so long as their son was actively pursuing topics and activities that interested him and that kept him out of mischief, the glittering prizes of academe were of no great importance. After all, the expectation remained that Bernard would join his father in the business where his knowledge of wireless and his rapidly improving engineering and technical skill would be great assets. With this in mind Gilbert began to supply radio equipment and changed the name of the firm from 'Oldland Cycles' to 'The Oldland Cycle and Radio Company.' For Bernard this alteration was an additional encouragement to end his schooldays as soon as possible and to devote the rest of his life to wireless and cricket.

Major M.J. Eaton, the headmaster of Kingswood, believed that regular use of the cane was essential for the maintenance of discipline. A quick rap on the knuckles would be administered for minor infringements of the rules; more serious offences would result in a formal rebuke and a public flogging in front of the entire school; the boys and girls were ordered to muster in the assembly hall to witness punishment, entirely for their own good. This regime would be regarded, today, as serious child abuse; but in 1925 Major Eaton was no different from most headmasters of the time; no doubt he had the best interests of his charges at heart, even when he was beating them; as he was fond of saying, it pained him to give just as much as it pained them to receive.

For all this, Eaton seems to have been a perceptive man who was sensitive to the abilities and promise of his pupils. In Bernard's case, in spite of the low level of achievement, he was impressed with his potential and he put pressure on Gilbert and Laura to encourage their son to remain at school beyond his fifteenth birthday and to take his school certificate. So it was that, in the autumn of 1928, instead of embarking on life in his father's firm, the reluctant student stayed on for one more year, determined that it should be his last. His determination was turned on its head by three crucial events.

As a lay preacher Gilbert Lovell would often receive visits from friends and acquaintances who wanted to discuss religious affairs or to seek spiritual guidance. A man called Champion was a regular visitor and one evening, soon after the start of this final year of school, he happened to call and found Bernard toiling over some incomprehensible mathematics homework; he was a schoolmaster by profession and as luck would have it this was his subject. Seeing his friend's son scratching his head and showing signs of exasperation, he asked the young man what was troubling him. He must have been a very good teacher, because he looked at the problem and, in no time at all, was able both to demonstrate the solution and to endow it with a clarity which was a revelation to the struggling student. A piece of work which had seemed dense and tedious was suddenly revealed to have a logical beauty that had never occurred to him; in the space of half an hour a completely new approach to mathematics was unveiled. The following morning, to the amazement of everyone, including his master, the boy regarded as the weakest in the class was the only one who had solved the problem; more important than that, it was clear that he understood it, even if they had no idea how he had come to do so. Never again did he struggle with the subject; his eyes had been opened and, for the first time, he began to enjoy it and to relish the challenges it presented.

Bernard had been brought up in a strict Methodist tradition and Sundays were dedicated to worship and to the glory of God. Years of sitting on a hard seat, being harangued, often at great length, by a succession of pulpit thumping evangelical preachers had rather taken the edge off his enjoyment of Chapel. Except when he was busy at the organ, he would relieve the monotony by surreptitiously reading a book, which he would bring secreted in his sheet music, anxiously watching out, lest his father should observe his lack of devotion. One Sunday, not long after the Champion episode, there was a visiting preacher, whose sermon suddenly whisked his concentration away from the book and engrossed his attention. The preacher's identity is long forgotten as is the text to which he was preaching; perhaps it was Genesis and the Creation, or St. John's sight of a new heaven and a new earth, in Revelation. Whatever it was, it led him to speak of Albert Einstein, relativity, the speed of light, and the relationship between time and space. The concepts he talked about had not previously crossed Bernard's horizon; they immediately excited his curiosity and imagination and awoke in him an embryonic attraction to science, which was soon to develop into a great passion. These two incidents, combined perhaps with a growing maturity, resulted in greater application and much improved results; but it was a third event in that autumn of 1928 which led, quite by chance, to a Damascene conversion and to a complete transformation in his outlook.

One morning, during school assembly, the master in charge of physics, Charles Howard, announced that he was taking a party of boys to a lecture to be given by Professor A.M. Tyndall, the head of physics at Bristol University; those who wished to come were to sign up at once. The prospect of escaping from an afternoon of lessons needed no second invitation and A.C.B. Lovell's name was one of the first on the list. Although Bristol was only 7 miles away, Bernard had rarely been there; his visits to the Colston Hall recitals and trips to cricket matches at Bath and Bristol were among his very few excursions beyond the environs of Oldland and Kingswood, so the expedition immediately took on the air of an adventure. His first sight of the University and the great physics laboratory, recently created through the generosity of the tobacco magnate Herbert Henry Wills, were stimulating enough even before he entered the lecture theatre; there he was stunned by the grandeur of the enormous room, the raised seating and an array of equipment the like of which he had never seen. When Professor Tyndall began his lecture, entitled 'The Electric Spark', Bernard was transported to a new world. In later years he never tired of recounting the experience of that lecture:

> There were electric sparks raging across the theatre, the hissing arc in the epidiascope projected light images onto the walls, he beamed ultra violet light across his teeth showing up the false ones, which looked almost black alongside the whiteness of his own, infra red rays were focused by a mirror and there was the dynamic energy of Tyndall himself. It all combined to create a mesmerizing effect. Many years later I discovered that he gave this as the Christmas Lecture at the Royal Institution. I think we witnessed the dress rehearsal.[4] As I walked home from the tram stop at Kingswood, I gazed at the brilliance of the stars, with fresh eyes and thought, for the first time about the heavens and our place in the Universe.

That evening all his dreams of an early departure from school to join his father's business evaporated, in the flash of the dazzling lighting effects. From the moment he left the lecture theatre he nurtured one overriding ambition, from which he never deviated for the next three years. He resolved to continue his education, to gain a place at Bristol University and to study physics under Professor Tyndall.

CHAPTER THREE

Bristol

The first hurdle to be overcome was breaking the news of his conversion to Gilbert and Laura. Just as Bernard had eagerly anticipated joining The Oldland Cycle and Radio Company, his father had looked forward to taking him on; with his knowledge of business and his son's technical expertise, the future looked promising. Whatever the initial disappointment may have been, it was fleeting and their support for their son's new ambitions quickly became as keen as it had been for his old ones.

The second hurdle was to apply himself at school, although this presented very little difficulty. Throughout his life, he was to show that once his interest was aroused, an unshakeable determination would ignite within him and drive him to overcome every obstacle. Now that he had set his sights on the University the need to devote his energies to his work was no exception. The tenor of his school reports altered from the less than enthusiastic examples already related to expressions of strong approval: 'Weak' and 'Needs to try harder' were replaced by 'Very good indeed' and 'Worked well'; 'Capable of doing much better' was proved to have been an accurate prophecy. Before long he had reached the top of his class and, in the summer of 1929, he gained credits in every subject of the School Certificate and thus qualified to remain at the school for another two years. That autumn, with the firm encouragement of Major Eaton and the continued support of his family, he moved confidently into the sixth form.

E.R. Brown, his new mathematics master, now became an important influence in his life. Bernard admired him greatly and the two formed a friendship, which was to endure long after both of them left Kingswood. In that sheltered community, Brown led a somewhat irregular life, being divorced, agnostic and a socialist, a combination which his young pupil found as riveting as it was unfamiliar. He often visited the Lovells and, perhaps surprisingly, got on extremely well with Gilbert who might have been expected to find such a man an anathema. His freedom of thought, his knowledge of philosophy and his political views were novel and exciting inspirations which helped to develop Bernard's intellectual curiosity; the stimulation they provided encouraged him to read extensively and to question received wisdom on topics well beyond the boundaries of the subject Brown was teaching him.

It was not, however, a case of all work and no play; he still found time for his old interests, including cricket. He was a good all-rounder, a seam bowler who generally batted at number six. As captain of the first eleven he helped to build up a team, which achieved good results, although his report at Easter 1931 contained Brown's comment: 'Should do well but must definitely not think of cricket when he is doing mathematics and science'. He evidently heeded this injunction because, some weeks after his last day at Kingswood, at the end of the summer term, he was overjoyed to learn that three years of hard work had been rewarded with a Higher School Certificate in physics, chemistry and mathematics. His results were so good that he was offered a place to read physics at Bristol, in the autumn, and was awarded a scholarship in the then princely sum of £60 per annum.[5] For a young man whose education had got off to such an unpromising start, this was a wonderful achievement.

Writing in 1927, H.V. Morton's impression of Bristol was that of "a city as fascinating as London, Bristol hides itself up alleys just as London does and is as generous with the unexpected; with sudden glimpses of old things; queer old buildings; alluring doorways, and – always – the sight of a ship lying landlocked between two streets."[6] Ships sailed into the heart of the medieval city, as they had done for centuries, and moored alongside warehouses and tramways. Over the River Avon hung the Clifton Suspension Bridge and the cathedral, the university and the massive tower of the physics laboratory, built in the grounds of the Royal Fort, rose majestically above the skyline. The centre of Bristol was destroyed by the Luftwaffe between November 1940 and April 1941; but in 1931, for a boy from a quiet country village, the university with the city which surrounded it was a magical kingdom. He could hardly believe his luck.

During his days as a student Bernard lived at home. Every morning he walked 2 miles to catch a train and then from Bristol station to the university and the lecture theatre which had so overwhelmed him three years before. His main honours course was physics but, during the first two years he also studied pure and applied mathematics, reverting full time to physics in the final year. Each evening he made the return journey to Oldland and then burnt the midnight oil with his books, wrestling with the beautiful mysteries of classical physics and mathematics. With only six students on his course, there was no shortage of space in the laboratories and no shortage of individual attention from the distinguished members of the faculty with whom they had daily contact for the next three years. He quickly struck up a close bond with Tyndall, who developed great respect for his abilities, in spite of Bernard's occasional tendency to allow impatience to get the better of him and to become somewhat irritable with the Professor and his ways.

Most notable among the other members of staff were the Professor of Theoretical Physics, Lennard-Jones, and his successor, in the final year, Professor Neville Mott who was to win the Nobel Prize for Physics in 1977. In a paper he wrote for the university archives many years later, Bernard recorded the transition from the old way to the new and conveyed something of the excitement he experienced in the physics department during this era of rapidly advancing scientific knowledge:

> The transference from the classical approach of Lennard-Jones to the modern wave mechanical and quantum outlook of Mott was staggering to a student beginning his third year. These years were the ones of the great discoveries in nuclear physics. The number of known particles was increased by the discovery of the positive electron and the neutron. It was quite usual for Skinner or Gurney to come to the lecture room carrying the issue of Nature which had arrived that morning and introduce us to something entirely new – such as the discovery of artificial radioactivity![7]

From the beginning of his time at Bristol, Bernard was doggedly single-minded that work must be his priority and in obedience to this resolve he even sacrificed his beloved cricket. One afternoon during his first term, he was in the library working on a problem set by his mathematics tutor James Vint, when he was approached by K.E.W. Ridley, the captain of the Bristol cricket team.

"Lovell," said Ridley, "I hear you are quite a good cricketer; you will, of course want to join the university team. We begin practice in the new year."

"I'm very sorry," replied Bernard, "I've come to university to work."

"Don't be so stupid," retorted Ridley. "The man who set you the problem you're working on bowls for us." But Bernard was immovable. Reflecting on this decision in later years, he found it hard to understand and probably regretted the missed opportunity, especially as there were other distractions from the tyranny of work to which he did succumb; it seems highly likely that he could have played cricket and still attained his academic goals.

Soon after his arrival at Bristol he struck up a friendship which was to have profound consequences. He knew Deryck Chesterman as one of his fellow students in the physics department; Deryck came and sat down next to him one pleasant autumn day, whilst he was eating his packed lunch in the garden of the Royal Fort. Bernard offered him an apple and they struck up a conversation which quickly revealed that they shared a mutual love of music. From that moment they were firm friends and spent much of their leisure time together. Deryck's background was very different from that of his new companion. He came from a well-to-do middle class family in Bath, where his father was a prominent figure and had served as mayor. He had been privately educated and was destined for Cambridge, until the exigencies of the depression frustrated his ambition and he had to settle for Bristol, which he regarded as second-best; this was in marked contrast to Bernard for whom the university was the fulfilment of his dreams. Fortunately Deryck had an optimistic temperament and he determined to make the best of it; he became and remained a lifelong companion and Bernard's closest male friend.

Not long after they met, Deryck suggested that they should attend an afternoon concert at the Pump Room in Bath. Tickets were obtained and Bernard was invited to lunch with Deryck's family before the event. That lunch provided an even more significant encounter than the shared picnic in the Royal Fort gardens. Deryck's fifteen-year-old sister Joyce was there. A lanky girl in a Guides uniform, which was covered in badges, she paid no more attention to Bernard than he did to her, fetching him a glass and bolting her lunch before rushing back to school; little did either suspect what fate had in store for them.

Much as he was enthralled by his studies, Bernard was not always the model student and sometimes let his ideas and enthusiasms run away with him. This was especially true when topics such as radio and electronics were on the agenda and his knowledge and expertise were ahead of those who were doing the teaching; he could be intolerant of their failings and had an annoying habit of butting in to put them right. Naturally this was something of an irritation to lecturers and tutors one of whom retorted: "Perhaps you would like to take over the lecture!" During his second year at the university Bernard kept a diary which reveals a spiky edge to his character.[8] The entry for November 1st 1932 records: "I objected to Dr. Lightfoot's method for demonstrating the motion of a particle at which point he said, well perhaps you will be good enough to demonstrate yours. I accepted the challenge." The reception of this acceptance by the other students is not recorded.

Even Tyndall was not immune from criticism. On 4th February 1933 he wrote: "I wish physics lecturers would tell us something we didn't know already. This morning we had Powell talking about particles as though we were ten-year-olds. Tyndall seems afraid to put a mathematical symbol on the board (I have already given him my views on this) and Sucksmith is doing thermionic valves!"[9] On 26th April Tyndall came in for further flack: "Tyndall is lecturing slower than ever with more 'ahs' and 'ums' than I can count."

In later life Bernard's recollection of his years at Bristol was one of constant work and of "being seized with a passion for physics". The diary reveals a less even picture of his life as a student; on the one hand, it shows that he often felt beset by trials and difficulties; on the other, it reveals that the work was not as unrelenting as his later memories suggest, with distractions being provided on many fronts, and particularly by music and cricket. There were certainly times when he was under a great deal of pressure and his account shows that he frequently became depressed and frustrated. On October 12th 1932: "Some days I feel possessed with a terrible feeling of depression. I had it at Easter – a general feeling of discontent." The following day he attended a German lecture, but the lecturer failed to turn up; "feeling much better and happier" he wrote; whether this was a consequence of not being subjected to the German lecture is unclear. On November 19th 1932 he was "in a really terrible state. I have absolutely no inclination to do anything whatsoever. I force myself to work because I must do something. But how terrible it all is. May it pass quickly and not return so often." But there were days when the

Working on a transformer at Bristol, circa 1935.

depression lifted and his spirits soared: "October 21 Physical Society presidential address 'Cosmic Rays.' Very interesting and enjoyable." The next day he was "astounded and amazed at the beauty of nature. Oh that these moments would stay longer with me." On February 4th 1933 he felt "exceptionally ill and worn out". The tenth was "a really terrible day the like of which I do not wish to see again. Spent all day with Venn [Harold Venn, the laboratory assistant] and Griff trying to make a spiral. Tremendously exasperated. Venn very annoyed and swearing. Finish up in same position as at start, with no spiral." And the next day: "Still feel most provoked and frustrated. Dropped pen and smashed nib in Powell's lecture. This is Dad's. Missed 18.50 train. What an ending to the week."

The strains of student life were clearly shared by others and tragedy struck the Faculty on 16th February 1933, when a chemistry student called Fysh hanged himself in the cloakroom. This was a dreadful shock to all the undergraduates, and Bernard, who records seeing the body laid out on the floor, describes a terrible atmosphere the following day with very few students about.

His own tiredness was to a certain extent self-inflicted and arose in part from his perennial passion for cricket. The Bodyline series between England and Australia, was taking place during these winter months; so after making the daily journeys to and from Bristol and working all day, he would slave over his books late into the night and then wake early, and tune in his home built wireless equipment, to listen to the test matches being broadcast from the other side of the world; he then reported detailed accounts of each day's play in the diary and commented, with great interest, on the growing diplomatic row between the two countries, about leg theory and the bowling of Harold Larwood.

In order to counteract the strength of the Australian batting line-up, and especially Donald Bradman, Douglas Jardine, the England captain, decided that his fast bowlers should concentrate on bowling short and on the leg stump, forcing the batsman to fend off the ball and risk sending a catch to the strong leg side field arrayed behind him. During the third Test Match at Adelaide, Woodfull, the Australian captain, received a severe blow under the heart and Oldfield was struck on the head and suffered a fracture to his skull. The Australian press and public were outraged and Bernard's diary comments provide an interesting English perspective from 10,000 miles away. The cricketing entries are punctuated with enthusiastic musical notes:

2nd December. The 1st test a joyous day. Begins with England 479 for six. Ends with Concert Yehudi Menhuin the 15 year old violin prodigy. Really unbelievable.

16th January. During the third test Oldfield scored 41 and then knocked out by Larwood. Amazing trouble over leg theory bowling Papers full of Woodful-Warner[10] incident. Seems to be serious trouble brewing.

21st January. Squabble over leg theory bowling reaches a head. At the end of last week Aussies sent a cable to MCC about 'body line' bowling accusing the tourists of unsporting play and that friendly relations between England and Australia were likely to be upset. Monday MCC sent a smashing reply which has apparently deeply impressed the Aussies. MCC stand behind Jardine and express willingness to cancel the remainder of the tour (but with deep reluctance). Makes Aussies look very small and childish. Further developments awaited with keen interest. But what a ridiculous situation.

5th February. Leg theory squabble continues. On Tuesday the Board of Control sent a conciliatory reply but MCC replied with an ultimatum that the word 'unsportsmanship' be withdrawn from the original. Even Cabinet ministers are now involved.

15th February. 51 runs for the Ashes this is wonderful. Met Chesterman off bus. Terribly excited about symphony concert. Mozart's 'Jupiter' and then Schnabel in the Emperor Concerto. Too wonderful for words.

16th February. Woke to the news 'Victory by 6 wickets'.

9th March. Alfred Cortot. Sonata in B minor Op 53 Chopin. It is impossible to say anything. Surely it is no ordinary human being who can play like this. The wonderful heights of Schnabel are undoubtedly surpassed.

The Bodyline row subsided as the test series progressed, but it rankled with the Australians for many years and led to changes in the laws of cricket which brought an early end to the short life of leg theory.

Once the test series was over, the extra sleep and the onset of "wonderful spring weather and the supreme glory of the morning" seem to have induced a much more cheerful frame of mind and he wrote on April 19th: "Finished treatise on high frequency resistance. I am tremendously pleased about this and regard it as a triumph. Never thought I should do it. The task seemed insurmountable." And on 25th April: "A IIa in Statics. III in Dynamics. Expected this but rather relieved because all the other honours people have thirds."

Cricket remained a very important component in his life. The diary records a number of visits to watch first-class matches, including trips to London for games at the Oval and Lords, where he saw Jack Hobbs score 111 against Middlesex and wrote: "Probably Hobbs' last innings before retiring but what a masterpiece".[11] Although he had refused to play for the university, his diary shows that, in 1933 he turned out quite regularly for other teams. He was commandeered to play for the university staff and on a glorious day he scored eleven runs and took four wickets; playing for Wick he scored a "long winded four out of forty-nine" before taking six wickets for nineteen runs; and he records a match between Kingswood School and the old boys in which he was out for a duck, but took six wickets and nearly achieved two hat tricks. "True cricket," he wrote of this game. "No strife and anxiety no five thousand barracking spectators, just our own happy family enjoying the game we all live for."

The diary also records regular visits throughout the year to concerts in London as well as Bristol. He heard Beethoven's 4th Symphony and 3rd Piano Concerto at the Queen's Hall and Beethoven's 5th Symphony at a "wonderful prom". On September 30th 1932 he wrote: "Prom. Beethoven's 9th Choral Symphony very wonderful. Surely there is nothing like this in the world. It embodies all I desire, so noble and great." And of another Promenade Concert on the following night: "What a night. I shall never forget it. Clifford Curzon and Schubert's *Wanderer Fantasie.* Amazing scenes of enthusiasm. Absolutely defies description." In Bristol he attended a concert given by the Halle Orchestra under Sir Hamilton Harty and was enchanted by Eva Turner. He heard Sibelius' 2nd Symphony and the *Don Juan* of Strauss and on 15th November he followed the score as Schnabel played Beethoven's C Major Piano Sonata, which was "inconceivably wonderful. As Chesterman said it was something infinitely bigger and greater than a man playing the piano." In the same concert he thought Florence Easton disappointing and described her voice as very poor. On another occasion he saw the young Horowitz playing Liszt's *Les Funérailles* which "was an experience never to be dimmed by the years."[12] On January 31st at an eagerly awaited concert at Bath: "Schnabel was wonderful. Schubert B major, Mozart F Major, Beethoven *Appasionata*. Had scores for everything. All to Chesterman's for tea."

His own love of the organ was fostered during these years as a result of an introduction, by Deryck Chesterman, to Raymond Jones who was at that time organist at St Paul's Church in Bath. The Church, which was to be destroyed by enemy action in 1942, had a fine organ and Bernard relished the opportunity of practicing in such a splendid setting. He contented himself at that stage with occasional visits to St Paul's, but after he completed his degree, he had regular lessons and sometimes had the chance to play on the organ in Bath Abbey where 'Jonah' Jones became assistant organist in 1935. This association cemented a lifelong friendship between the two men.

The habit of reading outside the range of subjects he was studying, a habit originally encouraged by E.R. Brown when he was at Kingswood, continued throughout his years as an undergraduate and became a lifelong passion. He wrote, in his diary that he was struggling through Arthur Eddington's *Nature of the Physical World* and could not understand him, but he read both Eddington and James Jeans, he marvelled at the discoveries being made by the Mount Wilson Telescope in the United States and he was enthralled to learn about Hubble's detection of extragalactic nebulae; above all, A.N. Whitehead's *Science and the Modern World* was a book which exerted a permanent influence on his life and thought.

In spite of his intermittent low spirits and the many distractions from work, he did well in the examinations at the end of the summer term. Writing on June 1st he said: "The physics paper was so easy that we are becoming suspicious", and on 16th June: "Physics IV too good to be true. Whatever the results, the papers have been fair." This was a welcome contrast to the Dynamics paper in March, which he had described as vile. The results did not disappoint and Bernard was well set for his final year for which, somewhat to his surprise, he was elected President of the Physics Society, although he declined an invitation to join the university Officers Training Corps.

Now that the labours of the term were at an end, there were holidays to be enjoyed with friends; one in Devon, with walks on the beaches, sunburn, cream teas, and trips to Ilfracombe and Clovelly; another in South Wales with morning walks on the mountain, picnics at the top and reading. But the tribulations he had suffered during the year had not dulled his eagerness to be busy and the idea of spending the whole of the long vacation away from the laboratory filled him with horror. He had managed to persuade two members of the research staff to allow him to help with some simple practical tasks and when he returned from the holidays, he went back to work for them. This experience confirmed to him the excitement of research into new ideas and the delights of achieving practical solutions to novel problems.

As the final year progressed, Bernard turned his attention to the future. In the spring of 1933 he applied to Imperial Chemical Industries for a job and on May 19th he received a letter offering an interview. His real ambition, however, encouraged by Tyndall, was to continue his studies, to obtain a doctorate and to pursue a career as a research physicist at Bristol. Even though it was he that had made the approach to ICI, he quickly declined the interview offer and he received a second letter from the company, dated May 22nd, which noted that he had decided to stay on at university and wished him luck for the future.[13] All he needed now was to achieve a first class degree.

When the final examinations arrived, they almost went horribly wrong. His knowledge of electronics was such that, in one paper, he got completely carried away; he spent so long on a single question that he failed to complete the paper in the allotted time and was, accordingly, heavily penalised by the examiner, who could only allocate so many marks to each question. His failure in that paper was compounded by what he later described as a dismal performance in his viva; during his years as an undergraduate he had become so absorbed with his own particular interests that he made the great mistake of neglecting those aspects of the course which bored him. One such subject, was the study of optics and, in particular, thick lenses; life being what it is, that very topic formed a major part of the questioning to which the committee subjected him and he was found wanting. It looked as though the first class honours he had coveted for so long and so desperately needed would be denied him. He was beside himself with anxiety when he attended The Degree Congregation for the crucial announcement, on June 30th 1934. The great and the good of Bristol University were assembled, his parents were in attendance and Tyndall himself was there to hear the results, read out by the Dean. The tension was unbearable, but when the moment came, and he heard his names, Alfred Charles Bernard Lovell, the relief which flooded through him was a true consolation for all the pain and anxiety he had suffered to attain his objective. The new Bachelor of Science First Class could hold up his head and see his proud mentor, Tyndall, smiling down upon him from the stage; and no doubt his father, steeped as he was in biblical texts, was thinking to himself: "This is my beloved son, in whom I am well pleased."

CHAPTER FOUR

The Graduate

"You did give us a fright, Lovell," pronounced Tyndall.

"I'm sorry, Sir, I feel it has been a rather inglorious affair," replied Bernard.

"Yes," said Tyndall, "the viva proved rather a sad ending. Professor Curtis said the best thing we could do was to forget we had ever interviewed this candidate!"[14]

There is no doubt that Bernard owed a huge debt of gratitude to Arthur Tyndall, even if he did not fully appreciate it at the time. Many years later, he had a chance meeting with Professor William Curtis, the external examiner who had presided over his disastrous viva. Somehow they made a connection with that inauspicious occasion and Curtis told him that it was only the steadfast support and advocacy of Tyndall, whose faith in his young protégé never wavered, that persuaded the committee to spare him the ignominy of a second. Nor did Tyndall's influence end there. As Professor of Physics, he was in a position to assist graduates who needed to obtain maintenance grants from the Department of Scientific and Industrial Research, in order to fund them whilst they worked on their PhD projects. Following his recommendation, Bernard was awarded £120 per annum and the University confirmed him as a postgraduate student; Tyndall was to be his supervisor; the deadline for delivery of his dissertation was October 1st 1936; his life for the next two years was neatly mapped out, to his considerable satisfaction.

Liberation from the oppressive regime of lectures, essays and exams came as a wonderful relief; now at last he had time to indulge in the delights of student life of which he had deprived himself during his undergraduate years. In Bernard's case the new-found freedom was greatly enhanced because, although most of the postgraduates were assigned to established research groups, he was going to be working alone, under the supervision of Dr. A.T.S. Appleyard, a senior physics lecturer, thus enjoying an independence which would not be inhibited by the intervention of others. Whether entrusting him with such a degree of autonomy was the consequence of Tyndall's belief in his abilities or an acknowledgement of his tendency to deal somewhat peremptorily with those who disagreed with him is far from clear; but giving him his head to work as his instincts dictated had obvious advantages and it may well be that both considerations influenced the choice.

Discussions with Appleyard and Tyndall led to a decision that Bernard should undertake research into the electrical conductivity of alkali metals, which had been a subject of investigation and uncertainty for forty years. It was known that the intensity of the photoelectric properties in alkali metals varied or disappeared completely when the metal was reduced to a thin film, but the reason for this behaviour was a mystery. The importance of the problem was that it caused a loss of power currents through the metal, particularly in the case of rubidium.[15] The anomaly was only observed in very thin layers of these metals, which had much greater resistivity to electric currents than they possessed in their bulk form; in other words, as the thickness of the metal was reduced to a film, its normal capacity for conducting electricity disappeared and it became highly resistive. The object of Bernard's investigation was to discover at what level of thickness the change appeared and, even more important, why it was happening at all.

The first task was to design and build the equipment. It was necessary to devise a method for depositing an atomically thin film of metal into a suitable container, under properly controlled conditions; the film would then be examined and measured. As luck would have it, Bristol University employed a man called John Burrow, who was a brilliant glass blower and one of the foremost experts in working with a recent invention, Pyrex glass. Johnny Burrow was enlisted to help and with his skill in glassblowing and Bernard's aptitude for intricate engineering, the product of many years constructing wireless sets and working with machine tools, they quickly produced the equipment he needed to start the experiments. Burrow was a practical man and once he had seen Bernard building vacuum pumps, a miniature galvanometer (for measuring small electrical currents), stands to hold the equipment, brackets to rest it on and clamps to secure it, he was very enthusiastic about the whole project; where Bernard was concerned nothing was too much trouble for him and over the next two years they became great friends.

Burrow made a series of Pyrex cylinders, with a complex arrangement of tubes, arms and small connecting chambers protruding from them; each one was designed so that it could be linked to a pump at one end and each was provided with a tiny aperture at the other, through which minute, almost microscopic, quantities of rubidium could be fired to build up a film on the inner surface of the cylinder, which was kept in a constant state of vacuum by the pump. Once this was done, the atomic thickness of the film was calculated and wire probes were used to test its conductivity. The results from the first experiments demonstrated that the resistivity of thin films of rubidium was very high when measured against the results from larger samples of the metal; this was precisely in line with all the previous learning on the subject; but why was this the case?

Throughout his life, one of Bernard's greatest strengths was an ability to apply his mind to difficult problems with imagination and insight. It occurred to him that the anomaly might be caused by impurities on the inner surface of the cylinder disturbing the conductive properties of the metal, when it was deposited in such small quantities. In consultation with Appleyard he decided to test this hypothesis. Burrow was asked to prepare a new set of Pyrex cylinders and Bernard set about making an electrically heated container within which the cylinders could be enveloped. Once this was done, the system would be heated in vacuum, for at least twenty-four hours, to between 250 and 500 degrees Centigrade. The whole operation was extremely delicate and there were many breakages and setbacks; the process required constant trial and resulted in frequent error; the services of the ever-patient Johnny Burrow were regularly called upon to provide more instruments; but once the rubidium was fired onto a flat surface in the thoroughly sterilised and cooled cylinder, further measurements were taken; it was immediately apparent that the conductivity of the thin film was identical to that which would be found in the metal in its bulk form. The results were absolutely consistent over many tests; it looked as though Bernard's instinct had been correct; the circumstantial evidence clearly indicated that the anomaly was caused by impurities within the cylinders; but Appleyard wanted proof and further analysis was required before the findings could be confirmed.

Burrow made yet another set of cylinders and the work began again. This time, once the uncontaminated film had been prepared and the consistency of the sample had been confirmed, impurities were introduced into the vacuum. As soon as this was done, the resistivity of the rubidium increased to the former levels and the cause of the anomaly was established beyond doubt. The experiments were repeated time and again and other alkali metals such as potassium and caesium were also tested, with the same effect. Bernard had successfully established that the impurities caused microscopic cracks in the surface of the metal film so that the normal conductive properties were lost. By dint of his hard work and constant application he was able to complete his thesis in good time for the deadline of October 1st 1936 and his conclusive findings were published in

Proceedings of the Royal Society[16] and in Volume 137 of *Nature*[17]. It had taken eighteen months of meticulous investigation to achieve, but a conundrum which had puzzled distinguished physicists for many years was resolved. In the concluding passages of his Royal Society paper he wrote:

> Minute amounts of impurity on the substrate give rise to anomalous results...The phenomenon of the decay of conductivity is discussed in terms of a break up of the film under surface tension forces.
> QED.

He had indeed worked very hard, and thoroughly deserved the PhD which he was now awarded; but, as he had found from the start, one of the great joys of research work was that he could follow his own, self imposed, routine, rather than being a slave to his tutors. The laboratory was open to him at all times, experiments could be done as easily in the early morning or late at night as during the day, and plenty of time was therefore available for cricket, tennis, organ lessons and university dances. At some of the latter events, the exigencies of his work had a tendency to interfere with tender encounters and several young ladies found that their partner for the evening had other things than romance on his mind, when they were obliged to accompany him to the laboratory and watch, whilst he made some urgent adjustment to his scientific equipment or checked that the latest batch of cylinders had not reached the melt-down point. The names of several girls appear in his diaries, Mary, Grace and Stella among them, but none merited more than a brief mention, except May: "Walk, during which I tell her that our friendship must return to its platonic state. Seems rather upset about it", as well she might be.

He had sacrificed the chance to play cricket for the University whilst he was an undergraduate, but began to make up for lost time as soon as he finished his degree course. Playing on the beautiful university ground, at Coombe Dingle, was an unalloyed pleasure and during the vacations he also turned out regularly for Bristol Optimists and for the village team at Wick. His diaries contain many descriptions of notable matches and his bowling and batting figures are recorded for each game. He was generally more successful with the ball than the bat, although he was often very self-critical. In a match against Shockerwick, on July 14th 1934, he took six wickets for 28 runs, even though he "bowled extremely badly and did not deserve them". Batting on a very muddy wicket at Wrington, on July 21st, the ball was spinning so much that: "the second came off the edge and went through the slips instead of the covers, the third got me in the stomach. The fifth I was confident of getting to the boundary but there was so much work on it that it came off the inside edge of my bat and went to third man." He had a good game on July 30th, making 25 not out and taking five wickets for 23 runs; and he posted some fine bowling figures in August: four wickets for 50 runs against a strong Sidmouth side which had recently beaten the MCC; and in another match for the Optimists he took twelve wickets in the match, 6 for 24 in the first innings and a remarkable 6 for 6 in six overs in the second. His batting did not live up to his bowling in this game as he was dismissed for 0 in the first innings and 2 in the second.

He now had the opportunity of going regularly to Bath, where he began to take weekly organ lessons from Jonah Jones. Jonah was full of admiration for his ability and was particularly struck by Bernard's playing of Bach, whose works were to become a lifelong passion. Gilbert Lovell had bought him a motor car shortly after he obtained his degree and several times each week, he would drive across the Clifton Suspension Bridge to practice on the organ at the Church in Leigh Woods, where he had befriended the vicar.

During his two years of postgraduate research, Bernard enjoyed these and other diversions to the full. The dark clouds which were beginning to loom in Europe had little effect on his youthful enthusiasm and his enjoyment of the pleasures of university life, although the presence of two German students who had fled from the Nazis gave some indication that all was not well in their native country. One of these students was a self-opinionated and irritating young man called Klaus Fuchs. Bernard took an instant dislike to him. Fuchs had become a communist and left Germany in 1933, after a violent clash with supporters of Hitler; Britain provided him with a refuge and the opportunity to complete his PhD at Bristol, where he studied under Neville Mott. In 1950, it emerged that he had repaid this generosity by passing atomic secrets to the Soviet Union. The news that he had been convicted of spying and sentenced to fourteen years imprisonment caused Bernard very little surprise and no sadness at all.

Since their brief encounter over lunch during his first term at Bristol, Joyce Chesterman and Bernard had not featured with any prominence in each other's lives. For him she was simply the schoolgirl sister of his great friend Deryck; for her he was an occasional visitor whom she tolerated with indifference. In the autumn of 1934 she began a three-year teaching course at a college in Bedford, so their meetings became even less frequent; but at some stage late in 1935 their paths crossed again and, for the first time, Bernard began to take notice of her; the lanky girl guide had blossomed into a lovely young woman, witty and intelligent with a dazzling smile and a gift for repartee which was extremely attractive; his interest was aroused and it was not long before the feelings he was beginning to harbour for her were reciprocated.

The Chesterman parents did not regard this impecunious young man of humble origins as an appropriate suitor for their beloved daughter and did everything they could to discourage the liaison. As frequently happens in such cases, parental opposition had precisely the opposite effect to that which was desired. The flame of ardour was fanned by the cold air which was constantly blown upon it; love blossomed and grew; their determination to be together strengthened in exact proportion to the hostility of the parents, who insisted that Joyce must continue her training. Undeterred by the obstacles, Bernard would drive to Bedford to visit her at college in term time; during the vacations elaborate subterfuges were devised for delicious clandestine assignations and secret trysts; in these they were much assisted by Deryck Chesterman, who was an enthusiastic supporter of his friend's courtship of his sister and gave them every encouragement, often helping to cover their tracks. As for Joyce, she was certainly not the sort of girl who would meekly succumb to parental pressure. By the middle of January 1936 they were hopelessly in love and each was convinced that life without the other would be unbearable. The constant separations were a great trial, but the blissful reunions more than made up for the pain of their partings, and Bernard's engagement diary for June 12th-15th and for July 4th-6th is boldly scored through, on each occasion, with the single entry: "JOYCE".[18]

The grant he had received from the DSIR was due to expire in the autumn of 1936 but with the help of Tyndall once again, he was awarded a Colston Research Fellowship and was already planning further work on the thin films, which had so preoccupied him for the past two years. Bernard saw, stretching ahead of him, a life of fascinating research, lecturing to students in the pleasant environs of Bristol University, cricketing through long summer days, practising and playing his beloved organ music with increasing skill and all this with the girl of his dreams permanently at his side, once she had qualified as a teacher in twelve months time. But these hopes were shattered one beautiful afternoon in July when he was about to play in a cricket match. Before he went out to bat, Tyndall spoke to him and launched a bombshell that exploded every expectation he had set his heart on.

"Lovell," said the Professor, "I think the time has come for you to leave Bristol. You need to broaden your horizons and test your scientific ability against tougher competition elsewhere. There are two openings you should look at. Patrick Blackett wants a young assistant at Birkbeck College to help with his research into cosmic rays and Professor Bragg has asked me to recommend someone for appointment as an assistant lecturer at Manchester. I suggest you apply for both posts immediately." Bernard was astounded. His whole life and all his attachments, including the most recent, had been centred on a radius of a few miles from Oldland Common; the idea of moving and making a career far away from home had never even occurred to him. That Tyndall, his great inspiration, his professor and mentor who had become through the years a dear and valued friend, that it was Tyndall who had made this suggestion was incomprehensible to him.

After much soul searching, discussions with his family and, no doubt, with Joyce, Bernard decided, reluctantly, that he had better apply for these positions and sent off letters to Blackett and Bragg. Of the two, there was no question as to which held the greater attraction. Patrick Blackett was a glamorous and heroic figure, who was regarded with awe by the young generation of physicists to which Bernard belonged. He had been a naval officer during the Great War and had fought with distinction at the Battle of Jutland; he had then studied under Rutherford, and he was now one of the most highly respected physicists of the day. To work for Blackett on his research into cosmic rays was an exceedingly appealing prospect, which would offer considerable consolation for the loss of all that he would be leaving behind. Just the thought of a move to Manchester, on the other hand, filled him with dread. If he was in London, there would at least be some chance of enticing Joyce up from Bedford for an evening at a theatre or concert; but to drag her to Manchester? The very idea stirred up feelings of deep gloom.

He received replies to both his letters, which offered him interviews on the same day, the afternoon of Thursday, August 1st. Accepting the invitation from Blackett at once, Bernard replied to Bragg's by informing him peremptorily that he could wait upon him the following morning; not that he had any intention of doing so, being entirely confident, with the vanity of youth, that Blackett would snap him up immediately. When the day came, he travelled to London, full of expectation, planning to return to Bristol after the interview and to set off on a cricket tour of the West Country on Friday morning. He was in a state of high excitement and was desperate to make a good impression; nothing had been left to chance; he had been studying Blackett's published papers on his ground-breaking cosmic ray research; and knowing Blackett's reputation as a committed socialist and his interest in Russia and in Marxist philosophy, he even took the precaution of reading Nikolai Berdyaev's biography of Dostoyevsky on the train and placed it prominently on the table during the meeting with Blackett, which went very well; he felt that they got on famously and that the job was in the bag.

At the end of the interview, to his consternation, the great man told him that he could not give him an answer at once, because he was due to see another candidate; he would let him have his decision in due course. Bernard was distraught; he realised that he would have to hedge his bets by going to the Manchester interview after all and must unscramble his arrangements for the next day. There were telephone calls to Joyce, who was at home waiting for news and to the organiser of the cricket tour who must have been delighted to hear that the first match would have to be played with ten men instead of the customary eleven.

It was dark when Bernard, tired and bad tempered, got off the evening train at Piccadilly station in Manchester. As he expected, it was pouring with rain and he tramped through the dismal streets, eventually finding somewhere to lay his head for a wretched and uncomfortable night. The next morning, at the precise time that he had hoped to be boarding the team bus in Bristol, he presented himself for the interview with Bragg and members of his staff. This meeting went even better than the one with Blackett the day before and ended with the immediate offer of a job as an assistant lecturer.

"It is very kind of you," responded the candidate, "but I would really rather work for Blackett in London. I shall have to let you know." A stunned silence greeted this unexpected announcement and the members of the committee did not know where to look; certainly not at the Professor, whose rivalry with Blackett was well known to all of them. Bragg was a most distinguished scientist who had won the Nobel Prize for Physics in 1915 at the age of only twenty-five; he must have been surprised at the impertinence of the young man but he did not turn a hair; he behaved like a gentleman and simply requested an answer in a few days.

Bernard caught the next train to Bristol, shaking the grime of Manchester off his shoes and promising himself that he would never set foot in the city again. He had a brief reunion with Joyce and then joined his cricket tour in time for the Saturday match, still confident that he would receive a positive answer from Blackett. As it happened, Blackett's letter of rejection did not reach him until the end of the tour, by which time Bragg, not having heard a word from Bernard, had telephoned Blackett, who told him that he was going to engage another young man from Cambridge. Thus it was through Blackett that Bragg discovered that he had a new assistant lecturer. When he read Blackett's letter, on his return home after the tour, Bernard was absolutely miserable, especially as Joyce had left

Bristol for a holiday with her family the day after his visit to Manchester and would not be returning for several weeks. He spoke to Neville Mott, who said:

"I hear you've been offered a job at Manchester."

"Yes," replied Bernard, "but I'm not going to take it."

"What?" exclaimed Mott. "Lovell, how could you refuse? You are mad. Manchester is a great university and Bragg is a great scientist. His predecessor was Rutherford. You will have the Halle Orchestra, the Free Trade Hall and cricket at Old Trafford. What more do you want?" Bernard realised that Mott was right and immediately wrote to Bragg to say that, if the post he had rejected was still open, he would like to accept it. With Joyce in Switzerland, he spent the next three weeks consoling himself playing cricket. Bragg replied kindly that he was very pleased to hear of the decision and that he quite understood the reasons for the delay in reaching it. In later years Bernard could never recall this episode without acute embarrassment at the way in which he had treated two such eminent men. To their great credit, neither of them ever reproached him for his conceit. Many years later, as he stood on the steps of the magnificent Victorian Town Hall and was presented with the Freedom of the City of Manchester he recalled, with deep shame and humility, that his youthful arrogance had nearly deprived him of every opportunity which life was to offer him.

At the end of September it was a disconsolate young assistant lecturer who set off for Manchester to take up his new post. Further separation from Joyce weighed heavily upon him and was only slightly alleviated by the somewhat more conciliatory attitude of her parents, who still insisted that there could be no engagement until she had completed her training. Accustomed as he was to the magnificent setting and facilities of the physics department at Bristol, the Manchester laboratories did nothing to cheer him up. The buildings were dark and gloomy and he was allocated a room in a basement with a window that looked out onto a brick wall. His digs were little better; all his life he had lived with his parents, surrounded by the pleasant countryside of Gloucestershire; now he was confined in the shadowy heart of a great industrial city, far from home, far from family, far from friends and, above all, far from Joyce. How on earth was he going to survive the experience?

CHAPTER FIVE

Manchester

Bernard Lovell's first four weeks in Manchester were among the most miserable of his life. The frustration at being rejected by Blackett still rankled; even the considerate letter, in which Blackett said that he had appointed the rival candidate, J. G. Wilson, because he was already familiar with his work on cosmic rays, was scant consolation for his disappointment; it seemed to him that the opportunity of a lifetime had slipped through his fingers, like a dropped catch. Quite apart from the dreariness of the Manchester laboratories, it quickly became apparent that they were heavily geared up for Professor Bragg's work on X-ray crystallography. This was an area of research which held no attractions for Bernard, important though it was and continued to be for our understanding of the nature of matter. In part, his lack of interest was due to a feeling that he had unfinished business in his research into thin films; in addition, as he was the first to acknowledge, throughout his life he was driven by a desire to investigate original ideas or to work on projects where others had failed, rather than to take forward and develop research which had already been pioneered.

This was one of the attractions of his work at Bristol; the problem of thin films had vexed scientists for years and the challenge he relished was to find a solution to it by the application of his individual ideas and initiative. Bragg was very understanding and was content that Bernard should carry on with the work he had been doing. The problem was that there was no Johnny Burrow in Manchester and, although he tried the services of a local glass blower, the equipment produced was not up to his requirements, not least because the Manchester man was unfamiliar with Pyrex. As always Burrow was willing to come to his aid, as far as he could at long distance; he continued to prepare the apparatus which was needed, although much of Bernard's work had to be done when he returned to Bristol for the vacations, and he did not complete these researches until Christmas 1937.

Within a few weeks of his arrival in Manchester, things began to look up. He left his digs and obtained a comfortable room in one of the university halls of residence and he met a man with whom he had much in common and who took him under his wing. Douglas Hartree was Professor of Applied Mathematics. He was also a great lover of music and he and his wife introduced Bernard to Manchester's vibrant musical society. They invited him to a musical evening at their home where they required him to play a Bach prelude and fugue for his supper; he obviously passed muster, because the two men became great friends and Hartree asked him to work with the wonderful machine which he had built and installed in the basement of the physics laboratory. The machine was a differential analyser, an early form of computer, which could solve highly complicated equations. Bernard spent a great deal of time with Hartree, using the machine to unravel increasingly complex mathematical problems. So impressed was he by Bernard's work, that sometime later, he was instrumental in guiding him into another productive change of direction, which was to have a profound influence on the rest of his life.

Towards the end of his first month in the new job, another glimmer appeared, to lighten the darkness. Joyce had decided that the half-term break from college would provide her with an opportunity to put pressure on her parents about her future with Bernard. She told him that she was going to confront them and insist that they should agree to a formal announcement of their engagement. Bernard left Manchester on Friday 31st October filled with a mixture of anticipation and dread. He knew that Joyce would be speaking to her parents as he drove; they had arranged that she should send him a telegram, to be collected at Lichfield post office, telling him the result of the conversation and as he sped along the Lichfield Road, with the spires of the magnificent cathedral ahead of him, he could barely contain his patience. At the post office he collected the telegram which contained wonderful news; the Chestermans had agreed that the young couple could announce their engagement at Christmas. When he arrived in Bath, Joyce was waiting to greet him and, for the rest of their lives, the city of Lichfield and the lovely spires of the cathedral held a special place in their hearts.

Suddenly life in Manchester did not seem nearly so bad. He was busy with lectures and teaching in the laboratories, when his work with Hartree and the complicated arrangements for transporting Johnny Burrow's beautiful Pyrex designs permitted; he would drive down to Bristol to collect them, except on one occasion when they risked shipment by train, only to find that an elaborate creation had shattered into a thousand fragments; Johnny was desolate at the waste of his labour, but was soon eagerly making a replacement. Klaus Fuchs had taken over some of the work at the Bristol end, so collaboration with the disagreeable German was forced upon Bernard; but in his new state of blissful happiness, nothing could dampen his spirits. When he returned home at the end of the autumn term, Joyce accompanied him to the Congregation where he was formally installed as a Doctor of Philosophy; after which, oblivious of the winter weather, he drove her out into the countryside and walked her up a hill so that he could slip the ring he had bought her onto the appropriate finger. It was the best and happiest of Christmas holidays for both of them.

Early in 1937 it was announced that Bragg was leaving Manchester to take up the directorship of the National Physical Office and speculation began over who would replace him as Langworthy Professor of Physics. It was a time of uncertainty, which lasted for six months, but Bernard decided, in consultation with Mott and Tyndall, that he should await developments before rushing off to seek another appointment. This proved to be a wise decision. Rumours as to the identity of Bragg's successor were rife. The first sign that a wonderful transformation was about take place came in a letter which Bernard received towards the end of September; it was from his great hero, Patrick Blackett. Hartree had told Blackett that Bernard was a little unsettled in his role as a researcher and that he might be interested in working on the cosmic ray experiments, which had been so tantalisingly dangled before him the previous year. He needed no second invitation and accepted with alacrity, little knowing that within weeks, the great man himself would be confirmed as his boss in charge of the physics department at Manchester.

By the time of Blackett's arrival, Bernard and Joyce were married. Her parents had been won over by their new son-in-law, not least because of his obvious devotion to their daughter. The wedding took place on 14th September 1937, at the Manvers Street Baptist Church in Bath; Jonah Jones played the organ; and the hymn whose authorship had given rise to Bernard's name, *Jesus thou joy of loving hearts*, was sung lustily by the happy families and friends crowded in for the service. They were both very young; Joyce, who had received the successful results of her final exams on the day of the wedding, was just twenty-one and Bernard was twenty-four; but there was no doubting their mutual adoration; never were marriage vows more willingly given and received; and their unalloyed happiness sustained them both through the next fifty-six years, only ending, as they promised one another, when they were parted by death.

The salary of an assistant lecturer was £300 per annum, which was enough, in 1937, to enable them to buy a house, 29 Parkwood Road, in Northenden, a suburb of Manchester where they lived for the next two years. It had a little garden and the seeds of their love of horticulture were

sown there, with the encouragement and advice of a keen gardener from
Bristol, Johnny Burrow, who was a man with many uses and talents. Joyce
was quickly welcomed into the fold of academic life and the Hartrees, in
particular, were extremely kind, introducing them to their many friends
and doing all they could to make them feel at home in their new
surroundings. When Blackett arrived, in November 1937, Joyce was as
enchanted by him as Bernard had hoped she would be; he was a brilliant,
witty, good-looking man and he and his wife immediately succumbed to
the charm of the assistant lecturer's bride. It was a bond of friendship
which endured for many years and enveloped Joyce as much as it did
Bernard. On one occasion, when asked to dinner, they were unable to find
a babysitter and Blackett's wife, Pat, told Joyce that if only one of them
could come they would prefer to see her. When Blackett was an old man,
he accompanied Joyce to a concert one evening and flirted with her
outrageously.

"Patrick," riposted Joyce, "you are the only man I would ever have left
Bernard for."

"Why didn't you?" asked Blackett.

"Because you never asked me," she replied, with her wonderful smile.

Blackett's arrival heralded a revolution in the physics department. His
energy and enthusiasm, coupled with his incomparable brilliance as a
physicist inspired everyone around him. He demanded the highest
standards of thought and argument and was intolerant of the second rate,
in any quarter; but he believed that his staff should have congenial
surroundings and the dreary premises were painted and lit up so that they
became a pleasure to work in. The crystallography equipment which had
filled every corner was quickly replaced with the apparatus of particle
physics and most of the crystallographers left, to carry on their research
elsewhere.

The new professor's famous photograph of the emergence of a proton
from alpha particles bombarding an oxygen nucleus was taken using an
adapted version of the expansion cloud chamber which had been invented
by C.T.R. Wilson in 1911. Using this device, Wilson had caused water
vapour to condense on the ions left by highly charged particles, so that
their movements through the chamber could be seen and their progress
observed. Blackett had built an automatic system, using Geiger counters to
trigger cameras as soon as a cosmic ray particle entered the chamber. One
of his students, a Chinese man called Hu Chien Shan, had built a smaller
chamber on this model, but he returned home, in order to fight for his
country, which was already at war with Japan. Even before Blackett's
arrival, Bernard was instructed to come to Birkbeck in order to dismantle

this piece of equipment and reassemble it in the laboratory in Manchester. For the next year and a half he was completely absorbed by the cloud chamber, which he nicknamed 'George', using it to track the path of cosmic rays, the high energy particles which invade the atmosphere of the Earth from outer space in vast quantities, observing their reaction on high impact with other particles in the chamber, photographing the results with a rather temperamental camera, and measuring their energies. When things went well he would make enthusiastic comments in his diary: "got very good distortionless tracks, including two beautiful showers, completely filling the chamber with particles. Very great excitement over this, but Blackett unfortunately away."[19]

A single particle, a mesotron, penetrates the cloud chamber through a lead plate. It strikes a brass box in the chamber projecting a show of particles beneath.

He modified George to his needs as he developed the techniques and he threw himself into this entirely new area of study, which was to lead him, ultimately, to his life's work. There were two short articles in *Nature* on these researches, but the main paper, *Shower Production by Penetrating Cosmic Rays*,[20] was not published until September 4th 1939, the day after Chamberlain's declaration of war, by which time he had been forced to lay his researches aside for the duration.

Loving the work as he did, he was extremely sensitive to anything which smacked of criticism about his progress. On May 12th 1938, he wrote in his diary: "Douglas said that he'd had an enquiry from Palmer at Hull about a position [for Bernard] on the staff. He'd spoken to Blackett and Blackett said it wouldn't hurt me to stay here another year." It was in his nature to take what others said to him at face value and he clearly regarded Blackett's reported remark as a sleight because he continued: "The tone of the conversation upset me very much and I felt very miserable and gutless for the rest of the evening." The next day his confidence was restored when he "saw Blackett early, who reassured me and made me very happy again. Blackett said I would be mad to think of going."[21]

It was a time of great happiness for the young Lovells. The bliss of their newly married state, the fascination which he felt for his research, the enjoyment of new friends and the expected birth of their first child combined to make them oblivious, to some extent, of the terrible dangers which lurked across the English Channel. There were walks in Lyme Park and weekends in the Lake District, where on 1st May 1938 it was "a beautiful afternoon, walking with J up Alcock Tarn above Grasmere" and they admired "superb views of the Langdales and Scarfell Pike behind".[22] Bernard returned to Manchester alone and on 2nd May recorded: "Quite fun getting one's own breakfast!" By the evening, however, he was missing Joyce and wrote: "Home to Lonely 29 at 10". So the next day he "came home early with flowers to get the house ready for J". He joined Didsbury Cricket Club and played there regularly for the next two summers, usually opening the bowling with considerable success, as he records in his diary; he took great delight in watching Bradman lead the Australian cricket team against Lancashire; but, to his desperate disappointment, the Old Trafford Test match in July was a "complete and official washout, without a ball being bowled! Then, after another downpour, the sun came out and mocked Manchester". There were trips to Stratford, where they saw *The Tempest*, and frequent concerts, with detailed programme notes made in the diary; they loved their "heavenly little home" and creating their first garden together; he wrote joyously of returning there with Joyce, after an evening with the Blacketts on a "superbly romantic night".

In August 1938, during a holiday in Wales, he made what was, perhaps, his first astronomical observation, when he recorded: "The moon and a planet (Jupitor?) [sic] rising over the hills in conjunction, a most superb sight",[23] showing an interest in the spectacle which was not, at that time, matched by knowledge of the subject or his spelling. It was to be many years before he began to learn about astronomy and then, as we shall see, he was taught by an amateur.

The invasion of the Rhineland, the Anschluss and the sabre-rattling of the Nazi regime seemed to be taking place a long way from home; it was hard to comprehend the danger of these signals at first or to believe that, once again, Europe would be plunged into war, even when Blackett insisted that: "There's a bloody smash coming and its coming soon."[24] The Munich crisis in September is closely followed in the diary, however, and on 23rd September he wrote: "very grave and terrible news…Troops are moving fast in Germany, so it looks like war this weekend." Then, on 24th: "Absolute jim-jams and horrors that nothing but a miracle can stop war this weekend. Chamberlain went to say goodbye to Hitler at 10.30 pm and came away at 1.20 am with a memorandum on what Hitler wants! Even this is a little less black than last night. Very little in the news tonight except that Europe is completely mobilised, but there is nothing to indicate the immediate imminence of hostilities – so I felt a little calmer."

On 26th September he wrote: "Most terribly distracted day ever. Thinking only of bombs and what I could do to make J and the unborn safe. Hitler is going to invade C-Slovak on Sat, of that there is no doubt at all. And Britain and France look like standing firm. Hitler made a most bloody speech at 8.30, absolutely full of vile hatred of Benes.[25] It was simply awful. Almost impossible to work in all this and there is no interest anyhow." And then on 30th September: "Could hardly bear to look at the *Guardian*, but there it was – Peace! It meant scarcely nothing, so unbearable was the relief…It seemed to me Hitler got all he asked for…Evening papers quite fantastic Peace Peace Peace with <u>almost</u> all the world rejoicing and wild scenes of enthusiasm. Chamberlain having signed another document with Hitler renouncing war between them and agreeing to consultation. But what a peace! Poor Czecho-slovakia. So wonderful to feel the glow of hope but what a nasty uneasy feeling of betrayal." He took Joyce to a George Formby film to celebrate, but his view that Britain and France had betrayed the people of Czechoslovakia was vindicated when the years of appeasement came to a shattering end less than twelve months later.

Back at work in Manchester on the 19th October, Bernard received a telephone call from Bath at 7.00 am telling him: "'a most beautiful little (I held my breath) <u>girl</u> has just been born into the World: Joyce has been simply marvellous.'" Evidently Joyce had her heart set on a boy because he continued: "Well! I hardly know what to think; wondering how livid J would be <u>really</u>."[26] In line with the custom of the time, there was no question of the father being present at the birth; indeed it is evident that there was no great urgency in him even setting eyes on the child. He spoke to Joyce on the telephone and received a letter from her two days later: "Charming letter from J, written in bed while the nurse was away, saying she couldn't help loving Susan, although she wasn't Bryan, because she was so funny." In the evening he took the train to Bath and saw his daughter for the first time, under the watchful eye of a rather ferocious nurse, who "took me to see Jennifer Susan asleep, looking like nothing on earth, but very sweet. J quite bright and merry but terrified of the nurse."[27] Joyce remained in Bath for four weeks, until the nurse departed and she rejoined her husband in Manchester, where they stayed for Susan's first Christmas.

In the early months of 1939 preparations were being made for civil defence; gas masks and blackout material were being manufactured on a huge scale, Anderson shelters were beginning to appear, but life continued much as before. Bernard was busy writing his first book *Science and Civilisation*, for which he was delighted to receive £50 when it was published on 10th July. In the laboratory Bernard and J.G. Wilson, Blackett's preferred candidate for the job at Birkbeck, set up two cloud chambers and photographed the impact of high energy cosmic ray particles entering them simultaneously; during the day, only Old Trafford and the Test Match between England and the West Indies could draw him away from this work; in the evening he and Joyce would meet friends to play tennis, go to the theatre in Manchester or drive over the hills to the Buxton Opera House. But the idyll could not last forever and he was, once again, writing pessimistic entries in the diary: "Europe preparing for war. Democracies at last look like standing up to Hitler", on 20th March, and: "Rumours of German moves on Poland. Chamberlain stated in the House that we would fight for Poland. This is good news at last, but what a world!" on the thirty-first.

Bernard's appointment as assistant lecturer was due to end in the autumn of 1939 and there was no possibility of a renewal; Blackett, however, did not want to lose him from his team and applied to the Department of Scientific and Industrial Research who offered him a fellowship to continue the work on cosmic rays. This held great attractions, because he would be released from the burden of teaching and would be able to concentrate on research. In the wake of this good news, his first assignment was to spend much of the summer vacation at an observatory at Pic du Midi, high in the Pyrenees. There his particle research could be continued in a more rarefied atmosphere, with less of the interference from the secondary particles which occur at lower altitudes.

Preparations for the trip were well advanced; a van was found and loaded with equipment including a cloud chamber and a small generator. On the morning of Saturday 29th July, he was outside the Schuster building in Manchester, making final preparations for the drive to Paris, where he was to pick up the French physicist Pierre Victor Auger, before travelling to the south. Just as he was about to depart, he received an urgent telephone call from Blackett: "Under no circumstances are you set off to France. I have got another job for you."

The nature of this job was not revealed to him. He was simply told that, in September, he would be going to a secret Air Ministry Station in Yorkshire; meanwhile he must report to Bawdsey Manor near Felixstowe, the headquarters of the Air Ministry Research Establishment, AMRE, on 14th August. Blackett gave no clear reason for the change of plan, merely telling Bernard that he would find out soon enough; but it was borne in upon him that the world was about to become a very different place; the reality of the danger to the peaceful existence he had been leading was immediately apparent. On 4th August, he made a final visit to the laboratory where he had worked for the last three years. Sadly he closed down George. As he looked round, he must have thought about the dismal beginnings of his tenure there, of the changes that those years had wrought in his life, of his wife, of his baby daughter and of the fascinating work he had been engaged in for the last eighteen months. No doubt we can allow him a nostalgic sigh, as he shuts down the expansion chamber, gathers his belongings, has one last glance across the room, turns off the light and locks the door; little does he know how many years are to pass before he can return to unlock it.

CHAPTER SIX

August 1939

If Bernard Lovell had been too engrossed in the joys of life to pay much more than passing attention to the portents from across the Channel, the same was certainly not true of his boss. For many years he had been one of those who foresaw the dangers presented by the rise of Hitler and he had been conscious, in particular, of how vulnerable Britain's defences were to the threat of attack from the air. Nor had he stood idly by, awaiting the onslaught. In addition to his many and onerous commitments to Birkbeck, to Manchester and to his own experimental scientific work, he was an active member of the Tizard Committee for the Scientific Study of Air Defence from its inception in 1935, and he became one of the great advocates of the development of radar in the years leading up to the Second World War.

Robert Watson-Watt is often referred to as the Father of Radar. In 1915, whilst working for the Meteorological Office at Ditton Park, he began to consider the possibility of bouncing radio signals off thunder clouds, in order to locate the position of storms. The original purpose of this work was to discover if predictions could be made, which might be used to help aircraft avoid the dangers presented to them by the weather, but it led him to a deeper study of the reflective properties of radio waves and he discovered that reflections could be recovered from the ionised regions of the upper atmosphere. From there it was but a short step to considering whether the system could be used to indicate the presence of objects in the sky, including aircraft. The implications of such a facility for the defence of the realm were obvious. Radio waves form part of the electromagnetic spectrum, which includes light, microwave, infrared and X-rays. All electromagnetic waves travel in a straight line at the speed of light, so that if they could be directed towards an aircraft and the reflection retrieved, the process would be virtually instantaneous and the aircraft could be detected when it was still many miles distant.

The Tizard Committee was set up in January 1935 under the chairmanship of Henry Tizard as a result of an initiative by H.E. Wimperis, the Director of Research at the Air Ministry.[28] The purpose of the committee was:

> To consider how far recent advances in scientific and technical knowledge can be used to strengthen the present methods of defence against hostile enemy attack.

As the 'present methods of defence' were virtually nonexistent, almost any strengthening would be a bonus and the committee's first inquiry of Watson-Watt, related to the possibility of a radio death ray, generally referred to in the Air Ministry as a 'Black Box', which they hoped might be used to destroy aircraft at a safe distance. This idea was an old chestnut and a popular one among the more optimistic pundits of the day, including those in the Air Ministry, which had offered £1,000 to anyone who invented a 'Black Box' that would kill a sheep at a range of one thousand yards.[29] Watson-Watt got his assistant, Wilkins, to do the calculations and immediately pronounced it to be a non-starter; but he did suggest that using radio waves to obtain a reflection or echo might make it possible to detect the presence of incoming aircraft. The committee was interested by this idea and asked Watson-Watt to arrange a demonstration.

On February 26th 1935 Albert Percival Rowe, the secretary to the committee, met Watson-Watt and Wilkins at the Empire Radio Station near Daventry, where the BBC had a powerful shortwave radio transmitter which could send out a continuous beam on a wavelength of 49 metres. Two aerials and a receiver were set up and linked to a cathode ray tube which would, if all went well, display the reflected signal from an aircraft crossing the beam. A Heyford bomber, flying 6 miles away at 2,000 feet, made four passes across the path of the signal; each pass appeared on the screen of the cathode ray tube; the demonstration was a complete success. Watson-Watt was puzzled by Rowe's reaction, noting that "he showed no detectable signs of excitement or elation".[30] Any disappointment he felt was dispelled when Rowe reported to the committee:

> It was demonstrated beyond doubt that electromagnetic energy is reflected from the metal components of an aircraft's structure and that it can be detected. Whether aircraft can be accurately located remains to be shown. No one seeing the demonstration could fail to be hopeful of detecting the existence and approximate bearing of aircraft approaching the coast.[31]

The Daventry experiment was a triumph and led directly to the development of radar facilities, which, four and a half years later, helped to save the country from invasion. And the development was swift; by the end of 1935, systems set up at Orfordness, in Suffolk, had successfully detected aircraft at a distance of 80 miles.[32]

By August 1939 Radio Direction Finding (RDF) had been installed at twenty-five locations, so that coverage stretched round the whole of the coastline from Portsmouth to the Firth of Forth. This system, known as the Chain Home (CH), provided the Air Ministry with the ability to detect incoming enemy aircraft up to 100 miles from the coast and was to give Fighter Command a vital advantage in the Battle of Britain; without this facility, the difficulties of intercepting the Luftwaffe would have been insurmountable and Hitler's ambitions for the invasion of Britain might well have been fulfilled. The extent of the secrecy about these developments, maintained for four years by all those involved in the creation of such a far-reaching shield, was little short of remarkable; no one among Blackett's friends or staff, including Bernard, who fell into both camps, had the slightest inkling of his involvement in defence, or his connection with the Air Ministry and the Tizard Committee, until the moment came when he recruited them into the wartime service of their country.

On 4th August Bernard and Joyce had shut up the house at 29 Parkwood Road, wondering when they would see it again. They drove down to Bath and on Sunday August 13th, Bernard travelled to Bawdsey Manor, completing the last leg of the journey in a launch across the mouth of the river Deben. Bawdsey occupied a magnificent position overlooking the estuary and, in spite of the imminence of war, it was a beautiful place in which to work. It was the first of the Air Ministry radar establishments and had been headed by Watson-Watt from 1936. As the forerunner of the CH network, it had become a place of enterprise, energy and hard work. On his arrival Bernard was encouraged by the sight of a cricket bag on the hall floor; the bag belonged to A.P. Rowe, who had succeeded Watson-Watt as the Superintendant of Bawdsey, but if he hoped for a game he was disappointed; even so, there was time for relaxation; during the summer months, high tide would invariably coincide with a break in routine and the young men and women who worked there were simultaneously overcome with the desire to take a plunge into the refreshing waters of the North Sea.

It was in this lovely place that Bernard and a group of twelve young scientists, hand-picked by Blackett, had their preliminary introduction to radar. For the next three days Rowe and his team demonstrated how the systems operated, with their powerful transmitters; these could generate radio waves at the rate of fifty pulses per second through the huge aerials positioned high up above the roof of the old manor house; any aircraft which flew through the field of their beams sent back echoes to cathode ray tubes at Bawdsey, so that their positions, height, distance speed and trajectory could quickly be calculated and the results forwarded to Fighter Command.

They also met E.V. 'Taffy' Bowen, who was in the process of developing the first airborne radar, work which had been instigated as a result of the foresight of Tizard and his committee as early as 1936. The committee were more than satisfied that the success of land-based radar would give Fighter Command the time they needed to get airborne and intercept enemy aircraft in daylight; but they realised that, even if the Luftwaffe was driven back and forced to abandon daylight raids, they were likely to resume the campaign by bombing at night; the RAF would be faced with the problem of finding bombers hidden by darkness and getting within a range which enabled them to be identified and destroyed before they had the chance to wreak the havoc which Hitler was determined to unleash on the mainland of Britain. This prescience of the Tizard Committee led to the decision to build miniature radar which could be fitted in defending aircraft. The visitors were given a brief overview of Bowen's work on this development, with a particular injunction from Rowe that they were being shown a "secret within a secret".

From Bawdsey the new recruits were taken to the Headquarters of Fighter Command at Stanmore in Middlesex. Here they were shown how the signals received from the CH stations around the coast could be coordinated into a swift and effective response to incoming bombers. There was a mock attack by French aircraft and the young women in the operations room swung into action, directing the dispatch of fighters to intercept the enemy, from the airfields under their control. The next day they went to Biggin Hill, where they saw the business end of the exercise and watched in fascination as a squadron of Hurricanes was scrambled in response to the messages which had been generated as a result of the original radar signals received at CH stations such as Bawdsey. It was all completely new to Bernard and he returned to Joyce and Susan full of enthusiasm for this new technology and eager to play his part in making it effective, in the event of war. He did not have long to wait.

He spent a week with the family, during which he wrote to Blackett with his impressions of the visit to Suffolk, expressing great interest in all he had seen. Blackett replied and told him Watson-Watt had approved his appointment to lead a team of scientists who would soon be going to Yorkshire. At that stage he was not informed precisely what he would be required to do there but things became clearer on 25th August, when he received a letter, telling him that he was to report to the Air Ministry Station at Staxton Wold, near Scarborough on the following Monday, August 28th. The weekend was spent relaxing with Joyce and their daughter. Then, on the afternoon of 27th August it was farewell and off to Yorkshire for whatever fate held in store for him.

In Scarborough Bernard stayed at a Victorian Boarding House in Albemarle Crescent. The following morning he presented himself, eager for duty, at Staxton Wold. But what was he supposed to be doing? The CH radar unit was fully staffed and had been operational for five months, large numbers of soldiers were arriving that very morning and were busy preparing the defences of the station and the group of young scientists felt entirely surplus to requirements. After a good deal of discussion and much hanging about, the warrant officer in charge of the RAF personnel agreed that they should read up on the instruction manuals and technical data and shadow members of staff to learn all they could about the operation of CH and the work of the station. The most striking features of the establishment were the steel towers which rose 360 feet above the site and carried the transmitter aerials. In common with all such units at that stage, these aerials were capable of detecting any incoming planes, except those at very low levels, such as mine-laying aircraft. The possibility of flying under the radar was well understood and work was continuing on adapting the equipment to deal with this problem; there was already a prototype known as CHL (Chain Home Low) and complete coverage was largely achieved early in 1940.

The first radar systems had operated on the 50-metre waveband, but this attracted so much interference from normal radio stations that it was unusable. By August 1939, every CH station was equipped with wavebands of less than 15 metres. The accuracy of the echoes to any given receiver might vary by 12 degrees but combining results from two or three neighbouring stations enabled the operations room at Stanmore to develop a very accurate idea of the exact location of incoming aircraft. Throughout the war these systems were being continually refined. One example of this was the development of Identification Friend or Foe normally referred to as IFF. In the early days such identification would depend almost entirely on educated guesses about the position of the intruder, coupled with the knowledge of what friendly planes were in the air and their approximate positions; as time went on, all aircraft were equipped with internal systems generating signals that could be recognised by land-based radar operators and the guesswork was removed from the equation.

The news of the non-aggression pact between Hitler and Stalin, on August 23rd, had sounded the most ominous of warnings throughout the world. Thus, on September 1st, the fourth morning at Staxton Wold, while

Bernard was continuing to familiarise himself with radar systems, the reports that Hitler had invaded Poland caused little surprise. It was clear to everyone that the crisis had arrived and if there was trepidation, there was also relief that the waiting was over; everyone knew what was going to happen next and could prepare themselves to face the future, if not with equanimity, then at least with fortitude.

At 11.15 on the morning of September 3rd, Bernard was in the operations room watching a pretty young radar operator in WAAF uniform go about her work, when the voice of Alvar Lidell came on the air:

"This is London. You will now hear a statement by the Prime Minister." The room fell silent, save for the hiss and crackle of the radar equipment, as Chamberlain's dry tones informed the nation that Germany had failed to respond to the government's ultimatum, and he spoke the fateful words:

"I have to tell you *now*, that no such undertaking has been received and that, consequently, this country *is* at war with Germany." The Prime Minister continued for several minutes before concluding: "Now, may God bless you all and may he defend the right, for it is evil things that we shall be fighting against. Brute force, bad faith, injustice, oppression and persecution. And against them I am certain that the right will prevail." There was a pause while Alvar Lidell returned to the microphone and said:

"That is the end of the Prime Minister's statement. Please stand by for important announcements, which will follow almost immediately." There was another long pause and then a peel of Church bells; the bells were succeeded by a series of terrifying announcements: places of entertainment and sports facilities must be closed with immediate effect and until further notice because, if they were hit by a bomb, large numbers of people would be killed or injured; gas masks were to be carried at all times; children were to be labelled like pieces of luggage; schools were to be closed; air raid warnings were explained and there was a particular injunction that, in the event of a gas attack, everyone must remain in their shelters until the gas had cleared; although no indication was given as to the method of identifying gas attacks or the means of discovering if the gas had cleared. The announcements ended with the National Anthem.

It was widely assumed that the moment war was declared there would be enemy bombers overhead within minutes. Everyone knew the fate of Polish cities only days before and of Guernica during the Spanish Civil War. In London, these forebodings were not dispelled by the immediate sounding of air raid sirens. At Staxton Wold, Bernard and the pretty young WAAF turned their attention back to the screen. He noticed immediately that it was full of echoes; the worst of fears were being fulfilled and a raid was already on the way. And yet the pretty young WAAF seemed very calm and did not react at all. Bernard was puzzled. This was not what he had witnessed in the hectic demonstrations at Bawdsey.

"Look at the screen," he said. "Aren't you going to transmit their positions to Stanway?"

"Oh those echoes aren't from aircraft," said the young lady; "they are at the wrong range and they are too short-lived. We were told they are just transient echoes from the ionosphere." At that very moment, as relief flooded through him and he felt a little foolish to have been alarmed, the germ of an idea flashed into his mind. Perhaps radio waves could be used to detect and study cosmic ray showers as they entered the upper atmosphere. "Echoes from the ionosphere." It was a phrase which was to live in his thoughts during six years of war, after which it would grow into a towering ambition that absorbed him for the rest of his life.

CHAPTER SEVEN

Radar

And then nothing happened. Staxton Wold was a pleasant enough place, but there was little to do there other than watching an empty cathode ray tube and keeping a log of everything that was not going on. Perhaps it was marginally less mind-numbing than watching paint dry; he was after all still learning about radar; but it was a close run thing and for a man such as Bernard, who was always busy on some exciting project, it was extremely frustrating. For nearly a week he took his turn monitoring the screens, sometimes on night duty, but he was beginning to wonder how much of it he could stand when, as so often in his life, Patrick Maynard Stuart Blackett came to the rescue. On September 7th he arrived at Staxton Wold to see what was happening and when he heard that the answer was very little, he said that he would find him a job in radar research. Two days later Bernard returned to Bath and spent a few carefree days with Joyce and Susan.

Obtaining a job was a matter of considerable importance, quite apart from his keenness to help the war effort. His university appointment was about to expire; the support he had been promised by the Department of Scientific and Industrial Research had been dependant on the aborted expedition to the Pyrenees and would no longer materialise; he would soon be out of work, with a wife and child to support and no salary. They returned to Manchester and the next two weeks were spent packing up the house, arranging for Joyce and Susan to return to her parents in Bath and making regular telephone calls to Blackett, to find out how he was getting on. Blackett was as good as his word and wrote to W.B. Lewis whom Rowe had appointed as his deputy at AMRE, which had moved to Scotland, because of fears that Bawdsey was vulnerable to air raids. He suggested that Bernard should be sent to work with Bowen on the development of air-interception systems: "I would be rather pleased," wrote Blackett, "as it would give him a personal contact with a branch of RDF in which I am particularly interested in connection with blind bombing." On September 20th Lewis signalled: "Come at once. Welcomed by Bowen at Scone airport near Perth."[33] On 27th September Bernard was told to report to

Lewis, in Dundee, as soon as possible. He arrived there on the 29th and was immediately sent on to join Bowen at Scone. His appointment as a junior scientific officer to the Air Ministry was confirmed; he had a job and something interesting to do. He was the first of a small number of scientists recruited to work on radar with Bowen, who was delighted to have them on his team and described their arrival in *Radar Days*: [34]

> It took them some time to get used to the rituals of government service and this was not made any easier by the survival situations in which we found ourselves. Moreover, they were not always allocated to the most glamorous jobs. For all that they took to the task with a will; what is more they were fresh and not suffering from the physical and mental strain which the pressures of the previous few months had brought to many of us. The first such recruit we received into the group was A.C.B. Lovell and we were blessed with several more in the months that followed.

Taffy Bowen had made remarkable progress in his work on air-interception radar, commonly referred to as AI. The land-based equipment, which Bernard had seen at Bawdsey and Staxton Wold, was huge and weighed many tons; the first requirement was to produce an apparatus which was small enough to carry in an aircraft and which weighed no more than a few hundred pounds. Bowen had succeeded in devising such a system, which was entirely self-contained, so that, even in the hours of darkness, the land-based stations could guide pilots to the general area where the enemy planes were to be found, at which point the on board equipment could, in theory, take over; the principal difficulty in perfecting such a system arose from the need to generate radio waves on much shorter wavelengths using much smaller equipment. This problem arises because the polar diagram, that is, the nature and shape of the radio beam, depends on the aperture of the aerial and on the wavelength. Like everything else in the electromagnetic spectrum, including light, radio signals travel in waves. The wavelength of a given signal is the distance from the peak of one wave to the peak of the next. Long wavelengths move in large waves on a wide beam and at a low frequency; short wavelengths are small, have a high frequency and travel on a narrow beam. For any given wavelength it is possible to obtain a narrower and more precise polar diagram, or beam shape, by increasing the size of the aerial; and for any given aerial, the polar diagram narrows as the wavelength is reduced; so what was required was a small aerial with an output on the lowest possible wavelength, giving the narrowest and most precise possible beam. On land the size of the aerial is not an issue; large aerials can be used to produce a narrow beam regardless of the wavelength; all that is necessary is to increase the size of the aerial to get a more precise beam. On an aircraft, the size of the aerial could not be increased and the trick was to devise a system with small aerials generating a low wavelength and producing a narrow beam; the best that had been achieved, at this stage, was a reduction of wavelength to 1.5 metres.

This wavelength, using the small aerial, provided a wide beam and the system was tricky to operate; two antennae were fitted to the aircraft, generating two such beams and the navigator had to calculate the direction and height of the incoming aircraft by comparing the returning echoes on his receiver. There were two further operational difficulties relating to the maximum range at which the enemy could be spotted and the minimum range at which the signal could be sustained; the former was a genuine problem, the latter was arguably illusory and was undoubtedly the cause of much argument.

The 1.5-metre waveband with the small aerial produced a wide beam; this meant that the height of the aircraft was also the maximum range at which an incoming plane could be detected; the reason for this was that, at that distance, the wide beam would hit the ground and the target at the same time, so the signal from the target would be hidden within the echoes from the ground. When flying at 10,000 feet, for example, the reflection from any airborne object more than 10,000 feet away would become muddled by the ground returns from below; as the normal flying height was no more than 15,000 feet, on board radar contact with enemy aircraft was restricted to a maximum of less than 3 miles; this could only be overcome if ground stations were able to guide fighters to within 3 miles of the target, which was beyond their capability at the beginning of the war.

The problem of minimum distance arose from the rather crude engineering of the original systems and the desire, at all costs, to avoid friendly fire being caused by inaccurate identification; it was also the primary cause of much hostility between Rowe and Bowen, which only ended in the autumn of 1940 when Tizard took Bowen to the United States, where he remained for the rest of the war. Tests carried out before the outbreak of war had satisfied the Royal Aircraft Establishment that even at night, positive visual identification could be made at a distance of 1,000 feet, in clear conditions. This was subsequently disputed in some quarters and Rowe took up the cudgels ordering Lewis to make improvements to Bowen's design, aimed at reducing the minimum distance at which the signal could be maintained to 600 feet. Bowen was already rather put out that he had been superseded by the appointment of Lewis as Rowe's deputy and he was not any happier when he discovered what

Lewis was up to. Lewis did, in fact, make modifications, which reduced the minimum distance to the required extent; but it is doubtful whether this work was actually needed, because Bowen later established that the common experience of night fighter pilots was that visual identification was made at between 1,500 and 1,200 feet from the target. It was unfortunate that this disagreement should have caused so much animosity but scientists are just as likely to have rows with their rivals as other men and sometimes more so.

Rowe was a somewhat peppery individual and did not take kindly to anyone who crossed his path. He was a bit of a stickler and, at times, unnecessarily awkward, especially with those who were under him. After the war he went to Australia and became, in due course, Vice Chancellor of the University of Adelaide, where he did not enjoy unqualified popularity; he was very intolerant of unruly students and, when the existence of the Himalayan yeti became a topic of popular speculation, his students dubbed him the Abominable Roweman. He was to show the pernickety side of his nature at Swanage in 1940, when he wrote to Bowen in the following terms:

Use of Canteen

I was astonished yesterday to find that a considerable number of staff are using the canteen for tea and other refreshments in the middle of the morning. No man in normal health needs refreshment in a morning so short as one from 8.45 am to 1 pm, and in general the canteen is not to be used in the morning. I think everyone knows that I am strongly in favour of tea in the afternoons. In most cases, however, it will save time if the tea is made in the laboratories by junior staff or by one of the very willing members of the typing pool.

Bowen's comment on this was: "The staff had met this kind of eccentricity before and, in their strictly practical way, they solved it by switching to coffee in the morning."[35] However, his overall assessment of Rowe as being no good as a manager is unfair and is not borne out by the facts; he was certainly correct in paying tribute to the "superlative dedication of the staff", but there is no doubt that Rowe was also a dedicated scientist and that he led AMRE and TRE[36] with great distinction through all six years of the war. Bad as the organisation was at the start of hostilities, it was symptomatic of a country groping its way into the chaos of war and was certainly no worse than that described by Evelyn Waugh in his satirical portrayal of army life, *Men at Arms*.

It was in this rather troubled atmosphere that Bernard was introduced to government service. Accustomed as he had become to academic research, where he was his own master and the only dictates were those of the experiment in hand, the world of the civil servant, in which the department is king, the staff are at the beck and call of their superiors, nothing can be done without prior authority and the simplest thing from paper and writing materials to equipment of any kind can only be obtained after proper requisition orders have been completed, took some getting used to. He quickly became absorbed in Bowen's work on AI and could see the urgent need to devise means of overcoming the problem of ground returns and making the system really effective. This, of course, is exactly what Bowen wanted and he explained to Bernard that the most urgent task was to find a way of operating AI using centimetre wavebands, in order to achieve the narrowest possible beam, which was so desperately needed to secure the optimum performance; he was instructed to work towards getting the waveband down towards 50 centimetres. He arrived for the second morning of work full of eagerness and energy, only to be told by Bowen's number two, Gerald Touch, who had been appointed by Rowe, that the priority was to install the existing transmitters and to get them working properly.

These AI units had been hurriedly built just before the outbreak of war, when the Air Ministry woke up to the fact that they needed to get Bowen's prototype operational as a matter of extreme urgency. An initial order for thirty transmitters had been rushed through and delivered to Scone, where the facilities were far from ideal for the fitting of precision equipment into the thirty Blenheim night fighters for which they were intended; there was a chronic shortage of equipment and the set up was very disorganised. For several weeks Bernard, Peter Ingleby and R.K. Beattie, Manchester colleagues who joined the establishment a few days after he did, were subjected to a constantly changing barrage of instructions. When Bowen was there they could get on with the research into centimetre radar, but when, as was often the case, Touch was in charge, suggestions that they should continue with this were met with:

"You've got to realise there's a war on. All efforts have to go into getting these 1.5-metre transmitters into operation." He continued to be a source of irritation, provoking this outburst in Bernard's diary:

Long argument with Touch about our ideas for bomb firing – he was most objectionable and obstructive. Bowen was very nice, apologised for Touch and told us to proceed.[37]

Soon after he started work at Scone, Bernard was taken on a test flight in one of the Blenheims which had been fitted with AI radar and another problem became immediately apparent. The cramped conditions, the cold in the aircraft, being dressed in a flying suit and sitting on the parachute which was strapped to his back, he understood for the first time how very different and how much more awkward the task of the radar operator was than he had ever imagined, whilst he was working on the equipment on the ground. It was a salutary lesson, which was to be reinforced during his frequent test flights over the next five years.

Even when they were able to get on with the research work they were hampered by the lack of facilities; they were working in an open hangar and, in particular, they desperately needed access to a library. Undeterred by these difficulties, Bernard and Peter Ingleby experimented on old equipment to devise a system with a shorter wavelength; they had some success and managed to get a transmitter working on a 1-metre wavelength, but at that stage they could proceed no further without studying the literature on the subject. Unfortunately, the nearest library was in Dundee and Gerald Touch would have none of it. It was a waste of time, there was a war on and they must get on with the job of making the existing equipment work, instead of messing about with experiments. Bernard could stand it no longer and fired off a blistering letter of complaint to Blackett:

As friend to friend, I thought you might find some unbiased views on the Air Ministry useful. To begin with, the general organisation and method of work used by the AM makes my head swim. It leads to persistent and inevitable bungling. I find it illogical and without the elements of common sense. At the beginning of the summer the group was told to get on with AI and design it for the Battle.[38] They did so and demonstrated in that machine. In June or July, they were told to fit twenty-two short-nosed Blenheims. They designed all the fittings, brackets, etc. Long-nosed Blenheims arrived. They redesigned the fittings and placed the apparatus near the pilot as per instructions. The first four arrived at Northolt. The C-in-C said he had ordered short nose Blenheims and the apparatus was not a bit of good in the front, it must be in the back for the rear gunner. Result, general chaos and further redesigning. The fitters (had) endeavoured to point out that the pilot could never operate the apparatus. They were told not to be obstructionist.

Other complaints cast aspersions on the ability of senior Air Ministry staff, who were after all his employers and he added, by way of a coda:

> By the peculiar AM system they have attained positions or which they are in no way suited.

He ended by saying that he was only trying to be helpful. Bernard was twenty-six years old whilst Blackett and all those in the upper hierarchy of the Air Ministry and Aeronautical Research, from Tizard to Rowe were distinguished men in their forties; writing such a letter was a high risk strategy. Nevertheless, Blackett's reply took a conciliatory tone.

He said that he was sorry everything in the garden was not quite as beautiful as he had expected and that he should not take minor troubles too seriously:

> You underestimate the difficulties of getting dispersal organisations going properly. You must be more tolerant too, especially at first till you have really achieved something in these technical fields – then you can criticise safely. One of the great things to remember is that all defence work like all service work is very much a matter of dealing with people – the qualities of the personnel are part of the experimental facts and it is no use getting too upset about them.

This was good advice, which had a calming effect; Bernard felt better for getting his troubles off his chest and appreciated the response; he had done what he could and that seemed to be the end of the matter. Blackett, however, was concerned about what had been reported to him and forwarded the letter to Tizard, telling him that the impression Bernard had got of conditions at Perth was depressing:

> It is only the huge importance of AI which makes me pass on these grumbles from Lovell. If you do pay a visit there they might be of use in suggesting things to look out for.

He asked him to destroy the letter to protect the identity of the writer. Tizard did not do so, but communicated the central complaints to Rowe, without naming the complainant.

The criticisms seem to have touched Rowe on a sore spot. He had already received one visit from Tizard, who had expressed concern that Bowen's experimental work was not being given the priority it deserved and he was more than a little irritated to receive a barrage of condemnation from some very junior member of his staff. It was clear to him that the perpetrator must be one of the three new boys from Manchester and he decided to interview them separately, asking each one if he had any suggestions for improvements. Peter Ingleby and R.K. Beattie either had no complaints or were discrete enough to remain silent about them; Bernard, on the other hand, was true to form and needed no second invitation; it quickly became obvious to Rowe that he had written the letter and, as he reported back to Tizard, he asked him to come and see him at Dundee. The Dundee meeting took place on October 26th, after which Rowe wrote to Tizard:

> I have spent an hour with him this afternoon. He clearly had no idea that I am aware that he has written to Blackett. Judging merely from the letter you quoted to me I expected to find that Lovell was a nasty piece of work who should be removed. I find, however that this is not the case. Many of the criticisms he raises are associated with the simultaneity of research, development, production and installation and with the natural alterations of mind of C-in-C Fighter Command as he feels his way to an operational solution.
>
> It was interesting that Lovell said that many of the things he felt critical about two weeks ago he now understands. At the same time he has a number of weighty criticisms which boil down to the fact that Perth has been separated from Dundee. There is no Test Room at Perth and no organisation for ordering and inspection of materials. There are many associated troubles caused by the separation. When a man says that everything is all wrong, I generally start by suggesting that he should put it right. This policy has worked in this instance and Lovell has gladly accepted the job of organising a test room and taking over contract procedure at St. Athan, to which Perth is moving next week. Bowen is happy with this arrangement. I feel convinced we shall make something of Lovell after his tactless start.

So, a chain of correspondence, which could have resulted in humiliation and dismissal for Bernard before he even got going, was concluded to mutual satisfaction on all sides, without him knowing anything of the involvement of Tizard. Four days later, Bowen's group left Scone for St. Athan, near Barry in South Wales.[39]

Whereas Perth had been less than satisfactory, St. Athan was nothing short of grim. Arriving as darkness closed in on the afternoon of 1st November, Bernard's diary describes a place which "looked foul with the dull evening and mud in the estuary". He found a dreary hotel but, even after a night's rest, things looked no better, especially when he and the rest of Bowen's research group turned up at the partially constructed aerodrome, which the Air Ministry was in the process of setting up as a training and maintenance establishment. They were greeted by a sea of mud and concrete and half a dozen gloomy hangars, which were overflowing with the four thousand personnel who were already on the station. The bemused staff had no idea that a group of scientists were about to descend upon them and even less idea what they should do with them or where to put them. Bowen sent everyone back to Barry to find lodgings and entered into protracted negotiations with the commanding officer who agreed to house them in one of the vast hangars, in which a canvas screen was hurriedly erected to create a makeshift laboratory. Eventually Bowen received orders that his group were to instruct one unit of engineers in the fitting and testing of airborne radars, after which they could return to their proper sphere of research and development.[40] Twenty-one Blenheims arrived from Scone and the work began.

It was a bitterly cold winter, there was no heating in the hangars, which were open to the elements, they had the most basic of tools and much of the equipment which was sent to them for installation was not fit for purpose; on one occasion they took a delivery of thirty receivers from Pye, which Bernard described as "absolute junk"; only six could be salvaged.[41] And it was not only Bernard who was horrified by the conditions. Bowen described them in similar terms, concluding his review of St. Athan:

> The conditions were simply appalling – and any member of the airborne group will say that this was by far the most unpleasant and least productive part of their lives. Here was one of the most sophisticated defence developments being introduced to the Royal Air Force and it was being done in conditions which would have produced a riot in a prison farm.[42]

The only release from this purgatory came with the arrival of Joyce and Susan from Bath. They rented a house in Barry where the pipes froze and remained frozen for two months, but at least they were together and love did much to assuage the frosts and discomforts of the winter.

Quite apart from the working conditions, Bowen and his team were still frustrated at the low priority being given to their research work, as opposed to the emphasis with which Rowe and Touch continued to insist on the programme of installation. Bowen and Rowe had a number of heated exchanges and Bernard, still blissfully unaware of the irritation which had been whipped up by his earlier correspondence with Blackett, fired off more letters expressing his concerns that the scientists on the staff were still being used as glorified fitters. On 14th December, Blackett brought Tizard and Watson-Watt to St. Athan to assess the situation. They were dismayed by what they observed and, within a few weeks, this visit lead directly to plans for redeployment. In spite of the inadequate amenities and of the cold, which was so intense on some days that simply holding a screwdriver was almost impossible, they began to make good progress with both the fitting and the instruction. In early December Bernard's involvement had been diverted from AI to testing and fitting another form of airborne radar, ASV or Air to Surface Vessel. This switch was triggered by an urgent signal that Bowen received in early December 1939, instructing him to install ASV units in a number of Hudson aircraft which had arrived at St Athan.

As early as 1937, Bowen had noted that his AI prototypes could accurately pick up the location of ships at sea. He developed a system using two sorts of aerial; one was a single antenna for long-range spotting of vessels and the other was a pair, with signals which could intersect each other for homing in on the target. At the start of the war, two of the three German pocket battleships, the *Graf Spee* and the *Deutschland*, were at sea and presented a serious danger to the Atlantic routes. The *Graf Spee* was scuttled by her captain, Langsdorff, on 17th December following the Battle of the River Plate, off Montevideo. Meanwhile, as Churchill described, "early in November the *Deutschland* slunk back to Germany."[43] This slinking back had been achieved without detection by British naval and air forces and resulted in immediate orders for planes to be equipped with ASV so that undetected passage would, in future, be more difficult, if not impossible. Three Coastal Command Hudsons were fitted and tested before Christmas; Bernard was on board one of these during a test flight on 21st December and recorded that the ASV worked magnificently over the Bristol Channel. This success was a fair reflection of the achievements of the whole group, as Bowen confirmed:

> Within a few months of our arrival, St. Athan was fitting one aircraft a day with either air-interception or sea-search radar and, as time went on, these figures were far exceeded.[44]

There was a brief respite from frozen pipes and constant work, while he spent Christmas in Bath with Joyce and Susan, before returning to St. Athan by the New Year.

Bernard's ASV test flight in December had gone perfectly, but on 7th

January his two young colleagues from Manchester were testing another Hudson in low visibility when it flew into the side of a mountain near Bridgend. All those on board, including Peter Ingleby and R.K. Beattie, were killed and, for the first time, the reality of the war and death was brought home to him with the sudden shock of an electric current. He was devastated. Both men had been younger than him, their deaths seemed brutally cruel, and they had provided his sole link to the peacetime work of the Manchester physics department. Joyce was on hand to comfort him and Blackett came to stay for a few days. But the most memorable and poignant inspiration was provided by the proud and dignified bearing of Peter Ingleby's father, whom he met for the first time when he came to Barry to collect his son's few belongings.

One afternoon during Blackett's visit, they walked with Joyce along the cliffs and for the first time Bernard talked to him about his ideas for using radar to study cosmic rays. He told him about his conversation with the WAAF on the day war was declared and described the further observations of rogue echoes which he had made during test flights at St. Athan. Blackett was fascinated by Joyce and became absorbed in a race with her to decipher Morse code signals from ships in the Bristol Channel. The score:

Former Girl Guide Lovell *10* Blackett R.N. Rtrd. *0*

Blackett was delighted but he had managed to pay enough attention to her husband's thoughts for his interest to be aroused and they continued the discussion late into the night. Blackett became very excited about the possibility of using radar to study the mysterious origins of high energy particles from the universe and freeing their cosmic ray research from the earthly bonds of the cloud chamber.

"This could be of fundamental significance," he said. "We might be dealing with something as important as Hubble's discovery of the redshift. You must write a paper about it and if the war ever ends it will be a good job for you to return to."

Bernard wasted no time, using every spare moment; he had no proper library facilities and was also preoccupied with his work at the base but some weeks later he sent what he described as a rather elementary paper to Blackett, who made amendments and refined it one evening, whilst taking refuge in an air raid shelter in London. Unknown to Bernard he then submitted the finished article and early in 1941 it was published. The paper concluded:

If the suggestion put forward here, that radio echoes should be detectable from cosmic ray showers, is substantiated by experiment, a new and powerful technique will be available for cosmic ray research, especially for the investigation of the energy spectrum at very high energies.[45]

Side by side at the head of the article appeared the names of the authors:

P.M.S. Blackett and A.C.B. Lovell

CHAPTER EIGHT

Return to Research

Blackett's visit in December 1939 was beginning to bear fruit and whilst he was staying with the Lovells, he told Bernard that part of Bowen's group was going to be moved and established elsewhere as a dedicated research team. The news that Gerald Touch was to remain with the technicians as a coordinator of installation and maintenance was the icing on the cake; he had been a constant brake on the exploration of centimetre wavebands and Bernard was pleased to be free of his control. The memory of the recent tragedy was still raw, but at least there was something to look forward to and his spirits were further restored when Blackett promised that he would send an alpha plus man to work with him. On 9th February the King and Queen paid them a visit giving, as Bowen recalled, "an enormous boost to a group which had been feeling the cold winds of adversity in more senses than one".[46]

When Blackett's alpha plus man, Alan Hodgkin, arrived on 26th February he was everything Bernard could have wished for; a brilliant scientist who later became Master of Trinity, President of the Royal Society and a Nobel Prize winner, Hodgkin was above all a kindred spirit; they were the same age as each other and struck up an immediate rapport. Touch had already transferred to the Royal Aircraft Establishment at Farnborough so they could embark on their work with no fear of being interrupted by comments about wasting time whilst there was a war on. They were joined by Blackett's cosmic ray technician A.H. Chapman and began to work in earnest.

The first task they set about was to build a large horn-shaped antenna, about 2 metres in length; using a new type of valve from GEC in conjunction with the horn, they managed to produce a narrow beam on a wavelength of 50 centimetres. An antenna of this size was far too big to fit to an aircraft and was immobile but it was a start and they persevered with several different horns, measuring the strength and shape of the beams and trying to devise a method of swinging them through the stationary horn so they would scan over a wide front. These efforts continued through March and at the beginning of April they were finally told that they would be joining the new Headquarters of AMRE, which was transferring from Dundee to Dorset, near the coastal resort of Swanage. Within a few days, Bernard was dispatched to reconnoitre the area and to locate Christchurch Aerodrome which had apparently had been allocated to them by the Ministry of Air Production.

On 10th April he drove to Worth Matravers. It was a glorious morning; the Dorset countryside, the sandy beaches and the sparkling sea looked a picture; this was a huge improvement on St. Athan and, even if the location of their headquarters was still somewhat short of facilities, wooden buildings were being erected and Joe Airey, the clerk of works, assured him that everything would be shipshape in time for their move on 4th May. Bernard and Airey then set off to find the aerodrome. Christchurch is about 5 miles from Worth Matravers but when they got there the existence of an airfield was not immediately apparent. They scouted round the village and its surroundings without success and finally resorted to asking in the local tobacconist where it was to be found. The request was met with puzzled expressions on the faces of the shopkeeper and his customers; there was a good deal of head-scratching and sucking in of breath.

"Aerodrome?" said the shopkeeper. "B'aint no aerodrome in these parts." Bernard and Airey continued to insist that there must be one somewhere and after several minutes the helpful purveyor of fine tobaccos suggested that perhaps the gentlemen were looking for the local flying club, which was closed for the duration. The gentlemen hardly thought so, but they followed his directions, which took them to a field surrounded by houses; there they found a disused café, a club room and a couple of small hangars containing two Tiger Moths. Surely this could not be the place they had been looking for. But it was. How on earth were they going to test fly Blenheims and other aircraft from this tiny grass patch? Back at St. Athan Bernard reported to Bowen, who was incandescent.

There was a single grass runway [Bowen recorded], too short for safety and surrounded on all sides by residences. At the western end was a tennis court, which was quickly demolished by a Hurricane that failed to clear the wire surround. This meant no tennis court and one less Hurricane to contribute to the Battle of Britain. There was nowhere for testing new radar equipment. We had already experienced totally inadequate facilities at Perth and St. Athan. Why this was repeated for a third time passes understanding. We were in the hands of people who had no conception about the requirements for sophisticated radar research.[47]

Bernard could not resist interceding, once again, with a higher authority. The new head of the Ministry of Air Production was Sir George Lee, who had taken over from Watson-Watt in January. Soon after his appointment he visited St. Athan and had a cordial discussion with the research team; perhaps Bernard's tendency to take people at face value and to see the best in them lulled him into a false sense of security that the director would welcome a telephone call from a junior boffin, expressing highly critical views about his department. Sir George did not entirely see the matter in that light; indeed, he took a dim view of such an approach and when Bernard told him that there was no aerodrome and nothing but a small flying field, he became very angry; he insisted that his staff could not possibly be mistaken and had selected the place with great care. If that was the case, their competence was sadly wanting; it was probably just as well that Bernard had no chance to make this very fair point as the director cut the conversation short, rather rudely, before he was able to do so. No doubt some poor telephone operator was castigated for putting this impertinent youngster through to the top man. Lee seems to have been a rather touchy individual and he did not last long in the job of director; on 24th October 1940, he told the distinguished electrical engineer, Sir Clifford Paterson, that he could not carry on due to interference from Watson-Watt.[48] Needless to say, Bernard's telephone call achieved nothing in the way of improvements. Fortunately, his intervention had no adverse repercussions either and soon afterwards he was informed that he had been promoted to the rank of 'Scientific Officer'.

The difficulty which the team assembled at Worth Matravers had to overcome was to create a system in the centimetre waveband, which was compact and light enough to be fitted to a plane and which could generate sufficient power to transmit and receive signals on a narrow beam. Hitherto, both the power of the signals and the sensitivity of the receiver reduced drastically as soon as the waveband fell below 1.5 metres; as we have seen, the effectiveness of that wavelength was severely circumscribed by the ground returns picked up ahead of the aircraft at a distance equal to or greater than the height at which it was flying. Although there was very little interest in exploring centimetre wavebands before the war, Bowen had considered and discussed the possibilities during the summer of 1939, with Sir Charles Wright, the director of Scientific Research at the Admiralty.[49] He realised that the only way of improving on the 1.5-metre system was to project forward with a narrow beam and he calculated that the optimum beam width was 10 degrees. The maximum aperture of the on board aerial would be 30 inches, through which a wavelength of 10 centimetres must be achieved; but this would require more powerful transmitters and more sensitive receivers than were currently available; in May 1940, siren voices continued to oppose his ideas and Rowe reported: "At least one person warned me almost daily of the folly of rushing into a centimetre application."[50] Had these voices been heeded, the long term consequences for Britain would have been disastrous.

On May 4th Bernard and Hodgkin arrived at Worth Matravers with a lorry, a trailer and several vans, all full of equipment. They set themselves up in a hut near the cliffs which had magnificent views across the bay and they were soon joined by a number of other scientists, including William Burcham, from Cambridge, H.W.B. Skinner from Bristol, and Philip Dee from the Cavendish Laboratory, who arrived on May 15th. Dee had been working at the Royal Aircraft Establishment before he was told to report to Rowe at Worth Matravers; on his arrival he met Rowe whom he found to be "a very self-important and conceited little man who shows some qualities of drive."[51] He also describes meeting "a very effervescent individual named Lovell who is full of righteous rage about St. Athan and the general chaos." Dee was appointed leader of the team and quickly set about restoring some order. Bernard and Hodgkin set up the horn antenna and soon began to make progress. By the end of the month, they had succeeded in producing enough power on an 11-centimetre wavelength, to enable them to measure the beam; they also made test transmissions through various materials, in order to find which should be used to cover the aerials when fitted onto an aircraft. On 5th June, Dee noted:

> Lovell has got a low power 10 cm glass magnetron[52] working in
> a field coffin for the polar diagram measurements. Much to
> Lovell's annoyance, everyone twiddles the knobs on every
> possible occasion, this being the first working apparatus.[53]

On June 9th they obtained a good reflection back from a sheet of tin, but they still needed to solve the problems of reducing the size of the aerial and increasing the power of the signal.

At the beginning of June they received a visit from Neville Mott who brought with him an antenna constructed from a wire grid fixed to the front of a sheet of metal. Tests with this were encouraging, but the solution to size came when, at Skinner's suggestion, Bernard made a paraboloid aerial, which was only 22 centimetres deep and could be fitted into the nose of an aircraft. The aerial was shaped like a bowl with a central dipole, or antenna; the angle of the sides of the bowl was such that signals would be bounced off them and reflected to the end of the dipole. When they tested it, they found that by moving the dipole 5 centimetres they could shift the line of the narrow beam by 8 degrees. Both the size of the aerial and the mobility of the signal could evidently be resolved and in his diary, Bernard wrote: "This makes me regard the aerial problem as 75% solved."[54] Dee found it hard to take the parabola seriously and on 14th June he wrote:

> Lovell is now measuring polar diagrams on 10 cm in the field outside his hut. His mirrors provide excellent targets for competition between Atkinson and myself of the throwing of large lumps of mud which collect outside the hut.[55]

One month later, on July 19th, the final breakthrough came with the arrival of the first Randall/Boot cavity magnetron from GEC, heralding a new era in the history of radar. "Britain shot into the lead in centimetre wave radar and, once in the lead, she maintained it quite easily until the end of the war."[56]

The klystron was invented in America at Stanford University in the 1930s. It comprised a vacuum tube in which alternating voltages caused clouds of electrons to become highly active. Resonant cavities then created microwave power from the energy of the electrons. Attempts had been made by Oliphant, at Birmingham University, to produce a high-powered klystron for use in centimetre radar, but this had not been successful. J.T. Randall and H.A. Boot were asked to work on another type of vacuum tube, the magnetron, to see if they could produce the necessary energy and they hit on the idea of using a solid block of copper drilled through with

A cavity magnetron.

cylindrical cavities, each connected to a larger central one.

A cathode in the centre of the block was heated to produce clouds of electrons, as in the klystron; the copper block was encased with a powerful magnet which subjected the electrons to magnetic forces creating electromagnetic fields and generating very high frequencies; these in turn reacted with the electrons to produce a powerful microwave signal. Today the system is present in every microwave oven in the world, but in 1940 it revolutionised radar. It was small, weighed only a few pounds and produced enough energy to generate centimetre radio waves with sufficient power to detect the enemy over large distances.[57]

Within a few days the cavity magnetron was attached to the paraboloid aerials and tests were carried out. Good, precise signals were immediately obtained from buildings a quarter of a mile away. They were much encouraged and mounted a double paraboloid on a swivel mechanism so that it could follow a moving target; the magnetron transmitter was attached to one and the receiver to the other. On 12th August, most of the group visited GEC at Birmingham, leaving Bernard and Bill Burcham to continue testing the equipment. At six o'clock in the evening they were still at work when an aircraft happened to fly through the line of the signal at a distance of several miles; to the astonishment of the two young scientists a clear reflection appeared in the cathode ray tube, the first echo of an aircraft in flight ever to be recorded on the 10-centimetre wavelength. When the rest of the group returned there was great excitement and the next day, with some anxiety, they recreated the experiment for the benefit of the whole establishment, including Rowe and Watson-Watt, who travelled down specially to witness the event. A fly past was arranged. But what if it went wrong? Perhaps it had been a fluke. The team all gathered at the hut, full of expectation and, as the aircraft came into view over the sea, the tension mounted. Burcham swung the paraboloid across the sky to follow it. For a few moments there was a breathless pause and then a huge cheer rose up as the echo from the aircraft appeared and the interception of the previous day was successfully repeated. It was a triumphant moment; Watson-Watt was wreathed in smiles and even the taciturn Rowe could not conceal his delight.

It was essential to test the accuracy of the signals and to see the effect, if any, of the presence of background material, so that evening a junior member of staff was asked to ride a bicycle across the front of the cliffs, which were several hundred yards away; he was carrying a sheet of metal and as the aerial followed his rather stately path the reflection which appeared on the receiver screen was precise and unaffected by any sign of ground returns from the cliffs behind him. The magnetron was producing the power needed to generate the narrow beam which they had been striving to obtain for months. The next step was to devise a system which would allow the paraboloid to scan the skies ahead of an aircraft. This had already been the subject of much debate; it was all very well to set up a system on the ground and prove that it could receive a reflection from a moving object which the operator could see and follow; it was a very different matter to equip a pilot with a self-contained unit transmitting a beam that would sweep through 180 degrees ahead to seek out the enemy. One afternoon in late August Bernard was driving to the airfield at Christchurch, when his passenger, Hodgkin, had a moment of inspiration; the solution was to rotate the paraboloid bowl in a spiral round the dipole aerial at a very high speed, deflecting the signal across a wide arc ahead of the aircraft. They were immediately convinced that this could be made to work and an order was placed with the engineering firm of Nash and Thompson at Kingston-on-Thames to make a paraboloid with a 28-inch diameter, which could spin at 1,000 revolutions per minute. Six weeks later the first scanner arrived. It produced the result they had hoped for and, after extensive testing, arrangements were made for the production of a system which could be fitted into the nose of a Blenheim. In March 1941, barely six months after the idea had sprung into Hodgkin's head, the first test flight was successfully accomplished. Some years after the war Bernard was asked how such novel and complex equipment had been produced so quickly in wartime.

"Nobody ever worried about the cost," he replied. "There were only two questions. Can you do it? And when can we have it?"

The first great test of the CH radar chain arose during the Battle of Britain in August and September 1940. Without the early warning system CH provided, Britain would have been defenceless; to intercept the enemy the RAF would have needed a huge force of fighters on permanent patrol and as the *Official History of the Royal Air Force 1939-45* acknowledged, this could not have been achieved with the scarce resources available.

> How could standing patrols, extravagant beyond measure in flying hours, and therefore in aircraft, men and everything else, be maintained at the requisite strength for the requisite length of time round every area to be protected? Only with a gigantic force could this be done – a force so enormous that it would leave us few resources for guns, tanks or ships and none at all for bombers.

In the daylight attacks of August and September, the constant stream of information from the CH radar defences allowed fighters to remain on the ground until they were warned of an attack; they then had enough time to take off and intercept the enemy. Hanbury Brown estimated that by eliminating the need to maintain standing patrols and taking to the skies only when attack was imminent, the warning systems increased the effective strength of our fighter force by at least three times.[58]

In August, the battle over southern England began to cause considerable disruption to the research work at Worth Matravers. There were frequent air raid warnings; one afternoon a bomb fell alarmingly close to the site and to the CH station nearby; it landed harmlessly in the sea and it is far from clear that it was a deliberate attack on a chosen target; but the near miss and the occasional sighting of a low-flying enemy plane led to a decision that this vital establishment must be moved to a less obvious and visible location. Not far away, at Langton Matravers, a girls' boarding school called Leeson House had been evacuated for the duration of the war and was lying empty. A large country house with a stable block, it provided ample accommodation for the equipment and staff and presented a more innocuous appearance to any hostile aircraft than the wooden huts and aerials at Worth. By the end of August, Bernard and the whole team were planning to move to Leeson House. Bernard's group took over part of the stable block and the work continued without the unwelcome interruptions from Adolf's pilots. Their centimetre AI, was set up on a trailer outside the stable block 250 feet above Swanage Bay with splendid views across to the Isle of Wight. At the beginning of October the system was able to detect a Blenheim at ranges of well over 6 miles.

Defeated by day, Hitler turned to night bombing raids, as Tizard and Watson-Watt had predicted. The airborne centimetre system did not become fully operational until March 1942[59] and, in the autumn and early winter of 1940, British defences were almost powerless against the onslaught; operating unaided, 1.5-metre AI did not enable night fighters to close in for the attack and they had virtually no success; when bombers reached the coast, there was no radar cover inland; the anti-aircraft batteries were not much more effective and the terrible destruction of London, Coventry and our other great cities proceeded almost without hindrance. The development of Ground Controlled Interception, GCI, in the late autumn, was the first step on the road to bringing the night attacks to an end. Using GCI, land-based radar operators could track the path of both the attacking bombers and the night fighters. By coordinating these signals with airborne AI systems, such as those fitted by Rowe and his team, pilots eventually learned to make interceptions at night; Blenheims were being superseded by Bristol Beaufighters, which were faster and had greater firepower, and by the spring of 1941 the defensive capability of the RAF was transformed; losses of ten per cent were being regularly inflicted on the Luftwaffe, and in May, when the combination of GCI and AI resulted in the destruction of over one hundred bombers, the campaign of regular night bombing was effectively brought to an end.

Soon after Bernard arrived in Swanage, he had been joined by Joyce and Susan. Many of the townsfolk had left, in fear of invasion; there was no shortage of property to rent, so they quickly found a house which suited them and settled in for a long stay. Joyce dug a vegetable patch in the garden, got to know the local shopkeepers and spent happy afternoons exploring the countryside and taking their daughter to the beach, which was not yet surrounded by barbed wire. Rationing of some commodities had been imposed on 8th January 1940, but at this stage of the war there was a plentiful supply of seafood and local farmers could still provide milk, eggs and vegetables, so they did not go hungry. The evacuation of Dunkirk and the fall of France brought the reality of war too close for comfort. Leaflets signed by the Prime Minister adjured everyone to "STAND FIRM" whilst the invasion was repelled: "The Home Guard, supported by strong mobile columns wherever the enemy's numbers require it, will immediately come to grips with the invaders and there is little doubt they will soon destroy them."[60] Camp beds, gas masks and iron rations were stowed in a cupboard underneath the stairs, which was popularly regarded as the safest domestic refuge from air raids; here the family would huddle by the light of a candle as enemy planes flew overhead. During the day Joyce started a school in the garage where she taught fifteen small children. In the evenings, air raid sirens permitting, there were tennis parties, visits to the local cinema and occasional dances in one of the local hotels. This was to be the pattern of home life for the next two years.

Following the testing of the first Nash and Thompson spiral scanner, it went into the development and production phase and Bernard's attention was directed back to perfecting the system of aerials and fine-tuning the signals which could be recovered from distant objects. A constant stream of ships crossed the bay between Swanage and the Isle of Wight and these provided the perfect targets for experiments, not least because signals were deflected away from the receiver by the surface of the sea but were clearly picked up and reflected back when they made contact with a vessel or the cliffs of the Isle of Wight, at a distance of 20 miles. On October 28th, two naval officers visited Leeson House and witnessed a demonstration; they were sufficiently impressed to report back to their superiors and a high-powered delegation arrived on November 8th and observed the echo from

HMS *Titlark* which was tracked at a distance of 13 miles. Three days later, on the 11th, a submarine, HMS *Usk*, was commandeered; echoes were recovered from 9 miles away whilst she was on the surface and, when she was partially submerged, the conning tower could still be detected at four and a half miles.

These tests were conducted both from Peveril Point, high above the town of Swanage, and from the pier, so that the effects could be demonstrated at different heights above sea level. The naval gentlemen were impressed, but suggested that the pitching and rolling of a ship at sea would make it impossible to obtain a consistent echo from another vessel. Bernard assured them that by using a cylindrical paraboloid this problem would be obviated and he was proved right with the result that, before Christmas, the equipment had been taken to the Royal Naval Signal School at Portsmouth. Within three months operational systems were undergoing sea trials and, in November 1941, 10-centimetre radar detected U-boat *U433*, which was duly sunk off Gibraltar. By the middle of 1942, nearly 250 Royal Navy ships had been fitted with the equipment.[61]

Bernard's research was now directed towards a further development of centimetre radar, the creation of an AI system which would locate an enemy aircraft and then lock onto it so that it could be followed and destroyed by blind firing from a safe range. Throughout 1941 he worked on this project with Freddie Williams, a former Manchester colleague, who had already distinguished himself in the development of IFF (Identification Friend or Foe), the operation of which was an essential complement to any blind firing system, if friendly fire was to be avoided. Together with F.J.U. Ritson, who had joined TRE at the start of the war, they set up their equipment on trailers at Leeson House and, in consultation with Metropolitan Vickers and Ferranti, produced a parabola which would scan continuously until it found a target, onto which an electronic circuit devised by Williams would enable the scanner to lock and follow. The new system was first tested successfully on May 24th, but as work proceeded they discovered that there was high speed fading of the return signal from the target; this affected the consistency of contact, and detailed visual analysis of the fading signals was required to establish why it was happening.

Bernard began by using a cine camera to film the cathode ray tube screen as the fading occurred, but this did not give enough information and he spent some time building a high speed camera to take rapid shots of the screen as echoes were being received. One day, whilst he was so engaged, Blackett paid him a visit and asked him what he was doing. Bernard explained that he was making a high speed camera to study the fading of the pulses from incoming aircraft.

"Well," said Blackett, "I think I've got a young man who may be able to help you." A few days later, on 17th July, Andrew Huxley appeared; a half-brother of Aldous Huxley, he was a brilliant physiologist who had worked with Hodgson and who was later to follow a very distinguished career, winning a Nobel Prize in 1963.

"Blackett sent me. I've come to help," said Huxley.

"Where's your equipment?" asked Bernard. Huxley pulled a small Leica camera out of his pocket and held it up.

"What are you going to do with that?"

"It's easy," replied Huxley. "I shall remove the lens, hold the camera in front of the cathode ray tube and pull out the film manually so it passes swiftly across the screen." He demonstrated his technique and to Bernard's astonishment the exposures which he generated provided exactly what was needed; the images of the pulses were separated and could be examined individually.[62] After several weeks analysing the large number of frames, Bernard was able to report that the system would need to rotate at 6,000 RPM to achieve the smooth operation needed for a constant signal.

The next problem was to adjust the equipment so that it would compensate for any erratic movements of the aircraft in which it was mounted. The Bristol Aircraft Company had no data as to this but Bernard discovered that the London Midland and Scottish Railway Company had a device with which they could measure the stability of trains when encountering uneven tracks. A long train journey to Watford and back and a short conversation with a Mr. W.M. Bond confirmed that the LMR equipment was exactly what he needed and arrangements were made to borrow it. The tests were carried out on October 7th and the information required to calibrate Lock Follow AI for use in a Beaufighter was obtained.

Flight trials began in October and continued until Christmas. Bernard, who was working very long hours, took up temporary residence in rudimentary accommodation on the little airfield at Christchurch and became accustomed to the daily discomfort of taking off and landing on the bumpy grass runway, in all weathers, and to the cramped and often freezing conditions within the aircraft during the test flights. At first the tests were largely unsuccessful and there were constant breakdowns of equipment or failures to find targets or both. A succession of VIPs, from the Duke of Kent downwards, left the airfield singularly unimpressed by what they had seen. By the middle of December, much better results were being obtained and blind firing with camera guns suggested that the system was already sufficiently accurate to promise a success rate of fifty per cent when firing live rounds at enemy aircraft. When Bernard and Joyce left Swanage and spent a happy Christmas in Bath, he was eagerly looking forward to getting the system into operational use during the course of 1942 and could hardly wait to return to work. But, as he was to discover, Fate, and Rowe, had other plans in store for him.

CHAPTER NINE

H2S

Reporting for duty on December 29th 1941, Bernard was greeted by an urgent summons to attend upon Rowe in his office. When he got there Rowe instructed him to stop working on the lock follow system forthwith. He was to take charge of a new development at Hurn airport near Bournemouth. The assignment was to devise a centimetre system for Blind Navigation or BN; the object was to provide Bomber Command with a facility which could deliver accurate bombing in low visibility and at night. Bernard expressed great reluctance to comply with this order; he had invested a year of toil on lock follow and he was very excited with the progress they were making; he told Rowe that he wanted to see the development through to its conclusion. He was also struck by the thought that his work so far had been concentrated on helping Fighter Command protect Britain from German bombers and he was troubled by the idea that the scientific expertise he had gained through that work would be devoted to the creation of equipment, which was bound to bring destruction and death to civilians – even if they were German. Two days later, Dee returned from leave and confirmed the order; he tried to sweeten the pill by taking Bernard to Hurn airport, which had recently been completed with facilities infinitely superior to those at Christchurch. Bernard was still unconvinced and the next morning he was summoned to a further meeting with Rowe and Dee. Once more he tried to explain his wish to continue with the lock follow work, but there was no spirit of compromise.

"There is no alternative," said Rowe. "You are to hand everything over at once and start work on Blind Navigation immediately." Rowe's account of these discussions was confined to the comment: "On 1st January 1942 Lovell was given charge of the H2S project and of the sister project ASV.[63] His turbulent spirit, high moral courage and boundless enthusiasm contributed greatly to the success of these devices."[64] Bernard's diary records that he was heartbroken and that Freddie Williams and Ritson were "terribly fed up".

It is not entirely certain how Blind Navigation acquired the name H2S;

the impetus for the change came from Professor Frederick Lindemann, Churchill's scientific adviser. He was concerned that the original name gave too much away about the nature of the equipment. R.V. Jones recorded Lindemann saying that it was a stinking matter that the device had not been produced earlier and so dubbed it H2S, after the scientific formula for hydrogen sulphide.[65] Rowe's recollection was that: "The code name of H2S chosen by Cherwell was associated with his desire that the equipment should be used for homing in on a target; Home Sweet Home."[66]

Whatever the source of the name, the source of the idea for a system of blind bombing arose from suspicions first harboured by Lindemann, as early as the closing months of 1940 when he told Churchill that he had doubts about the accuracy of Bomber Command's night attacks.[67] He pressed Churchill to authorise an investigation and a number of bombers were fitted with cameras so that a photographic record of their target areas and success rates could be made. The photographs were collected by the RAF Central Interpretation Unit at Medmenham in Buckinghamshire; it was here, in June 1941, that Lindemann's suspicions were confirmed. When he viewed the photographs, "he was aghast at what he saw: instead of being cheered by pictures of the bombers' targets either on fire or reduced to rubble, he found himself bleakly contemplating acres of green pastures that had been cratered by wasted bombs."[68]

In June 1941, Lindemann was created Lord Cherwell. With the authority of membership of the House of Lords added to his close relationship with Churchill, he was in a position to order a full investigation and sent his secretary, David Butt, to Medmenham to carry out an in-depth examination of the photographic records, which consisted of about 650 photographs of one hundred separate raids to twenty-eight targets on forty-eight nights, and to compare them with the claims of Bomber Command. The conclusion to his report was devastating:

1. Of those aircraft recorded as attacking their target, only one in three had got within 5 miles.

2. Over the French ports, the proportion was two in three; over Germany as a whole the proportion was one in four; over the Ruhr, it was only one in ten.

3. In the full moon, the proportion was two in five; in the new moon it was only one in fifteen.

4. In the absence of haze, the proportion is over one half, whereas over thick haze it is only one in fifteen.

5. An increase in the intensity of AA fire reduces the number of

aircraft getting within 5 miles of there in the ratio three to two.

6. All these figures relate only to aircraft recorded as *attacking* the target; the proportion of the total sorties which reached within 5 miles is less by one third.

The conclusion seems to be that only about one third of aircraft claiming to reach the target area actually reach it.[69]

Lindemann disclosed the results of the investigation to Churchill, who was appalled:

The results confirmed our fears. We learnt that although Bomber Command believed they had found the target two thirds of the crews actually failed to strike within 5 miles of it. It also appeared that the crews knew this, and were discouraged by the poor results of so much hazard. Unless we could improve on this there did not seem much use in continuing night bombing.[70]

On September 3rd 1943, Churchill sent a memo to the Chief of Air Staff: "This is a very serious paper and seems to require your most urgent attention. I await your proposals for action."[71]

TRE was already developing two radar systems for Bomber Command. One, known as GEE, provided a navigational capability; the other, called OBOE, was an aid to precision bombing. Although both were of considerable value, they shared the disadvantage of being land-based and of having a limited range, because their signals were restricted to about 300 miles by the curvature of the Earth; OBOE also exposed bombers to AA fire because it required them to fly for a considerable length of time in a straight line.[72] Cherwell had determined that far greater penetration into enemy territory was needed and that this would require a self-contained apparatus, which could be carried on the aircraft. With this object in mind, on 26th October 1941, he attended one of Rowe's regular Sunday meetings, known as Sunday Soviets. Rowe recalled:

Late in October 1941 I held a Sunday Soviet on how to help Bomber Command to bomb unseen targets. Lord Cherwell's insistence on great ranges of operation ruled out systems of the GEE and OBOE type which depended on ground transmissions from England. We therefore discussed the possibility of self-sufficient equipment in a bomber aircraft which might enable electric power lines to be followed or which might detect towns by virtue of the magnetic field associated with electrical installations.

The day ended sadly, for I recall that we went to our homes tired and without an idea.[73]

If Rowe took nothing positive away from the meeting, the same could not be said of Philip Dee, who was now in overall charge of the development of centimetre radar. Thinking about the problem a day or two later, he was suddenly struck by the significance of echoes from the town of Swanage, which had been picked up by the equipment at Leeson House; he also recalled the evening in August 1940 when a junior member of staff had cycled across the front of the cliffs with a sheet of metal, sending back a clear echo. He began to consider whether the narrow beam of the centimetre system would pick up reliable echoes from ground objects such as towns and factories. There was only one way to find out and he instructed Bernard O'Kane and Geoffrey Hensby to carry out tests. O'Kane worked for GEC and was seconded to TRE; Hensby had been an engineering apprentice at the Royal Aircraft Establishment, Farnborough, and joined TRE in November 1940. O'Kane and Hensby had been test flying the Blenheim fitted with the Nash and Thompson scanner, which they modified so that the beam was maintained at a steady angle of 10 degrees below the horizontal. On their first test flight they picked up a good signal from Southampton, when flying at a height of 5,000 feet; the outline of the town was clearly shown against the background of the sea and the surrounding countryside. The image did not look like a map in the conventional sense; rather the echoes created white marks on the screen which varied in extent and intensity depending on the nature of the Earth's surface being reflected at any given moment. Signals hitting the sea would be deflected away from the aircraft, leaving the screen black; some of those striking land would reflect back showing white markings on the cathode ray screen and, on the coastline, creating a defined edge between sea and land; the signals which encountered buildings and towns echoed with strongly marked white areas on the screen, clearly indicating the size and shape of the target.

During the next few weeks they made regular flights inland and, above the cloud cover at between five and ten thousand feet, they were able to pick out the echoes from individual towns. On 1st November they took a camera and photographed the screen as it displayed the echoes from military installations on Salisbury Plain and the coastline of the Bristol Channel. As soon as they landed at Christchurch, the negatives were printed and the prints, still wet, were shown to Dee and to Rowe. Rowe reacted excitedly with the words: "This is the turning point of the war."[74] When the news of the breakthrough reached the ears of Cherwell, he was

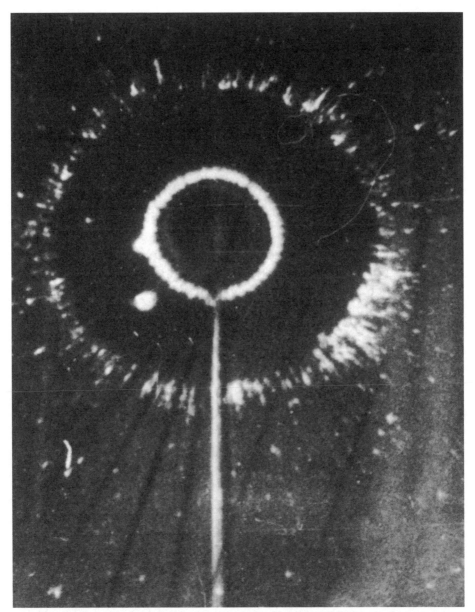

*Fishpond. The simulated attack by a Mosquito. The bearing of the aircraft is shown by
the straight line. The centre circle is the ground beneath. The small white mark below
left of the circle is the "attacker".*

eager to make swift progress with the system and very intolerant of delay;
he took the view that a simple aerial was all that was required and that this
could be fitted quickly into all aircraft; pilots would then have a convenient
map of the target on the screen and accurate bombing could commence at

once. Cherwell's optimism overlooked the need for flight trials and training, not least to establish that the echoes would be returned consistently from identifiable ground objects. A meeting with Sir Archibald Sinclair, the Secretary of State for Air, was arranged for 23rd December and further testing was ordered to determine "whether the signals obtained in separate flights could be definitely associated with specific ground objects". Cherwell insisted that a simultaneous assessment should also be made of the potential for a simple fixed aerial system.[75] This was the background to Bernard's appointment as leader of the H2S project; he had no choice other than to resign himself to the change and he took up his duties at once.

Sinclair had ordered that the scanning equipment should be fitted to one of the new four engine heavy bombers which were then being brought into service. Following the meeting of 23rd December, Dee, O'Kane and Hensby inspected the alternative aircraft and concluded that the Handley Page Halifax seemed to be most adaptable of the choices available. The modified AI equipment they had been using in the nose of the Blenheim could only scan ahead of the aircraft; Bernard and his team quickly came to the conclusion that this would not serve for H2S; what they needed was all-round vision which could be fed to a plan position indicator on board and provide the crew with a virtual map of the ground beneath them, through 360 degrees. Bernard, O'Kane and Hensby discussed the successful trials of the system in the nose of the Blenheim; they were confident that similar results could be achieved by mounting the new scanning system beneath the fuselage of a Halifax, in the centre of the plane. So it was that, on 4th January, three days after his appointment, Bernard and Bob King, the chief aircraft fitter at TRE, visited the Handley Page factory at Radlett in Hertfordshire

They were greeted by Frederick Handley Page and explained that they would need a modified Halifax on which the turret below the fuselage must be replaced with a Perspex cupola 8 feet long, 4 feet wide and 18 inches deep. Handley Page was incensed at the suggestion that the aircraft he had been developing for six years should to be vandalised in this way: "Put that under one of our bombers? That's out of the question," he said. "The device would ruin the performance and we would have to reduce the bomb load."

Bernard was tempted to respond that delivering fewer bombs accurately would be more useful to the war effort than dropping a larger load in the open countryside; fortunately, on this occasion, he kept his thoughts to himself; he was only twenty-eight and as a mere scientific officer he was in no position to argue with the distinguished manufacturer.[76] They left the factory empty-handed and returned to

Leeson House, where Bernard put a telephone call through to Cherwell, who assured him that there would be no delay; the matter was given the highest priority and on March 27th the first bespoke Halifax, V9977, complete with Perspex cupola mounted beneath it, landed at Hurn.

Halifax V9977 arrives at Hurn on 27 March 1942. The H2S cupola is beneath the RAF symbol.

During the first few weeks of 1942, O'Kane and Hensby were making the test flights ordered by Sinclair at the meeting on 23rd December. These tests in the Blenheim, with its forward looking equipment, were spectacularly successful. Flying at altitudes of between 5,000 and 10,000 feet they were able to confirm receiving echoes from Southampton, Bournemouth and Wolverhampton at ranges of up to 35 miles. They flew over the Black Mountains where no echo was received until they picked up the signal from Pontypool, and in Worcestershire, the town of Malvern was clearly definable from the surrounding hillsides; the results boosted their confidence that the transfer of the equipment to the Halifax would present no difficulties.[77] They already had the essential equipment; the centimetre transmitter was being manufactured; the receiver was satisfactory; everything was ready to set up and connect to the rotating scanner which would be fitted to the belly of the aircraft.

Because of anxieties about deploying the cavity magnetron over enemy territory, in case it should fall into their hands, hopes were still being harboured, in some quarters, that the system could operate just as well using the klystron, a device which was well known to German scientists. In order to test this possibility, O'Kane and Hensby reduced the sensitivity of the equipment in the Blenheim, so as to ape the performance obtainable with a klystron system. They concluded that: "range reduction was not sufficient to impair the usefulness of the apparatus". As time would show, this conclusion was not a reliable indicator of the effectiveness of the klystron, but it had the unfortunate result of prolonging the enthusiasm of the pro-klystron lobby, led by Cherwell; this caused delays in the months ahead before the final decision to use the magnetron was reached.

Towards the end of 1941, Group Captain Dudley Saward had been put in charge of a new radar department at Bomber Command headquarters in High Wycombe. Soon after the meeting of 23rd December, the Air Ministry placed an order for 50-centimetre scanners with EMI, under the leadership of the brilliant electrical engineer Alan Blumlein. So insistent was the Ministry that the existence of the magnetron must be kept secret, that the EMI specification required the use of the klystron as the power source for every unit. Fortunately for the future of the entire project the Ministry had instructed that TRE should be provided with two Halifax bombers so that testing of the equipment could proceed with all speed. When Saward visited TRE on 13th February 1942, he was already aware that the scientists there were convinced that the klystron would not be able to provide the power they needed. He was discussing the problem with Dee, when Bernard came into the office and expressed his views in characteristically forthright tones:

"They don't know what they are talking about at the Air Ministry," he said. "The klystron is no good at all. Without the power of the magnetron the transmitter will be useless. The Germans are no doubt already trying to develop one and might get it into action before we do. If we use the magnetron we will leave no productive capacity standing in Germany and they will not be able to make the bloody things." Saward was immediately convinced of the need for the magnetron. He said that the requirements for the new system were that it should have a range of 30 miles when flown at a height of 18,000 feet and that it must provide a clear image of the target for accurate bombing. He also agreed that both the Nash and Thompson magnetron device and the EMI unit fitted with the klystron should undergo trials at the same time, one in each Halifax, so that the performance could be compared.

In order to satisfy Cherwell, tests were also undertaken to establish whether a simple fixed aerial could provide the definition and range required for blind bombing. These tests were negative and the only remaining problem was to persuade Cherwell that the quick and easy solution he was demanding could not be achieved. With this object in mind, Burcham took Cherwell on a test flight, on 20th April. The demonstration was sufficiently unsuccessful to establish that there was no quick and easy solution and no alternative to extensive testing and a long period of development of the spiral scanner; as Burcham wrote in his diary:

> Took Lindemann for display of simple H2S. Not much good on RTB but range view showing quite good DF. Lot of interference from blowers. Demonstration probably had right effect.[78]

It did and Lindemann was convinced.

By this time the scanning equipment was ready for installation, which was completed by 16th April, when the first test flight was attempted; it was not successful due to the failure of the outer starboard engine to supply the power needed to operate the radar equipment; work continued overnight and the first successful flight took place on 17th April 1942, although the signals obtained were of poor range and quality and were a huge disappointment; the signals were intermittent, due to the higher altitude at which the Halifax was flown and the polar diagram, or the shape of the beam, proved to be very unreliable. To Bernard's consternation, instead of being able to make a calm and untroubled assessment, he was subjected to huge pressure by the sudden appearance of the Deputy Chief of Air Staff, who had come down to Hurn to observe the first flight. The problems continued for many weeks, with breakdowns and fading out of the signal and it was clear that much more detailed testing and adjustment was required before the system could become fully operational. The second Halifax, V9490, was fitted with the EMI klystron equipment by 14th May and the work continued with great intensity through the spring and early summer. Meanwhile the reality of war was brought much nearer to home.

One night in April the original TRE site at Worth Matravers was bombed and there was an attack on Swanage which destroyed the railway station and other buildings in the vicinity. Then, on the nights of April 24th and 25th there were huge air raids on the city of Bath, the home of Joyce's parents and many other members of her family. All communications were down and there were twenty-four hours of acute anxiety before a message was received from Bernard's parents that the Chesterman house had been bombed but that the family was safe. The following morning Bernard drove to Bath. It was a beautiful day, the countryside of Dorset and Somerset looked radiant and it was hard to believe that the world was being torn apart by war. As he got closer there were road blocks stopping all traffic, but using his knowledge of the byways and country lanes he was able to drive into the city, where he witnessed horrifying scenes of devastation. The roof of the Chesterman's house had been blown in and windows and doors were gaping open; the house next door had been destroyed as had many buildings on every side. It seemed as if only the Abbey had been spared and it stood as a great edifice in the midst of the destruction. He was told that four thousand people had been killed and over a thousand more were seriously injured. He managed to find his parents-in-law and late in the afternoon they set out on the journey back to Swanage. As they drove away from the city they passed crowds of people trooping along the roads to seek whatever shelter they could find in the open countryside, far away from the bombs. It was a pathetic sight; mothers with babies in their arms, aged grandparents helping to drag exhausted children along the road, carrying bits of bedding and baskets of food to sustain them through the long hours of darkness ahead, and everyone covered in the dust and grime of two nights of bombing. Any scruples which Bernard retained about attacking German towns and his work on H2S immediately evaporated.

The attacks on Worth Matravers and Swanage had been too close for comfort. On 27th February there had been a successful commando raid on a German radar station at Bruneval in Brittany[79] and the Air Ministry was worried about the possibility that the enemy might retaliate with a raid on TRE. No chances could be taken with such an important research facility and it was decided that a safer location must be found for the vital work going on at Leeson, Christchurch and Hurn. Until this was arranged steps were taken to protect the premises; barbed wire fences were quickly erected and armed guards were posted at night; all secret documents were taken inland, to places where they could be kept secure from enemy raids. Early in May it was announced that TRE was to be relocated in Malvern Boys College using the airfield at Defford, a few miles to the south of Worcester. On the 26th May, the entire establishment moved once again. Joyce had now had a second child, Bryan, and she remained in the house at Swanage until arrangements could be made for her to follow her husband to Malvern.

The logistics of moving the equipment which had been accumulated over the previous two years were a nightmare. Day after day of sorting it out and packing it safely for transportation to the school laboratory in Malvern and then unpacking and resorting it for continued use, were not alleviated by any pleasantness of the accommodation where they were billeted or by the friendliness of their hosts, most of whom were less than welcoming. Bernard's diary describes "a dark cavernous depressing house with hostile people" and the weather did not help being "all too wet and miserable". Rowe was to discover that:

Potential billetors fell ill with alarming regularity and the number of destitute aunts who were being given shelter in a few days time passed all bounds of reason. Some gave shelter on the understanding that billetees were in by ten o'clock at night while others gave it on the understanding that they stayed out, somewhere, until the same hour.[80]

It is hardly surprising that the good people of Malvern were less than keen on their new guests. The Boys' College had been evacuated early in the war, but Malvern was an unlikely target for an enemy raid and before long they returned. The school was initially selected in the erroneous belief that it was still unoccupied;[81] once the decision to move there had been approved by the War Cabinet no amount of protest or persuasion by the school, the headmaster, or the Board of Education had any effect. The boys had left the school for the Easter holidays and returned to find that they were moving again. Relations with the locals were not improved by the fact that, for reasons of secrecy, no one could tell them what these hundreds of newcomers were up to; for all they knew their activities would bring down German bombs upon a town which had been largely unaffected by the war.

The entire staff was to be fed centrally in the Winter Gardens, where the WVS were co-opted to provide the catering for a thousand people; there was considerable chaos in the organisation with very long queues at each meal, but the fare was good once they got to the front of the queue. After dinner on the first evening, Bernard, Hensby and A.C. Downing, who had continued to work on lock follow after Bernard's transfer to H2S, sought solace in a public house, before walking up the Worcestershire Beacon. But it was back to work the next morning.

The test flights made by Hensby and O'Kane in the Blenheim had established that the Nash and Thompson set up was capable of recording signals at distances in excess of 30 miles but, at first, the performance of the 360-degree scanner, fitted in the Halifax flying at a much greater altitude, continued to disappoint. Gaps and fades constantly occurred on the plan position indicator (PPI) and the team became increasingly anxious that, if there was no improvement, authority to deploy the magnetron over enemy territory would never be granted. In the second plane, the ranges obtained with the much less powerful klystron scanner were as bad as they had expected, in spite of the best endeavours of Blumlein and his team to provide the system with adequate power. There did not seem to be any reason why the magnetron should be unable to obtain signals at the required range, now revised downwards to 15 miles from the target.

As soon as they arrived in Malvern, Bernard, Hensby and O'Kane set up the equipment on a bench in the Science Laboratory and worked on it for several days, making careful adjustments to obtain a better performance. Simultaneously Blumlein's EMI team was working on improvements to their klystron. By the time the bench work was completed the two Halifax planes had arrived at Defford and the scanners were fitted for further flight tests; the results obtained from the magnetron scanner in Halifax V9977 were much more encouraging but, to the surprise of no one, the same could not be said of the tests in V9490; the klystron was not able to produce the power required to generate signals in the centimetre waveband; it became clear that O'Kane and Hensby had been over-optimistic about its capabilities during their earlier tests.

Throughout these upheavals, the programme was being given the highest priority from the highest authority. Cherwell's enthusiasm was replicated by that of his boss; the Prime Minister took a keen interest in the project and was as impatient as Cherwell to see it brought to a speedy conclusion, firing off a series of memos to the Secretary of State for Air:

14 Apr 42
Unless we can ensure that most of our bombs really do some damage it will be difficult to justify the pre-eminence we are according to this form of attack.

6 May 42
I am glad that the numerous matters raised in my memo of April 14 are in hand. I hope that a really large order for H2S has been placed and that nothing will be allowed to stand in the way of getting this apparatus punctually. If it fulfils expectations it should make a big difference in the coming winter.

7 June 42
I have learnt with pleasure that the preliminary trials of H2S have been extremely satisfactory.[82]

Quite how the Prime Minister had come to be informed that the progress was "extremely satisfactory" is far from clear; the news would have been something of a surprise to Bernard and his team. But by a cruel twist of fate the last of these memos was sent on the very day on which the H2S programme suffered a setback that was to delay production for many months.

CHAPTER TEN

Disaster and Triumph

The progress which had been made with the magnetron powered transmitter encouraged the EMI team to visit Defford so that they could compare the performance with that of the klystron system in R9490. On Friday 5th June 1942 Alan Blumlein and two of his colleagues, C.O. Browne and F. Blythen travelled down to Tewkesbury and put up at The Swan for the weekend. The next morning they drove over to Defford for a day of discussions with Bernard, O'Kane and Hensby about the effectiveness of the two equipments and the further developments that were needed. They returned to The Swan late on Saturday afternoon and spent a pleasant evening there, far away from the cares of war. Bernard and Geoffrey Hensby took an evening flight in the Halifax V9977 and were delighted by the much improved echoes which they received from Cheltenham, Gloucester and other towns, with better range and clarity being recorded than they had previously achieved.[83]

On Sunday morning Bernard asked Hensby and another member of the group, Pilot Officer C.E. Vincent, to organise a test flight for Blumlein and his team that afternoon. The arrangements were made and after lunch the three EMI scientists assembled at Defford. They boarded the plane at a quarter to three. As he climbed the steps Blumlein turned to Bernard, saying that they would only take a short flight and disappeared into the aircraft. V9977 took off at 2.51 pm; on board were Hensby, Vincent and Squadron Leader Sansom, from TRE; Blumlein, Blythen and Brown from EMI; and an RAF flight crew consisting of five men.

The weather and conditions on a beautiful summer afternoon were perfect for flying; the plane was in first-class condition and the passengers were eagerly anticipating their observations of the scanning equipment. After two hours V9977 had not returned and Bernard began to worry. At 5.00 pm he rang control and was told that they had not landed. For the next two and three quarter hours, there were increasingly frantic calls to control, the officers' mess, the commanding officer and other members of the RAF staff; they heard nothing, until 7.45 pm, when news came through that the plane had crashed. At 8.35 the full extent of the tragedy was confirmed: R9977 had come down in the Wye valley at about 4.20, an hour and a half after take-off. The plane had exploded on impact and every man on board was dead.

At nine o'clock in the evening it was still light and the commanding officer at Defford took Bernard and O'Kane to the site of the disaster. His diary for June 8th describes the scene which greeted them:

> Group Captain King drove O'Kane and myself down to salvage the apparatus. It was about 6 miles SW of Ross right in the Wye valley. It was a mass of charred wreckage, quite unbelievable. We salvaged some bits but there wasn't much except the magnetron recognisable. Arrived back 12.30 at Defford and finally Malvern at 2. Then Dee got me up – I didn't get back until 3.00 am. Today I don't feel as bad as I thought I should. Almost as though I am used to it with Ingleby and Beattie. The loss of Blumlein is a national disaster. God knows how much this will put back H2S.[84]

The shock and grief at the deaths of his trusted colleagues was hard to bear, and for a young man of twenty-eight the sight of eleven bodies "lifeless under sheets near the charred remains of a bomber in which I had flown the previous evening"[85] was horrifying. The four scientists who had perished had become personal friends and all shared with him a joint determination, working together to produce the instruments, which the country so desperately needed in the fight against Nazi Germany. Hensby was only twenty-three; Bernard had been in the plane only the day before and had asked him and Vincent to organise the flight; the anguish he felt at the death of his young friends haunted him for the rest of his life. Three days after the accident he wrote to Joyce, who was still living in the house at Swanage:

> The accident has left a great aching sore in our minds which is always there. We try to forget it by working hard and thinking that we just have to make a tremendous job of it to make up for that enormous sacrifice.

Nearly forty years later he wrote:

> For me Hensby was a tragic loss. At Birkbeck College, London, he had started research on cosmic rays before he joined the group. He was a fellow spirit, and on that depressing day of our arrival in

Malvern I wrote 'Hensby and I found a pub, drank a pint and then at 10 pm climbed up the Worcester Beacon and decided it was a marvellous place to experiment on.' The uninterrupted view eastward from the top of the beacon was later to lead to an idea destined to save the lives of many bomber crews, but not that of Hensby.[86]

At the age of ninety-seven he still felt the pain: "It was devastating," he told me in April 2011, sitting in his orthopaedic chair in the sitting room of his home in Cheshire; for seventy years hardly a day passed without him remembering the crash of V9977. The deaths of those eleven young men surely played a part in driving forward his dedication to science. His life's work endowed them with a fitting memorial.

The need for secrecy and the priorities of wartime Britain prevented a thorough investigation into the crash, which went entirely unreported in the press. An inadequate contemporary record concluded that, following the failure of the outer starboard engine, an attempt to restart it caused it to catch fire at an altitude of two to three thousand feet; the fire extinguishers failed to work and were probably empty; the plane lost height and crashed into the ground from 500 feet. Forty years later, W.H. Sleigh, a retired aeronautical engineer at the Royal Signals and Radar Establishment carried out an in-depth examination of the cause of the tragedy.

Sleigh found an eyewitness, Onslow Kirby, a farm worker who was standing only a few hundred yards from the crash site. He described seeing the plane with the starboard wing on fire, at a height of 350 feet; the wing broke off, the bomber rolled over and crashed upside down exploding into a fireball. Sleigh discussed the accident with former Rolls Royce engineers and concluded that it was caused by human error. A maintenance engineer had failed to ensure that a valve was fully locked, gases escaped into the systems resulting in the fire, the explosion and the crash which killed everyone on board.[87]

Mystery surrounds the failure of any one of the eleven men on board to bail out. It may be that there were no parachutes or too few to go round; there would have been very little time to react and perhaps, in the heat of the final catastrophe, there was a collective decision to remain together and trust to fate; all of them must have known that death was staring them in the face; at least, apart from the agony of anticipation, it was mercifully instantaneous when the aircraft hit the ground.

For several days a sense of despair pervaded the entire establishment. Two vital members of the team were dead and the only magnetron prototype had been destroyed. The three EMI scientists who were familiar with the klystron equipment in R9490 had also died. There seemed at first to be no way forward. The speed with which the pieces of the disaster were picked up was due, in no small part, to the determination of the Prime Minister that nothing should get in the way of progress. Churchill summoned a meeting for eleven o'clock on the morning of 17th June at which he intended to insist on the swift installation of H2S in a large number of aircraft. On the evening of 16th June, Bernard and Philip Dee arrived in London, only to find that the meeting had been cancelled because, as they discovered later, the Prime Minister flew to the United States for discussions with President Roosevelt. The meeting was reconvened on his return and took place on 3rd July at Number 10 Downing Street. As well as Bernard and Dee it was attended by the Secretary of State for Air, the Minister of Aircraft Production, Schoenberg, the head of EMI, Cherwell, Watson-Watt, the Assistant Chief of Air Staff, and the Commander-in-Chief of Bomber Command, 'Bomber Harris'. Sir Robert Renwick, who was chairman of a radar committee at the Air Ministry, in charge of coordinating research and development, was also present. They stood respectfully outside the door of the cabinet room, waiting for the Prime Minister. After some minutes he appeared, dressed in the ubiquitous siren suit and smoking an enormous cigar. "Good morning, Gentlemen, come in," he said, as he swept past them. They were all seated along one side of the cabinet table as Churchill stood opposite them with his back to the fireplace.

He announced that he must have two hundred H2S scanners installed by 15th October. He was told about the crash on 7th June and Schoenberg said that his firm could not do the necessary work on that time scale. The cigar was propelled over the Prime Minister's shoulder into the fireplace:

"We don't have objections in this room," he said. "I must have two hundred sets by October." Bernard explained that he had lost the only prototype and half his team in the crash.

"Now look here, young man," said Churchill. "You lost one bomber. We lost thirty over Cologne last night. I must have those equipments." He constantly pressed a buzzer on the table in front of him; minions would appear and he demanded to know where his notes were – they were before him on the table – and why there was no secretary to take minutes. This task descended upon the Minister of Aircraft Production, as the discussion raged on between Churchill's demands and the attempts of Bernard, Dee, Schoenberg and Watson-Watt to explain the difficulties; all such explanations were falling on a pair of very deaf ears and several more partially smoked cigars were projected violently over the prime-ministerial shoulders into the fireplace. A major general in full uniform appeared:

"The cabinet is waiting Prime Minister," he said.

"Tell them to wait," said Churchill as he turned to Cherwell. "What does the Professor think?"

"They can be built on breadboards!" said the Prof. What he meant by this obscure remark remained a mystery, but the Prime Minister was in no mood for compromise.

"What does the Air Marshal think?" he asked Harris.

"I must have them in Stirlings," was the reply. Finally the Prime Minister announced that he had to see the cabinet.

"You must now decide how to produce two hundred H2S sets by mid-October; it is our only means of inflicting damage on the enemy. The Prof says it can be done. Go into that anteroom and do not emerge except to tell me that I can have my squadrons equipped by October." The force of the great man's personality left little room for argument. There was no alternative but to agree, even if they were agreeing to the impossible. Churchill secured the promise he demanded and they left Downing Street feeling as if they had been put through a mangle.

The promise extracted by Churchill resulted in a period of frenetic activity for Bernard and his team. There was a constant round of visits to Nash and Thompson, EMI, and Handley Page and consultations with Renwick and the men from the Air Ministry. Harris had demanded that Stirling bombers should be fitted with the equipment, so Short Brothers was added to this list. The first priority was to secure permission for the use of the magnetron system. On 10th July, Tait and Cherwell arrived at Defford and after a day of heated argument Bernard recorded in his diary: "we have almost persuaded them to use the magnetron".[88] The final confirmation came on 15th July, when the Secretary of State for Air ordered that all work on the klystron should cease and that the two squadrons were to be fitted with the magnetron system, which could be used in action "if the Russians hold the line of the Volga."[89] Bernard had been confident enough to pre-empt this decision and a new prototype magnetron transmitter had already been fitted in the surviving Halifax.

On 3rd July, the team was greatly strengthened by the arrival at Defford of Don Bennett, an Australian who was later described as "perhaps the greatest flying expert in Bomber Command".[90] Bennett had been shot down over Norway in April 1942, but had escaped across the mountains to Sweden, from where he was returned to Britain. He was given command of the new Pathfinder Force, which was to use H2S to identify and mark targets. Bennett insisted that all flight testing should take place at night, with servicing and modification being carried out during the day. The whole team became immersed in work around the clock, testing and tweaking in the cramped and freezing conditions of the navigator's cockpit at 18,000 feet or fine-tuning the equipment on the ground between flights. Significant improvements in performance were achieved as the weeks passed, although the signals received at higher altitudes remained unreliable and difficult to interpret at times.

Sir Robert Renwick quickly realised that the timetable demanded by the Prime Minister was wholly unrealistic. He was in a very powerful position, having been appointed at the suggestion of Churchill with particular instructions that he should concentrate on the H2S programme and not get diverted by work on other apparatus.[91] Renwick and his assistant, Frank Sayers, became a vital conduit between TRE and the Air Ministry and provided a direct line of communication to Cherwell and the Prime Minister. Discussions with Renwick resulted in a schedule for equipping twenty-four Halifax and twenty-four Stirling bombers for the Pathfinder Force by the end of the year.[92] This was still a tall order and proved, in the end, to be optimistic, but at least the TRE team was now able to concentrate on a single system with a programmed target that had some chance of being achieved.

Another Halifax and a Stirling aircraft arrived at Defford; Saward ensured that the staff needed for testing were in plentiful supply and the work on refining and improving the performance of the scanners continued throughout the autumn. At the end of September, a Halifax, in which better but far from perfect results had been obtained, was sent to the Bomber Development Unit for tests; the response of the BDU navigators was anxiously awaited with considerable trepidation; the reaction when it was reported that the system was considered to be "valuable to a high extent both as a navigational aid and as an aid to locating targets"[93] was a mixture of surprise and relief. The comparative success of the BDU tests did much to counteract the depression which Bernard was beginning to feel at the negative attitude that was evident in some quarters. The Americans, in particular, were unconvinced by the viability of H2S and on a visit to TRE in July, Rabi, from the Massachusetts Institute of Technology, infuriated Bernard, Dee and the rest of the H2S group by announcing: "H2S is unscientific and unworkable" and that "if you persist with your plans the only result will be that the Germans will obtain the secret of the magnetron."[94]

The irritation which such remarks caused was soothed by the allocation of a family flat in Malvern and the great happiness of being reunited with Joyce and the two children. On 14th October Bernard received another much needed boost to his morale when Saward flew him from Defford to the BDU airfield in Cambridgeshire. There he spoke to the navigators who had been using the equipment in test flights; all of them expressed satisfaction with the results they were obtaining. In the evening, they went on to Lakenheath, where they saw a squadron of Stirlings take off on a mission to bomb Cologne. GEE was the only aid available to the bomber crews and, according to Saward, it had been jammed and would not help them that night. The hours dragged by as they waited for the return of the squadron. At last it arrived, much depleted by the German defences. At the debriefing of the surviving crews, it was clear that not one of them had even seen the target. It was a moment of revelation for Bernard who realised that they would have been infinitely better off with the imperfect system which he was working on, than they had been with nothing but the stars and a compass to guide them. He recorded in his diary that he was "now absolutely convinced of the necessity of H2S".[95]

EMI had promised to supply fifty sets for installation and, in spite of the difficulties caused by the loss of Blumlein, Blythen and Browne they delivered them on time. By the end of the year twelve sets had been fitted in Halifax bombers and another twelve, in accordance with the stipulation of Harris, in Stirlings; the Pathfinder Force would be ready as soon as O'Kane had trained enough navigators to use the system, with all its faults, to the best effect. The training was carried out early in the new year; all that was needed now was the chance to test the equipment in earnest.

With the defeat of the German armies at Stalingrad, the embargo on using H2S was lifted at the end of January, and on Friday 29th Bernard received a telephone call from O'Kane in which he signalled that they were about to go into action, with the words: "I advise you to take a weekend in the country." The next day he drove to Wyton where he was told that the Pathfinder Force was to lead an attack on Berlin. The last minute weather reports were very poor and a late decision was made to switch the target from Berlin to Hamburg. The twenty-four planes equipped with H2S took off at midnight, followed by a heavy contingent of Lancaster bombers. Following their departure a pall of apprehension hovered over the silent airfield; no news was expected until they returned; all that those left behind could do was wait. The weather was appalling and as zero hour approached fears on the ground for the safety of the airmen and the success of the mission intensified; the unbearable tension was not alleviated by the premature arrival of forty of the Lancasters and seven Pathfinders, all reporting that adverse weather conditions and equipment failures had prevented them from reaching the target area; several of the new equipments had failed to operate and it seemed as if the success of entire operation was in jeopardy.

At last, as dawn was approaching, there was something to celebrate; a

Halifax landed and was greeted by the anxious welcoming party. As the plane taxied to a halt, they could see the excited pilot giving an emphatic thumbs-up. The exhausted crew tumbled out of the aircraft and broke the news: the equipment had done its job; the docks of Hamburg had been unmistakeable on the radar, which showed them sticking out like fingers into the dark surroundings of the sea; towns and villages had been plainly indicated on the outward journey, greatly assisting in navigating to the target area; coastlines and estuaries were clearly defined; markers had been dropped; and, as the rest of the raiding party returned, they reported triumphantly that the main force had been able to drop their bomb loads accurately. The months of hard work and the sacrifice of Blumlein, Hensby and the others on V9977 had not been in vain; the system was far from perfect; operators continued to experience fading of the signals, especially at high altitudes; much depended on the skill level of each navigator; but bomber crews were now far better equipped to find and hit their targets; H2S had worked.

Following the first few raids Bernard received a telegram from the Commanding Officer of the Pathfinder Force at Wyton, Don Bennett, soon to be promoted to the rank of Air Vice Marshal:

> To Dr Lovell TRE   February 3rd 1943
> Heartiest congratulations from myself and other users to you and your collaborators in the development of the outstanding contribution to the war effort which has just been brought into action.[96]

The official assessments of the performance of the new system were better than anyone at TRE had dared to hope. Following the first raid Bomber Command concluded: "H2S is the most successful blind navigation and bombing aid yet devised."[97] On 9th February they produced a full report on the bombing of Hamburg, Cologne and Turin:

> On the operations under review, navigators were able to identify a large number of landmarks without difficulty and to obtain ranges and bearings from which to fix their position.
>
> The average maximum range at which landmarks were identified was in the order of 25 miles.
>
> Hamburg was very easily identified and the shape in the Cathode Ray tube was as expected.
>
> Navigators reported that:-
> Coastal towns and towns on estuaries and large rivers were

particularly easy to identify;

The picture obtained of large towns closely resembled the shapes given on the maps carried;

Some small towns showed up with more prominence than was expected.

In addition to the exceptional value of H2S for identification and bombing of the target, its great navigational value has been proved beyond all doubt.

The ease with which targets have been identified and attacked proves that if this device were introduced into as many heavy bombers as possible it would greatly increase the destructive power of the bomber force.[98]

This very positive assessment of the performance raises two questions: first, why was H2S not brought into operation sooner? Secondly, what effect would earlier deployment have had upon the course of the war?

The reluctance to use the system before the fall of Stalingrad was motivated by fears that if a magnetron got into enemy hands, German scientists would be able to work out how it was being used; once they had done so they could take countermeasures to jam the signals or make them ineffective and they would be able develop their own centimetre radar. As things turned out, these fears were without foundation.

In February 1943 a German scientist called Otto Hachenberg was sent to investigate radar equipment from a British bomber which had been shot down. Amongst the wreckage he recovered the remains of a device which he named 'Rotterdam' after the city where the bomber had crashed. The only part of it which was intact was the magnetron. Bernard knew nothing of this until 1977, when he visited Germany and met Professor Hachenberg who was his opposite number as Director of the Effelsberg radio telescope. Following a visit to the observatory, Hachenberg took the British contingent out to dinner and during the course of the evening suddenly remarked:

"I know what you were doing during the war, Lovell. You worked on radar in bombers."

"How on earth did you know that?" replied the astonished Bernard.

"We have our ways!" said Hachenberg, enigmatically. "As a young man working in Telefunken I was sent to investigate your equipment in a bomber that crashed near Rotterdam in 1943."[99]

"Were you surprised by it?" asked Bernard.

"Not really," replied the German professor. "We knew about the magnetron and we worked out what it was used for." Bernard asked why the Germans had not developed the magnetron themselves.

"We were ordered by Hitler to concentrate on the 1.5-centimetre waveband," was the reply.

It was not until the death of Hachenberg that Bernard was sent a copy of the report which the young German had written sixty years earlier, in May 1943. The report made it clear that, contrary to the belief of the Allies, the Germans already knew about the properties of the magnetron, which Hachenberg immediately recognised as a power source for producing radio waves in the centimetre waveband. A copy of Hachenberg's report is contained in the Lovell archives at the Imperial War Museum, alongside a partial translation;[100] it reveals that he was unable to fathom out precisely how the device worked. From information which was obtained by interrogating prisoners he understood that the system was capable of picking out rough features of the terrain beneath the aircraft, that it was difficult to operate, that towns and water surfaces could be identified and that Pathfinder planes used the system to mark targets for the bombers; there was also a possibility that the device could be used against U-boats. Even if they had obtained more information and had been capable of creating similar equipment, it is unlikely that the German scientists would have been allowed to do so, since, as Hachenberg had told Bernard over dinner, Hitler ordered concentration on longer wavelengths. That the German neglect of the significance of centimetric radar resulted from decisions at a high level is confirmed in a letter written to Bernard by Professor Wielebinski who sent him the Hachenberg report:

It is correct that in your conversation with Professor Hachenberg in 1977 he insisted that the principle of the magnetron was known in the Telefunken Company but by 'higher order' the engineers were told to continue the longer wavelength radar development rather than go to short cm waves.[101]

The prospect of German scientists being allowed to devote time and resources to develop and build a 'Rotterdam' of their own was, in reality, nonexistent. With the benefit of hindsight, it is clear that British and American anxieties about the magnetron falling into enemy hands were groundless; the magnetron system would have been operational much earlier if the brilliant EMI team led by Blumlein had not been forced to concentrate on the klystron; there was no need to delay its use over enemy territory; arguments about the benefits of strategic bombing remain to this day, but H2S could have been deployed over Germany, in the autumn of 1942; if it had been, such benefits as did result from strategic bombing would have begun to flow up to six months earlier than was in fact the case. Of the vital importance of the war at sea Churchill wrote:

> The Battle of the Atlantic was the dominating factor all through the war. Never for one moment could we forget that everything happening elsewhere, on land, at sea, or in the air, depended ultimately on its outcome, and amid all other cares we viewed its changing fortunes day by day with hope or apprehension.[102]

As we shall see, if the system had been used against U-boats during the winter of 1942-3, the loss of 1.5 million tons of shipping would have been prevented; the emasculation of the U-boat threat would have been attained by the end of 1942; German ascendency in the Battle of the Atlantic would have been ended much sooner; and the course of the war would have been dramatically altered.

CHAPTER ELEVEN

U-Boats and Rockets

The fall of France and the capture of the French ports had presented Hitler with the prize of access to the Bay of Biscay and Admiral Dönitz was quick to exploit this advantage by setting up bases, from which his U-boats could prey on the shipping lanes of the North Atlantic. For two years U-boat traffic across the bay was largely uninterrupted; they were sailing within the range of Coastal Command bombers and the breaking of the German Naval Enigma signals enabled British forces to find U-boats "at least as regards their general location".[103] This did not solve the problem, however, because if the Germans felt in any danger during daylight hours they could remain submerged, resurfacing to recharge their batteries at night, when, even if their general location was known, it proved very difficult to find them. The consequent destruction of shipping was a dangerous threat to Britain's ability to sustain the war effort.

In June 1942, Coastal Command was equipped with a new aid to night sorties over the bay. The invention of Wing Commander Humphrey de Verd Leigh, the Leigh Light, was a searchlight fixed beneath the fuselage of Wellington bombers which were also carrying ASV,[104] operating on the 1.5-metre waveband. In April 1941, tests of this equipment had shown that so long as the conning tower was visible a submarine could be spotted at a distance of up to 20 miles; the problem of ground returns did not occur over the sea which bounced the radio waves away from the ASV device, so that a clear signal from the U-boat would reflect back to the operator. Even on a dark night, an aircraft could home in on the echo until it was within a mile of the target. At that point the Leigh Light would illuminate the surface of the sea in the last few seconds of approach, so that the U-boat had no time to dive before being attacked. For a U-boat captain sailing under the security of a dark sky, the unheralded blaze of light and the furious bombardment which immediately followed was a terrifying prospect. The destruction of some twenty U-boats during June and July so alarmed commanders and their crews that they took to remaining submerged at night, surfacing during the day to recharge. This did expose them to danger from daylight attacks, but at least they could see the enemy coming and could either take evasive action by diving or have some chance of defending themselves by opening fire on the attackers. However the effectiveness of the U-boat campaign against Allied shipping was, for a time, severely curtailed and Dönitz recorded: "There being no defence against aircraft in the Bay of Biscay, the RAF can do as it pleases."[105]

By the autumn of 1942, German scientists had built a device that could pick up the 1.5-metre signals from Coastal Command radar equipments. This simple radio receiver, called Metox,[106] was mounted on the conning tower. "A beam was indicated by a pinging in the receiver and from August losses sharply declined."[107] It was quickly installed in the entire U-boat fleet, which was restored to its former position of being able to deploy safely on the surface at night, getting ample warning of the approach of hostile aircraft, so that they could dive to safety. The vital shipping losses in the North Atlantic began to rise once again. In the early months of 1943 the destruction escalated to an alarming level, 514,744 tons being lost in March alone.[108] Another solution to the U-boat threat was badly needed and the obvious one was to operate on a much shorter wavelength, which would not be detected by Metox.

Whilst Bernard's team had been working on H2S, another group at TRE was trying to develop a centimetre ASV system for Coastal Command; priority had been given to H2S, however, and there was no prospect that centimetre ASV would be ready in time to deal with the present crisis. On 30th September 1942, Dee and Bernard, immersed as they were in their work, were summoned to London for a meeting with Renwick. They were told that H2S must be installed in the ASV system which was being developed for Coastal Command as a matter of urgency.[109] The ASV group was to be disbanded and it would be necessary for some of the H2S equipments which were being prepared for Bomber Command to be reallocated to Coastal Command. These orders created a good deal of irritation on all sides: Bernard and his team were already snowed under with their efforts; at Bomber Command Harris was furious when he was told that some of his H2S sets were to be diverted for use against U-boats; Coastal Command were less than pleased that the group they had been working with was to be disbanded; Ferranti, who had been asked to manufacture the centimetre ASV, no longer had a contract; and the ASV team was broken up, some of them being sent to join Bernard and some elsewhere. However much argument these changes caused in the short term, the logic of the position was undeniable: H2S was ready for use and could be fitted in the Coastal Command Wellingtons, subject to some modifications and repositioning of the scanner beneath the nose of the aircraft; the centimetre ASV system would not be operational for many months; Renwick, was determined that H2S should be used in spite of the opposition of Cherwell, who suggested that rather than transferring any Bomber Command planes to combat U-boats, Coastal Command should make greater use of their existing aircraft by increasing the number of crews and working the planes round the clock – the wartime equivalent of hot-desking. Cherwell argued that:

> The best role for Coastal Command aircraft would be for the protection of the Atlantic convoys, and not for chasing elusive submarines in the Bay of Biscay. He also thought that neither operation justified diverting aircraft from attacks on Germany.[110]

Fortunately his opinion, which entirely accorded with the urgings of Harris, did not dictate the course of events and some Bomber Command planes and H2S equipments were made available for use over the Bay of Biscay, although the paranoia about keeping the secret of the magnetron meant that permission for deployment was not granted until after Bomber Command had begun to use it at the end of January 1943.

The Commander-in-Chief of Coastal Command, Sir Philip Joubert de la Ferte, was among those who lacked enthusiasm for the revised programme and several delays were caused by unnecessary demands from some of the officers serving under him. These problems were overcome, in spite of the additional load imposed on the H2S work force, by having to design and build the new system, and in the new year two Wellingtons were sent to Chivenor in North Devon for the training programme to begin under the guidance, once again, of Bernard O'Kane. By the end of February there were twelve Wellingtons, fitted out with H2S /ASV, and operational flights began. Sir John Slessor had replaced Joubert, which resulted in a much better relationship between TRE and Coastal Command, although the hostility of some of the officers remained. When the first two Wellingtons took off from Chivenor on the night of 1st March, Bernard waited for their return in the office of the Station Commander, Wing Commander Rowland Musson, whose antagonism epitomised the attitude of many in Coastal Command:

"What good do you think that gadget of yours is going to do out there?" he grumbled. "You ought to fly out and look for yourself at that great featureless expanse; then you would realise that your rotating thing would never stand a chance of catching a sub."[111] As it happened, no U-boat was spotted that night, but Richard Fortescue of TRE, who had flown in one of the aircraft to operate the radar, made a great impression;

his plane had been attacked by an enemy fighter and the instructions which he gave the pilot enabled them to escape; the reputation of the system amongst the Coastal Command crews soared. Musson was killed on 24th August 1943, when the Wellington he was flying crashed, whilst searching for U-boats.

It was not until 17th March that the first sighting of a U-boat was made at a range of 9 miles and no attack was possible on that night due to the fact that the Leigh Light jammed.[112] The next night there was a sighting at 7 miles, the Leigh Light did its job and the unsuspecting U-boat was successfully attacked with depth charges. The tide of the war against the U-boats had finally turned. There were thirteen attacks during the remainder of March, and twenty-four in April. The reaction of the German commanders mirrored that of the previous year and they began to surface during the day. Coastal Command forces were much stronger than they had been in the summer of 1942 and, by day and night, in May and June of 1943, they inflicted "an absolute slaughter".[113] The German submariners had no hiding place; they sustained insupportable destruction from which they never fully recovered and Allied shipping losses fell to 21,759 tons in June.[114]

It is clear that the Germans failed to understand how the British were able to find their submarines. Eberhard Rössler records that:

> At the end of July 1943, it was believed that the enemy could zero in on the receiver carried in the U-boats. This led to the order forbidding the use of Metox and the resumption of U-boat operations in the North Atlantic was postponed until new detection receivers had been fitted.[115]

As they were completely mistaken about the nature of the British device, even new detection receivers would have been worthless. Dönitz called off operations in the North Atlantic and later admitted that Germany had lost the Battle of the Atlantic.[116] Hitler had no choice but to approve the decision to withdraw U-boats, abandoning one of his most treasured hopes for victory.[117] Hitler and Goebbels both believed that the U-boat force, under the command of Dönitz was a devastating threat, which would enable Germany to win the war. But by 23rd September 1943 Hitler realised that Dönitz had been left with no alternative to the withdrawal of German submarines from the Atlantic. Nothing less would have saved the fleet from total destruction.

In spite of the success of the Coastal Command campaign there was a constant worry that it would not be long before the enemy refined their listening equipment to detect the centimetre signals and would, as in 1942, be able to avoid attack from the air. R.V. Jones, the head of the Air Ministry's Intelligence Branch, was also anxious that the regular interception and destruction of U-boats would lead the Germans to the conclusion that their Enigma code had been broken. At the request of the Naval Intelligence Division, Jones undertook the task of trying to mislead the enemy as to how the U-boats were being located:

> The basis of the deception was that we should give the impression that we were finding the U-boats, not by radar, or by the Enigma signals, but by infrared. I therefore provided a series of clues and this appears to have been successful; for not only were the Germans very slow in realising that we were using centimetre radar against them at sea, long after they had found it in our crashed bombers, but they also developed a most ingenious paint for their U-boats to camouflage against infrared as well as against visible light.
>
> Another hoax may also have played a part. A British prisoner of war under interrogation ingeniously told the Germans that our aircraft were homing on to some kind of radiation that was coming out of the 'Metox' receivers. It was a complete fabrication, but when the Germans investigated they found that radiation was indeed emitted from Metox receivers and they went to some trouble to suppress it.[118]

Jones did not know about Hitler's order to concentrate on 1.5-metre and longer radars, but he did highlight an obvious flaw in German communications, suggesting "a criminal lack of liaison between the German naval and air technical staffs." There was no evidence that the Germans were listening to 10-centimetre transmissions until the autumn of 1943, when they produced a device known as Naxos, which enabled them to pick up signals in the 10-centimetre waveband. By this time, work on further developments was already well advanced at TRE; the ability to keep ahead was symptomatic of the constant cooperation between the scientists, the services and the government throughout the war; there were, of course, disagreements and heated arguments; but there was always discussion and cooperation once decisions were reached. This was a stark contrast with the situation in Germany and as Bernard was to write:

> The delay in their understanding that the Coastal Command ASV was now radiating on a shorter wavelength illustrates the lack of

close liaison between the scientists and the operational staffs. It is inconceivable that such a delay could have occurred with the Allies where scientific/operational liaison was so close.[119]

This crucial flaw in the German war machine was confirmed by Albert Speer, writing about the rocket programme which he described as the biggest and most misguided project:

> Success was out of the question, for Hitler's principle of scattering responsibility meant that even scientific research teams were divided and often at odds with each other. The three branches of the armed forces and all other organisations, the SS, the postal system, and such, had separate research facilities.[120]

It would be difficult to overstate the crucial importance of H2S /ASV in the defeat of the U-boats. The Germans continued to try new methods of detection and developed new submarines, including the amusingly named 'Schnorkel', which was designed for speed under water and was equipped with a breathing tube and improved batteries to minimise the need for surfacing; but they failed to recover the momentum of the early years of the war; never again were the U-boats a threat to Allied victory. In *Closing the Ring* Churchill wrote:

> In the battle against the U-boats, the H2S apparatus, of which a number had been handed over somewhat reluctantly by our Bomber Command to Coastal Command, played a notable part.[121]

Dönitz had trumpeted the importance of U-boats to Hitler in the early days of the war:

> I am convinced that in the U-boat we have, and always have had, a weapon capable of dealing Britain a mortal blow at her most vulnerable spot.[122]

By May 1943, he was forced to report:

> We are at present facing the greatest crisis in Submarine warfare, since the enemy, by means of location devices, makes fighting impossible and is causing us heavy losses.[123]

Rowe summed up the vital strategic significance of its deployment in *One Story of Radar*:

> The greatest contribution made by radar to the success of the invasion of Europe and indeed to the whole war, was its decisive role in the defeat of the German U-boat fleet. Had not the submarine war been decisively won in 1943, the invasion of Europe could hardly have been successful. It is my personal opinion that it would not even have been attempted. One of the most astonishing facts of the whole war was that, with the Germans in possession of the Bay of Biscay ports, her submarines were unable to take more than a trifling toll of the vast armada which crossed the Atlantic or the vaster armada which sailed for Normandy in June 1944.

In June 1943, the Fuehrer himself announced in a radio broadcast: "The temporary setback to our U-boats is due to one single technical invention of our enemies."[124] Hitler was both right and wrong. One technical device had indeed enabled Coastal Command to pinpoint the position of the U-boats at night so that they could be destroyed; but the setback was not temporary, it was permanent.

As well as developing H2S so as to keep ahead of the enemy, by producing systems which operated on even shorter wavelengths, Bernard was engaged through 1943 on creating a more permanent answer to German countermeasures. One such solution involved increasing the power of the airborne transmitter so that the identification range of enemy aircraft would be extended, at the same time providing the navigator with the means to reduce the strength of the signal as the aircraft got closer to the target; the idea of this was that the German operator, seeing an apparently constant signal would not realise that it was closing in by the minute, once again maintaining the element of surprise.[125] And the inspiration to develop new techniques extended to every aspect of operational need throughout the services.

On 18th April, 1943, Dudley Saward paid one of his frequent visits to Malvern. He stayed overnight with Bernard and Joyce and in the evening, they drove round the hills to the Westminster Arms. After dinner Saward said that he would like to walk back and Joyce drove home, leaving the men as they set out to climb the Beacon. Saward seemed very preoccupied. When they reached the top they stopped to admire the view and talked. Saward said that there were serious worries about the number of bombers being shot down by German fighters attacking from behind and below;

existing systems were failing to give warning of these attacks and the losses were mounting. Whilst he was talking Bernard gazed across the countryside to the east and suddenly recalled something which Geoffrey Hensby had said, when they were standing on the same spot, just a few weeks before Hensby was killed in the crash of Halifax V9977.

The young man had noted the magnificence of the view and commented that he believed there was no high ground between the point where they were standing and the Urals. The moment he recalled the words, Bernard was struck with an idea about the empty space between a bomber flying at 15,000 feet and the ground beneath it. H2S was set up to look at the ground; why not create a separate display unit which would give the rear gunner a scan of the empty space? Any approaching aircraft would show up as a blip on the cathode ray screen and warn the gunner of the imminent danger. The next morning he asked Saward to send him a mechanic to build the display unit, which was successfully tested within a few weeks. On 27th May Saward was taken on a flight and he was able to see the clear signal of a Mosquito making a mock attack from behind and below. Two days later Renwick placed a large order for the system, code named 'Fishpond'; these were flying over Germany by the autumn. Less than twelve months after his tragically early death, Geoffrey Hensby's chance remark gave rise to an idea which was destined to save the lives of many hundreds of British airmen.

As the battle against the U-boats was coming to its successful conclusion, the Pathfinder Force and H2S were involved in another event of great strategic importance.

On 19th December 1942 R.V. Jones received a telegram from a reliable source in Stockholm:

Overheard conversation between Prof Fauner of Berlin Technische Hochschule and an engineer Stefan Szenassion a new German weapon. Weapon is a rocket containing five tons of explosive with a maximum range of 200 kilometres with a danger area of 10 kilometres square.

A second telegram dated 12th January 1943 revealed:

The Germans have constructed a new factory at Peenemunde, on the Baltic, where new weapons are manufactured. The weapon is in the form of a rocket which has been fired from the testing ground.[126]

In April the Prime Minister was warned of the possible rocket attacks and he appointed his son-in-law, Duncan Sandys, to investigate. Sandys had a meeting with Cherwell, who said that he thought there was nothing in it; this view may have been coloured by his dislike of Sandys and he remained sceptical about the reports.[127] Good photographic reconnaissance revealed what appeared to be two rockets of considerable size and further intelligence reports were returned which indicated the development of pilotless planes as well as rockets. On 29th June the Prime Minister convened a meeting to discuss the extent of the threat. The Chiefs of Staff, Alanbrooke, Sandys, senior members of the cabinet and others attended and, in spite of Cherwell's opposition, it was decided that no chances could be taken. As Alanbrooke recorded in his diary, they concluded that a definite threat existed and that the Peenemunde experimental station should be bombed at the earliest possible date.[128] Meanwhile, unknown to anyone present, events in Germany had entirely justified their decision.

On 7th June 1943 Albert Speer invited Wernher von Braun, the leading scientist at Peenemunde, to Hitler's headquarters. The Fuehrer was shown a colour film of a great rocket rising from its pad and disappearing into the stratosphere. He was greatly impressed by the film, which fired his febrile imagination. Back in his bunker he became quite ecstatic about the possibilities. "This is a measure that can decide the war. And what encouragement to the home front when we attack the English with it! This is the decisive weapon of the war."[129] So excited was Hitler at the prospect of unleashing the world's first weapons of mass destruction that he insisted on paying a visit to the establishment at Peenemunde, which took place on 10th June. After the visit he triumphantly announced to his generals that London would be razed to the ground by Christmas and that Britain would be forced to capitulate. Orders were given for large-scale production of both the V-1 and the V-2, which would be launched against London and the south coast ports. October 20th was fixed as zero day for the rocket attacks to begin;[130] but in little more than two months, all these hopes were extinguished.

On 17th August planes of the Pathfinder Force, fitted with H2S, guided 570 bombers to Peenemunde. The Pathfinders marked the target and nearly 2,000 tons of bombs were successfully and accurately dropped. Churchill described the results of the raid as being of:

> Capital importance. But for this raid and the subsequent attacks on the launching pads in France, Hitler's bombardment of London by rockets might well have started early in 1944.[131]

There was substantial damage, over seven hundred people were killed, including Thiel, the expert on propulsion, and Walther, the chief engineer; many of the plans and drawings were destroyed and the fear of further attacks on Hitler's pet project, at Peenemunde and elsewhere, led the Germans to take the manufacture underground in the Harz Mountains, causing them further disruption and delay.

The precise extent to which the attack at Peenemunde delayed the flying bomb programme is a matter for conjecture; even the least generous commentators have settled for a period of two months and others, such as Joubert, estimated it as six.[132] There were a number of factors which contributed to the delay, including serious defects in the V-2 which took time to remedy.[133] What is beyond dispute is that before Peenemunde Hitler ordered that the campaign must begin on 20th October and predicted the destruction of London by Christmas; following the raid his hopes were postponed by eight months and his prediction was never fulfilled. On any objective view, the success of the attack was a substantial setback to Hitler's plans, both from the physical and psychological viewpoint and because of the loss of key personnel; his prophecy about capitulation was shredded and by the time the first V-1 was deployed the invasion was well under way. For all the fear they created and for all the damage they did, V-1 and V-2 had no strategic importance, and were vengeance weapons, as Elizabeth Longford justly described them.[134]

Eisenhower summed up the enormous importance of the demise of Hitler's expectations:

> If the German had succeeded in perfecting and using these weapons six months earlier than he did, our invasion of Europe would have proved exceedingly difficult, perhaps impossible. I feel sure that if they had succeeded in using these weapons over a six-months period, and particularly if they had made the Portsmouth-Southampton area one of their principle targets, 'Overlord' might have been written off.[135]

Leading the Peenemunde raid, the Pathfinder Force, guided by H2S, put down accurate markers for the bombers which followed in their wake. The triumphant results of the attack delivered a severe blow to Hitler's hopes of winning the war and played a vital role in the ultimate victory of the Allies.

CHAPTER TWELVE

The Road to Victory

As H2S went into full production and sets were fitted to bombers on a large scale, other possible uses for it began to emerge. On 21st March 1943, a delegation from Combined Operations arrived at TRE to enquire whether H2S could be adapted for use on landing craft. A few weeks later came a request to prepare a demonstration which took place on 9th May. A scanner was rigged up on a landing craft, 36 feet above sea level. Bernard accompanied the Combined Forces officers and recorded in his diary that, on a rather rough day, low-lying coastlines appeared at ranges of 10-15 miles and features such as the harbour at Bembridge were clearly defined.[136] The demonstration was repeated a few days later for the benefit of the Chief of Combined Operations, Lord Louis Mountbatten, who was sufficiently impressed to place an immediate order for twenty scanners to be built at TRE. Within a few weeks these were delivered and the equipment was used during the invasion of Sicily on 10th July. Large-scale production of the system was taken over by the Admiralty Signals Department and on 6th June 1944 they were used on many of the landing craft as they approached the Normandy beaches.

The early success of H2S owed much to the brilliant leadership and training of Bennett. Problems with uneven display continued, however, and these became even more evident when the system was fitted in Lancaster bombers operating at much greater heights than the Halifax and Stirling. Constant experiments under very difficult conditions, at these high altitudes, led to significant improvements. The enhanced performance was confirmed, at the end of July, by the precision of the raids on Hamburg, resulting in massive devastation and terrifying firestorms which raged through the city. The raid on 24th July was the first occasion on which Bomber Command had used 'Window;' this entailed the dropping of bundles of aluminium foil in order to confuse German radar operators, who mistook the clouds of foil for bombers.[137] The deceit worked brilliantly, the consequent loss of bombers was much reduced and the combined effect of Window and H2S being deployed in the same operation was a marked success; but the accuracy attained by using H2S over Hamburg was not repeated during the attack on Berlin in September:

> The revolutionary factor in the battle of Hamburg was the release of Window, but the attack also signalised the most rewarding employment of H2S. The Battle of Berlin on the other hand began and continued without corresponding new advantages.[138]

It was apparent that the 10-centimetre system was of much greater use over places such as Hamburg and Peenemunde, where there was a clear contrast between the reflections from sea and land, giving operators a virtual map, than there was over inland targets such as the German capital. The obvious answer to this problem was to reduce the wavelength and work had already begun on the production of a 3-centimetre H2S scanner, which was tested in a Stirling on 11th March 1943. As work on this system progressed, a serious dispute erupted at TRE with American scientists who had also been attempting to perfect a 3-centimetre system.

Early in June, a delegation from the Massachusetts Institute of Technology, led by the director, Lee DuBridge, came to London and tried to persuade the Air Ministry of the benefits of fitting their version of 3-centimetre radar into British bombers. When he heard of this request, Bernard was incandescent with rage, not least because only one year before, Rabi, DuBridge's colleague from MIT, had the effrontery to describe H2S as unscientific and unworkable; now the Americans were trying to sell a system of their own to our Bomber Command. Dee and Saward were also less than impressed by the American approach and the situation had all the makings of a major row. On 7th June Watson-Watt chaired a meeting at the Air Ministry, which was attended by Cherwell, Dee, Bernard, the American delegation and others; following an afternoon of furious argument, Bernard was able to record in his diary:

> After much breathtaking suspense it was agreed that the British proposal should be accepted and that the target should be 3 SQUADRONS BY CHRISTMAS 1943![139]

Anger about the MIT approach to the Air Ministry was exacerbated by the fact that TRE was already deeply involved in the difficult task of equipping American Flying Fortresses with H2S. On 15th March, the Chief of Air Staff, Portal, had received a request from General Eaker, the Commanding Officer of American 8th Bomber Command, for this work to be carried out. On the 18th, the very day of the first successful attack by a Wellington on a U-boat, Bernard was busy at Chivenor, supervising preparations for Coastal Command, when he received an urgent summons to return to Defford to meet 8th Bomber Command officers. Their requirements were explained and although his small team was already inundated with work, the importance of giving help to the Americans was impressed upon him and there was no alternative but to agree.

The Flying Fortress operated at 30,000 feet and all the problems which were being experienced in producing accurate signals for Bomber Command were greatly increased at this altitude. Testing put an enormous strain on technicians, who had to endure the effects of freezing conditions and lack of oxygen whilst they worked; one of Bernard's team soon ended up in hospital with pneumonia and later in the year another perished during a test flight. Gradually the signals improved, the training of American navigators progressed and on 27th September and 2nd October the H2S Flying Fortresses put down marker flares through cloud over the North Sea port of Emden. The markers guided 300 Fortresses and Liberators which carried out a successful attack causing severe damage to the submarine construction yards, the port and other areas of the city.[140] But not all sorties were so successful.

Soon after the September raids on Berlin, Dudley Saward showed Bernard a photograph of the image of the city as it appeared on the cathode ray tube of a Pathfinder. It presented a depressing picture showing a large mass of blurred light with no definition at all to help the navigator. Saward produced a map and they noted the lakes, the Tegeler See and the Wansee to the west, the Rivers Havel and Spree and the network of canals running through the city. If they could only get 3-centimetre H2S working satisfactorily there seemed to be every chance that much more precise reflections could be obtained, using the shorelines of the water features as markers.

The objective of having two squadrons of Lancasters with the new system fitted by November was hopelessly optimistic, but Saward, Bernard and Bennett determined that, failing all else, they would prepare and equip six Lancasters by the middle of the month. Saward arranged for the planes to be sent to Defford and they were fitted with experimental equipments, which had been tested constantly in Stirlings for three months, with significant improvements. Although Harris, Renwick and a few others knew what was being planned, it was all done without any kind of official sanction or finance. By 17th November, Bennett had his six Lancasters. They flew over Berlin and the rivers, the lakes and Templehof aerodrome could be seen on the screens as clearly as on a map. Both the range and the definition were greatly improved and from November 1943, Berlin,

Leipzig and other cities were marked for the bombers, with devastating effect. Large sections of Berlin were destroyed, the Reichstag was set ablaze, munitions factories were attacked and it seemed to many Germans that the accuracy of some of the bombing was so precise that traitors and fifth columnists must have pointed the way for the bombers. The destruction was such that they felt as though they had been plunged into hell.

Attempts to provide an increasingly versatile array of features continued throughout 1944. Scanners were provided with stabilisers so as to maintain a consistent signal as planes banked and weaved to avoid attack or home in on a target; there were constant improvements to the picture on the plan position indicator; a huge 6-foot scanner called 'whirligig' was constructed. These developments were often dogged by rows and criticism. When H2S worked, all was well, but whenever it was less than perfect, whether as a result of poor operator training, or the failure of the Air Ministry to provide essential equipment, it was the system which came in for censure. Sometimes the disagreements were rather acrimonious. When Slessor visited TRE in October 1943, Bernard told him that two hundred 3-centimetre systems for ASV had been handed over to the Air Ministry many weeks previously, but that none had been fitted. Slessor penned a furious letter to the Secretary of State for Air, Sir Archibald Sinclair:

> This is either crass stupidity or pettifogging obstructionism of the worst kind I have ever encountered in this war. No one but a congenital idiot could imagine that our 3cm equipment would be of any value if there was no appropriately fitted antisubmarine aircraft to use it.[141]

The letter had the desired effect to the extent of provoking a summons for Bernard to attend a meeting in the War Cabinet Office on 27th October. Saundby, the Deputy Chief of Air Staff, Slessor, Bennett and Watson-Watt were all present. Following a long discussion Saundby reluctantly agreed to allocate enough 3-centimetre equipments for one Coastal Command squadron. Bernard returned to Malvern thinking that his day had not been wasted. He was greeted by Rowe, who did not look happy.

"You haven't done very well, Lovell," said Rowe.

"Why not?" replied Bernard. "Coastal are being given enough for one squadron."

"No they are not," retorted Rowe. "Harris telephoned the Prime Minister and got the decision reversed."[142]

In March 1944, following the failure of the Ministry to place official orders for stabilised scanners, Bernard penned a memo to Dee and Rowe which included a comment that the Director of Communications Development, Air Commodore Leedham, should be shot. Unfortunately this perfectly reasonable recommendation was leaked to the DCD himself and easy relations with the Ministry were not enhanced.[143]

Nor were the insults a one-way traffic. After one of Rowe's Sunday soviets on 26th March 1944, he sent some suggestions to Harris about his attitude to TRE, which was not always as constructive as might have been hoped. Harris regarded Rowe's comments as less than helpful and sent a reply which shared a common feature with many of the bombs he had dropped before he had the benefit of H2S; it fell some way short – on compromise: "Tell TRE to mind their own bloody business. They remind me of a lot of pimply prima donnas trying to get into the limelight."

Rowe responded: "If he wants a battle he can have it." He then initiated a 'Get rid of Harris' campaign which came to a climax with a meeting on April 22nd chaired by Saundby to discuss 'Policy in regard to future use of H2S'.[144] Predictably enough, the attempt to unseat Harris was doomed to failure, but the meeting was the culmination of these disputes and it did result in the installation of some of the improved TRE equipments. Throughout 1944, as more and more bombers were fitted with H2S, greater accuracy was achieved and losses were much reduced, especially amongst those planes which were also fitted with 'Fishpond' to warn rear gunners of the approach of enemy fighters. During the last seven months of hostilities, over 100,000 sorties rained massive destruction on cities deep inside enemy territory with aircraft losses of less than one percent being recorded.[145]

In 1939, Bernard Lovell had been assigned to work on radar for TRE. At first this new field appeared to him as a fascinating extension of his scientific life. Before long the deaths of young colleagues, the fall of France, the Battle of Britain, the Blitz and the destruction he saw in Bath, brought the brutality of warfare vividly to life. In February 1945, five and a half years of unrelenting work, seven days a week, with no vacations took their toll; he became ill, diagnosed as suffering from nervous exhaustion and he was ordered to rest for four weeks. He was immediately given leave of absence from TRE, only returning to duty shortly before VE day. His war was effectively over.

The exigencies of war led to enormous advances in scientific knowledge and achievement; many of the devices which were turned to use in battle had been created by scientists in peacetime with no notion of their potential for adaptation in time of war. Robert Watson-Watt's work in the Meteorological Office had given birth to radar, but it was the threat of war that led to the rapid building of radar systems for use in defence and attack. When Rutherford split the atom his ideas were guided by a quest for knowledge about the nature of matter; in the maelstrom of war, the atom bomb brought death and devastation to Hiroshima and Nagasaki on a hitherto unimaginable scale. Wernher von Braun's interest in rocket technology was motivated by the possibilities of space travel, long before he became technical director of Hitler's missile programme; it is fortunate for mankind that the invention of the atomic bomb and the ability to deploy missiles occurred on opposite sides of the conflict.

The experience of scientists such as Bernard Lovell highlights the eternal dilemma between the progress of civilisation and the destructive power which progress can unleash. Thirty-five years after the end of the war, he wrote about the moral dilemma posed by the search for new ideas and the expansion of scientific inquiry:

> The devices of science, especially those involved in the penetration into the innermost structure of the atom and the remotest parts of time and space, have led to means of mass destruction never before available to mankind. This is a special crisis for the modern world, a material dilemma arising from the paradox that the search for knowledge has become dissociated from the search for wisdom. The hope of our generation is to re-establish, as St. Thomas Aquinas did seven hundred years ago, the fabric of man's attempt to comprehend the Universe.[146]

The war brought together groups of scientists of extraordinary brilliance, who had been pursuing their own peacetime research in university laboratories; it wove their energies into the structure of wartime establishments, where their collective endeavour led to incredibly rapid advances, which would have taken far longer to achieve if they had continued to work as individuals. German scientists were no less clever than their British counterparts; it was the successful union between scientists, civil servants, engineers, manufacturers and the government which gave Britain a huge advantage over the enemy. At TRE Dee and Rowe collected a glittering array of talent; men such as Hodgkin and Huxley, both, future Nobel Prize winners who served as Presidents of the Royal Society; Bennett "the greatest flying expert in Bomber Command"; Blumlein the brilliant engineer, whose life was so tragically cut short; and Bernard Lovell himself. Together they worked for six years on ideas and projects which had a major impact on the progress of the war and on Allied victory.

The original purpose to which radar was put was primarily defensive. At the start of the war, the Chain Home Command served as an early warning system which enabled fighters to intercept enemy bombers before they reached their targets. Until the autumn of 1940 this gave the RAF such an advantage that the Battle of Britain was won and the daylight raids of British cities were largely ineffective. With the commencement of night bombing the enemy gained an ascendency that was maintained until the combination of GCI,[147] and 1.5-metre airborne radar forced an end to the campaign in May 1941. Throughout this period, the deployment of radar was designed to save British lives and any questions about the morality of killing German pilots were subsumed in the knowledge that they were being killed to protect Britain from attack. As centimetre radar came into use and H2S was developed for aggressive purposes, the scientists were far too busy to ponder or debate the morality of bombing enemy towns and cities; the Germans, after all, had visited death and destruction on British civilians and they just got on with the job.

In later years Bernard gave much thought to the dichotomy between the needs and the consequences of war and he was, at times, troubled by the extent to which his work had been instrumental in air raids which caused the deaths of many thousands of people. Whilst researching for *Echoes of War*, in 1990, he was greatly moved when he came across the report of the Police President of Hamburg on the raids of July and August 1943 and the terrifying firestorm that engulfed the city:

> The streets were covered with hundreds of corpses. Mothers with their children, youths, old men, burnt, charred, untouched and clothed, naked with a waxen pallor like dummies in a shop window, they lay in every posture, quiet and peaceful or cramped, the death struggle shown in the expression on their faces...No flight of imagination will ever succeed in describing the gruesome scenes of horror...Posterity can only bow its head in honour of the fate of these innocents, sacrificed in the murderous lust of a sadistic enemy.[148]

Such an account brought home to him the true nature of war and confirmed that the revulsion of each side at the brutality of the other was matched in equal measure. As he told Naim Attallah, in an interview in 1992:

> It was chilling to think that it was the planes that carried our equipment which actually marked out those cities for bombing.

But then I immediately had the consoling thought, illustrative of the dividing line between good and evil: the device used to destroy German cities saved us from starvation. Of course the dividing line in most of science is a very thin one.[149]

As well as the destruction of the U-boat threat, consolation was to be found in the beneficial consequences which flowed from actions such as the Peenemunde raid, from the development of airborne radar for Fighter Command, which saved so many British lives from night attacks by German bombers, and the deployment of the 'Fishpond' system in the protection of British bombers from enemy fighters. As he wrote in his autobiography:

I became increasingly thankful that the device for which I reluctantly accepted responsibility at the end of 1941 helped save as many lives as it destroyed.[150]

The development of ballistic missiles in the post-war years confirmed Bernard's thinking about the perennial dilemma between the beneficial and negative consequences of scientific enquiry and mankind's constant fluctuation between the forces of good and evil. In 1979 he wrote:

Vast empires have been created by force in the name of freedom and religion, and eventually they have been destroyed by force or decadence. The present state of mankind has been developed by the unstable, complex interaction of the intellectual power of a rather small number of individuals, coeval with the group instincts of greed.[151]

These ideas take on renewed significance in an age when hostile and volatile regimes, ruled by despotic psychopaths such as Kim Jong-un in North Korea and Mahmoud Ahmadinejad in Iran, have developed nuclear weapons.

On 8th May 1945, Bernard was treated to a curious but happy postscript to the years of conflict. Dudley Saward drove him to Whaddon Hall, in Buckinghamshire, explaining that the Brigadier wanted to thank him.

"What on earth for?" asked a puzzled Bernard.

"Well, unknown to you," said Saward, "they have been using some of your equipments for getting agents in and out of occupied territory." They arrived at Whaddon and were greeted by Brigadier Richard Gambier-

Parry and his officers who were generous in their praise of the contribution which H2S had made towards their secret and dangerous work. Whilst they were there they heard the BBC announcement of the German unconditional surrender.

The huge contribution which radar made to the Allied victory in World War II is beyond question:

> Until the introduction of radar, there was in Bomber Command no regular and reliable method of making fixes (on targets)…Without radar the bulk of Bomber Command would have continued to fail to find the target area, and on many occasions those that did would have been unable to hit the target.[152]

> H2S was certainly the most widely useful aid to navigation and bomb-aiming which was ever produced for Bomber Command during the War.[153]

> GEE, OBOE, H2S and G-H, were products of the allied genius of Anglo-American scientists and technicians. All had their limitations and disadvantages and some had a revolutionary effect on the ability of Bomber Command to find and hit its targets.[154]

The value of radar to the Allied war machine was summed up in a report of the Royal Commission on Awards to Inventors:

> At four critical periods of the war, radar made a major contribution to success:
> 1. in the Battle of Britain;
> 2. in defence against night bombing on which the enemy concentrated after his defeat in the Battle of Britain;
> 3. in dealing with the submarine menace;
> 4. in enabling our bombers to reach their objectives in Germany and to drop their bombs with a high degree of accuracy.[155]

Bernard Lovell played an important part in each of those achievements and the work he did was acknowledged in two letters he received in 1945. One, dated 13th September, was from Air Marshal Victor Tait, the Director General of Signals at the Air Ministry:

> I would like to express to you the very great appreciation of the Royal Air Force for the magnificent work you did for us during the past war years.

The radar equipments, especially H2S, which you developed and saw into operational use in the RAF were one of the main factors in making the Air Force so effective in the destruction of German armed forces. We especially appreciate the grand cooperation we have always received from you and the way you always were prepared to hear our troubles and help us with advice or technical solutions to our problems.[156]

The other letter, written whilst he was on sick leave from TRE in February 1945, was in response to his request to return to duty. It was from A.P. Rowe:

The trouble with us all when we get overtired is that we hang on. You need have nothing whatever on your conscience; if you never did a stroke of work for the rest of your life you would have justified your existence.

Never do a stroke of work for the rest of his life? He had barely started.

CHAPTER THIRTEEN

Cosmic Meteors

Bernard Lovell's return to Manchester in 1945 was the very antithesis of his arrival there in 1936. Then he had dragged himself off the train, seething with frustration at his failure to secure an immediate appointment from Patrick Blackett; he had spurned the post offered to him by Bragg, with a churlish arrogance that he could never recall without a blush of shame; when he finally accepted it, he hauled himself north with a degree of enthusiasm that would have done credit to Jonah entering the mouth of the whale; a rather naive young man, who had enjoyed a cosseted and sheltered life, he had arrived, lonely and alone, to work in surroundings which he regarded as dreary and uninviting. But at least he had a job.

In the three years he spent there he had grown to know and love the city. He had begun his married life there; the recollection of delight in his young bride, of the friendships they had made, of the fascinating work he had done in his laboratory, of the games of cricket at Didsbury and the matches he had watched at Old Trafford and of the concerts he had heard at the Free Trade Hall had sustained him through six long years of war; he was now a man in the prime of life, toughened by tragedy, but full of hope for the future; he was enraptured with his adored and adoring wife and their two enchanting children; the once despised university soared triumphantly in the midst of its bomb damaged surroundings; he was eager to get back to work as soon as he could; but his assistant lectureship had expired in September 1939 and there was no job for him to go to.

There were other opportunities to explore. He was asked to remain on the staff at TRE, but had no wish to do so; he applied for a job with ICI, but was appalled at the lack of research facilities and beat a hasty retreat as soon as the interview was over; he was tempted by the prospect of employment at the Christie Hospital in Manchester, where new treatments for cancer were being developed; but he was conscious that he did not have the knowledge of nuclear physics which the work demanded. His old professor, Tyndall, recommended that he should take up the offer of a post at Manchester; he had doubts about his ability to return to academic work and teaching after so long an absence; he was worried, too, that the Manchester physics department, without the leadership of Blackett to inspire and encourage him, would be an anticlimax after the exhilaration of his wartime activities. And then he heard that Blackett was planning to leave the Admiralty, where he was in charge of naval research, and return to Manchester as Professor of Physics. His mind was made up in a trice, he accepted a job as a lecturer in physics, and he and Joyce bought a small house at Timperley, 6 Fairview Road.

He returned to his laboratory, fizzing with anticipation. As he pushed open the door it creaked on rusty hinges and he recalled the last glance he had cast over it before turning the key in the lock in 1939 reflecting, for a moment, on the great events of the intervening years. The room and everything it contained, including 'George', were just as he had left them, save for the thick coat of dust which covered every surface; whilst the human armies of the world had been hell-bent on destruction, armies of spiders had constructed an intricate network of cobwebs, which now obscured the light from the windows and spanned every nook and cranny of the dingy interior. Armed with dusters and a mop, Bernard embarked on a major clean up.

As soon as the laboratory was habitable he set about restoring the cloud chamber, relishing anew the enjoyment of working with his own hands on delicate apparatus. After a few days he found that he needed a part; but who was to order it and who would pay? At TRE he had been able to obtain delivery of a Lancaster bomber at a moment's notice by the simple expedient of a brief telephone call, leaving the tedious question of funding to be handled by others. Now the university requisitioning department claimed to be short of money and for want of a small part George would not work. The arrival of Blackett put an immediate end to his dilemma.

"Why are you messing around with the cloud chamber?" said Blackett. "We agreed we would employ radio echoes to detect cosmic rays. Have you forgotten?" In the excitement of getting back to his laboratory, Bernard had not given it a thought. In no time at all, Blackett produced a copy of their Royal Society paper from 1941 and instructed Bernard to get on with it. Reading the paper again was all the stimulus he needed and he knew exactly how to get hold of the equipment. During the last months of the war he had met James Hey at the Army Operational Research Group at Byfleet, where he was in charge of anti-aircraft units, using gun-laying radar to home in on enemy bombers. The system operated on a wavelength of 4.2 metres with precise direction-finding Yagi aerials and a powerful transmitter to push out the radio signal towards incoming planes. This was exactly what Bernard needed for attempting to detect cosmic rays as they entered the upper atmosphere. He telephoned Hey and asked him whether, now that the war was over, there was a redundant system which he could borrow. Hey told him that he would be delighted to help; no one had any use for the equipment and it was being tipped down disused mineshafts. Some days later soldiers from Hey's unit arrived with two heavily laden trailers; they parked outside the physics department and set up the apparatus on the trailers.

The Yagi aerials were fixed to the roof of the two cabins which housed the transmitter and the receiver, the cathode ray tube was placed alongside the diesel generator and in no time at all Bernard had the radar up and running. Manchester had then, as it does today, a very busy network of electric trams. These vehicles were nothing less than trains driven by overhead electricity and running down the streets on tracks, to the constant hazard of unwary pedestrians; unfortunately their presence also proved fatal to the detection of cosmic rays or of any signals at all, except those emitted by the electric power cables and by the sparks, which flew off the wires with monotonous regularity. It was immediately clear that as a location for observing the ionosphere the centre of Manchester was entirely useless. Bernard tried to obtain a better response during the early hours of the morning one night in November, but the results were no better; it was obvious that he needed a place in the open countryside where there would be little or no interference with the radio signals.

Later the same day, in the staff common room, he bumped into the bursar, R.A. Rainford, who was curious to know why the courtyard outside the physics labs was congested with hardware. Bernard explained his problem and Rainford suggested that he should inspect a piece of land owned by the University near the village of Lymm, some 12 miles to the south-west of the city. With his customary zeal, Bernard jumped into his car and drove off to survey the site. The moment he saw the fields he realised that he had been dispatched on a wild goose chase; they were overhung with a mass of pylons and wires, which were hissing in the pouring rain. Feeling very disappointed and rather cross he drove back to the university.

After lunch the next day he repaired once more to the common room and told Rainford the result of his expedition. The bursar pulled on his pipe thoughtfully for a moment before using it to point at a bearded man swigging a post-prandial pint of beer in preparation for his afternoon lecture.

"Try him," said Rainford. "That's Frederick Sansome, the Head of Botany. They have some fields a few miles south. It could be exactly what you want." Bernard approached the beard and introduced himself.

"Are you responsible for that radar equipment?" enquired Sansome. Fearful that he was about to be castigated for taking over the yard Bernard replied that he was.

"How absolutely fascinating!" said the botanist, with reassuring enthusiasm. "I have been interested in radio since I was a lad. You must give me a demonstration at once." Bernard told him about the interference and explained that he was looking for a clear site in the open countryside. He also mentioned that he had a great interest in gardening and the two men were quickly embroiled in an animated discussion about plants and trees. They got on like a house on fire and Sansome suggested that he might have the very place Bernard was looking for his research.

"It is about 20 miles south in the heart of the Cheshire plain, at a place called Jodrell Bank. We use it as a nursery. It's a bit remote and there is no electricity. There's not much going on at this time of year. Why don't you take a look at it." Remoteness and a lack of electricity were exactly what Bernard required; he thanked his new friend, asked him how to get there and the following morning set off, once again, in his car.

It was a foggy day, but armed with Sansome's directions Bernard soon found himself driving through trees down a muddy track, identified by a small sign at the entrance as the University of Manchester Jodrell Bank Experimental Grounds. Indications of experimental activity were not readily apparent; he emerged from the trees and stopped outside a couple of crude huts; in one of these two jovial gardeners, Alf Dean and Frank Foden, were sitting beside a cosy stove enjoying their mid-morning brew of tea. Bernard joined them for a few minutes, spent some time reconnoitring the site, which extended over eleven acres, and drove back to Manchester scarcely able to contain his delight at finding the perfect location and determined that the Jodrell Bank Grounds should swiftly justify their experimental pretensions in the search for cosmic rays.

He sought out Sansome, who was delighted that the expedition had been so successful. As far as he was concerned Bernard was welcome to set up his equipment there. All that was needed now was permission from the University and who better to obtain it than Professor Patrick Maynard Stewart Blackett, who promised to speak to the Vice Chancellor, Sir John Stopford, at the earliest opportunity. A day or two later Blackett sent for Bernard and gave him the welcome news that Stopford had agreed that he could go to Jodrell Bank for two weeks.

Hey's men were dispatched once again to effect the removal. Everything was carefully dismantled and the trailers were towed out to Jodrell, where the next two days were spent dragging them into position through the December mud and reassembling the equipment ready for use. At last, on the evening of 12th December 1945, the work was complete and Bernard was left alone as darkness fell. He made a last check of his newly acquired system before he locked the gate for the night, eagerly anticipating that, six long years after his conversation with the pretty young WAAF at Staxton Wold, he would be detecting cosmic rays as they entered the upper atmosphere. He returned soon after dawn and tried to start the generator by turning the massive handle provided for the purpose. He could barely move it and, even with the combined help of Alf and Frank, no spark of life could be coaxed out of the machine.

The restorative effects of a pot of strong tea and a warm stove soon galvanised the jovial gardeners into suggesting that outside assistance was required. This arrived in the ample shape of the local farmer Ted Moston. Ted was the man who knew all about engines, his help was immediately enlisted and by nightfall, to Bernard's consternation, he had completely dismantled the generator, which was lying in pieces on the frozen ground. It was a disconsolate cosmic ray researcher who drove back to 6 Fairview Road; another day had been wasted and he began to wonder how he would get hold of a replacement for the generator. He need not have worried; fixing motors was meat and drink to Ted and the next morning he identified the problem, which was caused by ice in the fuel pipes; at the end of the day the machine was finally in full working order and Bernard felt confident that he would soon be observing cosmic ray echoes on the cathode ray tube.

It was late on the afternoon of 14th December before he finally had the aerials pointing high into the sky and switched on the power. Almost at once, to his great delight, he began to see echoes flitting across the screen. This was the moment and there they were, just as he and Blackett had predicted in their paper in 1942; particles from the depths of space entering the atmosphere and appearing as if by magic on his little screen in the middle of a boggy field. The signals flashed onto the screen and disappeared in an instant; but there seemed to be many more echoes than he had anticipated; two or three a day would have been a result and Bernard was seeing ten or twelve every hour. Were they really cosmic rays or was he picking up some other unexplained signals? He consulted Blackett who suggested that he should talk to Hey about his experience of any such occurrences during the war. This turned out to be good idea and it produced an unpredicted explanation.

During the early years of the war Hey's gun-laying equipments had been used to detect enemy bombers and to assist the aim of anti-aircraft gun crews whose job it was to destroy them. When the Germans began to launch V-1 flying bombs, in June 1944, the aerials were adjusted to pick up their signals as they flew low over the Channel, so that RAF fighters could locate and attack them, often by tipping their wings and sending them plunging into the sea. British pilots had some success with this hazardous pastime, but the V-1 menace was substantial and, by the time all the launch bases had been captured, three months later, over six thousand people had been killed and many more wounded.

The V-2 rockets were not operational until September, in large measure as a result of the damage inflicted on the programme by the Peenemunde raid. Their range was much greater than that of the V-1s and, as the world's first ballistic missiles, they flew at a height of 60 miles above the surface of the Earth, dropping in on London in a matter of minutes. There was no means of attacking these frightening and destructive weapons but Hey's radar units were once again called into action, this time to operate as an early warning system which at least gave terrified citizens a few minutes to take cover before being blown into oblivion.

Hey and his teams began to experience problems from phantom echoes when signals were received but no rockets arrived; this caused frequent false alarms and needless panic. At first he thought they must be emanating from missiles that had fallen short of the target and dropped harmlessly into the English Channel; soon, however, his operation was coordinated with agents working behind enemy lines and it was confirmed that, on these occasions, no V-2s had in fact been launched. Hey was intrigued and began to investigate the possibility that the signals were coming from some natural source rather than the German rockets. His enquiries led him to the idea that the phantom echoes might be caused by meteors and he obtained a paper written before the war by an American scientist, A.M. Skellett, discussing the ionising effects of meteors entering the ionosphere.[157] Hey had been instructed to prepare a secret report on his findings and he now gave a copy of it to Bernard,[158] who quickly appreciated that some, at least, of the transient echoes he had seen must have come from meteors.

Bernard was a physicist who knew next to nothing about meteors and even less about astronomy. His interest in using radar to scan the heavens had been focused entirely upon searching for ionisation trails left by massed clouds of particles from space as they entered the atmosphere. He now realised that it was essential to turn his attention towards meteors in order to understand how he could isolate and identify their signals from those emitted, as he thought, by cosmic rays. What he discovered took him to a completely new branch of scientific enquiry and cosmic rays, which had been his constant preoccupation for almost ten years, were quickly consigned to the annals of his early life as a scientist. But where was he to start?

At that time there were very few books on astronomy available in England and almost no literature on the subject of meteors. Nor did Bernard know any professional astronomers and those with whom he made contact had little interest in meteors. He consulted Blackett and was advised to speak to Nicolai Herlofson, a Norwegian, who had settled in England after escaping from his native country when the Germans arrived in 1940. Blackett appeared to think that because Herlofson was a meteorologist he might be able to help. Bernard was sceptical about this and was never entirely sure whether Blackett's suggestion arose from an erroneous belief that meteorologists studied meteors; but he arranged to meet Herlofson who turned up at Jodrell Bank one afternoon in the spring of 1946. Bernard was well aware that meteorology concerned the weather and had nothing to do with meteors, so he was not in the least surprised when the young Norwegian told him that he knew no more about them than his host. He did, however, have information which proved to be invaluable.

Herlofson told him that asking professional astronomers about meteors was pointless; they had neither the time nor the inclination to focus their precious telescopes upon streaks of light which flashed across the sky in a fraction of a second and which were visible to the naked eye; they left this work entirely to the amateurs and he suggested that Bernard should contact the British Astronomical Association, which had a strong contingent of amateur astronomers. The secretary of this august body was only too happy to help and gave Bernard an introduction to John Philip Manning Prentice, a solicitor from Stowmarket in Suffolk, who had studied meteors for many years and had been in charge of the Association's meteor section since 1923.

Manning Prentice made his name in astronomical circles in 1934. On the night of 12th December he was out in the dark Suffolk countryside, observing the annual arrival of the Geminid meteor shower. At one point he took a short break and when he returned to his watch he immediately noticed an alteration in the appearance of the head of the constellation Draco in the northern sky. He realised that he was seeing something quite remarkable; forsaking the meteor vigil, he jumped into his car and drove straight back to Stowmarket from where he telephoned the Royal Observatory at Greenwich. They trained a telescope onto the object and before dawn obtained two photographs of the early stages of an emerging nova,[159] which was later named Nova Herculis; the report of this discovery in *The Times* followed by a leading article on the value of amateur

1. *Above:* Captain Laura and the Ladies of Kingswood, circa 1912.

2. *Right:* Bernard Lovell, aged about six, circa 1919.

3. *Above:* Escape from parental disapproval. Joyce and Bernard picnic at Pavenham in Bedfordshire, summer 1936.

4. *Left:* Joyce and Bernard married at last, 14 September 1937.

5. *Right:* Bernard and Joyce with all their children at The Quinta, summer mid-1950s.

6. *Below:* The Physics Department at Bristol, 1935. Lovell is in the back row, second from the right. A.M. Tyndall sits centre front. Of particular note is Klaus Fuchs, second row, third from left, who was imprisoned after the war as a traitor for revealing atomic secrets to the Russians.

7. *Above:* Patrick Blackett flanked by Lovell on his left and L. Rosenfeld on his right, at the University of Manchester, 1949.

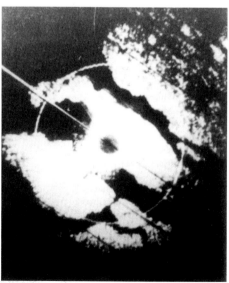

8. *Left:* Rotterdam as displayed on an H2S radar screen. Much skill was needed to interpret the signals.

9. *Above:* The Leigh Light illuminates the terrifying last moments for a U-boat crew. *Courtesy of Mark Postlethwaite.*

10. *Below:* Jodrell Bank on 12 December 1945. The first equipment arrives.

11. *Above:* Perseid meteor shower over the Mount Lemmon Sky Center, Arizona. The radiant point of the shower, the dark centre, can be seen clearly. *Courtesy of Adam Block, USA.*

12. *Below:* Autumn 1955. None of the planned changes have been made, they are still merely in the design stage.

13. *Right:* June 1957. Steel plates are welded to the surface of the bowl.

14. *Left:* Bernard Lovell and Charles Husband on 20 June 1957, the day the Telescope moves for the first time.

15. *Above:* The control room at Jodrell Bank, November 1958. Courtesy of Wayne Young.

16. *Left:* Princess Margaret sends a royal command to Pioneer V, 18 March 1960.

astronomers[160] gained Prentice a herculean reputation in the amateur hierarchy. When Bernard met him, twelve years later, he had built up a network of enthusiastic meteor watchers across the country.

At their first meeting Bernard was immediately struck by the country solicitor's extraordinary depth of knowledge and his great enthusiasm. Prentice explained that the incidence of sporadic meteors occurs throughout the year; but at certain times the Earth's orbit takes it through the debris shed by comets, which have travelled from the outer reaches of the solar system and passed close to the Sun. When this occurs, showers of meteors can be seen with the naked eye as the debris enters the atmosphere and burns up; as it evaporates, the meteor leaves a trail of ionised particles, coincident with its trail of light; radio signals directed at the line of the trail would be reflected back by the particles and could be observed on a cathode ray tube, like the echoes from an aircraft. Bernard would need only to train his radar equipment on those parts of the sky where the showers were visible; any radio signals that were emitted would be travelling at the same speed as the light from the burning meteors, and if signals and light were observed at the same moment, it would be reasonable to conclude that they came from the same source. The arrival of the Perseid meteor shower in August would provide the first opportunity for this experiment and Prentice said that he would be delighted to come to Jodrell to assist. By the time he arrived the establishment had grown.

Now that Bernard was tucked away in the depths of Cheshire, the university authorities seem to have forgotten that the original plan was for a stay of two weeks. Blackett was a constant support. He was an enthusiastic advocate of the new research capabilities which radar presented and was equally excited at the prospects both for cosmic ray research and the study of meteors. In December 1945, he managed to obtain a block grant from the Department of Scientific and Industrial Research (the DSIR) and encouraged Bernard to recruit two former members of TRE, John Atherton Clegg and one C.J. Banwell, a New Zealander, who joined him early in the new year. With additions to the staff there arose an urgent need for more equipment and, once again, wartime connections proved to be of vital importance.

The ordnance requirements of a country fighting a world war were enormous. Now that hostilities were over, there were vast quantities of hardware for which there was no use and no market; much of this was gently rotting away or being broken up and buried. Bernard was able draw on his contacts to obtain equipment at a minimal cost or even, on occasions, for nothing but the trouble of collecting it. Clegg was an expert on aerials, but he also enjoyed driving around the country picking up machinery, returning to Jodrell in triumph, for all the world, like a glorified scrap dealer. In this way they acquired a large quantity of valuable ex-service gear for scarcely any outlay beyond the fuel needed to drive the trucks. The greatest triumph was the acquisition of a huge vehicle known as a Park Royal which carried a large cabin.

They decided to house this beast in a distant field, about four hundred yards beyond the huts and some distance from the end of a stone track they had laid to improve access to the receiver aerials, which had already been located there. Rather optimistically they had tried to extend the track manually, using a couple of spades, but they quickly realised that this would take weeks to complete and they enlisted Ted Moston to scoop it out with a bucket attached to the front of his tractor. They ordered in several lorry loads of stone and, after a couple of days work, the track was ready for use. When the Park Royal arrived, with Clegg proudly at the wheel, he made it to the end of the new track only to find that the last hundred yards were extremely boggy and could not support the weight of the vehicle which sank up to the axles in a thick bed of mud. There it remained for several years, serving as the control centre of operations.

The arrival of Manning Prentice at the end of July provided a marked contrast with the arrays of equipment which had been transported to Jodrell in the preceding months. He drove up in an open-topped Morris loaded with nothing more than an overnight bag, a celestial globe, a deck chair, a couple of star atlases and a flying suit. When asked where his gear was he pointed laconically towards the car; evidently that was all he needed; and the system of observation could hardly have been more simple. Soon after sunset, Prentice set up his deck chair and reclined there in an almost horizontal position, with a small torch, a pen, a writing pad and a piece of string resting on his knees; the flying suit was for use in inclement weather. Sometime after midnight, the constellation of Perseus rose above the eastern horizon; the Perseid meteor shower became visible, emerging from that sector of the sky and radiating out in all directions from a central point. The moment he saw a meteor, Prentice would hold the string out at arm's length to mark the track it had taken; he would then identify the background stars across which it had travelled and write down the path, the time and the magnitude, using the torch to illuminate the paper. The receiving aerials were directed towards the shower to pick up radio signals and Bernard's team sat inside the Park Royal cabin in relays, observing the echoes as they appeared on the cathode ray tube.

When Prentice saw a meteor he called out to the radar-watchers, who would record any echoes which coincided with the shouts; Clegg, Banwell or Bernard would deliver complimentary shouts when they saw an echo;

thus they were soon able to conclude that there was a definite correlation between the visual and the radio spectra. Any doubt that they were receiving echoes from meteors was effectively removed. As the intensity of the showers built up there were many shouts which did coincide with echoes, but others for which no echoes were seen and some echoes were not accompanied by any visual sightings; were these signals from meteors which were too faint for the eye or could they be from cosmic rays? The puzzle was not solved for many years, at which point it was finally concluded that the search for cosmic rays could never have succeeded with the equipment they were using. The Perseid showers continued for over two weeks, with the most prolific bursts being observed on the night of 14th August. Each morning, daybreak heralded a sense of anticlimax that the display was over; the restless days passed with agonising slowness in the eager anticipation of the night watch ahead. Bernard brought a deck chair from home; night after night, sitting in the field outside the Park Royal, he listened in wonder as Prentice talked about the stars, reeled off the names of each down to the fifth magnitude, pointed out the constellations and conducted him on stellar rambles across the darkened sky; he was mesmerised by the country solicitor's encyclopaedic knowledge of the heavens; as they watched through those warm summer nights he was transported into realms of unimagined beauty, learning his astronomy at the side of the gifted amateur.

Duty and demanding partners called Prentice back to his legal practice. Before he returned to Suffolk, he told Bernard that he believed there would be a superb opportunity to build on the Perseid observations in October, when the Earth was expected to cross the orbit of a periodic comet, which was first observed by Michel Giacobini in 1900 and then by Ernst Zinner in 1913. In 1926 he had seen spectacular meteor showers as the Earth passed through the tail of the comet. The comet returns every six years but his observations in 1933 had been badly hampered by cloudy skies and, in 1939, the Earth crossed the expected orbit before it arrived, so there were no meteors to observe. The perihelion of Giacobini-Zinner[161] was expected to occur again on 18th September, and it was hoped that the Earth would cross its orbit only fifteen days later.[162] Prentice predicted that the concentration of debris from the tail, so soon after the comet had passed that point, would provide a display of unparalleled intensity from 9th October. He would not be able to return to Jodrell for this exciting event, but he would be observing it in Suffolk and believed that, if the skies were clear, it would provide a superb opportunity to make further comparisons between the visual sightings and radio signals.

The aerials which Bernard and his team had been using were fixed, although they could be spun round in the horizontal, or azimuth, plane by turning the cabins on which they were mounted; so an aerial which was set at an angle of 40 degrees to the horizon could be spun through 360 degrees at that angle, but could not be lowered or elevated as it was going round. If a fully steerable unit were obtained, which could rotate on its base and be elevated and lowered through the vertical, they would have a much more effective system to work with. By raising or lowering the angle to the horizon at the same time as rotating the aerials they could observe any part of the sky as the need arose. After a good deal of wrangling they managed to borrow an army searchlight, which Clegg adapted by fitting an aerial on a narrow beam; this new and flexible instrument was ready for use by the time of the expected arrival of the Giacobinid meteor showers.

On the evening of 9th October, there was a brilliantly clear sky. Soon after dusk Banwell, Clegg and Bernard took up their stations in and alongside the Park Royal and waited impatiently, gazing up at the darkening sky. As the hours ticked away very little happened; there were the usual sporadic meteors, which were seen and picked up on the cathode ray tube at a rate of three or four every hour; there were dogs barking rather persistently on a nearby farm; they heard the melancholy calls of a barn owl and saw a couple of foxes hurrying by, no doubt intent on slaughtering a few of farmer Moston's chickens; but there was no great array of shooting stars and they began to question the accuracy of Manning Prentice's calculations. Blackett was in attendance but with nothing much going on he became bored and departed shortly before midnight, on the pretext that he had to travel to London the next morning. Leaving when he did, he missed the start of a thrilling display by only a few minutes.

Soon after midnight it began, slowly at first but then quickly building up to a crescendo of extraordinary pyrotechnics, the like of which none of the watchers had ever witnessed. Before long the sky was ablaze with streaks of light pouring out from the radiant point, shooting across the background of the dark sky, the stars and the Milky Way, and racing towards them like tracer bullets fired from a celestial machine gun.

At the height of the shower the meteors were so prolific that they were unable to count them; by three o'clock they were seeing them at a rate in excess of one thousand per hour, corresponding closely, so far as they could keep up, with the number of signals appearing on the cathode ray tube. It was an unforgettable sight which Bernard was to recall to his last days, saying, at the age of ninety-eight: "It was like being bowled at by great streaks of meteors." At that moment, star-struck though they were by the heavenly fireworks, they had the presence of mind to turn the beam of the aerial away from the lines taken by the blazing meteors and direct them towards the dark radiant point at the centre, with the result that the echoes on the tube dropped instantly from more than a thousand an hour almost to zero. The echoes that had been returned when the transmitter was aimed at 90 degrees to the trails of the meteors disappeared altogether when the outgoing signal was directed into the forward path of the emerging debris as it entered the atmosphere before bursting into flames and spreading out from the centre. Here was the final proof; there could be no doubt that the echoes they were receiving emanated from the meteors as the signals struck their fiery ionised trails at an angle approaching 90 degrees; when the signal was moved away directly into the path of the oncoming objects, very few echoes were recorded; the conclusion was drawn that only meteors of exceptionally high energy would return a signal which was meeting them head on; but as soon as the aerials were turned back towards the line of the trails, the echoes were there with all their former intensity. Radio astronomy was born.[163]

As dawn approached the frenzy abated and the three scientists, spent with the exertions and the elation of the night's activity collapsed in exhaustion. But Bernard and Clegg had lectures to deliver in Manchester and were obliged to gird up their loins for the day job with no time to rest. In Bernard's case, the euphoria he had experienced carried him through the day's work; although, as he freely admitted, the scheduled lecture topics were thrown over and given up to waves of Giacobinid fervour.

Throughout the autumn they attended to their university duties during the day and almost every night, whatever the weather, they rushed to Jodrell to observe the next in the sequence of annual meteor showers; the Giacobinids were followed by the Taurids, the Leonids and the Biclids.[164] On clear nights they would take turns to sit outside calling out the visual observations, whilst the echoes on the cathode ray tube were monitored, noted and photographed. When the skies were cloudy they could all take shelter in the comparative comfort of the Park Royal and concentrate on the electronic results of the radio signals. In December they were joined once again by Manning Prentice, who donned his flying suit for the return of the Geminids which, twelve months earlier, Bernard had mistaken for cosmic ray showers. The observation of meteors had become an obsession.

On 13th December 1946, Bernard was invited to address a meeting of the Royal Astronomical Society at Burlington House. The proceedings, as reported in *The Observatory* magazine,[165] were presided over by the President, Professor H.H. Plaskett, FRS. The account has a charming Pickwickian flavour, although Bernard approached the task with considerable apprehension. The audience consisted almost entirely of men who were steeped in the traditions of Galileo, Newton and Herschel, the first President of the RAS, traditions which were based on direct observations with the naked eye and the use of optical telescopes. How would they react to a Johnny-come-lately with new and alien methods, which had nothing to do with looking at stars but relied on picking up radio signals on a screen?

Manning Prentice presented the first paper and spoke about the visual observations of the Giacobinids in 1946. He then turned to the "remarkable technical advances in radio echo observations of the Giacobinids. We knew that about thirty per cent of the echoes which we had been getting from our previous work must have been due to meteors below naked-eye visibility. We had also realised the limitations of the apparatus previously used, which was adapted for ionospheric soundings and not for astronomical observation, and had constructed a directional aerial for work on meteor streams". He concluded his remarks with a wonderful build up for the next speaker:

"It is obvious that this beautiful new technique represents a major advance in this field of observation. Indeed we are, like the first possessors of the telescope, unexpectedly armed with new powers of observation. With your permission, Mr. President, I will ask Dr. A.C.B. Lovell to continue." Bernard stood up and began. Any diffidence he felt was quickly dispelled by his deep fascination for his subject and the obvious interest and curiosity of his audience. He told them that the extent of the shower was contained in a short compass between midnight and 6.00 am and continued:

"The transient echo rate at the start of this period was 0.3 per minute. The rate increased with great rapidity and reached a maximum of 168 per minute at 03.40. This period of peak activity was extremely short; within five minutes of the peak it was fifty per minute and by 06.00 it had fallen to the normal rate of 0.03. The passage of the shower was thus associated with an increase of five thousand times in the transient echo rate." When Bernard finished there was warm applause and then Hey presented a paper on his findings, after which the meeting was thrown open to the floor. There were questions and contributions from members, including Sir Edward Appleton, Mr. Naismith, Professor Chapman and Dr. Mervyn Ellison, an Irish astronomer, whose claim to have seen a meteor which lasted for nine minutes was peremptorily dealt with by Dr. Lovell:

"In our experiments a duration of as much as ninety seconds is quite exceptional. In 17,000 observations we have only found three echoes with durations of this length."

Soon after that the Rev. Dr. M. Davidson complained that he had difficulty hearing one of the replies and the President, perhaps suspecting that the Reverend Doctor had been listening with his eyes closed, regretfully ended the discussion in view of the lateness of the hour. He asked the members to return their thanks to the speakers and concluded that they had "presented an entirely new field of astronomic research."

The day following the RAS meeting marked the anniversary of Bernard's first tentative observations at Jodrell Bank. In twelve months, almost without realising it, he had become an astronomer.

CHAPTER FOURTEEN

Radio Astronomer

The exhilarating developments at Jodrell during 1946 were accompanied by a mixed bag of events on the personal front. Bernard's salary was increased to £650 per annum; with child benefit of £150 this was far less than he could have commanded in industry, but they managed and the joy of his work more than made up for any financial anxieties. During the winter he had again been very unwell and on medical advice his tonsils were removed on 6th April. The operation caused excruciating pain, as he wrote in his intermittent diary,[166] but his general health improved and by August he had put on over a stone in weight. On 26th May he received a letter from the Prime Minister asking if he would agree to his name being recommended for the award of an OBE, in recognition of his work during the war. At 5.30 on the morning of 23rd June, Joyce gave birth to their third child, Judith Ann, and the family celebrations were increased by the announcement of his OBE in the honours list the following day. Susan was "growing apace" and enjoying school but Bryan was rather in the wars. Bernard described one "agonising event":

> The week before Whitsun I shut Bryan's finger in the car door and cut the top off it. I was inconsolable and yet poor Bryan was very brave, fortunately all has gone very well and it now does not seem half so bad as we feared. It seems to be a straight cut from the top of the finger to the bottom of the nail and shows all signs of healing well.[167]

There was more pain for Bryan in the autumn, when he fell off a wall and broke his arm; once again he was very brave and made a full recovery in due course.

During the early months of 1946, for the only time in their long friendship, Bernard and Blackett had a major disagreement, which might have had fatal consequences for Bernard and the whole Jodrell project. The origin of the contretemps lay in an error in their joint paper on cosmic rays, which had been published in *Proceedings of the Royal Society* in 1941. Neither of them had noticed a small but important inaccuracy in one of the formulae cited in the paper; indeed they failed to realised that the mistake had crept in until T.L. Eckersley, an ionospheric scientist, helpfully took it upon himself to write to Blackett and point out the elementary blunder, which fundamentally undermined some of their conclusions.[168] Blackett was furious. Even though he had failed to spot the error himself and, having rewritten it in a shelter during an air raid, may actually have been responsible for it, it was young Lovell who got it in the neck; any mitigation advanced, along the lines of having been preoccupied with vital radar work at the time, fell on deaf ears. In Blackett's eyes Bernard had involved him in a schoolboy howler and he expressed forceful opinions about the latter's scientific ability.

Unknown to Bernard, Blackett was at this time involved in a serious dispute with the Prime Minister, Clement Attlee, on the subject of British neutrality in the arms race, which Blackett was promoting in opposition to government policy. The disagreement resulted in his isolation from the central role he had occupied as an adviser to the government and dissatisfaction at this state of affairs no doubt contributed to his rather extreme reaction over the cosmic ray paper. In due course, the full force of his ire was turned towards the failures of the government and the usual cordial relationship with his protégé was soon restored. Blackett asked him to write a full report of everything that had been going on at Jodrell over the winter months; the positive developments which he was able to describe and the work which had been done by Clegg and Banwell, even when he was ill, were more than enough to mollify his boss, who was, once again, eager to help in any way he could.

Although the 1946 research concentrated on meteors, it did lead to other interesting and important observations. On 25th July, as they were preparing for the eagerly awaited Perseid meteor shower, a violent blaze of unexpected signals appeared on the cathode ray tube, obliterating all the usual echoes. So great and persistent was this intrusion that Bernard's initial reaction was to assume it was the result of a failure in the system. The equipment was examined and found to be operating perfectly; so what was the cause of the temporary interruption of their signals? Once again, the wartime recollections of James Hey provided a clue. In February 1942, radar operators experienced a sudden influx of extraneous signals, which wiped out the echoes they were receiving from incoming aircraft; the immediate suspicion was that the radar had been jammed by the enemy and Hey was called in to investigate. He found that the maximum interference seemed to emanate from the direction of the Sun; the Royal

Observatory confirmed that a massive solar flare was taking place and he concluded that this had emitted very strong radio signals, which caused the disruption to the anti-aircraft radars. When Hey published these findings in 1946,[169] they were greeted sceptically by many radio experts, including Sir Edward Appleton, then the Secretary of the DSIR and a future Nobel Laureate. His analysis was confirmed, however, by the incident at Jodrell on the 25th July, which coincided precisely with another great solar flare. This discovery was to provide a strong impetus towards the early development of radio astronomy.

As the year progressed they continued to assemble a variety of equipment, which was housed in a motley collection of huts, cabins and randomly constructed tin shacks. Clegg and Bernard realised that a much more sensitive aerial was required to continue their research into cosmic rays and they decided to build a makeshift tower for this purpose, using old scaffolding tubes set in concrete; they dug the holes out by hand and, not having access to a mixer, used buckets to prepare the concrete. During the summer they completed the base of the tower to a height of about 30 feet, but the project was then abandoned, not least because from the top it looked a long way down to the ground. The skeletal construction was left standing as a mere monument to their endeavours. Any random visitor to the site who asked what was going on there would have been amazed to hear that these muddy fields and ramshackle structures represented the cutting edge of a new era of scientific enquiry. It was becoming clear that a large injection of cash would be needed in the ensuing year, if they were going to make further progress with their research.

Having abandoned the tower aerial, Clegg and Bernard discussed the way forward and concluded that what they really needed was a large paraboloid with a tall aerial at its centre. The paraboloid could be constructed on the ground which lay between the Park Royal and the boundary fence, a distance of about eighty yards. The structure would be circular and would rise to 24 feet in height at the outer edge; the diameter would be 218 feet; it would be supported by scaffolding, with a series of steel cables being stretched from the top of the perimeter down to ground level at the centre to form a large bowl. These cables would be used as the framework to support the reflecting surface; in an ideal world, this would have been formed with metal sheets; but it was decided, in the interests of economy, to lay a lattice work of wires across the cables running all the way round the interior, with a gap of 8 inches between each wire; with the 4-metre wavelength they were planning to use, this would achieve the reflection they needed, whilst losing only a small proportion of the signals through the gaps in the wires. The instrument would be completed with a central mast 126 feet in height, to which would be attached the focus of the aerial; signals would be reflected from the surface of the paraboloid to the focal point; from there they would be transmitted electronically along wires connected to the cathode ray tubes. There were no formal plans and no costings or estimates, but the construction of the mast began in the late summer, when they managed to scrounge a wooden frame which had once supported a coastal defence aerial during the war. It had reached a height of 20 feet when they decided to suspend work for the winter.

It was at this moment in the autumn of 1946 that Blackett introduced Bernard to D.A. Spencer, who was a member of the DSIR committee responsible for approving university research grants. One Saturday morning, Spencer came to see what was going on at Jodrell Bank; he was intrigued by the 20-foot wooden structure which was standing on its own in the middle of the field. Bernard explained what they were attempting to do and said that he needed a steel tube, which would be supported by the wooden frame; the height of the tube would be 126 feet and the aerial's focus would be fixed to the top of it. Spencer let it slip that this was precisely the kind of work which the department was keen to support. Bernard needed no second invitation; he seized his chance and asked for a grant of £1,000, which was immediately agreed. He could hardly believe his luck. Now, at last, he felt that he had the resources to build the great paraboloid with the power and sensitivity he needed to find his cosmic ray showers; the search, which had drawn a complete blank with the aerials they had so far used, could continue. The DSIR money would enable them to build it, using makeshift materials and their own labour; but it was impractical to resume work until the spring and the observation of meteor showers, with the searchlight aerial, continued throughout the winter.

The Aquarid shower in May 1947 was expected to mark a break in their surveillance until the return of the Perseids in August. The Aquarids appear shortly before dawn and early one morning the watch proceeded uneventfully until the shower had passed through at 7.30. They were about to pack up and go home for a well earned breakfast, when they noticed that the rate of the echoes, instead of reducing to two or three an hour, accelerated to a very high level. They were identical in nature to those which they been analysing for the last six months. It was suddenly borne in upon them that they were looking at the echoes from a hitherto unknown phenomenon, a daylight meteor shower. The watch continued during the ensuing days and weeks and it rapidly became apparent that the Earth was moving through vast clouds of debris; the meteors this debris generated had, until now, remained unseen by virtue of the daylight prevailing at the time of their encounter with the Earth's atmosphere; quite by chance the radar signals had stumbled upon a new field of observation, which kept them busy for months.

Late in the evening of 15th August 1947, another unexpected event manifested itself whilst they were observing the Perseid shower, which had come round for its annual visit. Shortly after midnight the cathode ray tube began to fill up with strange new echoes, the like of which they had never before seen; the signals were scattered across the screen like confetti and unlike the transient meteor echoes, which invariably disappeared quickly, they remained visible for many minutes. John Clegg and a young New Zealander, Clifton Ellyett, were with Bernard at the time and they all piled down the steps of the cabin to see what might be causing the interference. It was a beautiful night and the moment they got outside they were confronted by the magnificent sight of the Aurora Borealis in all its glory, arching high into the sky from the northern horizon. None of them had seen it before and they stood gazing up at the breathtaking patterns of green and red light streaking across the darkness of the heavens. They realised that the radio signals, like the light, were spontaneous electromagnetic emissions from the Aurora, generated by the collision of vast numbers of energetic particles. Quickly they directed the searchlight aerial towards the north and stared at the cathode ray tube, transfixed by the dramatic increase in the signals pouring in.

After twenty extraordinary minutes the Aurora faded. As it did so, the signals also subsided, leaving them in no doubt at all that they had been caused by the wonderful event they had just witnessed. Another line of research had opened up; as with the solar flares, the random signals they had received from the Aurora suggested the possibility of scanning the skies to find radio emissions, as opposed to transmitting radio beams at specific objects and waiting for the echoes; it was another step beyond radar, into the realms of radio astronomy. The three astonished scientists immediately wrote a brief account of the event, which was published in *Nature* in September.[170]

The original two week visit to Jodrell Bank had now extended, on a completely *ad hoc* basis, to eighteen months and the university authorities began to ask questions. Why were Lovell and Clegg spending so much time away from their duties? What was the purpose of their research? On whose authority were they operating? The pressure for an explanation was building up and Patrick Blackett decided that it was time to arrange a visit from the Vice Chancellor, Sir John Stopford. The importance of making a good impression was not lost on Bernard, who viewed the prospect of entertaining the VC with considerable trepidation. He knew very well that an unfavourable impression would herald disaster; he was anxious to convince his visitor that the work they were doing was worthwhile; and he was cautiously hopeful that, if things went well, he could secure approval for his schemes and the money to carry them out. It was June and he was especially keen that Sir John should get to Jodrell at an early hour, when he could show him the signals from the newly discovered daytime meteor showers.

The day of the visit dawned just as he would have wished; the mists cleared as Sir John and Blackett arrived. It was a glorious summer morning. They were ushered from the warm June sunshine into the dark interior of the Park Royal in perfect time to witness a mass of echoes flashing across the cathode ray tube. Bernard explained the significance of their recently discovered phenomenon and from that moment, the Vice Chancellor became a passionate supporter of the project. Within a few weeks he had persuaded the University Council that Bernard was indeed running an important facility; if adequate funding and the proper level of support were provided there was every prospect that Jodrell Bank would prove to be a valuable asset which would greatly enhance the reputation of the University. This was the first of many visits Sir John made over the next eight years, during which time his enthusiasm for the University of Manchester's new observatory never wavered.

The work on the great paraboloid had begun as planned in the spring of 1947 and good progress was made under the expert control of a new addition to the staff. Ted Baker provided the establishment with skills which, hitherto, had been sadly lacking; he was a fully trained practical engineer, who had been a foreman in the Rolls Royce aero engine factory during the war and had then obtained a job at the university as a workshop technician. A colleague suggested that Ted would be a the ideal person to oversee the construction of the paraboloid and Bernard agreed; at last they would have a man who knew how to build things and, which was equally important, had a head for heights. An association was formed which was to last for many years.

The first thing Ted Baker did was to insist on the purchase of a concrete mixer and things began to happen; as the summer progressed the structure of the paraboloid rose steadily from its foundations; a tubular steel mast was acquired; it was fixed to the wooden frame and raised to its full height of 126 feet; all hands were enlisted to help weave the lattice of wires round the mast and across the cables forming the reflective surface; even wives and children were recruited and worked at ground level beneath the lower parts of the bowl, securing the wires to each cable starting from the centre; Bernard, Clegg and Banwell spent many hours perched on top of a lorry attaching wire to the upper parts of the structure as they were driven in stately circles underneath the circumference. By November the work was complete; the paraboloid was primed to reflect signals; on top of the mast, an array of dipoles[171] at the focal point was standing by to receive them; the electronic connections were made and the transit telescope, as it came to be called, was finally ready. They switched it on and began to transmit, waiting with bated breath for the expected echoes from cosmic rays.

The entire *raison d'être* for the construction of the new instrument, which now occupied some 34,344.34 square feet, give or take πr^2, was the desire to capture the hitherto elusive signals from large showers of high energy particles, as they entered the Earth's atmosphere. But none arrived. There were occasional echoes from meteors, but not a cosmic ray was in sight. They had a fixed aerial of enormous power, by far the most powerful instrument of its type in the world, it was working perfectly but it was failing to deliver the very thing they had designed it for. After a few days they noticed unexplained radio signals from another source. These signals rose and fell dramatically every twenty-four hours, as Earth's rotation took the narrow beam through the Milky Way, when it was positioned directly overhead in the zenith. Could these radio signals be from unknown and unseen objects far out in the galaxy? Suddenly, their frustration at the failure to find cosmic ray echoes was forgotten.

The human eye can see that part of the electromagnetic spectrum which lies between the infrared and ultraviolet. We call this light and, since *Homo sapiens* first trod the Earth, our ancestors have been able to observe the sun, the moon, the planets and the stars by virtue of the light they emit or reflect. The means of observation of the heavens remained unchanged through the millennia; from Aristotle and Ptolemy to Tycho Brahe, Galileo, Newton and Hubble the human eye was the window to the stars. Telescopes allowed astronomers to see more and to delve deeper into space by picking up fainter light from more distant objects; but at the beginning of the twentieth century, most still believed that the entire universe consisted of a spherical Milky Way, with the solar system at its heart, extending across twenty thousand light years.[172] After the Great War, the light-gathering capability of the 100-inch optical telescope at Mount Wilson in California, the Hooker telescope, transformed this parochial view of the cosmos. Observations with the Hooker disclosed that the Milky Way is a spiralling disc 100,000 light years across, containing several thousand million stars;[173] so far from being at the centre, the solar system is positioned in one of the arms of the spiral and is closer to the outer reaches of the galaxy than to the middle. Using this great instrument in 1922-3, Edwin Hubble confirmed an idea first mooted by William

Herschel in the nineteenth century; Hubble's observations proved that the faint nebulae originally seen by Herschel were much too remote to be within the Milky Way; they were in fact massive galaxies, similar to but entirely separated from our own. In less than two years, the perennial belief that we were in the centre of a solitary galaxy with nothing beyond its boundaries was shattered. In spite of these huge advances, our powers of observation remained circumscribed by being confined to that part of the spectrum visible to the eye and by the need for clear, dark skies to reveal the glory of the stars. It was generally believed that the light from stars and galaxies was the only means by which they could be studied. No one had considered that the heavenly bodies might emit radio waves which could be picked up and analysed on Earth in the same way as light.

In 1931, Karl Jansky, an American working for the Bell Telephone Laboratory, made the chance discovery of radio signals which seemed to originate from the centre of the galaxy, in the constellation of Sagittarius. With brilliant acuity, he observed that these radio waves became perceptible every twenty-three hours and fifty-six minutes, the exact time it takes for the Earth to rotate through the background of the stars, known as a sidereal day; in other words, it was a consistent signal coming regularly from the same remote point, presumably associated with some unseen object. To Jansky's disappointment his employers refused to finance a prolonged study and his death on 14th February 1950, at the age of only forty-five, meant that he did not live to witness the true significance of his discovery; but his findings were widely reported at the time[174] and were well known to astronomers throughout the world. It was left to another young American, Grote Reber, who was intrigued by the Jansky reports, to investigate further. In 1937 Reber built a steerable paraboloid in the backyard of his suburban house at Wheaton Illinois; it was 30 feet across and must have taken up most of the yard, but with this homemade device he was able to confirm Jansky's discovery. He used this instrument to make a map of radio signals from the sky. Ten years on at Jodrell, it was obvious to Clegg and Bernard that they too had chanced upon a mysterious stellar radio source; but how they wished that they could follow it as it passed out of the narrow beam of their fixed paraboloid. The transit telescope had the power, but it lacked the flexibility of the searchlight aerial.

In order to develop research into this new field, it was imperative to get an exact idea of the polar diagram of the transit telescope, i.e. the size and shape of its radio beam. For this purpose, Bernard was able to call in a few promises from old friends at TRE and, in the spring of 1948, he borrowed a plane and a pilot, who spent several weeks flying over and around Jodrell Bank at a height of 3,000 feet, no doubt causing considerable irritation to

The 218-foot transit telescope with a 165-foot aerial at the centre.

the locals, both human and bovine, although no drop in milk yields is recorded. During these flights he enlisted the help of a PhD student, Victor Hughes, who spent many hours logging the signals from the plane, until they were confident that they had an accurate graph of the polar diagram. Armed with this information, Hughes spent the following months completing his thesis by creating charts of those areas of the sky which passed through the beam. By the end of the year a clear picture had emerged of the range of the investigations which could be undertaken with the transit telescope.

From the beginning of their work on meteors, Bernard's team had concentrated on the great showers and, although they often observed the echoes of sporadic meteors they paid little attention to them. There were frequent contacts and meetings with other scientists in the field, many of whom visited Jodrell Bank and it soon became apparent that there was strong disagreement about the origin of sporadic meteors. There was no doubt that the showers were caused by the residue of comets and that they were heliocentric, i.e. in orbit round the solar system; every so often, and in many cases annually, their trajectory brings them into contact with the Earth resulting in the meteor showers, as we have seen. When it came to the sporadic meteors, however, one set of scientists believed that they too were heliocentric and contained within the solar system, while others took the opposite view and were convinced that they were occasional visitors from outer space, coming under the fleeting influence of the Sun's gravity before flying off again on endless journeys to the farthest reaches of the universe. This was not an insignificant issue because, if it could be established that sporadic meteors did come from interstellar regions, they might provide valuable information about the nature and incidence of matter in space.

Bernard was aware of the existence of this dispute, which had been the subject of learned papers and scientific articles. The true ferocity of the argument was brought home to him in September 1948, when three of the principal protagonists attended a high-powered conference, which Blackett had arranged in Manchester. Dr. Ernst Öpik, whose grandson Lembit is a well known politician and former Member of Parliament, was an Estonian who had fled from his native country in 1944, ahead of the advancing Russian armies. A distinguished astronomer, he had recently taken up a post at Armagh Observatory, in Northern Ireland, and had long held a particular interest in sporadic meteors, which he believed originated in a vast cloud of matter far beyond the solar system. In the early 1930s Öpik was visiting professor at Harvard University and led a meteor expedition in the Arizona desert, which recorded more than 20,000 meteors in eighteen months. On his return to Estonia, he had made further meteor studies between 1934 and 1940. He postulated a theory that the sporadic meteors were moving at very high velocities and were, accordingly, of interstellar origin. He also invented a so-called 'rocking camera', which he used in conjunction with a system of mirrors to photograph meteors; he calculated that sixty per cent of all the sporadic meteors came from outside the solar system.

Dr. John Guy Porter was the director of the computing section of the British Astronomical Society. His calculations were based on a huge body of visual observations by many British astronomers, including Manning Prentice; they led him firmly to the view that all meteors were orbiting the Sun within the solar system. Also attending the conference was Fred Whipple, Director of the Smithsonian Astrophysical Observatory and Professor of Astronomy at Harvard, whose studies had led him to an entirely neutral position, sitting on the fence pending convincing evidence from one side or the other. One morning during the conference, Bernard drove these three eminent gentlemen out to Jodrell to show them the work that he was doing there. As they were walking round, enjoying the September sunshine, a furious row erupted between Öpik and Porter, who had made some derogatory remark about his opponent's 'rocking camera'. Bernard and Whipple looked on in amazement as the raging argument descended to vulgar abuse, more redolent of a drunken quarrel in the nearby Red Lion public house, than of a civilised disagreement between two scholarly scientists. To calm the situation down, Whipple gently suggested that Bernard might be able to settle the dispute by using his radio equipment to establish the velocity of the meteors in question. All agreed that this was a good idea and peace was restored.

The receivers and the cathode ray tube in the Park Royal had already been adapted to record the velocity of the shower meteors with reasonable accuracy. This was the key to the solution. It was known that the maximum velocity of objects in closed orbit, travelling round the Sun at the same distance as the Earth, is 42.2 kilometres per second; if an object had a greater velocity than this, it must be a temporary visitor to the solar system. By taking an accurate measurement of a meteor at its point of entry to the atmosphere, the problem of its origin could be solved. The Earth moves round the Sun at a speed of 29.8 kilometres per second. If the combined velocity of the meteor and the Earth in head-on collision, did not exceed 72 kilometres per second at the point of impact, it could be concluded that it was in heliocentric orbit, within the solar system. If the combined speed exceeded seventy-two, the meteor must have been travelling faster than 42.2 kilometres per second, which would prove that it had an open orbit and had come from the interstellar region.

The work began on 18th September and continued for several hours each morning until 18th December. The searchlight aerial was directed towards the east so that any meteors entering its field would be meeting the Earth almost head on and the combined speed of the two could be measured, in the same way as the joint speed of two cars driving towards each other; an automatic camera recorded all the echoes which appeared on the cathode ray screen; by analysing the photographs the speed of each meteor could be worked out. At the end of three months they had been able to measure sixty-seven meteors, none of which were travelling more than 42.2 kilometres per second; not a single interstellar meteor had been detected. Bernard was delighted. He had, by means of a simple if time-consuming experiment, solved a riddle which had caused much dissension between three men whom he liked and admired. In a state of high excitement he wrote to each of them, enclosing copies of the results. In due course he received three replies.

The first, from Ernst Öpik read: "Your results confirm my measurements that the meteors are from interstellar space." The second was from Parker who wrote: "Your results leave no doubt that the meteors are contained within the solar system." And what of Professor Whipple? – "Your results are indecisive but give promise of a valuable contribution to the subject":[175] still firmly on the fence.

Whether Öpik's response was evidence of the existence of the 'cheeky' disposition observed, many years later, in his grandson is a moot point; he certainly reconsidered his initial reaction to Bernard's news, because he subsequently expressed fierce objections to the results, saying that the experiment had been biased in favour of the British scientists and that they had been concentrating only on meteors of low velocity. If they would take the trouble to examine those of higher velocity, which were the ones he had studied with his rocking camera, they would disabuse themselves of their erroneous conclusions. Bernard's team had, in fact, approached their research with completely open minds, but Öpik's challenge was so robust that it stung them into further efforts. Over the next three years they repeated the whole exercise each spring and autumn, with a succession of larger aerials, longer wavelengths and more powerful transmitters. The last of these experiments ended in December 1951, by which time they had used thousands of feet of film, during nearly six hundred hours of observations and had recorded the velocities of 1,095 sporadic meteors, not one of which was travelling at a speed greater than 42.2 kilometres per second. Any residual doubts were effectively removed and the overwhelming evidence established that, like their more gregarious brothers the meteor showers, they too were in heliocentric orbit around the Sun. The results were published in a series of papers in *Monthly Notices of the Royal Astronomical Society*.[176] But although Bernard was happy that he had reached the end of a long road, his satisfaction was tinged with melancholy. He liked Öpik and was rather sad that a fellow scientist's treasured theory had been demolished; he also harboured a wistful sensation, that if the opposite result had been proved, it might have provided him with a fascinating opportunity for further investigation.

Long before this dispute was finally laid to rest, the transit telescope was starting to pull its weight in the brave new world of radio astronomy. That this occurred is due, in no small way, to the arrival of another wartime associate, Robert Hanbury Brown. Hanbury Brown was one of the most brilliant electronic engineers in the world. He had been a member of Bowen's team at Orfordness before the war and had worked in radar throughout the hostilities, both in Britain and America. In 1947 he became a partner in Robert Watson-Watt's consultancy, which advised airlines on radar and radio aids to navigation and was also involved with the embryonic television industry. In 1949, Watson-Watt announced that he was dissolving the partnership and moving to Canada; his partners were less than enthusiastic about this development, but they were forced to accede to it and Hanbury Brown found himself out of a job. He was thirty-two and, although he had long experience and expertise in electronics and with radar and radio, he felt that he lacked the formal qualifications which he needed to pursue an academic career. Following an unsuccessful application to an American university, he wrote to another former radar man, Freddie Williams, who was now Professor of Electrical Engineering at Manchester. Williams immediately realised that Hanbury Brown would be ideally suited to the work being done at Jodrell and, after a telephone call to Bernard, a visit was arranged. On 24th May 1949, Bernard met Hanbury Brown off the train at Goostrey and took him on a guided tour of the experimental station. He was extremely impressed and was particularly attracted to the opportunities offered by the transit telescope. The only problem was funding and Blackett and Williams applied to ICI for a research fellowship; the award was announced on 2nd June and Hanbury Brown started work in September.

Research undertaken by Hey at Malvern, by Martin Ryle and Francis Graham-Smith at Cambridge and by Bolton and Stanley in Australia had revealed the presence of a number of discrete radio sources from different places in the sky. The only one of these that could be linked with a visible object was a signal from the region of the Crab Nebula, which is the remnant of the supernova explosion observed by Chinese astronomers in 1054AD Among the other sources, the strongest signals were in the constellations of Cygnus and Cassiopeia, but no visible object appeared to coincide with either of them. It was generally considered that these mysterious phenomena were dark 'radio stars' within the galaxy, producing signals from the invisible part of the electromagnetic spectrum as opposed to the light emitted by regular stars. Almost no one believed that radio signals of any importance came from outside the Milky Way.

Hanbury Brown built a highly sensitive receiver to use in conjunction with the transit telescope and connected it to the focus with coaxial cable,[177] which he soldered to the main feed whilst perched precariously on the top of the mast, a task he was not anxious to repeat. Soon after he arrived at Jodrell, he was joined on the staff by Cyril Hazard, with whom he began the search for cosmic radiation. They were enthralled by the results as they recorded the radio waves pouring in from the 2-degree strip of sky through which the beam was swept by the rotation of the Earth. They marvelled at the nightly increase of the signal from the Milky Way; but they saw no answer to the question of the origin of the radiation. Was it entirely confined to our galaxy, as most astronomers believed? Or could they obtain evidence that it came from the universe beyond? Like Bernard and Clegg, they quickly became frustrated with the fixed beam which was restricting their observations to that small section of the cosmos immediately overhead.

They were mulling over this conundrum one afternoon, when Hanbury Brown was struck by a bold idea. If they could move the focus away from the vertical they might be able to attract signals from each side of their current field. The tubular steel mast was secured by eighteen cables which acted as guy ropes attached to the top, radiating like a wagon wheel to fixed moorings on the ground. If they loosened two or three cables on one side, perhaps they could move the mast by tightening the same number on the opposite side. It was risky; the mast might collapse one way or be pulled over the other, causing serious injury or death to any unsuspecting passer-by. Even worse, it might bend or snap off, wreaking havoc to the whole system. They thought about it for some time before they decided that it was a viable proposition, if extreme care was taken, and then plucked up the courage to tell Bernard what they wanted to do to his telescope. Fortunately, the boss was in a receptive mood and immediately saw the possibilities.

They wasted no time. That evening, as darkness fell, they began to adjust the angle of the mast. Very gingerly the cables were eased off on one side and, simultaneously tightened on the other; and it began to move. In 1771 the French astronomer, Messier, logged the Andromeda Nebula as M31 in his celestial map. Throughout the centuries it was thought that M31 was an amorphous cloud of matter hovering in the Milky Way, close to the constellation from which it takes its name. In 1922, Ernst Öpik estimated that it lay much further away in the outer universe; this idea was confirmed by Hubble in 1925, when his observations at Mount Wilson established beyond doubt that it is a completely separate galaxy, with a spiral disc shape similar to our own; it is now known to be two and a half million light years away; it is the largest galaxy in our group and, of the billions of galaxies in the universe, it is one of the very few which is visible with the naked eye. Hanbury Brown and Hazard realised that Andromeda was less than 10 degrees to one side of the strip of sky through which the beam of the transit telescope was swept on its nightly journey. In their discussions with Bernard it was decided that they should take a calculated chance and move the focus far enough from the zenith to cover M31; if they succeeded it was hoped that they could manipulate the mooring cables and track the galaxy for a few minutes each night.

Just as a larger optical telescope is able to capture images from ever more distant sources of light, so a larger radio telescope can detect fainter signals from ever more distant sources of radio waves. With his 30-foot paraboloid, Reber had been unable to establish whether M31 was sending out signals such as those received from the Milky Way. The transit telescope was seven times the size of Reber's and there was good reason to think that it would pick up any radiation which was being emitted. Every night, in all weathers, they moved the mast, inch by inch away from the vertical, bringing another area of sky into focus; every night the beam got closer and closer to the path of the great Andromeda galaxy.

After days of delicate manoeuvring they managed to tilt the mast 15 degrees from the centre point on either side, safely achieving a remarkable range of 30 degrees. At last they could begin their experiment. For three months, during the early autumn of 1950, frequently struggling with dreadful weather, they tracked radio frequencies from Andromeda, using a wavelength of 1.89 metres. During this time, they obtained ninety records, of which twenty were affected by heavy rain storms. Of the remainder, fifty established the existence of a radio source in the centre of the nebula and they concluded that: "The apparent dimensions of the source are consistent with a source of radio frequency radiation of size comparable with the main body of the nebula M31...From the results it appears evident that radio emissions from M31 are being received on Earth."[178] The characteristics of the signals were very similar to those which had been observed in the Milky Way. Sixty-three years after Heinrich Hertz proved the existence of electromagnetic radio waves, the experiment had recorded signals from outside the galaxy. For the first time in 13 billion years, a direct connection had been made between man and the universe. The age of the radio astronomer had arrived.[179]

CHAPTER FIFTEEN

A Steerable Paraboloid

The triumphant achievements of Hanbury Brown and Hazard, using the gerry-built but superbly effective transit telescope, provided the final impetus towards a plan that had been bubbling away in the background for nearly two years. If this fixed and unwieldy system could produce such stunning results, what could not be done with an even larger, fully steerable paraboloid? The sky, it seemed quite literally, would be the limit. Francis Graham-Smith, who was to succeed Bernard as director of Jodrell Bank more than thirty years later, explains the driving force behind this ambitious scheme: "He had a gut feeling, an insight which told him that if you build a really big and sensitive instrument you will find something with it. At first it was cosmic rays, but within a short time other possibilities opened up, as he knew they would. It was an extraordinary and unique insight. No one else had reached that conclusion."

Bernard first broached the subject with Blackett, in the autumn of 1948, at a time when the main purpose of the Jodrell establishment was still the search for cosmic rays. The work which had been done by Victor Hughes and the charts of the heavens which he had been able to prepare were an early indication of the wider possibilities; armed only with these charts and his customary enthusiasm, Bernard evidently had little difficulty in persuading Blackett that the plan was, at the very least, worthy of investigation. He had not the first idea how he would set about building such a structure, but he was determined to try. After all, had he not created steerable paraboloids which could operate at 20,000 feet in Lancaster bombers? How difficult could it be to build a similar instrument on terra firma, even allowing for the minor distinction that it would have to be two hundred times the size of its airborne counterpart?

Once he had received Blackett's blessing, Bernard threw himself into a frantic round of visits and discussions with construction companies and engineers.[180] There were letters to Dorman Long, who said they were too busy, and to a manufacturer of telescope mirrors, Grubb Parsons of Newcastle, whose Mr. George Sissons came to Jodrell and was wildly excited about the idea, saying that it could be done for £50,000; he went away and had a drawing of an aluminium structure prepared by Head Wrightson; the drawing was accompanied by a covering letter in which Mr. Sissons contradicted his earlier suggestion and said that it would cost a lot more than £50,000. Bernard also consulted F.D. Roberts from the London firm of Coubro and Scrutton; Roberts had supplied the design and the materials for the transit telescope mast and seemed to promise much. He sent his Mr. Turtle who opined that the problem was not a difficult one; following a second visit by Coubro and Scrutton, Mr. Roberts also had second thoughts about the undertaking; he wrote that it was a job for a leading structural engineer, suggesting approaches to Dorman Long, who had already said no, and Vickers Armstrong who proved to be a little less than enthusiastic.

Bernard was starting to feel a bit discouraged when, towards the end of July 1949, Roberts wrote to him again and said that he had been in touch with a consulting engineer who was keen to take on the whole project. Cue for entry, stage right, of Henry Charles Husband from the firm Husband and Company, consulting engineers of Sheffield and London. Roberts brought Husband to Jodrell on the afternoon of 8th September 1949, where he and Bernard met for the first time standing, appropriately, alongside the transit telescope. Bernard explained what he wanted and Husband said that it would be about as difficult as throwing a swing bridge across the River Thames at Westminster; whether this analogy was intended to reassure or to provide a warning of choppy waters ahead is not entirely clear; but the two men got on very well at this first meeting and, later in the year, Roberts provided some rough sketches which Husband had prepared; the surface of the bowl was to be formed with strained copper wire mesh and the suggested estimate was in the region of £45,000.

No proper plans and no realistic idea of the cost of the project had emerged from these rather chaotic discussions; but towards the end of the year Blackett, who was anxious to take matters forward, suggested that a high-powered committee of astronomers should be formed under the auspices of the Royal Astronomical Society. His ostensible rationale for setting up this group was the need for a forum, which would strive to maintain for Britain the early advantage created by the discoveries of Ryle at Cambridge, Hey at Malvern and Lovell at Jodrell. His real motive was to advance Bernard's idea, to build support in the highest scientific circles and to move on to coherent proposals for planning and delivery. He instructed Bernard to prepare a joint paper with Hey and Ryle; the three of them met for this purpose on 18th January and compiled a programme for the development of radio astronomy over the next five years. Bernard decided to attach an appendix of his own, with preliminary drawings, optimistically presenting it as a scheme for: "A large radio telescope which might be constructed in the near future." Ryle objected on the ground that the additional material would diminish the effect of the main document. From Bernard's point of view removing it had the fortunate if unintended consequence that, when it was put before the committee as a separate paper, its significance was greatly enhanced.

On 10th February 1950, the inaugural meeting was held at Burlington House, under the chairmanship of William Greaves, the Astronomer Royal for Scotland. Hey, Ryle, Blackett, Prentice, J.A. Ratcliffe from Cambridge, and H.W. Newton of the Royal Greenwich Observatory were present, as well as Bernard. Sir Edward Appleton the principal of Edinburgh University and H.S.W. Massey of UCL were absent and Mervyn Ellison, the Irishman, acted as secretary. In his eagerness, Bernard fully expected that Blackett would be his chief mediator and advocate; he was alarmed and bewildered when his mentor assiduously avoided any indication that he approved of the scheme. It was left to Bernard to make the running and, in the absence of specific proposals from Ryle or Hey, he was given a free rein. The minutes record that:

> Dr. Lovell then asked for consideration of his project for building in this country the 250ft. parabolic receiver so mounted that it could be swung round to any region of the sky. Preliminary drawings and a memorandum were submitted. After some discussion it was agreed that this was a matter of great importance for the future of Radio Astronomy in Britain and that the matter should be placed first on the agenda of the next meeting.[181]

It was decided that the next meeting would take place in Sir Edward Appleton's official apartments at the University of Edinburgh. The Astronomer Royal, Sir Harold Spencer Jones, was invited to join the committee and during the next two weeks, Patrick Blackett wasted no opportunity to remind Bernard of the crucial importance of making a good impression and of being fully prepared to deal with any questions which the distinguished members might throw at him. He drafted a more detailed memorandum with two sets of drawings, one which had been commissioned from Head Wrightson, by George Sissons, and the other drawn up by Charles Husband. These were circulated in good time before the date, which had been fixed for 27th February. The memorandum did not include any detailed costings nor even a rough estimate of the funds which might be required to build the telescope.

As the day of the meeting approached, Bernard was filled with foreboding. What if the Astronomer Royal was against the idea? What if he was asked a question he had not anticipated and could not answer? An uncomfortable journey on the night-train to Scotland and the instructions Blackett gave him whilst they were standing on a freezing platform at Carstairs at 6.00 am, waiting for their connection to Edinburgh, did nothing to calm his fears. He had planned to make a strong pitch for the telescope to be built at Jodrell and was thoroughly alarmed when Blackett told him to think again:

"You will emphasise to the committee that you are not putting forward this plan on behalf of yourself as something to be built at Jodrell, but as a project for the UK with the committee to decide the best place to build it."[182] This advice from his prime supporter threw Bernard into a state of dismay. If Blackett was not with him how could he possibly persuade the other members about the merits of his plan? As the train approached Edinburgh, he did some rapid redrafting of his presentation notes, but he was overflowing with doubts and felt increasingly nervous at the ordeal ahead. By 2.15, when they arrived at Sir Edward's imposing rooms, he was in a high state of nervous excitement.

Greaves once again took the chair and called the meeting to order. Appleton, Blackett, the Astronomer Royal, Hey and Ellison were present but, to Bernard's amazement, neither Martin Ryle nor Jack Ratcliffe was there to represent the interests of the Cambridge group. Ryle had produced a paper in which he described his work with an interferometer, a device which used two fairly small receiving dishes, placed some distance apart from each other, working together to increase the power of the signals; but the Cambridge scheme could not compete with the scale or ambition of Bernard's and the techniques being used were still at the development stage. It was quickly decided that Ryle's paper and another one produced by Hey should be discussed at the next meeting. This was the moment. The chairman turned to Bernard, and asked him to explain his proposal for a large, fully steerable, paraboloid telescope. As he developed his theme, building it like a long innings, his confidence grew. His brief notes[183] recall that he was pressed very strongly on all points including the advantages of his plan over the cheaper system being developed by Ryle; but his preparation had been thorough, he dealt with every ball they bowled at him with aplomb and his defence remained solid and unshaken.

From start to finish he did as Blackett had instructed, not overplaying his hand and studiously avoiding any suggestion that this was a personal proposal to build the telescope at Jodrell. When he sat down, Blackett took up the argument, endorsing the remarks made by Professor Lovell, just as Bernard had expected he would; all went well until he expressed the view that the telescope could be constructed in a number of places, including the Royal Observatory at Herstmonceux, which might be the best site of all. Bernard was incredulous. He had been listening complacently to Blackett's helpful remarks, but at this suggestion he bristled with indignation; he was on the point of springing to his feet in a furious protest, with consequences that would have been fatal to his hopes. Fortunately he managed to control the violence of his emotions and the instantaneous reaction through the room demonstrated how well Blackett had judged the mood of the meeting and how astutely he had handled his irrepressible protégé. Had he allowed Bernard to go in with all guns blazing in support of a telescope at Jodrell, the response of his erudite audience, accustomed as they were to the careful weighing of evidence and sagacious decision making, would have been negative or even hostile. By gently dropping the Herstmonceux proposal into his measured argument, he obtained precisely the response he had been hoping for all along. Without a moment's hesitation the chairman announced that if the telescope was to be built anywhere it must be built at Jodrell Bank and he moved swiftly to call for the committee to decide:

"I now ask every member attending the meeting to give his decision as to whether support should be given to the construction of the instrument and whether a very serious effort should be made to obtain the money."[184] The money was not a topic with which the committee had been troubled, to any great extent. Bernard mentioned figures of between £50,000 and £100,000, but only in passing, and not one of the brilliant scientists gathered in Edinburgh on that frosty afternoon had a notion of the cost of the enterprise they were debating. They were there to evaluate high scientific aspirations and mundane questions of price could not be allowed to sully the mind or cloud the judgement. As each member pronounced his agreement with Bernard's proposal, his wildest hopes soared. The final endorsement came from Sir Edward Appleton:

"I am impressed by the wide range of problems in astronomy and geophysics which Professor Lovell has listed as capable of solution by a radio telescope of this size. But I am even more impressed by the possible uses of this instrument in fields of research which we cannot yet envisage."[185]

With this ringing endorsement it was unanimously agreed that an immediate application for funding should be submitted to the DSIR and that the Council of the RAS should be urged to support the project. It was a happy Bernard who travelled back to Manchester that night, accompanied by the brilliant architect of his success, Patrick Blackett.

In the immediate afterglow of Edinburgh, George Sissons encouraged Bernard to make contact with F.J. Dean, the managing director of Head Wrightson's special projects department. Of the two designs which had been put before the committee, Bernard's initial preference lay with the Head Wrightson version, which was to be built in aluminium and looked particularly elegant. Dean indicated that his firm would charge £900 to provide a preliminary estimate; on 20th March, the University Council agreed to underwrite this expense and Head Wrightson were instructed to proceed. For the next two months, in spite of a constant stream of letters and frequent promises that delivery of the estimate was imminent, no concrete proposals were produced. In May, desperate for a response, Bernard took Blackett to Slough to meet Dean. The encounter was not a success. Dean had been severely disabled by war injuries and appeared to Bernard to be "a little bit of a crank".[186] The charm of the original plan was its simplicity but it was now overlaid with a variety of complex additions, which added hugely to the cost; this had soared tenfold from the £50,000 originally mentioned by Sisson to a figure in excess of half a million. Blackett was furious at this immense and unexpected increase; he insisted that the size of the paraboloid would have to be reduced. Bernard argued that this would undermine the whole purpose of the scheme and little progress was made. It was arranged that Dean would fly up to Manchester on 27th June with amended plans and a more realistic estimate. The day came; Blackett arrived, but there was no sign of Dean; enquiries were made with Head Wrightson who said that he no longer worked for the company and that his department had been disbanded. The two scientists were more than a little irritated, in due course the University refused to pay Head Wrightson the £900, and Bernard finally entered into full negotiations with Charles Husband.

Even whilst the Head Wrightson fiasco was in full swing, communication with Husband had continued. On 3rd April 1950 F.D. Roberts wrote to Bernard quoting Husband's current estimate that the 250-foot paraboloid could be constructed for £59,000. This was £14,000 more than his original suggestion but, Bernard recorded that, when challenged, Roberts replied: "The professional pride of my consultants has been somewhat hurt by your insinuations that they are unable to guess how much the instrument will cost."[187] The use of the word "guess" does not appear to have caused any anxiety about the accuracy of the estimate and arrangements were made for a further meeting with Husband. He arrived at Jodrell Bank on 14th June and explained that his standard fee for the completion of the design work was £3,000, with a further sum of £300 to cover the cost of sinking a borehole. His preliminary estimate had been raised again, on the grounds of an increase in the depth of the bowl and a reduction to 2 inches in the size of the copper mesh; it now stood at £120,000, which Husband described as "reasonably safe", although he added a rider to this questionably comforting prediction, emphasising that: "For anything as unusual as this a design in much more detail than we have prepared already is essential in order to obtain firm tenders for carrying out the scheme."[188] Based on these figures, which were less than twenty-five percent of the half a million pounds quoted by Head Wrightson in May, an immediate application was made to the DSIR for a grant of £3,300 to pay for the design and the borehole. The supporting documents sent with the application included an endorsement from the Royal Astronomical Society, in the following terms:

> The RAS strongly endorses the proposal for the erection of a steerable paraboloid of 250-foot diameter. In the Council's opinion the investigations undertaken are of high scientific importance including the systematic survey of the isolated reaches and the general background of galactic radio emission, the study of the spectrum of the galactic and solar radiation, the extension of the meteor programme to meteors fainter than 6th magnitude, the further investigation of auroral phenomena and the measurement of the reflected pulses from the Moon, the planets and the solar corpuscular streams. The Council is impressed by the consideration that the construction of the proposed paraboloid would permit the continuation in the UK of new methods of astronomical research, which have been greatly developed by the skill of scientists in the UK and which are independent of climactic conditions.[189]

Only one week later, on 22nd June, Bernard was invited to London to make his presentation to the research grants committee of the DSIR. The composition of the committee could not have been more promising if he had picked it himself. Philip Dee was the chairman, several other wartime colleagues were members and the Secretary of the DSIR was Sir Ben Lockspeiser, a close associate of Patrick Blackett. Lockspeiser later claimed that, in line with his usual practice when considering applications from "any enthusiastic scientific research worker", he had mentally doubled the estimate of £120,000.[190] Whether this claim was true or made with the benefit of hindsight, it would have been more accurate if he had applied a multiple of six to the original figure. The committee had no hesitation in supporting the enthusiastic scientific researcher and authority was granted for the design work to be carried out by Husband, at a cost of £3,300. Neither Husband nor the committee had any idea that the negotiations with Head Wrightson were still current; it was, perhaps, fortunate, that they collapsed the following week before anyone found out about them.

It was a beautiful afternoon as Bernard skipped out of the DSIR offices and into Trafalgar Square. Looking up at Nelson's column, he indulged himself with the glorious reflection that the supporting towers of his telescope would be 185 feet tall, the same height as the top of the great naval hero's tricorn hat. A digital survey more than fifty-five years later established that he had done less than justice to the impressive size of the towers; they did indeed rise to 185 feet, but the top of Nelson's hat is a mere 169 feet 3 inches from the ground.

In order to appreciate the extraordinary feat which the building of the telescope represented, it will be helpful to have some appreciation of the scale and sensitivity of the instrument at the time of its completion in 1957.

The size of the finished article is immense. We see it, shortly before completion, in the middle of a field which it is sharing with a herd of cows, as it towers above the surrounding countryside. The bowl is 250 feet across, it is 70 feet deep and the top of the rim is 215 feet from the ground when the bowl is level. It is supported on two enormous towers. Each tower houses the machinery and the electric motors that tilt the bowl through 180 degrees across the sky (in elevation or declination). Each tower stands on six bogies running on two circular railway tracks with an inner diameter of 320

A herd of cows look on unphased as the Telescope moves for the first time,
20 June 1957

feet round which the entire structure spins like a top through 360 degrees, driven by electric motors at the base of each tower. The tracks bear the whole weight of the instrument, more than 2,000 tons, but it must not deviate from its path so much as a fraction of an inch as the carefully tapered wheels on the bogies revolve. By coordinating the tilting of the bowl with the spinning of the telescope, it can be pointed to any part of the sky.

The shape of the paraboloid enables radio signals gathered by the surface to be reflected with great precision to the focus, at the top of the central tower 126 feet above the middle of the bowl; the focus contains a radio receiver; this converts the radio waves into electrical signals which are conveyed by underground cables running through a tunnel from the centre of the telescope to the control room, 200 yards away. Finally the electrical signals are converted into optical images which appear on the screens.

The construction of the telescope required the solution to four major problems:

1. it was necessary to make a paraboloid reflector with a diameter of 250 feet, in such a way that it would retain its shape when it moved and would not be susceptible to extraneous movement by wind, temperature conditions, sun, rain, frost or snow;

2. the driving system for moving the paraboloid in any direction needed to be sufficiently powerful to control the telescope with great precision under all conditions;

3. the controls had to be capable of being set so that they could follow any object automatically, regardless of the momentum of the object, its direction of travel, the daily rotation of the Earth or the orbit of Earth round the Sun;

4. no instrument of this size and with this mobility had ever been built before, so the design and specifications had to be such as could be followed by manufacturers and construction firms with no previous experience.

The exceptional power and sensitivity of the instrument required that it should have a very high level of stability in all conditions, it must be stiff enough to hold its shape throughout its massive structure and it must be able to maintain both the stability and the stiffness even in the highest gusts of wind. The original design envisaged that it would operate on wavelengths of 1 metre or above, which would have permitted a tolerance to movement of 6 or 7 inches. During the early stages of development, radio astronomers began to detect hydrogen emissions from the Milky Way on a wavelength of 21 centimetres. If the telescope was going to be an effective instrument, it became essential that the design should be modified to accommodate short, high frequency wavelengths. This required a far more accurate and sensitive reflecting surface than could be provided by the 2-inch mesh, which was abandoned regardless of the cost, in favour of solid steel. The surface of the bowl was now laid on 2,200 angle iron purlins, each of which was precisely curved so that it lay absolutely true. The purlins were continuously welded to the 7,100 3-foot by 3-foot steel plates and each plate was welded to its neighbours at the edges. The effects of wind were extensively tested and calculated using a wind tunnel at the National Physics Laboratory with an exact model of the proposed telescope, scaled down to one percent of the actual size. The lower part of the bowl was only held at the central point, so that it could expand and contract with the inevitable variations of temperature; when the bowl expanded, it exerted a pressure which was taken up by the trunnion bearings connecting the bowl to the towers and by deflection of the towers themselves. Each tower stood on two bogies, powered by electric motors to carry the instrument round the tracks; each tower had another two bogies on either side, to carry the supporting stanchion legs to keep the towers upright.

The movement of the telescope was controlled by an analogue computer designed by J.G Davies, who had joined Bernard's team in 1947. The system he devised measured and monitored the actual position of the telescope at any given time, taking account of the Earth's rotation and orbit; it would also calculate the required position, that is, the position of the object under observation; the difference between the two measurements was then fed into the control system of the driving motors in the towers and on the bogies. The required position was continuously calculated, using a sidereal clock (completing its full cycle every twenty-three hours and fifty-six minutes) so that the position and path of a star could be ascertained and the information could be fed to the motors which automatically moved the telescope to follow it. In addition to the main control room, a small laboratory was suspended from the bottom of the bowl, 100 feet above the ground.

Once the euphoria of obtaining consent from the DSIR for the design study had abated, it was time for the serious work to begin and they had to wrestle with the difficulties which the above specifications dictated. Any hopes that they would be allowed to get on with the job undisturbed by extraneous troubles, were soon dissipated; meanwhile, one of the first problems was solved by a suggestion made by Patrick Blackett during a discussion about the mechanism for moving the bowl on its axis, in elevation and declination. Blackett realised that the method of gun-aiming on a naval vessel pitching and rolling in heavy seas mirrored some of the difficulties which would be encountered in 'aiming' the telescope. He advised Bernard to visit the Admiralty Gunnery Division at Teddington in Middlesex, and on 20th July, accompanied by Husband, he went there to a meet J.M. Ford. Ford recommended that they should ask Metropolitan Vickers to design the control system and that they might be able to use gear racks from redundant guns to drive the elevation of the bowl. Two weeks later, Husband went to the ship breaking yard of Thomas Ward at Inverkeithing in Fife. They were in the process of breaking up two battleships, the *Revenge* and the *Royal Sovereign*. Husband was shown three of the rack and pinion mechanisms used to rotate the guns, which they were offered for £250, little more than their scrap value. Even though they were still at the design stage and might never need this beautifully engineered machinery, they decided to take a chance and agreed to buy it. Then they then had to move the racks 280 miles back to Cheshire; each one was 27 feet in diameter and the cost of the transport was four times the price of the racks. The DSIR refused to help, but Bernard was able to persuade the University that they had obtained a real bargain and he was allowed to take the money out of his annual research budget.

For the rest of the year there was a constant round of meetings, telephone calls, drafting and correspondence between Bernard and Husband; the pattern was set and, for the next seven years, hardly a day passed without them being in communication. Bernard also became preoccupied with producing a detailed description of the proposal, which would form part of the material sent to the DSIR when the time came to make the full application. This document was the cornerstone of the submission. It was not professionally produced but was typed on eighty loose leaf sheets of paper. It was illustrated with poor quality photographs and rather crude drawings. Seventy copies were required; a stencil was created for each page and seventy copies of each stencil were made with a manually operated duplicating machine. The 5,600 pages were sorted and stapled together before being placed in rudimentary blue bindings embossed with the title 'A Steerable Radio Telescope'. It was a laborious process, but it did provide a comprehensive guide to the project and, as such, it served its purpose. On 20th March 1951, Husband's designs and estimates were submitted to the DSIR, supported by 'The Blue Book', as it had come to be known.[191]

A short forward indicated that Husband and Co. had now carried out designs and obtained estimates for all parts of the work. This was followed by an introduction, in Chapter One, which argued that Britain's overcast skies prevented her from "regaining our birthright, for the work of Herschel and Rosse". It described the adaptation of wartime techniques for the peaceful pursuit of the new science of radio astronomy, which was impervious to adverse weather and could also make observations in daylight; these techniques had led to a remarkable sequence of discoveries, which had returned Britain to a position of high eminence in the field. They included finding radio stars, the study of solar flares, discovery of radio emissions from Andromeda, observation of intense radio activity from areas of sky which were devoid of visible objects, solving the dispute about sporadic meteors, the daytime meteor showers and the detection of vast volumes of debris within the solar system. There was further work to be done on solar activity and the Moon and the real hope, thereafter, of studying the planets and the universe beyond the Milky Way.

What was needed to take these discoveries further was, of course, a huge steerable radio telescope, the advantages of which were set out in Chapter Two. In summary the benefits were that it would be extremely powerful, that it could cover any area of the sky and that it would have a greater capacity than any of its rivals, at home or abroad. Subsequent chapters dealt with sources of power, location, a number of potential problems, such as interference from electric cables and local development plans and an all important chapter, headed 'Financial Proposals'. These helpfully reminded the research grants committee that the estimate in June 1950 had been £123,300. The submissions continued in a bold vein stating that, due to increasing costs and underestimates, this figure had risen; more money was needed for foundations, drive mechanisms, control mechanisms, the reduction of the mesh size from 4 square inches to 2 square inches, the rise in the price of steel and other unspecified items. As a result, in the nine months between June 1950 and March 1951, the estimated cost had increased to £259,030. The book concluded by repeating the strong endorsement from the Royal Astronomical Society, which had been included in the preliminary application the previous year.[192]

Blackett expressed considerable annoyance at this huge increase and once more advocated that the scale and ambition of the enterprise should be curtailed. He considered that the likelihood of obtaining a grant of £259,000 was insignificant and that a much smaller instrument with a diameter of 100 feet would still allow very significant research. Bernard was in no mood for compromise and argued, somewhat disingenuously, that the increase had been caused by rising costs. In truth this only represented about £20,000 of the additional expense. Husband had substantially underestimated the price of the foundations in his original estimate; they later decided that a mesh of 4-by-4 inches would result in a significant loss of signal through the surface; the 2-by-2-inch copper mesh with which it was to be replaced was much more expensive; it also added significantly to the weight which the structure would have to carry; this in turn reduced the stability of the instrument and increased the potential effect of severe wind, so more steelwork was needed for support.

Week after week they eagerly awaited a response from the DSIR and week after week they received no news at all. There was a great deal of lobbying behind the scenes and they certainly had powerful friends. Blackett's influence was crucial and did not waver, in spite of his reservations. In July 1951, he arranged for Henry Tizard to visit Jodrell. Bernard first met Tizard when he had taught his son at Bristol and their relationship remained strong through the years at TRE. Lord Simon, the Chairman of the University Council was an industrialist and a politician who had been Chairman of BBC Trust. Sir John Stopford, Vice Chancellor of Manchester University, was a distinguished physician and anatomist, a fellow of the Royal Society and crucially, as it turned out, Vice Chairman of the Nuffield Foundation; he had close contacts with the DSIR and with Lockspeiser, who was also firmly behind the project. Lord Woolton, the Chancellor of the University, had been Chairman of the Conservative Party since 1945, and in the new government formed by Churchill in October 1951, he joined the cabinet as Lord President of the Council, and was a powerful supporter, although, as we shall see, his support was ephemeral and waned quickly when it conflicted with his own agenda.

The delay was unbearable, but they began to receive optimistic signals at the turn of the year and early in 1952 they were instructed to prepare a revised estimate. The price of steel had risen sharply and they were horrified to find that this had pushed up the construction cost a further £76,000; the projected total now stood at £335,000. Husband prepared new estimates which spread the cost over three and a half years rather than the two and a half originally envisaged; although this manoeuvre massaged the increase to some extent, they could not help but think that their worst fears were about to be realised. There was a further agonising delay until one afternoon just before Easter, when Bernard received a cryptic telephone call from Blackett who simply said: "You're through." He could hardly believe it. A letter from the DSIR, confirmed that the cost of building his great steerable paraboloid was to be shared equally between the Department and the Nuffield Foundation. He had not known of Stopford's connection with Nuffield and he read through the document in a complete daze. The revised estimate was nearly three times the figure provided in June 1950 and had grown almost sevenfold since the

Edinburgh meeting; but there were only two conditions of the grant: a board of visitors was to be appointed to oversee the operation of the telescope; and Bernard must see the project through and then remain in charge for at least five years. It might have saved a great deal of trouble if the visitors had taken up their duties at once to oversee the construction. As for Bernard, after all he had been through to get to this point, he had no intention of going anywhere.

With three children by 1948, the house in Fallowfield had become too small for comfort and Bernard was spending so much of his time at Jodrell Bank that it seemed sensible to move to the country and travel into Manchester when he needed to. In May he had noticed an advertisement in the *Manchester Guardian* for the sale of a house with some acres of land at the village of Swettenham, only 2 miles from Jodrell. One afternoon Bernard and Joyce drove to Swettenham to view the property. To this day a narrow lane marked "no through road" leads to the village, which contains a few houses, a tiny church and a public house called the Swettenham Arms. The Quinta, as the house they were viewing was called, stands at the edge of the village just beyond the pub, with fine views across a small valley. As soon as they saw it they fell in love with it. The auction was scheduled for that very afternoon and full of hope and expectation they hurried to the George Hotel at Knutsford, where it was to be held. When they failed to get the house they wended their way home to Fairview Road feeling sad and deflated. That evening, to their surprise and delight, they received a telephone call from the vendor who told them that he did not like the successful bidder and he wanted them to have the house; quite how he had squared this with the purchaser is a mystery. One month later they moved in and it became the hub of their family life for the next sixty-four years. It was in this lovely place that Bernard received the letter confirming the DSIR grant, on Good Friday, 1952. It was a very happy Easter at The Quinta.

The plans submitted to the DSIR indicated that the telescope would be built on a field identified as Field 80, which the University had purchased from a Miss Robinson. Her farm had been in the family for several generations and she was reluctant to sell any of it; in due course she was persuaded, after which she became most amenable and allowed work to begin, even before the sale was completed. Husband sent in his contractors to drill boreholes so that he could establish the quality of the subsoil and the depth to which the foundations would have to be sunk. So the land was acquired and work began even before the funds had been approved. But Field 80 was not Bernard's preferred site for the telescope; that honour belonged to Field 132, which had better access and was more conveniently placed in relation to the transit telescope and the existing buildings. Unfortunately, this field did not belong to the University either; it was part of Blackden Farm, the property of Mrs. Massey, a widow with four sons; she was of good Cheshire farming stock and was not inclined to sell any part of her family's heritage. Her death, early in 1952, fired the starting gun for an unseemly family quarrel in which Bernard, rather unwisely, allowed himself to become involved.

The farm was left to Mrs. Massey's sons. The three oldest, Hubert, Rex and George, had farms of their own, but the youngest, Eric, had continued to live at home and farmed the land with his mother for several years. The situation was a classic recipe for sibling rivalry, even without the complication of Bernard's wish to build the telescope on Field 132. He discussed the possibility of the University buying the field with Rainford, the bursar, who agreed to investigate. Shortly after this the grant from the DSIR and Nuffield was approved, and Husband, who was quite content to build on Field 80, began to make preparations and instructed contractors to begin work early in May. The University approached the brothers, who were all executors of their mother's estate, and made a generous offer to buy the whole farm, with vacant possession. The offer was quite acceptable to Hubert, Rex and George; Eric, on the other hand, stood to lose his home and his livelihood and he expressed vigorous objections. In a spirit of compromise the University attempted to broker a deal which would satisfy all parties and made an alternative offer; they would buy Field 132 and leave Eric as the sitting tenant of the rest of the farm. This idea provoked howls of anger from the other three; one moment they thought they would be receiving a good vacant possession price for their inheritance, the next they were going to be left with their younger brother as the sitting tenant and a reduced acreage to take to the market. Eric was not happy either and said that he had no intention of agreeing to the sale of a single acre, to the University or anyone else.

Bernard had arranged that Husband should start work on the foundations no later than 1st July. It was now nearly the end of May; he could contain his patience no longer and before any further mediation could be attempted, he launched himself into the fray.[193] On 23rd May Eric complained that Husband's men had been trespassing on his land and the next morning Bernard visited him to try and get him to see reason; the mission was a failure and Eric told him that he would not agree to sell. A few days later the brothers said they were prepared to compromise by selling a total of 40 acres, including Field 132, leaving Eric with the tenancy of the rest of the farm. Eric refused to countenance the idea. Bernard suggested swapping Field 80 in exchange for Field 132, but this proposal found favour with no one and the squabbling continued. On 12th June he talked to Eric Massey who was in the middle of a field mowing his hay. He said he was happy to sell the field, but predicted that his brothers would not agree because they wanted a good price for whole farm. On 28th June Bernard had another long discussion with Eric and his wife; they agreed to a sale of the farm providing they were given a long lease and a low rent on everything except Field 132, which he said he was now prepared to give up. Eric said he would square it with his brothers, but shortly before midnight Bernard was awoken by the ringing of the telephone; it was Eric, who had no doubt spent the evening considering the position over several pints of Robinsons bitter; he informed Bernard that he had changed his mind and was not prepared to sell a single acre.

The following day, Bernard, who was becoming "increasingly annoyed at the situation", decided to visit each brother in turn in order to arrange a meeting with them at the office of their solicitor, Barclay May. Hubert, who was haymaking in a remote field, seemed very reasonable; Rex was out, but his wife felt sure he would attend; George said he would be there; but Eric flatly refused to attend any meetings. On 30th June the three older brothers and Bernard met at the solicitor's office, where it was agreed that court action should be taken to force a sale, regardless of the views of the unfortunate Eric. Counsel's opinion was obtained. They were advised that they would be able to get Eric excluded as a trustee as he had an interest in retaining the farm, which conflicted with the interests of the other beneficiaries. Proceedings were commenced and, on 24th July, Bernard received a telephone call from May telling him that the High Court in London had ordered the sale of the farm to the University. If Bernard hoped that this decision would bring about a quick resolution of his problems, he was to be sadly disappointed in the coming weeks. His impatience had driven him to become embroiled in matters which he should have left to others and the aftershocks of the minor earthquake his intervention had orchestrated continued.

Two days after the hearing in London, Eric Massey's wife telephoned him. She insisted that they had no idea what was going on and that Eric believed Barclay May was bluffing about taking the affair to court. She said he was convinced that his brothers would see sense eventually and would compromise. Ten minutes later he received a call from Eric who was violently abusive, swore at Bernard, called him a double-crosser and said that the farm would only be sold over his dead body.

"Never in my life have I received such a call. He told me I was backing the wrong side and that we would never get the field as he wants it and it is his farm. There were veiled threats and he said that if we take it further it would be the worse for me and the University. I became very alarmed and rang the solicitor, who reported my anxieties to the police."[194] Predictably enough the Cheshire Constabulary were not interested; an officer did visit Eric Massey some days later and then came to see Bernard and told him that, as it was a civil matter, there was nothing he could do. The brothers were apparently having some pangs of conscience about their treatment of Eric; they said they were most reluctant to become involved in evicting him and refused to sign the contract; they thought that the eviction should be effected by the University. Attempts to persuade them to sign the contract continued through August, including a "long discussion with Hubert who was on top of a stack of oats, loading a cart". The agreement to sell the farm to the University for £12,500 was finally completed on 22nd August and Husband's men gained entry, pegged out the site of the telescope and the buildings and erected a workman's hut in the field. Eric was nowhere to be seen. Calm was finally restored and they could build the telescope on the field of their choice. But they had not reckoned with the determination of the irate farmer.

The next morning the workmen returned to find that the hut was lying

Troubles with the locals. The caption originally read: "Popular Misconceptions - Life Down in the Country". COURTESY OF PUNCH LIMITED.

upside down in a ditch; the marker pegs had been pulled out of the ground and thrown down alongside the hut and a herd of cows was in occupation of Field 132, accompanied by a rather ferocious bull. Once again the police were called and a couple of officers arrived. They did not stay long. One hostile glance from the beast was more than enough to see off the boys in blue, and the bull and his ladies were left in full possession of the field.

That evening there was another lengthy telephone call from a very cross Mrs. Massey.[195] She said that her husband, or 'Daddy' as she called him, would fight all the way and go to prison if necessary. Bernard tried to reason with her and made particular reference to the ferocious bull on the rampage. Mrs. Massey retorted that the bull was not really ferocious. When Bernard pointed out that it was fierce enough to frighten off the workmen, the redoubtable lady made a caustic comment about the lack of courage of "Manchester men". Bernard changed tack and informed her that Eric was breaking the law because the field now belonged to the University. She enquired how Daddy was to get across the field to cut his corn.

"He will only have to ask and I will give him permission," said Bernard.

"After thirty-six years he's got to ask permission to put cows in his own field," protested Mrs. Massey. "He's prepared to go to prison to support what's right. You're on the wrong side – the side that's greedy, aren't you? The brothers will demand £3,000 for the stock and Daddy will end up with nothing." The deadlock continued and four days later the diary entry for 28th July reads:

"Bull still in possession and hut in the ditch. Husband rang and was very amused, saying it reminded him of stories of farmers in the days of building railways. He would advise the contractors to take plenty of men with them, including someone who knew about bulls and to engage a strong night watchman." The University made the helpful suggestion that someone should drive out the bull but they did not put up a volunteer. Then, as unexpectedly as it had arrived, the bull was removed and, on 1st September, work could commence. The row rumbled on for months but eventually cordial relations were resumed and the Masseys and the telescope rubbed along together quite happily for many years.

Chapter Sixteen

How to Build a Telescope

Husband's investigation of the subsoil had revealed that, underneath the fertile grassland, there were 40 feet of wet running sand, with another 20 feet of clay and sand before a solid bed was reached to support the 160 piles of reinforced concrete which would form the foundations for the telescope. The piles were to be drilled down from the bottom of a huge circular trench 6 feet deep, 20 feet wide and 350 feet in diameter. Once they were all installed the trench could be filled with reinforced concrete on which the railway tracks would be laid to take the full weight of the telescope. The depth of the piles was dictated partly by the huge weight that they would have to support and partly by the need for the perfect stability that was required throughout the length of the tracks. The delays caused by the land dispute meant that the work began at least two months later than intended. It had been hoped that all the piles and the concrete for the trench would be in place before the onset of winter, so that construction of the railway tracks could be completed by the spring of 1953. The postponement of the start date until early September meant that this ambitious target could not be met; there were constant problems caused by water filling up the holes drilled for the concrete piles; only two dozen had been completed before winter set in.

The depression caused by these delays was compounded by the need, as early as February 1953, to go cap in hand to the DSIR asking for more money. It was clear from revised estimates that an additional sum of £92,000 would be required to complete the construction. Of this increase, twenty per cent was due to rising costs but most of the extra money was the consequence of over-optimistic estimates in the original figures, unsatisfactory design features, alterations to the design which meant that more steel was required and the decision to reduce the size of the mesh even further, this time to 2 inches by 1 inch. This decision was made following the discovery, by astronomers around the world, of 21-centimetre radio emissions from clouds of neutral hydrogen gas within the Milky Way. The study of these emissions would reveal a great deal about the presence and properties of hydrogen in the universe; the inability to operate at wavelengths as short as 20 centimetres would considerably curtail the effectiveness of the new telescope; to cater for this development it was essential to fit a smaller mesh. The diary for the 20th February explains the increases:

> The figures from Husband show a required increase in capital expenditure of 32%, over £92,000. The main breakdown shows that 20% of this is due to rises in engineering costs since the original schedule and the remainder is mainly due to the fact that the weight of the structure has now come out at 1,200 instead of 1,000 tons in the original plan. The major items of increase are the £39,000 representing 37% on the structural steel work and £19,000 representing 32% on the driving system. A good deal of the latter is due to the fact that the original design for the pivot was completely unsatisfactory, an increase from £5,700 to £12,000. The mesh itself is to cost £20,000 instead of £12,000, this being an increase of 67% and in the new estimates £4,500 has been included for painting. I wrote to Evans summarising the position and saying I would bring the detailed estimates on the individual items with me on Tuesday.[196]

On 25th February the request for the additional money was sent to the DSIR, with the new estimates setting out the detail. They were explained mainly on the basis of rising costs, with any adjustments being kept within the agreed margin of ten percent.

> Yesterday afternoon I met Evans and Fryer of the DSIR and presented them with the revised schedule showing an additional sum needed of £92,000. They were of course somewhat shattered, but I think I managed to convince them after a great deal of hard talking, that the increase was mainly due to rising cost and that we had in fact done quite well to keep the other increases down to 10 percent...On returning home I phoned Rainford, as agreed. He had received my schedule and thought it told quite a good story. He promised to give all the support needed when he went to the DSIR today. I asked Rainford to be most circumspect in what he told the DSIR especially with regard to increased costs.

Bernard conceded, in later years, that the argument he had presented to the DSIR was "a bit thin".[197] It may have fallen somewhat short of full disclosure as to the cause of the projected increases, but the figures were set out in the estimates, and his success was a tribute to his powers of advocacy. Evans, the Assistant Secretary to the DSIR, said that the Department did not have the money and that it would take two or three months to reach a decision; even as the spring weather permitted work on the piles to restart, a period of acute anxiety lay ahead. On 4th March Rainford was highly critical of Husband for failing to build contingency funding into his estimates. At the end of the month the Nuffield Foundation agreed to pay another £32,000 but insisted that the balance would have to be provided by the DSIR. The feeling of gloom is summed up in a diary entry for 2nd April:

> Last Easter was the time of the announcement the grant had been made. A year later, on this stormy afternoon the site is almost deserted. It is piled with mounds of earth and on the whole is somewhat depressing. There is little to show for the vast amounts of steel and concrete already sunk into the ground.[198]

On 6th May, there was a difficult appearance before a rather hostile committee, whose composition had changed since the time of the original grant twelve months earlier. They insisted that a further report should be obtained on the question of the stability of the instrument in windy conditions; this was provided by Professor W.A. Mair and on 21st May Bernard received a telephone call from Evans at the DSIR. The advisory council had agreed to provide the extra money, with "a very big BUT". They were concerned at the size of the increase and warned that it might be impossible to provide funds for any further increases, should they arise. If more money was needed the University would have to raise it. On 1st June a total of £104,000 was confirmed, with the important rider that no more could be provided in future.

In later years he was to make light of the enormous anxieties caused by these pressures remarking, with a twinkle in his eye:

"The cost increased dramatically, far above what we had expected – But I didn't tell anybody! If I had, the telescope would never have been built. And by the time they did realise, so much steel had been constructed that it was too late to close us down." And if you asked him why the Department did not keep control of the spending, he would say: "They had no idea what was going on." But at the time these worries were acute and the DSIR and the University were at least as responsible as Husband and Bernard, whose principal aim was to build the best possible instrument. As Husband wrote in a letter to Rainford: "Professor Lovell's sole interests, quite properly, are the use of the telescope, and the earliest possible date at which it can be completed."[199] In fact the records show that the University was kept very well informed: at any stage they could have vetoed changes and settled for an inferior instrument if they had chosen to do so; and from start to finish they were responsible for failing to manage the finances and keep a check on spending.

During the planning and execution of the project, neither the DSIR nor the University asked to see accounts and there was no proper scrutiny of the costs. Financial control over expenditure was conspicuous for its absence throughout the five and a half years which it took to build the telescope, a criticism for which all sides must share the blame. As Bernard frankly admitted, he had neither the competence nor the experience to handle complex financial problems.[200] During these years he was completely absorbed, or even obsessed, by his determination to fulfil his dream, to the extent that any obstacle had to be overcome by any means. Nothing else mattered. Nor was he helped by the players mentioned above taking the elementary precautions of checking whether he knew anything about finance or of appointing someone who did know to oversee the development. When more money was deemed to be necessary, an application was made and, in due course the funds were provided; that was the system, or lack of a system, under which everyone operated until the telescope was built.

By the time the additional funds were promised, all 160 piles had been completed; soon the trench would be filled with reinforced concrete, the evenness of the surface would be measured and prepared to the necessary precision, they could start to lay the railway track and the telescope would begin to rise. Things were looking up both financially and on the construction front, but other worries about construction elsewhere were beginning to emerge.

Once the decision was made on the position of the telescope and other buildings, the necessary planning consents were obtained without any difficulty; but even as work began there were worrying reports of plans to relocate large numbers of people, categorised as 'Manchester overspill', in the Cheshire countryside. One of the principal attractions of Jodrell as the site for the telescope was its isolation. There were no large developments or towns within 6 miles and the electricity supplies to local farms and villages were provided without the need for high voltage power lines and pylons. The incursion of significant centres of population close to the telescope would severely affect its ability to operate. The original reports did not give much cause for concern, because the areas preferred by Manchester Council were the villages of Lymm and Mobberley, which were closer to Manchester and outside a 6-mile radius from Jodrell.

Cheshire County Council was strongly opposed to the development of these villages, however, and was said to favour the encroachment of Congleton into the countryside to the north-west of the town; this would bring it well within the zone which Bernard was anxious to protect. The first diary entry to mention the possibility of development at Congleton appears on 4th November 1952; during the ensuing year the controversy sprang into life with the announcement of a public inquiry to decide whether the Cheshire County Council objections should be overturned. Bernard made immediate representations, through the agency of the DSIR. He was assured that there was no immediate cause for concern because the inquiry was to concentrate on Lymm and Mobberley and would not be considering the question of Congleton.

The Member of Parliament for the Knutsford Division, Lt. Col. Walter Bromley-Davenport, was strongly opposed to the plans for a new town at Mobberley. The story of his departure from the Whips Office following an incident in the House of Commons is well known; believing a gentleman lurking in the corridor to be a Conservative Member, who should have been in the Division Lobby on a three line whip, he aimed a sharp kick at the offender's backside projecting him down the stairs; unfortunately the well padded posterior with which the Colonel's highly polished size-nine connected belonged not to an Honourable Member but to the Belgian Ambassador; this explains, in part, why he resigned the next morning but it is not the whole story. His position as a government Whip had prevented him from voicing his opposition to the Mobberley development openly. Resignation gave him the freedom to represent the interests of his constituents with his customary vigour and as they were very unhappy that their village should become a haven for the unwanted residents of Manchester, they were delighted to have his unstinting support. From the earliest days, however, Walter Bromley-Davenport had been an enthusiastic advocate of the radio telescope, which was in his constituency, and his resistance to development at Congleton was in no way weakened by his stance on Mobberley.

The diary entry for 14th August 1953 reports a visit from the Bromley-Davenports and their house party. The visitor's book at Capesthorne Hall reveals that the party included Lord Selkirk, the Paymaster General, which was useful, and Walter Bromley-Davenport's American brother-in-law, William Jeanes, who was on a visit with his children Bill and Helen. "There was much discussion about the Manchester overspill and the effect on Jodrell Bank. It was a very successful afternoon. Mrs. Bromley-Davenport (Walter's formidable mother, Lillian) has promised to arrange for a deputation from the planning department to come over and see what is going on and the member asked me to send him a map and some notes." These were posted a few days later, pointing out the importance of keeping development and traffic to a minimum and of only very limited industrial development within the 6-mile zone.

Bernard had been "particularly impressed by Mrs. Bromley-Davenport's attitude", and on 27th October the promised visit of the planning committee took place. According to the diary it opened the eyes of the visitors to the project and its importance; the wooing of the County Council members continued over lunch with Mrs. Bromley-Davenport at her home, 'The Kennels'. It was no longer thought likely that the Manchester overspill would be located at Congleton but lobbying continued through the autumn. A few days later it was reported that Frederick Errol MP, the Member for Altrincham was going to ask a hostile, if rather convoluted, question in the House suggesting that:

> The DSIR should withhold any further grant from its funds for the construction of the radio telescope...until the Minister is satisfied that the public money so expended will not be wasted by satellite town development reducing the value of the telescope.

Bernard fired off a suggested supplementary question to Bromley-Davenport, asking the Minister to ensure that in the national interest the radio telescope should be completed as a matter of urgency and that no satellite town development should be allowed to prejudice its performance. In the event the supplementary was not needed; Erroll failed to catch the Speaker's eye, and on 17th November 1953, there was a brusque response in a written answer from the Parliamentary Secretary at the Ministry of Works, J.R. Bevins:

> No. I have consulted my right hon. friend the Minister of Housing and Local Government, who sees no reason to believe that any town development which may be proposed in the Congleton area could not be so sited as to avoid electrical interference with the radio telescope at Jodrell Bank.[201]

The planning controversy continued to be a troublesome distraction for many years. In October 1954, it was finally announced that the applications for new towns at Lymm and Mobberley had been refused; the decision provided a spark that rekindled the Congleton debate. Manchester Council entered discussions with Cheshire County Council about the possibility of moving 50,000 people to Congleton and establishing industries there to keep them in employment. In a state of great alarm, Bernard fired off a memorandum to the DSIR, reminding them of the importance of maintaining planning restrictions. This memorandum was leaked to the local press and a furious campaign began which was highly critical of Bernard and the telescope and made wild allegations, including the suggestion that he wanted all domestic televisions to be banned from the area. The Congleton plan for development to the north-west of the town was apparently linked to a new sewage system which the Council was keen to construct. It was also motivated by a desire to create jobs and Bernard was placed in an embarrassing position by the fact that a near neighbour, Laurie Hargreaves, wanted to build a factory there and had already spent £100,000 acquiring the land; he made it clear that he would be fighting any restrictions on planning tooth and nail.

In order to put forward his case and win some friends, Bernard agreed to speak to the Congleton Rotary Club, on 6th June 1955. It was a Monday evening and he expected that a couple of dozen influential burghers might attend the meeting. When he arrived he was rather taken aback to find that the venue had been moved to the hall of a local school, which was packed with townspeople, all baying for blood. He managed to make his speech, in spite of hostile interruptions, after which the meeting was thrown open to the floor. There was "a barrage of questions about the West Heath development and so on".[202] Laurie Hargreaves spoke and was enthusiastically acclaimed for his laudable ambitions to bring employment to the town and Bernard was berated by a red-faced councillor shaking with rage, who pointed at him and bellowed:

"You have sterilised the whole of the West Heath sewerage scheme. Why don't you go to the Sahara?" Quite what the African desert had to do with the price of sewage was not immediately apparent, but it was a most uncomfortable evening for Bernard and did not bode well for the future of his enterprise. Nor did the reception he received in his mail and from the local press make him any happier; the attacks became very personal and for many years he steered well clear of Congleton.

Attempts to reach a compromise, which incorporated the Hargreaves factory, were rebuffed by the local council; they enlisted help from the Member for Macclesfield, Air Commodore Arthur Harvey MP, who asked another parliamentary question:

By what authority is the Department of Industrial and Scientific Research imposing limitations on private and local authority house building in the Congleton Area?[203]

A rather inconclusive written answer from Bevins was tabled on 12th July. Thereafter the Parliamentary Secretary to the Ministry of Housing and Local Government, Bill Deedes, invited all parties to a meeting at the House of Commons on 26th July. Bernard and Rainford attended on behalf of the University with members of the DSIR. They were joined by Harvey, the Congleton town clerk, the surveyor, two councillors, the clerk to Cheshire County Council, the chief planning officer and various other officials, all eager to make their representations to Deedes. They did not get far. As soon as Vere-Harvey opened the proceedings, by proposing that the telescope should be built elsewhere, the Minister brushed him aside saying that the government would not consider such a suggestion and that it was a waste of time discussing it. The town council delegation descended to personal abuse but Deedes would have none of it; by the end of the afternoon the local authority was left with no alternative but to settle for the very compromise which had been rejected out of hand only a few weeks earlier.

The Congleton planners remained a constant thorn in the Jodrell side, but following this meeting relations with the County Council improved greatly. It was agreed that in local villages and farms there could be a reasonable amount of infilling and that modest extensions to property and buildings should be permitted, particularly for agricultural purposes. As time went on, Bernard often found himself appearing before planning inquiries to justify refusals of consent. Although these interventions made him unpopular with applicants and developers, those who live in East Cheshire today owe him a deep debt of gratitude that the countryside between Knutsford and Macclesfield, bounded by Alderley Edge to the north and the Potteries to the south has remained largely unspoiled for sixty years.

These struggles achieved the goal of reducing interference from extraneous sources, although unexplained signals were sometimes received. On one such occasion, Bernard became intensely irritated by signals which interfered with his observations for several nights at precisely eleven o'clock. The source was never explained, but the signals were of a kind that might be caused by the ignition system of a motorcycle, being revved up constantly for a period of twenty minutes. Bernard used this story at a planning inquiry on 8th February 1964 to illustrate the problems that can result from terrestrial interference. He told the inquiry that the interference was affecting observations of a star ten light years away and produced records of the signals; by way of analogy he commented that it was as if a young man had taken his girlfriend home on his motorcycle but was unable to drag himself away from her and kept revving the engine to keep it going. On hearing this, a young reporter from the local paper became very excited and rushed out of the room with a scoop which appeared the next morning in the world's press under headlines such as: "Scientist uses telescope to spy on courting couple" and "Young lover blots out a star".

In Ohio, the *Toledo Blade* reported:

Sir Bernard said of the interference: 'It happens every night at about the same time. We were able to pinpoint the source of the interference very precisely. If only I could find out whose motorcycle that was I would get it suppressed.'[204]

The identity of the young couple has never been discovered.

Similar disputes arose over the years with the electricity authorities about the erection of high voltage power lines. The first of these was resolved at a very satisfactory meeting in the Ministry of Fuel and Power on 7th October 1952. The room was packed with representatives of the authority. When the Minister came in he looked round in surprise and asked who they all were. His secretary replied that they were from the Electricity Board.

"Where are the university people?" asked the Minister. His official pointed to Bernard, sitting alone in the corner. The Minister cast a steely eye over the array of electricity men. "Haven't they got any work to do?" he grunted. It was a very good start and at the end of the meeting, the Authority was instructed to erect their line to suit the requirements of the Jodrell Bank Experimental Station. Another proposal in 1954 would have brought a line of pylons within 2 miles of the telescope; as a perfectly viable alternative route was already in existence some miles further away, Bernard argued that the second line was entirely unnecessary. Common sense prevailed and the new pylons were not erected. Some years later, British Railways decided to electrify the main line between London and Manchester. The line passed very close to Jodrell and Bernard was exceedingly worried about the interference it would cause. He sent for Francis Graham-Smith, who had recently joined the staff and enlisted his help; the future Astronomer Royal was dispatched to the railway embankment, where he spent an entire afternoon in the company of nettles and brambles monitoring the trains with a radio receiver. There were plenty of them; he recalls that as each train passed droppers on the wires that carried the electricity were lifted and gave off sparks which you could hear clicking on the receiver. Something had to be done and urgent meetings were arranged with the directors of the railway company. The

British Rail Directors were far more accommodating than the local authorities and the electrical companies had been. They arranged for Graham-Smith to go for a ride in a locomotive with recording equipment; modifications to the system were quickly agreed and they welded every connection on the stretch of line near the telescope – they sent their men down, of course, they did not do it themselves. This had the desired effect and the radio emissions were suppressed. The results of these various disputes can be fairly summarised as: Jodrell Bank 4, Public Authorities 0.

The expectation that the tracks would be laid by the spring of 1953 had proved hopelessly optimistic and work on them did not begin until the end of January the following year. The diary entry for 17th February 1954 describes the progress as being agonisingly slow, but by 15th March they were finally laid. All that was needed now was the bogies; once they were on the tracks, construction of the towers could begin.

The driving motors for the bogies and for the rotating mechanism in each of the towers were to be built by Metropolitan Vickers, who had quoted £28,600 for the work in the autumn of 1951; this was the figure on which the estimates of 1952 and 1953 were based and it had been accepted by the DSIR. In December 1953, without consultation or warning, the price was unilaterally doubled. Bernard and Husband were speechless with rage and on 21st December Rainford accompanied Bernard to Trafford Park to meet Willis Jackson, a director of Metropolitan Vickers who had, at one time, been a professor of electrical engineering at Manchester.[205] They hoped that he could be persuaded either to reduce the price or to treat the surplus as a donation to the University. They were to be disappointed. Jackson said that if the price had doubled in two years it could only be because the specification had been changed; there was no substance in this allegation nor had the firm ever suggested that the figure approved by the DSIR was too low or inaccurate; it was clear that the original quote was the result of reckless guesswork on the part of a company that wished to be associated with the project and put in an unrealistically low quote to secure the contract; in the end their cavalier attitude deprived them of the opportunity to be involved at all.

On 6th January Rainford received a telephone call from Jackson reporting that an investigation had been carried out; the quotation was perfectly in order and there was no excess profit which the company could forgo. He sought to justify the position by claiming that the original figure was just a rough estimate; he did not explain why Metropolitan Vickers had failed to revise the figure for more than two years. On 27th January Rainford and Bernard had another meeting with Jackson who told them that the company was satisfied that the estimates were reasonable. He added that he had met Lockspeiser in his club and told him of the problem. Lockspeiser exploded and said that Manchester would not get another penny out of the DSIR.[206] Bernard began to feel desperate; with costs spiralling and no prospect of further funds he even suggested using tractors to pull the telescope round the tracks and a winch system to elevate the bowl manually. Anything to save money and get the instrument built.

Early in 1954 Husband made an approach to the German company Siemens which provided a much lower estimate than the price now being demanded by Metropolitan Vickers. There was strong opposition to employing a German company from Lord Simon and Sir Raymond Streat, who was to succeed Simon as Chairman of the University Council. It was not until June 1956 that the order for the motors was finally placed with the Loughborough firm Brush, who promised to deliver by the following spring. The promise was honoured on time and on budget by 1st May 1957, a mere five and a half years after the original estimate from Metropolitan Vickers had been approved by the DSIR.

The chaotic way in which the commissioning and eventual delivery of the motors occurred was mirrored in every aspect of the telescope's construction. In September 1953, a letter from Bernard to Rainford set out a detailed timetable. At the conclusion the position was summed up as follows:

> From the above it will be seen that the most probable general programme is:
> completion of steelwork erection by autumn 1954,
> completion of entire instrument by summer 1955.[207]

But steelwork could not even start without two huge cranes which were required to lift it and the cranes could not operate until thousands of tons of stone had been brought in to provide them with firm foundations. No one seems to have spotted this until January 1954 and it was late February before the first lorry loads arrived. The cost of buying and transporting the stone was well in excess of £3,000; this figure had never been included in the estimates, an omission which no one thought about until 15th March, by which time 1,500 tons had already been laid.[208] The erection of the first crane began in April; labour problems created further delays and the cranes were not ready until the middle of July, just in time for the construction workers to take their annual holidays in Blackpool. Work on the telescope finally began on 10th August but the building of the first tower did not start until October, by which time, according to the programme, "the steelwork erection" should have been complete.

The naval gun racks and pinions through which the telescope would be driven in elevation were to be supported by a massive cantilever girder running between the opposing towers and cradling the bowl as it was turned. In order to ensure the stability of the bowl it had been decided that this girder must be made deeper and stronger than originally planned. On 14th August Bernard returned from a short cricket tour to find a letter from Husband who had calculated that the extra weight of the new girder would make it necessary to strengthen other parts of the structure as well. This meant that a great deal more steel would be needed, adding substantially to the cost and he had decided that a different system of support should be used. His plan was to replace the cantilever girder with a semicircular framework which would run round the back of the bowl. This was a radical alteration and no doubt it would have been prudent to discuss it with the DSIR and the University; but it was August, Rainford was away, Stopford, the Vice Chancellor, was in hospital and a few days later Bernard had to attend a conference in Holland. In any event, at that stage it seemed that the new design would lead to a reduction in the amount of steel; the modification was essential for the effective operation of the instrument and was entirely in line with the common objective, which was the creation of a large fully steerable paraboloid; even though the modification represented an obvious change in the appearance of the instrument it did not seem that it would be significantly more expensive than the original girder.

A second important and, in this case, costly change in design was the decision to use steel sheets instead of wire mesh for the reflective surface. This idea metamorphosed over a period of many months. It was not a simple proposal which could be put to the DSIR with a neat application for further funding; it somehow grew out of a chain of unpredicted events, with consequences that only became fully apparent as the final links were added. In February 1954, following a meeting of the Aeronautical Research Council in London, Bernard had a discussion with a wartime colleague, Robert Cockburn, who was now working in the Air Ministry. Cockburn suggested that, with appropriate adjustments, the telescope could operate on very short wavelengths to detect guided missiles. Both Husband and Bernard were enthusiastic about this idea, not least because it presented the prospect of an additional source of funding and future revenue. The main requirement would be the use of an even smaller mesh and strengthening of the structure to cope with the extra weight. Cockburn was told that it would cost £46,000 and the expectation was that the Ministry of Defence would pay for it. Two months later Cockburn informed Bernard that the funding could not be justified. It was typical of the way in which the telescope project was managed that, by this time, Husband had agreed the details and cost of the new mesh with the manufacturers; so they would have the benefit for the more sensitive system but no money to pay for it.

The next problem became clear in the autumn of 1954. The manufacturers found that when strips of mesh were being joined to each other there was a severe loss of electrical conductivity across the joints. A number of solutions were discussed, but the obvious answer was to substitute steel plates for the mesh to make a solid reflecting surface. This was an attractive alternative for Husband, because it would improve the strength of the structure; and from the scientific point of view it had the great advantage of preventing any loss of signal even with very short wavelengths of very high frequency. But the steel would be very expensive.

The extent of the financial chaos in the autumn would have been obvious at once to any competent accountant. Of the £390,000 actually allocated, £165,000 had already been spent, with very little to show for it above ground. And the projected costs continued their relentless rise, with no plans for controlling them and vague hopes that the money to cover the deficit would be found somehow. The DSIR, the Nuffield Foundation, the University or God would provide. There was much agonising over the increasing expense, as reflected in a diary entry on 28th October 1954:

Rainford and Smith, the Chief Financial Officer of the DSIR, came to discuss the financial position. The visit placed me in an extremely awkward position since Smith made a very plausible case for requiring a fairly accurate indication of the over-expenditure in which we are likely to be involved. This of course is exactly what I wished to avoid at this juncture. I made a very strong point in a letter that I did not wish to undertake further guesses as to the total amount of any such over-expenditure. However there was no escape since the request from the DSIR was so obviously very reasonable. They have a limited amount of money to spend in the 5 year grant from the Treasury. And it was evident they could not instruct us to proceed with the expenditure of another £30,000 unless they knew what further sums were likely to be involved. I was full of foreboding. It was left that I should discuss it with Husband...It is of very great importance that we should present this case purely on the basis of increased costs and not give any indication that there had been any increased tonnage due to the modification of the bowl. Discussed Husband's view that the membrane should now be of stainless steel. This was later changed to mild steel, which could be painted and was much cheaper. Husband agreed about presenting the new budget on the basis of increased costs.[209]

This passage is very revealing on a number of levels. It shows a willingness, on the part of both Bernard and Husband, to drive forward the great work they had embarked regardless of the cost and even if it meant not being entirely frank about the cause of the increases. They were also fully aware of the financial constraints under which they were having to operate and were prepared to make economies where they could. The informal nature of the visit from the bursar and the man who was responsible to the Department for the financial arrangements is indicative of the lack of financial control or management from those who held the purse strings. Smith's use of the words "fairly accurate indication" and "likely" expenditure were a case in point. As has already been observed, there was no request for proper accounts, even though Smith was told of the decision to construct the membrane from stainless steel; there was merely a general question about the eventual cost. Had fully costed requests for more money been made, the whole enterprise would have become bogged down in a bureaucratic quagmire, while decisions were taken by committee, and the telescope would never have been finished. The fact that the Department was content to proceed in this *ad hoc* way can be seen from another diary entry on 22nd December 1954:

> Called at DSIR and was told, to happy surprise that the advisory council had decided that every effort should be made to finish the telescope in its fully steerable form. Had been prepared for gloomy news, so very happy. Must make sure the request from Rainford is not for more than £50,000. If it was £60,000 DSIR will get rather annoyed.[210]

The last entry of the year is a handwritten note: "Huge progress. Surely now the telescope will be finished, perhaps even in 1955."[211] So everyone was happy. But not for long.

As early as January 1955, the planned changes gave rise to another serious difficulty. Tests carried out in the wind tunnel at the National Physics Laboratory, using a model with a solid steel bowl, revealed violent oscillations, even at wind speeds no higher than 40 miles per hour. As usual, Husband was able to come up with a cure but, as usual, the cure meant more expense. What he proposed was the addition of a 'bicycle wheel' running beneath the semicircular framework of girders at right angles to the axis of the bowl. As the bowl moved, the wheel girder would bear down on large hydraulic rubber wheels, which would absorb the oscillations created by the wind.

Taken together, the new design features provided the perfect solution to a number of scientific and engineering problems; but there was still no idea of the final cost and it was late in 1955 before manufacturers had been identified and estimates obtained. By this time it was apparent that the whole structure would require 440 tons of extra steel, the price of which had increased by £21 per ton. The full horror was revealed and they realised that the telescope was going to cost £250,000 more than they had been allocated to build it.

In these darkest of days with the estimates spiralling out of control Bernard had derived great comfort from a comment made by S.H. Smith, the Chief Financial Officer to the DSIR, when he paid another visit to Jodrell in the autumn of 1955. Throughout the day there were long and excruciating discussions about the financial situation. Late in the afternoon Smith was gazing thoughtfully out of the control room window watching the autumnal sunshine flickering across the massive towers and the scaffolding. After a few minutes, he turned to Bernard and said: "The strength of your position, Lovell, is that huge mass of steel." So much money had already been thrown at the enterprise, that calling a halt was quite out of the question. No one who had been involved with any aspect of the Jodrell Bank enterprise could have contemplated the prospect of such a massive structure standing half-built in the middle of a field, as a permanent memorial to the folly of those who had countenanced the project. So the building was bound to continue – but before long they would be looking for scapegoats.

The DSIR had £50,000 in reserve. Smith indicated that it might be possible to provide half of the remaining balance, on a pound for pound basis, if the University could match the payment; so the University and the DSIR would have to find £100,000 each. This proposal received guarded support from Rainford, but it was subject to confirmation on both sides and following the meeting the Department decided to set up a committee of inquiry to examine the causes of the deficit. The University summoned the officers to a lunch at which Bernard was put through the mill; it was clear, however, that there was no appetite for abandoning the telescope and he was instructed to set about raising the money. He embarked on this task with his customary impetuous enthusiasm, writing letters to friends, to anyone he knew who could remotely be categorised as a captain of industry and to every ministry and organisation with which he had the slightest contact. He even applied to the Royal Society, of which he had been elected a fellow in March, to ask whether some of the funds allocated to Jodrell Bank for International Geophysical Year, scheduled for 1957, could be diverted towards the construction.

These efforts began to bear fruit when Lord Simon brought the entire board of directors of Henry Simon Ltd.[212] to Jodrell on a freezing afternoon in November. After a tour of the site Bernard took his distinguished visitors down into the cable tunnel which led from the central pivot beneath the telescope to the control building where Joyce was preparing tea. They negotiated the 200 yards of subterranean passages, only to find that the exit door had been locked on the outside. By the time Bernard had rushed back to the entrance door; that too had been locked by some helpful member of the security staff. He was trapped in a dank and dingy tunnel with Simon and the twelve members of his board who were being kept from their refreshments. The omens for a donation from Henry Simon did not look good. After much shouting and banging they were released and Joyce's tea must have been superb, because Simon telephoned the very next morning, to report that the visit had been a great success and that the board had agreed to donate £10,000.

On 10th of December, without any warning, the Vice Chancellor, Stopford, sent for Bernard and reprimanded him severely for his efforts. Bernard pointed out that he had been instructed to organise an appeal and that he had received almost instantaneous support in the form of £10,000 from Lord Simon. Stopford insisted that only preliminary enquiries had been sanctioned. This was news to the Professor. He was in no doubt that he had been ordered to raise the money, as the new Chairman of the University Council, Sir Raymond Streat, later confirmed to him. He felt both disappointed and puzzled that he should be blamed for doing exactly what he was told to do. Stopford said that people who had already contributed to other appeals were irritated at being approached for money again. After the meeting Rainford told Bernard that Stopford, Simon and Lord Woolton were at loggerheads about an appeal sponsored by the latter to raise £1,000,000 for student accommodation.[213] Simon had refused to subscribe and Woolton was very angry when he heard about his donation to Jodrell Bank; but Bernard was not told that it was Woolton who had vetoed the Jodrell appeal.

Woolton attached great importance to his scheme and took particular pride in having one of the halls named in his honour.[214] Having raised nearly £900,000 he was intensely unhappy about anything which might make it more difficult to reach his target. When he learned that the Professor of Astronomy was trying to raise a sum which was but a fraction of his own total, he complained to Stopford, and this was the real reason for the volte-face on fundraising for the telescope. The University seems to have thought that Woolton's intervention was a matter for secrecy both at the time and in perpetuity. In 1980 Bernard wrote to the current Vice Chancellor, Sir Arthur Armitage, asking for access to the files from the period when the telescope was being built. He wanted, among other things, to understand why the Jodrell appeal had been ordered and then proscribed. Armitage asked Mansfield Cooper, Stopford's deputy at the time, to examine the files; they were silent about the reasons for the decision. He sent Armitage a full account of how Woolton and the University had prohibited Bernard's attempts to raise the money. He plainly did not want the truth to come out, however, and concluded with the advice: "I cannot feel that any good would come from making these old controversies live again." Armitage agreed and his reply to Bernard's enquiry sanitised the Mansfield Cooper explanation by redacting the Woolton connection in its entirety.

To make sure that the story did not see the light of day, Armitage placed this 1980 correspondence with the Vice Chancellor's files for 1957-58.[215] These files had already been classified as restricted documents, which were not to be disclosed to Bernard and were to remain secret until after his death. As we shall see, the university authorities were determined that the reputation of the University was paramount and that it must not be tarnished by suggestions that they had mismanaged the Jodrell Bank Telescope project; blame was to be deflected towards the engineer and the Professor of Astronomy, regardless of the truth. Anything which might reflect badly on the University and its officers was buried in the convenient grave of restricted access to the 1957-58 files. In 1955 they had ordered their Chief Scientist to launch an appeal and then countermanded the order for extraneous reasons; Mansfield Cooper and Armitage decided that such untidy management should not become public knowledge and the 1980 papers were put in the 1957-58 files, where the story lay undisturbed for another thirty-three years.[216]

The committee of inquiry set up by the DSIR met at Jodrell Bank on 18th January 1956 under the chairmanship of Mansfield Cooper. On the following day Bernard and Husband were grilled for eight hours and the members concluded their investigation on the 20th. The Council of the DSIR met in March, but for many months there was no announcement of their findings. Various rumours were circulated; it was believed that Smith's pound for pound proposal would be accepted, even though the deficit was now expected to amount to £260,000 over and above the £50,000 which the Department had in reserve; but it became known that matters had been referred to the Treasury and it seemed likely that the Public Accounts

Committee would investigate the deficits. It was not until August 1956 that the Treasury approved the arrangement that the DSIR and the University should each contribute £130,000. The offer was hedged round with four pages of conditions. Of these, the most contentious was that the University must undertake to provide a written guarantee, backed up by counsel's opinion, that steps would commence to recover the money, if necessary by instituting legal proceedings against Husband and Co., the contractors, the suppliers, the manufacturers, old Uncle Tom Cobley and all. Until this point no one had contemplated litigation and the requirement became a cause of considerable indignation at the University, where it was felt that issuing writs would amount to an admission that they had lost control and were not capable of handling large sums of money.[217] There was also a general feeling, that the DSIR and the Treasury were in fear of the Public Accounts Committee and were watching their own backs. Bernard believed that the conditions were being made "by men whose first concern was the preservation of their own skins, who had no concept of the likely consequences of their actions and whose horizon was limited by the walls of their offices".[218] No such undertaking was ever given.

Following the Cooper inquiry, the DSIR insisted that a site committee must be appointed to oversee the operation. The terms of reference were to get on with the job within the £260,000 limit, which was still awaiting approval from the DSIR.[219] Sir Charles Renold, a businessman and a member of the University Council was appointed as chairman and he visited Jodrell for the first time on 12th April 1956. The committee met at regular intervals over the next eighteen months; a great deal of time and effort was expended; the meetings tended to be long and argumentative; but as often happens in such cases, they had very little effect on the building of the telescope. Construction work continued to be punctuated with delays in delivery from suppliers, regular strike action by the workers and refusal to work in adverse weather conditions. This catalogue of problems culminated on 23rd December 1956, when the welders packed up for Christmas and did not return until the spring.

It was not until 5th March 1957 that the findings of the DSIR committee of inquiry were published in the annual report of the Comptroller and Auditor General, Sir Frank Tribe; it made for very unhappy reading. "He spilled the whole story of the chaos surrounding the telescope," records a despairing entry in the diary on 6th March; "the newspapers are having a field day."[220] The headlines proclaimed that the cost had more than doubled to £700,000 and leading articles expressed outrage that public money was being wasted on a project which was suddenly being cast in the role of white elephant. The report also "recorded a very unsatisfactory position as between the University and their consultants Husband and Co". Criticism of Husband at this juncture was very unfortunate, because he had recently agreed to forgo some of his fees in order to avoid adverse publicity. "And now he has the publicity. At present he is in Ceylon, but Rainford fears the worst." He had returned by 25th March, when the diary records: "Husband, of course is beside himself". And a few days later:

> The situation is very tricky – he is sending in fee notes exceeding those under the original contract. The University would not pay because this would indicate their agreement to the revised design. Every letter about this was referred to the solicitors before dispatch. Husband has now written to the University to ask if they intend to pay and if not could he be told in writing. He would then take appropriate action. I asked if this meant he would stop the job, but I was told that it is more likely that writs would be flying around.[221]

Two weeks after the Tribe report, on 21st March 1957, the Public Accounts Committee began to hear evidence.

Work continued in spite of these troubles, although it was constantly interrupted by a spate of problems ranging from severe weather and striking steel erectors to failures of delivery and faulty equipment. Nevertheless the telescope continued to rise and by October the framework was complete.

Gradually during the winter the instrument was released from the shackles of 90 miles of scaffolding and the trunnion bearings, attached to the great gun racks at the top of the towers, took the weight of the skeletal bowl. The towers rested on their bogies, which were patiently awaiting the installation of the Brush engines that were to drive them. On 1st February 1957 hydraulic jacks were used to push the bogies a few inches with satisfactory results; everything seemed to be in order. The tortuous riveting of the steel plates to the surface of the bowl ground on through the winter and into the spring until the arrival of the motors which were installed at the top of the towers and in the bogies in May.

On 12th June Bernard and Joyce were enjoying a wonderful holiday with all five children in North Wales. It was a glorious morning and Bernard took Susan, Bryan and Judy for a walk up Snowden. Late in the afternoon they returned to the house to be greeted with the news that the bogies had driven the telescope round the track. The next morning a letter arrived from Bernard's secretary, Maureen Patrick:

Dear Professor Lovell,

We have just seen the telescope move 20 yards – it was most exciting and the suspense was terrific! In fact it is now being moved back to its original position. Everything seemed to go very smoothly.[222]

Back from the holidays on 20th June, as the rising sun broke through the early morning mist to herald a beautiful summer day, the decision was taken to drive the bowl for the first time. Bernard arrived at Jodrell after a hurried breakfast, to find Husband was already there, having driven across the Pennines from Sheffield. The conditions were perfect, not a cloud in the sky, not a breath of wind stirring the treetops. Joyce brought a friend to witness the historic event. At half past ten they were standing with Bernard in the shade of an oak tree. The thrilling hum of the motors drifted across in the still air and they stared up in rapture as, almost imperceptibly at first, the bowl revolved on its axis. It was a magnificent sight. Inch by inch, the huge paraboloid rotated majestically through 10 degrees from the zenith. At midday the engines were restarted and it turned again through 30 degrees; everything worked to perfection.

Nearly eight years had passed since the afternoon when Bernard, standing with Charles Husband beside the transit telescope, dreamed of the possibilities. It was eighteen years since the fateful Sunday morning at Staxton Wold, when the transient echoes on the radar screen had aroused his curiosity and fired his imagination. As he gazed up at the wonderful instrument they had created, the years of toil, of worry, of planning and of disappointment melted away; even the black cloud of the long expected report from the Public Accounts Committee was forgotten. This was the future; they had done what they set out to do and nothing that happened afterwards would ever take away from him the memory of those first moments when the telescope began to move.

CHAPTER SEVENTEEN

Called to Account

When he addressed the Royal Society of Arts on 5th August 1955, Bernard had been optimistic about the progress of the construction. In the conclusion to his paper he summed up his hopes for the new science of radio astronomy and spoke optimistically about the progress of the development:

> British astronomy achieved distinction in the eighteenth and nineteenth centuries, when the Earl of Rosse and Sir William Herschel pioneered the construction of large telescopes. Their leadership was doomed to capitulation to those living in a more favourable climate and in this century the world has looked to the American continent for the startling advances in our knowledge of the universe. Now, by a strange twist of fate, the devices of war have been transformed into a revolutionary method for the exploration of space, independent of cloud or fog. In the study of the universe Britain can once more compete without handicap. The greatest radio telescope in the world will soon be operating within these shores and scientists everywhere, with great confidence watch it rise to completion.[223]

Two years later, much remained to be done before the telescope would be fully operational. The computer systems were not ready, the cables for connecting them to the motors had not arrived, the steel membrane was incomplete and the electronic position indicators were not yet working; but at the end of July, makeshift devices were used to position and manoeuvre the instrument and to record the very first observations from 2nd August. The results were excellent, at least as good as they had hoped and the expectation that all the remaining work could be finished within a few weeks filled everyone with excitement. It was at this moment, on 13th August 1957, as they were on the verge of bringing their great work to a triumphant conclusion that "the dreaded PAC report came out",[224] and the full weight of the Establishment, the press and public opinion fell upon them like the crack of doom.

It was extremely unfortunate that Ben Lockspeiser, who had been involved with the telescope from the start and was an enthusiastic supporter, retired as Secretary of the DSIR shortly before the Public Accounts Committee met on 21st March 1957. He was succeeded by Dr. Harry Melville who had been Professor of Chemistry at Birmingham. Melville was not a physicist, knew nothing about radio astronomy or engineering, and only spent one short February afternoon at Jodrell Bank before he gave evidence to the committee. His lack of knowledge made it inevitable that his testimony was riddled with inaccuracies and gave a wholly false impression of the relationship between Husband and Bernard. He claimed,[225] in the clearest possible terms, that Husband had made major changes to the design without consulting anyone, including Bernard. As scarcely a day had gone by for the past five years when the two men had not communicated and as every change in design was discussed in detail and agreed between them, this evidence displayed an astonishing degree of ignorance on the part of the civil servant who was now in charge of the department responsible for providing grants. And his evidence was unequivocal:

Mr. George Benson MP (Chairman): Who had changed the design without obtaining the approval of the University, the engineering consultant or Professor Lovell?

Dr. Melville: Oh, no, quite clearly the engineering consultant changed the design without the concurrence of the University.

Benson: Without even consulting the University?

Melville: Without consulting the University.

Benson: Is that transverse circle one of the things he introduced?

Melville: Yes, that is one of the new features which, of course, has added to the complexity of the instrument.

Benson: He designed that on his own without consulting anybody?

Melville: Yes.

Benson: And without advising them that it would materially increase the cost?

Melville: Yes.

Benson: That is rather unusual, is it not?

Melville: It is unusual but this is a rather unusual structure, of course.

Benson: It may be, but even with unusual structures the engineer does not go off on his own responsibility and enormously increase the expense without telling anybody.

Melville: Quite.[226]

Soon afterwards his claims became even more ludicrous:

Benson: This alteration was made entirely without consultation?

Melville: Yes.

Benson: Professor Lovell lives on the spot, presumably?

Melville: Oh, yes, he lives in the apartments.

Benson: He must have known what was going on. Was he not consulted?

Melville: No, he was not consulted as far as we know.

The fact that there were no apartments does not seem to have troubled Melville in the slightest; perhaps he was thinking of the swinging laboratory hanging below the bowl. During further questioning he expressed uncertainty about the name of Husband's company, was unsure whether his employees were scientists as well as engineers, could not say what advice the Department had taken about the estimated costs and had no idea who would own the telescope once it was finished. In spite of the unsatisfactory nature of his evidence, the committee did not challenge any of his assertions, nor did they see fit to call the two principle players or a representative of the University. On the uninformed evidence of one man, the blame was laid almost entirely at the door of the consultant, whose fees were said to be based on a percentage of the total cost, giving him an alleged motive for inflating it; in effect they accused him of dishonesty and convicted him in his absence.

The committee was certainly very concerned that the University had not properly controlled the expenditure and criticised the Department for not inquiring more closely into the systems of control for the whole project. But the villain of the piece was Charles Husband:

Your committee were disturbed to learn that in making a substantial grant from public funds towards the cost of such a novel and expensive project the Department did not see fit to inquire more closely into the University's arrangement with the consultant engineers over the design and construction work. They are particularly surprised to be told that the consulting engineers, before introducing substantial modifications in a novel and costly scientific instrument, had not followed the common-sense course of discussing their plans with the eminent scientist who was in charge of the project. Your committee regard as highly unsatisfactory the state of affairs in which it was possible for the project to be altered substantially at greatly increased cost without the consent and approval of the Department or of the University, or even of discussion with the scientist in charge.[227]

Had they known that the bursar and the officers of the University knew about the design changes and the increases in cost and that they could have prohibited them, the committee's concern would have transformed rapidly into condemnation. The university authorities were very anxious to ensure that the Public Accounts Committee remained unaware of the extent of their knowledge and involvement. It suited them to have the blame thrown onto Husband and they made it their business to conceal the truth.

The Vice Chancellor's 'withheld' files for 1957-8 contain a number of papers from earlier years, which can only have been placed there to keep them from prying eyes. One such document is a report dated 25th October 1955, which tells us much about the true extent of the University's knowledge of the escalating expense of the instrument. On 8th February 1954 the bursar and the Professor of Radio Astronomy informally warned officers of the Department that because of errors in estimating and further costs rises, especially for the drive mechanisms, more money would be required unless the idea for a fully steerable telescope was abandoned. Husband's revised estimate of £441,846 was submitted to Rainford in November 1954 in a detailed document which set out both the original cost and the increase in respect of each item. The University did not trouble the DSIR with the detail; Rainford simply delivered another unofficial warning to the Department and he did nothing at all to restrict the planned work. On 10th January 1955 an additional payment of £50,000 was agreed by the Department. In March 1955, "Husband gave the first hint of considerable changes". On 4th and 5th April there were long discussions between Bernard, Rainford and Husband about important design changes including the addition of the bicycle wheel girder, as well as the new braking system which would cost £13,300. Husband spoke of the increased tonnage of steel, and additional costs of £70,000 were discussed in full. Rainford asked him to obtain further estimates, but said nothing to the Department. There were the usual delays in extracting figures from suppliers and contractors. The estimate was sent to the University on 22nd September with a revised total of £569,567. Rainford did not disclose this document to the Department either. On 15th October Husband provided a further updated estimate of £630,059.

This time Rainford did forward the figures to the Department, claiming that it had become clear during the preceding weeks that the design had been changed without university approval. As Rainford had been kept abreast of all the changes as they arose, the truth of this assertion was, to say the least, a matter for debate.

At every stage, Husband and Bernard had discussed alterations to the telescope, which were invariably designed to improve performance and make it fit for the purpose for which it had been commissioned. There was also a regular line of communication between Rainford and Husband, who exchanged more than a thousand letters about the telescope; this correspondence included many requests to attend meetings with the DSIR so that he could provide direct explanations of what was happening. On 25th March 1955 he wrote to Rainford in the following terms:

> I have come to the conclusion that for reasons concerned with the control of expenditure it is extremely desirable that I should attend all future meetings to discuss engineering requirements and estimates with the DSIR.

On 31st March he repeated the request:

> My great concern at the moment is because I have never attended any meetings with the DSIR and just do not know how far the re-design of the telescope has been reported to them.

On 15th July 1955:

> I fully appreciate that our own agreement is with the University, but in view of the possible damage to our own reputation with the DSIR (who presumably are responsible for paying us) may we attend all technical discussions which take place with the Department.

This plea was followed up on the 20th:

> There seems to be a major matter of policy involved which may require clearing with the DSIR. It would be entirely wrong to present the latest estimates and tenders on any other basis than a major change of design.[228]

These letters can have left Rainford in no doubt that there had been important changes in the design of the telescope and that they had serious implications as to the cost.

Why Rainford did not take up Husband's suggestions or even respond to them is mystery. Perhaps he was worried that the Department would not sanction the alterations or would baulk at the increased costs but the fact is that, both through the scientist in charge and through the bursar, the University was well aware of what was going on throughout the period of construction. It should be stressed that all that had been done at this stage was to alter the design; the only parts of the telescope structure which had been built by the autumn of 1955 were the two towers, mounted on their bogies as originally envisaged. Had they wished to, Rainford and the University could have brought work to a halt and prevented the new plans from being activated; as Mansfield Cooper noted on the 14th February 1958: "If this had been done when R.A.R. [Rainford] first became alarmed, the drift [in financial control] might well have been stopped long ago."[229] Likewise, the Department could have closed the project down in October 1955, if they were not prepared to countenance the increases; by then they were in the same position as the University and were in full possession of the facts; no additional expense had actually been incurred; they could have insisted that the University must stick to the original specification, even if it meant building an inferior instrument; they chose not to take this course. The documents from 1955 were buried in the 1957-8 file and none of this was explained to the Public Accounts Committee in March 1957; by the time they met, the structure was almost complete and that fact, in combination with the wholly inaccurate picture painted by Melville, caused them to believe that construction based on the revised plans had been completed without the knowledge of the University. The committee was led into serious error.

Husband's reaction to the Tribe report, in March 1957, was not the first occasion on which he had shown himself to be a rather touchy individual who was quick to take up the cudgels at any perceived slight. In 1955, Bernard presented a paper about the telescope at the Royal Society of Arts and Husband took umbrage because he considered that his role had not been adequately recognised in the lecture. He tried to insist that Bernard should make amends for the lacuna by writing a letter to *The Times* saying that the entire credit for the design should go to Husband and Co. and particularly to Charles Husband himself. In declining to do so, Bernard wrote what he hoped was a conciliatory letter; this provoked a furious reply from the thin-skinned consulting engineer, who made a personal attack on Bernard and insisted that he had been sidelined. Eventually the row petered out and, before long, the two men were once again working together quite happily.

But if this incident and the Tribe report had pricked Husband's equanimity, the press coverage of Melville's claim that he made changes without consulting his clients and that he did so for personal gain unleashed a volcano of fury which threatened the very future of the entire enterprise. As soon as the reports appeared, he telephoned Bernard and demanded that he should write a letter to *The Times* without delay and refute the allegations, or else! The "or else" was a threat to sue Bernard personally if he did not write the letter. Bernard was quite prepared to do so and to put the record straight. He had already been interviewed by the *Daily Telegraph*, on the 14th and confirmed that he had been in almost daily contact with Husband for five years and that no major changes had been made without consultation. He told Husband that he would follow this up with a letter to *The Times* once he had cleared it with the Vice Chancellor. Husband accepted that this was a reasonable request and said that he would await the response with interest.

Mansfield Cooper was away on holiday but Rainford told Bernard that he could not possibly send such a letter, on the grounds that the report of the PAC was subject to privilege and could not be controverted. This advice was nothing short of drivel, particularly bearing in mind that Bernard's denial was already on public record. Rainford knew very well that the allegations made in the report were untrue and there was no legitimate reason to prohibit the writing of a letter to correct the glaring errors. He consulted the Vice Chancellor, on his return from holiday. Mansfield Cooper was a professor of law and it is inconceivable that he genuinely thought that public criticism of the PAC was prohibited; if he did he had no business to hold the distinguished positions he enjoyed. In spite of this, he confirmed Rainford's advice to Bernard, who accepted it in good faith, as was his wont when dealing with people he trusted. This was the first move in a cynical campaign by university officers to silence the inventor of the great scientific instrument, which had been built under their auspices. They too had been the subject of criticism by the committee for failing to keep control of the project; but if they concentrated the heat on Husband and Bernard there was every chance that they could protect their own reputations, so they imposed a gagging order.

As soon as the embargo on *The Times* letter was communicated to Husband, he made a "very nasty telephone call"[230] to Rainford, during which he said that, if Bernard did not write the letter, he would "drag the information out of him in the witness box". This threat was without substance, as Rainford and Mansfield Cooper must have known. Husband had no cause of action against Bernard and any attempt to sue him would have been struck out at the first hurdle; his quarrel was with Melville and the PAC; their allegations against him had indeed been made under the cloak of parliamentary privilege, so he could not sue them either; it was all bluster. But the engineer's threat provided the perfect foil to keep Bernard on tenterhooks and to set the creators of the telescope at each other's throats. Divide and rule was the order of the day. The officers lost no time in passing on Husband's threat to Bernard, who once again accepted what they told him at face value; Mansfield Cooper was a lawyer, after all, and must know what he was talking about. For many months they used the spurious menace of litigation to hold him in line, as a shield to protect the University and its officers from censure.

That the wall of criticism should crash so forcefully upon two men whose invention, enterprise and dedication had shaped this marvellous instrument, just when it was on the point of fulfilling its purpose, was a strangely cruel trick of providence that caused Bernard much anguish both at the time and when he recalled it in later years. They had worked together since 1952 and at the very moment when their efforts were about to bear fruit, instead of uniting to rejoice in their achievement, they were driven apart by the misconceived condemnation of Parliament, the press and the public. Bernard was told that he must not speak to Husband except in the presence of the university solicitor. They were obtaining superb results[231] from the early observations, even though they were still operating on a restricted basis, but the situation was so fraught with apprehension that it was a huge relief to Bernard, on 24th August, to travel to Boulder, Colorado, for a conference of the International Union of Radio Science.

During this conference the *New York Times* reported a speech made by President Khrushchev in which he proclaimed the successful test, on 21st August, of an intercontinental ballistic missile, which had been fired more than 3,500 miles and had landed within its target area. He boasted that the results showed that it was possible to direct missiles to any part of the world. That the Russians had been able to launch such a missile before the United States was ready to do so was a matter of considerable surprise and alarm across the world and especially in America, where it was confidently believed that the Soviet Union was well behind in the space race. In 1955, both countries had announced that they intended to launch Earth satellites during International Geophysical Year.[232] The Americans had postponed the launch date of their satellite, Vanguard, and it seemed clear to Bernard that they would not be ready for many months. It now looked as though the Soviets were on the point of fulfilling their prediction and would beat the Americans to it. He mentioned this to John Hagen, the Director of the Vanguard project, whilst he was at the conference; in spite of Khrushchev's announcement Hagen insisted that the Russians did not have the capability and that the

American programme was on track. But the reality of the danger from nuclear attack spread fear through the people of the western world.

On his return to Jodrell Bank, in mid-September, the hostility of the press was unabated. Bernard found that the atmosphere was "exceedingly disturbed". Many of his university colleagues seemed less than supportive and were quick to criticise the cost of the telescope, not least because they feared that the publicity which had been generated by the PAC report might have an adverse effect on funding for their own areas of research; the hostility of some members of the faculty made for very unhappy visits to the Manchester staff room and he was forced to avoid going there; but the attitude of colleagues was the least of his worries. Everything on the site at Jodrell was on hold; the bowl was still not complete and the workmen had gone on strike, once again, because they had not been paid. Worse still, the newspapers had got hold of the story from the contractors and were reporting that this great monument to waste was on the verge of bankruptcy. On 24th September the diary records his fury at the impotence of the site committee to get anything moving; the links between the driving motors and the control room were still not complete; Husband "continued to find every opportunity for not doing things"; and the engineer from Brush refused to continue working on the motors as long as he had "the University people breathing down his neck". There was also "a vicious exchange between Husband and me about this and several other matters". The precise nature of the matters is not specified, but things took a turn for the better on 1st October when the engineers returned. By the evening, the telescope was "being driven in azimuth from the control room…it was a wonderful sight in the evening sky".[233] They had taken a major step forward and hoped that tests on the elevation motors would start on Friday 4th October; this would surely be an exhilarating event and Bernard could only pray that the date would mark a turning point in their fortunes. And so it did; but not for a moment did he anticipate what destiny had in store for him on that remarkable day.

CHAPTER EIGHTEEN

Sputnik

On the morning of 4th October 1957, the world woke up to the news that the Russians had placed a satellite in orbit around the Earth. For the first time, man had shaken off the chains of gravity and escaped from the atmosphere of our planet. It was an astonishing achievement and it was greeted, at first, with incredulity, even though it had been heralded in a broadcast by Moscow Radio, on 18th September, and by the announcement on 1st October of the frequencies on which the satellite, Sputnik 1, would transmit. In the United States the event was initially regarded sceptically, not least because the Russians claimed that the satellite weighed 184 pounds, infinitely heavier than its proposed American rival, Vanguard, which weighed in at no more than 3 pounds. Once they had got over the initial shock, President Eisenhower and his spokesmen said that they had seen it coming but, as Alistair Cooke reported, this assurance was "drowned by the astonishment of scientists, the defensive surprise of the Pentagon and the angry cries of the Democrats".[234] Eisenhower adopted a more measured approach, at a press conference on 9th October, when he said that the United States would not be stampeded from the path of steady development; he pointed out that the Russian capture of German scientists from Peenemunde, at the end of the war, had enabled them to concentrate on ballistic missiles, whereas American efforts had been focused on aerodynamics. Whether this was much comfort to the great American public as they contemplated the presence of a Russian satellite flying across the Land of the Free is a moot point.

The launch of Sputnik 1 was the cue for frenzied activity from the media, who descended upon Jodrell Bank expecting news of signals direct from the satellite. Bernard adopted a somewhat snooty attitude towards using the telescope to pick up a series of bleeps, which could be detected by any small receiver. He had been told the news in a telephone call which awoke him in the early hours of the morning and, when he arrived at Jodrell, he was very surprised to find the ladies and gentlemen of the press camped out there, demanding a statement and a demonstration of the telescope's potential. He had been anticipating this event for some time and could not understand the commotion which now surrounded it.

Using the telescope to pick up the signal from Sputnik was not on Bernard's agenda, in spite of the urgings of Husband, who told the press that the instrument was operational and wrote furious letters to Bernard and Mansfield Cooper complaining at the lack of activity; Bernard responded with equal fury at the impertinence of a mere engineer presuming to tell him how to manage his telescope. The fact is that the contractors were in possession of the site, the telescope could not be driven from the control room, there were no cables to connect the computers to the driving mechanisms and they had run out of money. During preceding months, small radar systems had been used successfully to obtain echoes from the Moon. By analysing these echoes a technique was developed for measuring the density of electrons between Earth and the Moon. As part of the programme for the telescope during International Geophysical Year, plans had been laid to use this method in conjunction with the eagerly anticipated American satellite. By bouncing a radar beam off the satellite as it orbited outside the atmosphere it would be possible to measure the density of the electrons between the Earth and the satellite; a simple process of subtraction would then give an accurate measurement of the volume of electrons between the satellite and the Moon, providing important information about the nature of interplanetary space. Now there was a Russian satellite in orbit, with no sign of the American version and a telescope which was not ready to track its path.

Monday morning began early with a telephone call from Robert Cockburn, who was now the Controller of Guided Weapons and Electronics at the Ministry of Supply; it was a call that transformed the fortunes of the telescope. Cockburn said that not a single facility in the western world had been able to detect or track the carrier rocket, which was believed to be an Intercontinental Ballistic Missile. Could Bernard use the telescope to find it? The request threw him a lifeline and he needed no second invitation to grasp hold of it. Here, at last, was a real task to perform and an opportunity to show the world what the instrument was capable of doing. The story of Jodrell Bank was changed in an instant and the call initiated a vital association involving highly secret operations and the defence of the realm. But nothing could be done with a telescope that was not in commission and urgent discussions began with the consulting engineer. Husband had predicted that it would take at least two weeks to get everything in working order but Bernard needed to use it at once, if not sooner. He told Husband that if everyone came back to work and the systems were completed, he would be able to drive the telescope with the computer to try and find the carrier rocket. The challenge galvanised Husband and his differences with Bernard were put aside for the time being. The Brush engineer was persuaded to return and a round of frantic activity began. The press picked up on the absence of high frequency cables and reports appeared in the papers the next day. There was no money to pay for them, but Sir John Dean of the Telegraph Construction Company read the reports and immediately telephoned Bernard offering to donate as much coaxial cable as he needed. It arrived at Crewe station on Wednesday evening. Soon after midnight all the connections had been made, the computers were driving the telescope and radar echoes were being obtained from the Moon. Two weeks work had been accomplished in forty-eight hours and all they had to do now was find the rocket. At that crucial moment the system developed a fault.

After hours of work they failed to find out what was wrong and disaster was staring them in the face when Dr. Stanley Greenhow, who had been working at Jodrell since 1948, approached Bernard and produced some calculations he had scribbled down on the back of an envelope. Greenhow had been using a 4-metre transmitter to study meteors and suggested that, if it was hoisted up to the swinging laboratory, it could be used to find the rocket. The small transmitter was lifted into place and on Thursday evening, with the huge gain in the signal obtained from the massive reflecting surface, a beam was directed towards the expected path of the missile. Nothing was seen, but on Friday the receiver was adjusted and that night they obtained what Bernard described as a vague and inconclusive echo.

On the evening of October 12th everything was ready for a further attempt. Bernard was in the laboratory watching the usual echoes from meteors in a desultory way. Just before midnight they got a superb track off the carrier rocket as it crossed England. A spectacular echo appeared on one side of the screen and moved rapidly across the time base. This was what they had been waiting for, the unmistakeable echo of the ICBM travelling across the Lake District and out towards the North Sea at 17,000 mph. As they watched its passage across the screen everyone in the laboratory was electrified. Bryan Lovell was standing next to his father; at that time he was showing more interest in the arts than in science and as the echo disappeared from the screen Bernard turned to him and said:

"If the sight of that doesn't turn you into a scientist, nothing ever will!"

The control room is packed with reporters. A photograph of the echo is quickly developed and arrangements are made to project it onto a screen in the lecture theatre, which is soon bursting at the seams with journalists and photographers jostling and pushing to find a seat, squatting on the steps or standing pressed against the walls in the crush. We are sitting at the

Tracking an ICBM, 12 October 1957.

front of the darkened house in the midst of a spellbound throng of animated people; we see the Professor, with his shadow vividly silhouetted on the screen, pointing to the upper of two thick black lines running across it. This line, he explains, is recording the distance of the rocket and the lower one shows the strength of the signal at each point as it crosses the screen. "It provides us with a gold mine of information and is one of the most dramatic things I have ever seen," he tells us. When questioned about the event, he says that the rocket was observed for thirteen seconds as it passed over the Lake District at a height of 125 miles and that this telescope is the only instrument in the western world that has been able to find and track the Russian Intercontinental Ballistic Missile. He ends the impromptu news conference with a plea for the future of the facility:

"The government has been treating us like criminals because of the over-expenditure. Even now we are very worried about obtaining the funds to make full use of the telescope. Perhaps the powers that be will finally understand its importance." The media are impressed. The next day the telescope is front page news across the world. In place of the usual diatribes about wasting public money, peons of praise are heaped upon the professor, the engineer and their teams; this ICBM could have been carrying a missile, they suggest; without the telescope no one would have known about it until it struck; by then it would have been too late; the telescope is a vital instrument of early warning; a swift solution must be found to the financial debacle.

In the succeeding days the lecture theatre continues to be packed with reporters, as Bernard gives press conferences and demonstrations twice nightly. The little canteen cannot cope with the numbers. He receives a distraught note from the lady in charge of the catering: "Dr. Lovell, I am very sorry to say there were no eggs this morning. I left eight meat pies for supper. I am also sorry that there is no bacon left as we only have 1 lb. a week and it is due tomorrow." The media circus does not have to starve for long as friends, families and the local WRVS come to their aid. In one night the reputation of the telescope has been rescued from oblivion. From Middlesex Hospital, a young nurse who is just beginning her training reports that her father has become a hero overnight; she is no longer being called Susan Lovell; she has been nicknamed 'Miss Jodrell Bank 1957'.

A few weeks earlier Bernard felt friendless and bereft. Now, as well as the adulation of the press, he began to find that he had friends in high places. On the 16th of October, a letter appeared in *The Times*, from one of his wartime colleagues, Sir Robert Renwick, President of the Radar Association:

This instrument has now demonstrated its powers by detecting the satellite by radar. It appears that it is the only installation in the UK and possibly in the western world, which is capable of establishing contact with the Russian Satellite. The astonishing thing about this new telescope is that the Director of Jodrell Bank had to depend on the timely gift from industry of some polythene cables in order to bring this instrument into operation for this purpose.

The publicity which the satellite has drawn to the radio telescope has revealed a depressing financial situation and it is disturbing to learn that Manchester University, which has had the courage to proceed with the erection of this instrument, is now under stricture from the government because this project has exceeded the original estimate by some £250,000, a sum considerably less than that expended on a single modern bomber. It should not have been necessary for Professor Lovell to depend on last minute charity...this unique installation has become the envy of the world. It is to be hoped that one result of the satellite will be the clear demonstration that the telescope is a national asset of high importance and that Manchester University will immediately be provided with adequate funds.[235]

Renwick quickly followed up this opening salvo with a letter to the Prime Minister, Harold Macmillan, dated 22nd October, enclosing a note on the telescope which had been prepared by Bernard and setting out the importance for both Britain and America of "the information that can be gathered for defence purposes from these early radar contacts with the rocket and satellite".[236] He suggested that the instrument would be of immense value for defence both to Britain and America and urged the provision of sufficient funds to enable the effective operation of the telescope. Renwick and Bernard went to 10 Downing Street for a meeting with the Prime Minister's Private Secretary, P.S. de Zulueta, and the lobbying began to bear fruit when Macmillan himself said in the House of Commons:

> Honourable Members will have seen that within the last few days our great radio telescope at Jodrell Bank has successfully tracked the Sputnik's carrier rocket.[237]

This was not the first occasion on which there had been discussions with the government about the defence capabilities of the telescope. The abortive contacts with Cockburn in 1955 had taken place at the same time as talks with the Ministry of Defence; this is clear from secret correspondence with the MOD,[238] in connection with the Congleton planning issue. On June 15th 1955, a letter from Bernard to H.S. Young at the Directorate of Scientific Intelligence requested help in opposing the major industrial development being planned in Congleton.[239] On 20th June, Young wrote to Dr. Blount at the DSIR saying that Bernard had "undertaken certain important commitments and it should be possible for Lovell to detect missiles on the Russian guided weapons range and he has undertaken in the future to put his mirror on sentry duty for intelligence purposes. This is vital from the country's point of view and would provide a very economical way of getting intelligence. Information of this type obviously cannot come out in a public inquiry...It might be possible for you to pass a hint or two to the Ministry of Housing and Local Government."

Blount responded that the best approach would be a direct request from the MOD to the Ministry of Housing and on 11th July Sir Frederick Brundrett KBE, the chairman of the Defence Research Policy Committee, wrote to Dame Evelyn Sharpe DBE, the Permanent Secretary to the Ministry of Housing, asking for her help by opposing the Congleton plans.

The next day an irate Dame Evelyn telephoned Brundrett and told him that "Lovell has already agreed to the encroachment and it is public knowledge that he has agreed." This assertion was clearly based on misinformation because, as we have seen, Bernard had done no more than suggest a compromise which had been rejected by the local authority; it was only after the meeting with Bill Deedes on 26th July that the planners were forced to agree to a greatly reduced scheme. Having received the Dame's inaccurate missive, Brundrett sent Young a sharp letter expressing unflattering views about Bernard's apparent volte-face. Young responded with a cryptic note: "I can only apologise for having worried you, but one could hardly have expected this. Next time I see the gentleman I will assault him with a blunt instrument!" It is to be presumed that Young learned the true state of affairs before he carried out this threat; certainly there are no records of such a crime being committed and correspondence between Young and Bernard continued on a cordial basis for many years.

These exchanges did have an unfortunate sequel early in 1957 when Bernard wrote to Young, on the 14th March, prior to the hearing of the Public Accounts Committee, asking whether he would "put in a word to someone at a high level so that the PAC soft pedals [on Jodrell] and the Treasury feels disposed to give the all clear to the DSIR to meet half the deficit as they agreed a year ago." As ill luck would have it, Young was away and a note was sent to Bernard in the following terms:

As Young has gone on leave for a week he has asked me to deal with your letter of 14th March. I have asked Sir Frederick Brundrett to put in a word with the Treasury about the importance of your telescope to us and the Ministry of Supply. I have not yet heard any results, but if I get anything before Thursday (the day of the PAC hearing) I will telephone you.

G.L. Tunney

No such telephone call was received. It seems safe to assume that the crusty Sir Frederick resisted the temptation to make favourable comments about Bernard or his telescope.

Before long it became apparent that even the Soviet Union did not possess the equipment to keep track of the hardware they had sent into space. On Saturday 26th October, a telegram from Moscow was delivered to Jodrell. The Russians had lost their rocket; could Jodrell Bank help them to find it? They evidently expected that this task would take some time because they provided an approximate location where they expected it to be on Monday. Within six hours it had been found, 1,000 miles away flying

Financial woes. The caption originally read: "Jolly demoralizing tracking other people's satellites AND on something that isn't paid for yet." COURTESY OF PUNCH LIMITED.

over the Arctic. "TELESCOPE TRIUMPHS" trumpeted the headlines. International cooperation in space had begun with a resounding success for British scientists.

By this time the batteries of the satellite had run down and, over the next few weeks, it gradually declined towards the Earth and eventually burnt up as it re-entered the atmosphere. Meanwhile, on 2nd November, Sputnik 2 hit the stratosphere. This time, a small dog named Laika was chained into the capsule and was catapulted into space, with a one-way ticket to oblivion. Laika was a stray who had wandered about the streets of Moscow before being taken in and prepared for her last adventure. For many years the Soviets claimed that Laika, which means 'barker' in Russian, had lived happily in space for over a week. In 2002, however, the Russian biologist Dr. Dimitri Malashenkov told a World Space Congress in Houston that the poor creature had been attached to monitors before blast off. All signs of life were extinguished between five and seven hours later and analysis of the monitors revealed that Laika had died from overheating and the effects of stress. The news that a dog had been sent into orbit aroused both interest and anger around the world. At Jodrell, the main transmitters had been repaired and, with everything in perfect order, the telescope was used to follow the satellite and the launch rocket to great effect.

The Russian space programme had been run in tandem with the development of military hardware and ballistic missiles; it had benefitted greatly from the cooperative approach. In contrast, Eisenhower had determined to maintain a strict division between the peaceful exploration of space and the exigencies of weapons manufacture and defence. The American space programme suffered a severe setback from this decision, hence the much greater progress made by the Soviet Union. The successful launch of the Sputniks spurred the Americans into action and the inappropriately named Vanguard programme was rushed to completion with disastrous results. The first American attempt was made on 6th December 1957. It was an ignominious failure. The satellite itself was about the size of a grapefruit and when the countdown ended, the world's press and television cameras were treated to the sight of the rocket rising a few feet from the launch pad before it collapsed and exploded with spectacular effect. The satellite was thrown clear in the explosion; it came to rest in some bushes and immediately started to transmit a strong signal. The press had no mercy and headline writers round the world made the most of their opportunity for ridicule, variously dubbing Vanguard 'Pfftnik' in the *Waco Herald*, 'Spätnik' in *Die Wiener Zeitung*, 'Flopnik' in the *London Daily Herald*, and 'Unclesamnik Kaputnik' in the *Washington Daily News*.

On the very day of the Vanguard fiasco, President Khrushchev announced that the Sputnik carrier rocket had landed in the United States. He said that the Americans did not want to give it back and, being "a pretty straight sort of guy", he declared that if the boot had been on the other foot he would have returned an American rocket without hesitation. The American Ambassador to Moscow pronounced: "It's the first I've heard of it." *The Times* reported that Professor A.C.B. Lovell, of Jodrell Bank, had confirmed that the rocket re-entered the atmosphere above the United States during its 879th orbit of the Earth and immediately burnt up in the atmosphere. So the Soviets and the Americans were both correct, after a fashion, and the Sputnik 1 story was brought to an amicable conclusion.

The last regular entry in the diary that Bernard had kept for five years was made on 2nd October 1957. It was full of despair at the terrible difficulties which were still surrounding him. The next and final entry, on New Year's Day 1958,[240] strikes a very different note: "Two days after the last entry the Russians launched their first satellite. All life changed immediately." And so it had. Public perception transformed the telescope from pariah to saviour of the West. The Jodrell Bank Diary concluded: "1958 opened with a telegram of good wishes from Moscow which thanked us for our satellite observations which we sent them." But in spite of the adulation of the press, the praise of politicians from the Prime Minister downwards, and the pride of the public in a great national achievement, the burden of debt, the criticisms of the PAC, and the hostility of Charles Husband still hung round Bernard's neck like millstones. He had derived great pleasure and satisfaction from the achievements of the past three months, but it was a pleasure which was imbued with anxiety, and the gloss of satisfaction was tarnished by fear of the future.

The lobbying continued into the new year and there were many allies as well as siren voices prophesying doom. Foremost amongst the latter was Melville, whose misconceived and inaccurate evidence had been largely responsible for the damning PAC report. On 29th January, he took it upon himself to write to Mansfield Cooper, the Vice Chancellor, complaining that: "Professor Lovell has made yet another unofficial move to obtain support for his cause in an unorthodox way through a personal letter to Sir Robert Renwick and later through an interview with one of the Prime Minister's Private Secretaries."[241] He enclosed copies of Bernard's letter and of Renwick's letter to the Prime Minister and concluded that: "lobbying of this kind can only make life more difficult for all of us", by which he presumably meant for himself. The ensuing correspondence shows that his letter did him no credit and, as we shall see, it was not long before he had to eat a very large helping of humble pie.

CHAPTER NINETEEN

Resurrection

In spite of the sensational achievements of the telescope, the University continued to insist that the gagging order imposed on Bernard in August must remain in place. All that was required to satisfy Husband was a letter to *The Times* stating that the PAC had got it wrong, as they had, and that there had been constant communication between Husband and the scientist in charge of the project, throughout the period of construction. There was no conceivable reason to forbid the writing of such a letter other than the determination of the university officers to avoid any more criticism falling upon them. The report had highlighted their lack of financial control and, as we have seen, they could have brought work to a halt had they chosen to do so. The main thrust of the criticism had been falsely directed against Husband for his alleged failure to communicate. This was an excellent result for the University and the officers; any admission that there had indeed been regular consultation between the engineer and the scientist acting as their agent would invite a shift in the blame to include them. This was the last thing they wanted and if pressure remained focused on Bernard and Husband they were confident that they would escape further censure.

The pressure was such that Bernard wrote a letter of resignation but the Vice Chancellor sent for him and refused to accept it. He realised that he was going to have to sweat it out and the University decided that this situation should be maintained. The principle consideration for the University was to avoid criticism and the best way of doing so was to turn up the heat on Bernard. Mansfield Cooper and Rainford had told him that he must not, under any circumstances, refute the findings of the Public Accounts Committee, on the spurious grounds that to do so would be a breach of parliamentary privilege. They fostered the fear that Husband would sue him, and they would not allow him to adopt the simple expedient of going public with the truth. The advice that he should maintain silence on the topic was reiterated time and again, even though they knew that the committee had got it wrong. On 23rd October Mansfield Cooper wrote to him:

Our negotiations with the DSIR are at a critical stage. I enjoin you to be extremely cautious in any statement you make to the Press. Say as little as you possibly can, and nothing at all I think on relations between the University and the engineers.[242]

On 30th January he wrote forbidding "any unorthodox approaches to the financial powers" and proscribing contact "with Renwick or anyone else. I think we must work at the moment through DSIR". On the 2nd February Streat wrote to Sir Charles Renold that, in view of the threat of criticism of the University, he had "sent a note to Lovell enjoining the most strict caution in whatever press comments he makes". Two days later, Mansfield Cooper told Bernard that he might be asked by Husband's solicitors to write a letter setting out the extent of consultations with the engineer and concluded:

"Do not write such a letter without further consultation with me."

It is not difficult to imagine the searing anxiety that all this must have caused. Bernard knew that he and Husband had been traduced by the findings; he knew the truth; he knew he had only to speak out to break free from the turmoil; yet this was the very thing he was not allowed to do. The directives to maintain silence on these matters were invariably couched in firm but soothing tones. Streat, in particular, appeared to offer kindly, almost avuncular, support and assured him of the unremitting efforts that were being made to help him. He told Bernard that he must not hesitate to call him if he wanted to discuss anything. But the velvet glove of compassion concealed a mailed fist that was ready to smash into him if needed – in the nicest possible way, of course.

On Sunday the 9th February, Streat's diary tells of a telephone call from Professor Lovell,[243] who said that he was deeply troubled by remarks made to him by the Vice Chancellor the previous morning. Mansfield Cooper had been summoned to appear before the Public Accounts Committee. He had warned Bernard that some of his letters to Husband were equivocal and might be interpreted as showing that he had misled the University about the nature and extent of alterations. This was a fair point. Bernard's focus was always on the central goal of building the best possible instrument in the shortest possible time and this led, on occasions, to mixed messages. On 26th April 1954 he wrote:

The practical situation is that I cannot engage in modifications to the steelwork which will increase the cost. It may be possible for you to introduce minor modifications without exceeding the present estimate in which case we shall be very glad for them to be introduced.

By way of contrast on 30th July 1954:

> We must at all cost avoid being forced into any formal revision of the contract at this stage. These issues on money will be far easier to face when the structure is nearer to completion next year. If any major financial issue were raised at this stage it might cause a serious hindrance in the progress of the work.[244]

As we have seen, the changes being discussed were proposed modifications intended to improve the design and function of the instrument. At the time when the final cost increases were disclosed to the Department, in October 1955, none of the new features had been constructed; they were mere plans, which could have been abandoned. The fact is that, although there were alterations and improvements to the design, not a penny of extra money was actually spent without the full knowledge of both the University and the DSIR. In his later evidence to the reconvened Public Accounts Committee, Mansfield Cooper confirmed this and said:

> The point was that the money was not spent and Professor Lovell has never had the power to spend a halfpenny on this and every halfpenny must go through the Bursar's department.

He also made it clear that, although anyone can make errors, Bernard's probity could not be impeached.[245]

Bernard told Streat on the telephone that he was very worried and feared that the Vice Chancellor might "throw him to the wolves". Streat agreed to call on the Lovells that afternoon and he arrived at The Quinta with his wife in time for tea. While Joyce entertained Doris Streat, Bernard took Sir Raymond into his study.

It was a dark and gloomy afternoon. As he sat in front of the cosy fire, drinking his tea and toying with a crumpet, the Chairman of the Council was all velvet glove, oozing with sympathy. He told Bernard that the Council believed Husband was about to serve a writ on him for defamation, claiming damages of up to £1 million. Of course the University would do everything it could to help and would support him to the hilt all the way through the litigation; but there was very little expectation that the action could be defended successfully; the adverse findings of the PAC against Husband had never been denied and Bernard would certainly lose.

"What would happen then?" asked Bernard.

"Well then," continued the velvet glove, "I fear that you would be condemned in damages of up to £1 million." Bernard was stunned.

"I don't have £1 million," he said. "I wouldn't be able to pay."

"In that case, my dear fellow, I am afraid that you will face imprisonment." The blow crashed in. The mailed fist did its work and settled back into the velvet. "Goodness! Is that the time? We had better be going. Thanks for the tea." And away they went, leaving Bernard prostrated with horror as he sank back into his chair.

Joyce came in and Bernard told her what had happened. As always she provided a haven of tranquil support and did what she could to console him. After a few minutes she went to find the children and asked them to come with her at once because their father had something to tell them. All five were at home, full of youthful chatter and laughter. They realised that something serious had occurred; the laughter was silenced and they followed her into the study.

"I want you to know that Father has done nothing wrong," said Joyce. Then Bernard broke the terrible news. He told them about the crisis at Jodrell and said that if it was not resolved he might very well be sent to prison. It took a moment for the words to sink in before the girls all burst into tears. Bryan recalls being absolutely livid. He was furious at the injustice that could visit such a fate upon their beloved father at the height of his fame and success.

Streat's terrible pronouncement was both wicked and untrue. Bernard had not defamed Husband who, in spite of his protests, had no cause of action against him. Even if he did sue, Streat must have known that imprisonment for civil debt was finally abolished in 1869, the year before the death of its most passionate adversary, Charles Dickens; the Fleet and the Marshalsea prisons had been closed for more than one hundred years. Although Streat's diary refers to the tea party and to the conversation about Husband, it does not mention the £1 million or the question of imprisonment; this is hardly surprising as they are not the sort of falsehoods a man would boast about, even in his private diary. There is no reason to suppose that the idea emanated from anyone other than Streat and there are no contemporary references to the visit in the university files. On the 14th February he wrote of the "grim prospect facing the University" and his fear of any criticism that would "show us up as incompetent administrators"[246] – as they were. The only conclusion one can reach is that Streat, in line with the rest of the university hierarchy, was so determined to silence Bernard that he was prepared to say anything that he judged would promote that aim, including putting the frighteners on him. Hidden in the 1958-59 files, Mansfield Cooper's 1979 note to Sir Arthur Armitage records his view of the matter: "I am led to think that 'the third of a million pounds' [sic] and the reference to imprisonment were the consequence of Streat having mulled it over and felt the direst of warnings to be necessary."[247] There can be no other explanation for uttering such deliberate and untrue threats.

And the 'direst of warnings' had dire consequences both for Bernard and for his family. It was his misfortune that he trusted Streat and took the threat of incarceration at face value. In later years he even wrote of his profound gratitude for the kindly way in which Sir Raymond had spoken to him and he praised him for the support he believed he was giving.[248] But the fear of being sent to prison was genuine and it caused him great torment both at the time and for the rest of his life. Within a few weeks, Melville changed his evidence and Husband and Bernard were cleared of blame by the Public Accounts Committee; but the belief that he had been facing imprisonment and the traumatic fear which it caused him haunted him to the end of his days. The family shared his pain at the memory of Sir Raymond Streat's visit and the story featured in his son Bryan's moving and eloquent address at Bernard's funeral in August 2012.

On the 10th February, Husband sent Melville a memorandum setting out the full extent of his consultations with Bernard and the University during the years of construction. The document was clear and irrefutable. It referred to the thousands of letters which had passed between them, quoting many passages and conversations which established the truth beyond a peradventure. The University had been fully involved in the process and the letters between Rainford and Husband showed that the University knew as much about what was being planned as Bernard and that they did nothing to curtail the plans. Rainford made a positive decision not to inform the Department of the details until the final estimates were presented in October 1955. Even then neither the DSIR nor the University called a halt, although they knew the full extent of the design changes and the cost implications which they caused. Husband's memorandum ended:

> Husband and Co. hope that the Public Accounts Committee will think that, in the light of the representations which have been set out herein, the statements contained in the report, which have been so damaging to Messrs Husband and Co., do not represent a true view of the actual events at Jodrell Bank nor of the conduct of the consulting engineer.[249]

On the 28th February, Melville finally accepted that he had got it wrong and wrote to the PAC withdrawing his earlier evidence. He said he had not intended to imply that no discussions on the scientific aspects of the design took place; this was a remarkable claim in the face of his assertions the year before that Husband had made the design changes without consulting anybody and that Bernard was unaware of them. He was forced to concede that there had been extensive consultation between Husband and Professor Lovell and concluded his letter: "So far as my previous evidence may have been misleading, I wish to offer the fullest apology to the committee."[250] Misleading? It was completely wrong.

As a result of this ignominious capitulation by the secretary to the DSIR, who had recently been awarded a knighthood, the committee summoned Rainford and Mansfield Cooper to appear before them on 18th March 1958. Both men were quick on their feet and somewhat slippery when it came to answering the difficult questions about their failures to keep control and the extent of their knowledge. Fortunately for them the main emphasis was on Melville's retraction but there was much obfuscation during the evidence. Melville tried to excuse himself by claiming that when he said there was no consultation he did so because he had misunderstood the question. Mansfield Cooper prepared a note for his evidence in which he made the false claim: "The University were not aware until some time after the further expenditure occurred that it had happened."[251] When he was asked about Professor Lovell living on the site he replied, "Would it be proper to make a correction there? Professor Lovell does not live on the site. That crept into your minutes last year", thereby craftily finessing the truth which was that Melville had presented Bernard's living quarters as an established fact. The chairman, Sir George Benson tried to put a further gloss on this by suggesting that Melville had been speaking figuratively; that he had merely meant to infer that the Professor spent a great deal of time there. As Melville had said, in terms, that the Professor "lives in the apartments" Benson's suggestion lent new meaning to the entire concept of papering over the cracks.

Rainford and Mansfield Cooper continued to maintain that the substantial changes were made without university approval, in spite of the clear evidence to the contrary. Even twenty-one years later the Vice Chancellor's determination to hide the facts is evident in the note he prepared for Sir Arthur Armitage: "I would not recommend that any direct access be afforded to these files at the present time."[252] In the end the chairman did acknowledge the committee's embarrassment that they had been so badly misled: "We are quite conscious that we have a difficult problem of our own in dealing with the evidence and the report of last year." No more adverse findings were drawn in their report which was finally published on 24th July. Husband was completely exonerated: "In view of this further evidence, it is clear that the evidence given to the committee of last session was gravely inaccurate and misleading, and that there was in fact the fullest collaboration on scientific and technical matters between the consultants and the Professor."[253]

These important concessions satisfied Husband. His reputation had been cleared and there was no bar to the release of the grant to pay off half the debt of £260,000 as had been agreed in 1956. No conditions were attached, beyond a requirement that the satisfactory functioning of the telescope must be certified by the University, which issued this ringing endorsement: "The radio telescope is doing the work for which it was conceived and doing it more expeditiously and over a greater range than was thought possible a few years ago."[254] The money was paid to the University. Now all they needed was the other half.

Even as they turned their minds to raising the money, additional costs continued to mount up. The United Steel Structural Company presented a final bill which demanded £124,405 above their original quotation. Husband went into battle and reported that the Company might be prepared to waive their claim to the excess as a donation to support the construction of the telescope. On 11th July 1958 the Chairman of United Steel, Sir Walter Benton-Jones, visited Jodrell Bank at the invitation of the University. So impressed was the Baronet by what he saw that, in due course, he persuaded his board of directors that the honour of being associated with such a marvellous project was cheap at the price of £124,405; the debt was duly written off as a gift and another acute financial problem was duly solved.

The stress caused by these events was alleviated to some extent by exciting developments in the space race and by an unexpected but deeply gratifying invitation from the BBC to present the Reith Lectures in the autumn. On 31st January 1958 the American satellite Explorer 1 was launched into orbit, using an adapted military ballistic rocket, Juno 1, which had been designed by Wernher von Braun. Von Braun arrived in America after the war, and the expertise he had acquired in designing the V1 and V2 missiles was put to good use by his adopted country. In 1956 he was appointed Technical Director of the Army Ballistic Missile Agency. ABMA was taken over by the National Aeronautics Space Administration, NASA, in October 1958 and von Braun played a key role in the American space programme. Explorer 1 transmitted data for thirty-one days until the batteries failed, and was the first element in a successful programme which fulfilled Eisenhower's stated determination to have a satellite in orbit during International Geophysical Year.

Early in April Bernard received an unexpected visit from a US Air Force colonel who told him, in the strictest confidence, that the Americans had just built an Atlas missile and that they intended to use it, in the near future, to send a rocket to the Moon. The Colonel explained that this programme was vital in order to restore the prestige of the United States following the success of Sputnik and the Vanguard disaster, but that they had no way of tracking the rocket once it was launched. Could Bernard and Jodrell help? Bernard said that he would be delighted, but that he would have to consult the university authorities first.

"There is no time for that," said the Colonel. "I need an immediate answer and I am flying back to the States at once." He also reminded Bernard of the need for absolute secrecy.

"All right then," said Bernard, "we will run it under the auspices of the IGY." The Colonel said that he was delighted to do business and departed, promising that the necessary equipment would be shipped over in due course. Bernard confided in John Davies, whose help would be essential for tracking the rocket. Nothing more was heard and the secret was kept until July, when a huge amount of equipment arrived, accompanied by a group of American technicians. It had been flown to Burtonwood near Liverpool and was packed in boxes which were emblazoned with large labels reading:

Project Able US Air Force
Jodrell Bank Radio Telescope
SECRET

It was not long before a sharp eyed reporter spotted a scoop. The telephone began to ring, rumours spread and in no time at all the press had the story. On 25th July, the press proclaimed: "Jodrell Bank and journey to the Moon."

The launch date was fixed for 17th August when Bernard was in Moscow at a conference of the International Astronomical Union. At the appointed hour he managed to find a telephone that worked in the lobby of his hotel and wrestled with the complexities of the Russian state telephone system. Eventually he got through to Jodrell on a very poor line and eagerly asked for news. It was a massive anticlimax. The rocket had been launched at Cape Canaveral but eighty seconds into its flight it exploded somewhere over the Atlantic. It had not risen above the Jodrell Bank horizon and no contact was made.

On Saturday 11th October the successor, Pioneer 1, was ready. At Jodrell there had been careful preparations and the telescope had been fine-tuned by following one of the Explorer satellites as it orbited the Earth. Lift-off was scheduled for 8.42, Jodrell time. As the moment approached, tension mounted in the control room and among the reporters and camera crews packed into every available corner of the building. Contact was made as soon as the rocket rose above the horizon and Bernard emerged from the control room to announce the successful launch. Wreathed in smiles, he said that the telescope had picked up the signal at 8.52 and that everything was going according to plan. All that day they tracked the rocket as it sped on its way, deeper and deeper into the unknown regions of space. The watching media looked on in amazement as the great telescope followed its path, turning in azimuth and elevation, under the direction of the computers. When the rocket set over the horizon that evening, it had travelled 60,000 miles but it had become apparent that it was off course by at least 10 degrees.

Early on Sunday morning, when Pioneer 1 was almost 80,000 miles from launch, the fuel supply ran out. At that point the velocity was 34,000 feet per second. This was 1,250 feet per second short of the velocity required to break free of the influence of gravity and the spaceship began to fall back. There was a retro rocket on board which had been designed to fire it into orbit round the Moon, if it ever got there. An attempt to ignite this device and to put the spacecraft into Earth orbit failed; shortly afterwards, Pioneer 1 plunged to destruction as it re-entered the atmosphere and burnt up above the Pacific. It had not reached its target, but the achievement was nevertheless a remarkable one. It had travelled further into space than any previous probe and put the Americans in front of the Russians for the first time, if only by a short head. The telescope followed the rocket throughout and the mission provided important information about magnetic fields in space and the nature of particles trapped within the Earth's sphere of gravity. According to the *Daily Telegraph*'s special correspondent at Cape Canaveral, there was generous praise from the Americans for the contribution the telescope had made to the success of the flight and the quality of the information which Jodrell Bank had sent them.

There were two more American attempts to reach the Moon that year. Pioneer 2 was launched on 8th November but only travelled 1,000 miles before it failed. On 6th December Pioneer 3 flew nearly 70,000 miles towards the Moon; then, like Pioneer 1, it ran out of fuel before it had reached escape velocity and burnt up as it fell back into the atmosphere. The Soviet scientists were spurred on by the American attempts. During Bernard's visit to Moscow in August he asked them if they had a programme for sending a rocket to the Moon but did not receive a direct answer; the party line was that no attempt would be made until the Russian space experts could be sure of success. On January 2nd 1959 they launched their first moon rocket, Lunik 1. Bernard was sitting quietly in his study at home, listening to a Bach fugue on the wireless when he was disturbed by a telephone call telling him that the Russian space probe was on the way to the Moon. Bach was immediately abandoned to the airwaves and he jumped into his car and headed for Jodrell.

The Russians had announced the frequencies on which the spacecraft would be transmitting but, in spite of many hours work, Bernard and his team were unable to pick up a signal. This failure was widely broadcast around the world and within a few days rumours began to circulate that the launch of Lunik 1 was a Russian invention designed to terrify the West; the rocket did not exist; the Russians did not have the knowledge or technology to perform such a feat. Foremost among the detractors was an American scientific writer, Lloyd Mallen, the father of a long line of space travel deniers. Mallen was a serial denier of many widely accepted beliefs, including the existence of Russian nuclear weapons and the connection between smoking and lung cancer. He wrote several books and no doubt made a good living out of being a professional sceptic; but he was as wrong about Lunik 1 as he was about everything else. Although Jodrell Bank failed to find the Russian rocket, the Jet Propulsion Laboratory at NASA did receive a weak signal, eight hours after it had passed within 3,750 miles of the Moon. Having missed the target by this tiny margin, Lunik 1 set off on a timeless journey round the Sun, travelling in an orbit which lies between those of the Earth and Mars. Fifty-three years on, the Russian spaceship still carries on orbiting.

This extraordinary feat placed the Russians in pole position from the beginning of 1959, a position they would not relinquish easily. Bernard was evidently disappointed that he had not been given notice of the Lunik 1 mission by his Russian friends, with whom he had established a good relationship during his visit to Moscow in August 1958. He wrote to congratulate them on their achievement and asked to be kept informed in future. He received the following reply:

2/11/1959

Dear Prof. Lovell,

Many thanks for your good wishes.

We often think of our lovely discussion in Moscow, but we hope you forgive us for not mentioning the date of the space rocket!

With best wishes from us both,

Anna Kapitza[255]

In a letter to Anna's husband, Pyotr Kapitza, dated 21st February 1959, Bernard expanded on his complaint by saying that he felt he had been misled during conversations during the preceding August. He expressed a sincere wish to cooperate in any way with future space probes and pointed out that it would be helpful to receive prior notice of the coordinates in order to assist in the tracking of missiles. He also referred to the fact that the inability to obtain signals from Lunik 1 had led to doubts being expressed in some quarters about the truth of the Russian space probe. "What are we expected to believe if we cannot make direct scientific observation?"[256] He had no further reply until 12th September 1959.[257]

It was one of the last Saturdays of the cricket season and Bernard was preparing to turn out for the village of Chelford, where he was the team captain. His bat, pads, whites and other necessary accoutrements were all packed in his cricket bag and he was about to depart for the ground when all the telephones started to ring. He answered the Jodrell direct line with one hand and the house telephone with the other. The excited voices of his assistant in his left ear and a journalist in his right told him that the Russians had launched another moon rocket.

"I'm sorry," he said, speaking into both telephones at the same time. "There's nothing I can do about it, I'm going to play cricket." With that he hung up, jumped into his car and set off for the cricket ground. He was still feeling rather offended that he had been ignored by the Russians in January and felt no inclination at all to divert the telescope away from the important scientific research which was currently underway. Joyce was in charge of the tea ladies that day and when she arrived at the ground she insisted on speaking to her husband. He would not forsake his cricket for the Russians, but it was a different thing when Joyce commanded him and he left the field at once.

"You have no idea what is going on," she said. "The telephone never stops ringing at home, the press is hounding us and the Americans at Jodrell are getting extremely agitated. You will have to do something about it." Bernard agreed that he would call at Jodrell on his way home; but even his beloved could not keep him away from the game for long. At six o'clock he arrived at the telescope. The American team in particular was delighted to see him. All afternoon they had been berated by their bosses in Washington asking for information and they had been labouring to describe exactly what it meant when they told them that the Professor was playing cricket.

"What the devil is cricket?" asked the men in Washington.

"It's kinda like baseball," replied the Jodrell team.

"But the Limeys don't play baseball," said Washington.

"No, but they do play cricket."

"But what the devil is cricket?" the conversations continued in circular vein all afternoon.

Bernard still felt little inclination to do anything but he went into his office where he found a long trail of paper hanging out of the telex machine. He picked it up. It was a message from the Russians giving the frequencies of the transmitter on the space ship and the calculations of the azimuth and elevation required for Jodrell to follow it. The exact time of impact with the Moon was said to be at 10.01 the following evening. The precision of the calculations and the confidence of the prediction stirred Bernard into action; the information had come late in the day, but his Russian friends had not forgotten him after all. It would be churlish to spurn their overture; what a coup it would be if they did hit the Moon this time; how left out he would feel if he did not get involved.

He summoned John Davies to Jodrell and put the research programme on hold. Fortunately the aerial which was being used operated on the correct frequency and as soon as Davies arrived they set up the systems. Almost at once they were rewarded with a clear signal from the Russian spacecraft and began to take measurements. Lunik 2 was directly on course for the Moon. Throughout the night and all day on Sunday the watch continued, punctured by regular demands for information from the press and urgent calls from across the Atlantic. The American bosses could hardly believe what was happening; the Russians just did not have the capability did they? As ten o'clock approached the tension mounted. All the signs were that the rocket was still on course; they had a strong bleeping signal; everything was in working order as the minutes ticked slowly away.

They counted down the seconds. At 10.01 precisely everyone in the laboratory held their breath; the world was waiting; but the signal continued to bleep. The seconds passed and at 10.02 they were wondering what had happened. Had their calculations been wrong? Perhaps the rocket had missed the Moon. Even now, perhaps, it was speeding on into space to join its predecessor in an eternal journey round the Sun. Another twenty-three seconds slipped by and suddenly the signal stopped. There was a moment of silence and then pandemonium broke out. A BBC microphone was held in front of Bernard as he was asked what had happened. "We're inclined to believe that the Lunik probe must have hit the Moon," was his understated reply. That was all they needed. Cameras flashed in from all sides, every available telephone was commandeered; the story rocketed round the world; the Russians had landed a spacecraft on the Moon. As Professor Lovell said, it was a brilliant achievement and a clear demonstration of the advanced state of Russian science and technology.

The timing of Lunik 2 was no coincidence. Within a few days President Khrushchev was due to fly to the United States for an official visit. The success of the moon rocket provided him with a wonderful opportunity to pull rank on his hosts. He did not waste it, arriving in Washington beaming with delight, much to the annoyance of Richard Milhous Nixon, the Vice President, who was reported as saying that no one really knew the rocket was on the Moon. Nixon was not the only doubter. Lloyd Mallen jumped back onto the bandwagon he had started and sent a message to Jodrell Bank alleging that the Lunik 2 expedition was a "Big Red Lie".[258] He received a telegram in reply on 15th September:

> Position of rocket signals did not agree with that of moon until end of period STOP Doppler record proves that rocket did hit the moon STOP JG Davies STOP Jodrell Bank

During the last stages of the flight of Lunik 2 John Davies made the inspired decision to measure the Doppler shift from the rocket as it accelerated into the gravitational field of the Moon. The Doppler Effect is familiar to all of us from sound waves. The wail of a police siren travelling towards us has a high pitch because it is moving on a shorter wavelength. As soon as the police car passes us, the longer wavelengths of the receding siren lower the pitch. The principle is identical in the electromagnetic field. The longer wavelength of the light from objects moving away from us causes visible light to move towards the red end of the spectrum; this phenomenon is known as the redshift and the faster the movement the greater the shift. By studying the redshift of galaxies the astronomer can determine their rate of recession and, therefore, the rate of the expansion of the universe. Likewise with radio waves; if the object emitting them is accelerating away from the receiver the frequency increases as the object recedes. By measuring the wavelength of the rocket flying away from Earth and towards the Moon, Davies calculated its speed and the line of approach; this measurement, combined with the abrupt halt of the signal proved beyond any rational doubt that the Russians scored a bull's-eye. And they had not finished yet.

On 4th October Lunik 3 was launched. Bernard was in the States where he had been invited to the proposed launching of another Pioneer which was intended to orbit the Moon. Before he even arrived the rocket had exploded on the launch pad. Denting American pride was becoming a favourite Russian sport and they were delighted that the start of their latest mission coincided with another failure. As if the fact of a successful launch was not enough, Lunik 3 was destined for the very same voyage that had been planned for the ill-fated Pioneer. The science correspondent of TASS took great delight in reminding the Americans that, only a few weeks earlier they had been boasting of flying round the Moon during the month of October. By the time Bernard returned to Jodrell Bank on the sixth, the Russian craft had travelled round the Moon and sent back the first photographs of the hidden side.

At the end of November Bernard received a letter from the President of the Soviet Academy of Sciences, Professor Nesmeyanov, thanking him for his assistance in tracking the Lunik probes and asking him to send the data which had been recorded at Jodrell back to Moscow. Bernard was happy to oblige. It was evident that, for all their success, the Russians' ability to follow the progress of their flights was very limited. This was confirmed many years later by a senior Soviet scientist who told him that they had not been able to track their spacecraft and were forced to rely on Jodrell Bank. His contribution to their efforts was not forgotten. In March 2013 the distinguished Russian scientist, Roald Sagdeev, who now lives in the United States, wrote:

> I remember how much he was admired among my mentors and peers in Soviet Academy. He was very courageous to extend the helping hand to Soviets in Space at the peak of the Cold War and at the time they indeed needed the deep space communication connection to their own spacecraft. But it was Bernard Lovell who pioneered this type of cooperation.[259]

In March 1960, the American fight back began in earnest. NASA planned to send a Pioneer rocket into deep space equipped with instruments designed to gather information about magnetic fields and the nature of matter in the solar system. In order to operate across the vast distances envisaged, the space craft would have to be under the control of an instrument which was sufficiently powerful to transmit the command signals. Like their Russian counterparts, the Americans turned to Jodrell for help. The preparations had been going on for months. Equipment was sent from the States, the aerials were redesigned and a powerful transmitter was fitted in the base of the bowl. The launch date was set for the tenth but a fuel problem developed during the countdown and it was aborted seventy seconds before lift-off. The next day the fault had been repaired and at Cape Canaveral the rockets were fired up for a perfect launch. Twenty-five minutes later Pioneer 5 had covered 5,000 miles. A large contingent of British and American scientists was gathered at Jodrell Bank. At 1.25 precisely a button was pressed and a signal was transmitted to the spacecraft. It worked to perfection, igniting the fuses of the explosive bolts that connected the carrier rocket to the probe. Immediately the signals changed and they knew that Pioneer 5 was flying alone, on its way and on course.

The following evening it flew past the Moon and within a week it had travelled nearly one and a half million miles, responding to commands and sending back signals as it went. On 18th March, the Queen's sister, Princess Margaret, came to Jodrell Bank. She had met Bernard at a lunch party whilst she was staying with her friends, Sebastian and Mona Ferranti. Bernard invited her to Jodrell and, by happy coincidence, her visit coincided with the flight of Pioneer 5. Whilst she was in the control room she was asked to press the button and issue a Royal Command to the space craft – one assumes that it was obeyed.

By the beginning of May the probe was 8 million miles from Earth and a signal was sent to it that switched on a much more powerful transmitter. This continued to send information until 26th June when the batteries failed and Pioneer 5 fell silent forever. At that moment it was 22 million miles from Earth. For more than three months it had continued to respond to commands and it sent back important data about many things, including magnetic fields, cosmic ray activity and solar flares. The data was received at Jodrell, where an enlarged group of Americans was still working with Bernard and his team, forwarding it to NASA for further investigation and analysis. The mission and the cooperation between American and British scientists had been an unqualified success. On 7th July, Bernard was invited to the White House, where he received the thanks of President Eisenhower, who presented him with a musical box from the grateful people of America. It only played one tune, *God Save the Queen*, and the box was an exact model of Pioneer 5. The model is still in the possession of the Lovell family. The original remains in perpetual orbit round the Sun.

Throughout this period attempts to find a solution to the financial deficit continued. On 28th November 1958 the University launched an appeal to raise £150,000. It was not an unqualified success. The press was now unanimous in championing Jodrell but large donations from industry and commerce were slow to arrive and less generous than had been anticipated. The industrialists who attended fundraising events enjoyed the hospitality and expressed full support for the telescope; but many considered that the government should pay for such a valuable national asset and were reluctant to subscribe. This view was widely shared by the public. Thousands of letters were written to Members of Parliament and government ministers demanding that the financial turmoil should be sorted out. Lord Hailsham, the Minister of Science, was bombarded with correspondence and, when he visited Jodrell he greeted Bernard with the words: "You're the fellow making my life a misery. Every morning my desk is piled with letters from people I don't know telling me I ought to pay off your debt." Bernard assured him that the University were not behind this campaign and intended to raise the money without further government help, as had been agreed with the DSIR. After a good lunch and a tour of the telescope the Noble Lord was mollified and returned to London impressed by what he had seen.

By the summer of 1959 the appeal had raised £65,000, some of which came through donations from members of the public. The Lovell papers at the Royal Society contain letters from many such donors. There were gifts from individuals, both friends and strangers; his neighbour Betty Lockett, sent a cheque for £20; Alice M. Bumstead, a widow from Dorset who evidently knew her Bible, sent "a mite". Dorothy Sayer enclosed a postal order from her daughter Pammy who had bought it with her pocket money; Pammy wrote: "I thought my money would be a little help towards the cost and I hope you get enough money soon to balance your budget." Anthony Kent of Form 4A, New Close Primary School, in Wiltshire, sent fifteen shillings saved by his class, saying: "We are amazed at the things you have done with your telescope." Bernard was very touched by these gifts, every one of which was acknowledged with a personal note of thanks. There were so many individual contributions that the sum they raised was far from insignificant; but even when they were added to the larger donations from industrialists, they were still a long way short of its target. The appeal centred on organising a number of fundraising events at Jodrell and, from time to time, individual donors were entertained to lunch and a tour of the facility. On 29th March 1959 the bursar brought just such a visitor to Jodrell. She was an attractive young lady and she arrived with an apparently respectable financial adviser. She introduced herself as Shirley Sayaha, the daughter of a rich businessman with interests in India. She was very pretty, Bernard was more than happy to show her round, and they provided her with the finest fare the canteen could rustle up. Miss Sayaha was enthralled by everything she saw. Before she left, she instructed her adviser to inform the Professor that she had decided to donate £10,000 to the appeal and another £10,000 for the research programme. Bernard was beside himself with excitement. He drove home to share the wonderful news with Joyce and began thinking of the most cost-effective way of allocating these new funds.

Several weeks passed before they heard from Miss Sayaha again. When they did it was in the form of a telephone call from the financial adviser who said that the young lady had been using that name in order to protect her identity from predatory fundraisers; she had now given him permission to inform Bernard that her real name was Lady de Montford. Her

Ladyship would be out of the country for a few months, he said, but on her return, in November, she would attend to the small matter of the donation at once. November came and went and no cheque arrived. Bernard began to doubt the veracity of the charming young lady; as the months passed he put his hopes aside and forgot the incident.

On 28th April 1960 he was sitting in his office browsing through *The Times* and enjoying a mid-morning cup of coffee. The news for the day was of little interest until he got to page nine, when his eye caught sight of a headline which almost made him fall off his chair: "Typist poses as Lady de Montford". The typist was said to be the daughter of a retired greengrocer from Lewisham in South East London. She sometimes claimed to be Shirley Sahaya [sic] and that her father was an Anglo-Indian gentleman with large interests in the subcontinent, while she lived in a fashionable street in Chelsea. Now she had appeared in court charged with theft and fraud. Her most recent exploit involved an elaborate plot to obtain money from Sidney Cabot, a New Zealander who had played rugby for the All Blacks. She had managed to obtain his chequebook and used it to fund an extravagant lifestyle. She asked for five other offences to be taken into consideration. The magistrate, Mr. T.F. Davies, described her as a menace and sentenced her to six months imprisonment. Bernard did not get the money, but felt relieved to have had a lucky escape at no greater cost than a canteen lunch.

The collaboration between Jodrell Bank and the American space programme led to a deal between the University and NASA which provided a regular income. The use of the telescope during the Pioneer 5 mission paid a substantial dividend and, by March 1960, the deficit had reduced to £50,000. Pressure on the government continued with questions in the House and articles in the press, which condemned the failure to support a great national facility and the disgrace of having to rely on American money. All pleas fell on very deaf ears and the difficulty seemed to be beyond resolution.

A few days after the launch of Pioneer 5 Bernard received a telephone call. It was put through to him by his secretary, Anthea Hollinshead, who sensed that something important was about to happen and could not resist listening in.

"Is that Professor Lovell?" inquired a voice at the other end of the telephone.

"Yes."

"Lord Nuffield wants to speak to you, would you hold the line please?" A few moments later he heard Nuffield's voice.

"Nuffield here. Is that Lovell?"

"Yes, my Lord."

"How much do you owe on that telescope of yours?"

"I think about fifty or sixty thousand."

"Is that all? I'll send you a cheque." When Bernard tried to thank him, Nuffield interrupted: "That's all right my boy. You haven't done too badly."

In the event Nuffield sent two cheques for £25,000 each. One was drawn on the Nuffield Foundation. The other was drawn on his personal account. With the payment of this money the final burden of debt was lifted. It had taken three years, but the telescope had been raised from the dead.

CHAPTER TWENTY

Reith Lecturer

On the 28th February 1958 Bernard arrived at Jodrell to prepare for the day's work and found on his desk an envelope of official appearance, embossed with the words 'British Broadcasting Corporation'. Inside the envelope was a letter from Sir Ian Jacob, the Director General, inviting him to present the annual Reith Lectures in the autumn. To say that he was astonished would be to understate his reaction by a substantial margin. It was a daunting prospect. Bertrand Russell had given the first series of lectures in 1948 and nine brilliant and eminent men had followed in his footsteps. Bernard would be the eleventh Reith lecturer. He immediately telephoned Joyce to ask her what she thought about it. Without a moment's hesitation she answered in her customary forthright way:

"Of course you must do it." In spite of his initial feelings of trepidation he had no hesitation in following her advice and wrote to Sir Ian at once that he was "greatly honoured and delighted to accept". In his letter, the Director General had set out the purpose of the series which was "to promote an opportunity for someone in the van of contemporary thought to make an individual contribution to a subject that should receive wide and serious attention".[260] Pondering these words as he wrote his reply he felt that this was a clear demonstration of faith in him and in the great project which had absorbed him for so many years. The announcement that he was to give the lectures provoked a flood of letters congratulating him. One in particular must have caused him both satisfaction and amusement; it was from Neville Mott, who wrote applauding the public recognition of his achievements and added: "It is a smack in the eye for the Treasury types."

In 1955, he had made a broadcast on Christmas Eve in which he discussed the difficult questions thrown up by the conflicts between religion and science in the modern world. The theme of this talk was that man had grown to fear science and to despair of religion: "We fear science because we feel it might destroy us; and we despair of religion because we no longer feel able to prepare man to face the contemporary world."

Religious belief had failed to embrace the advance of science, particularly in grappling with the problems of evolution and the origin of the universe. He decided that he would try to develop these ideas in the series of Reith Lectures, which was to be called 'The Individual and the Universe'.

Discussions began with the BBC and he met the producer, Kenneth Brown, who asked him to send the first two lectures by the end of August. In July he prepared a draft for the first lecture and felt quite pleased with the result. Obviously it would need some fine-tuning and no doubt Brown would subject it to editorial scrutiny, but it was a good start. Walter Hingston, the information officer of the DSIR came to stay for a weekend and one evening, after dinner, Joyce suggested that he should read the lecture to them. Bernard fetched the manuscript from his study and his wife and their guest settled down in front of a cosy fire. Then Bernard began. He kept an eye on his audience as he read and felt that he was holding them in the palm of his hand; certainly they were hanging on his every word and looked bright and interested; it was extremely gratifying to have such a reception for his work. He spoke for half an hour and, as he finished, looked at his two spectators in eager anticipation of their reaction. It was not quite what he expected.

"Is that the only copy?" inquired Joyce. Bernard replied that it was and she asked him to pass it over to her. She glanced through it, got up and tossed it into the fire. "That will never do," she said. "You would have sent them all to sleep in the first five minutes. Now you can start again." Hingston looked a little surprised at the turn of events, but murmured his agreement with Joyce's opinion. For a moment Bernard gazed in horror at the burning paper but he knew immediately that she was right. He had condensed his thoughts for the whole series into that first half-hour script and it was a muddled concertina of ideas randomly cobbled together. So he followed the noble example set by Thomas Carlyle on being told that John Stuart Mill's maid had burnt his manuscript of *The French Revolution*: he turned on his heel, went to his study, sat down at his desk and started all over again.

Kenneth Brown received the first two scripts on time, but his reaction to them caused a deep disagreement between lecturer and producer. As he had planned, Bernard's argument dealt with the fundamental dilemma of the dichotomy between the advancement of science and orthodox religious doctrine. Brown sent him a lengthy document in response in which he rejected any suggestion that cosmology or science could clash with religious thought; conflict between them was impossible because the two disciplines were entirely separate from one another and had no common denominator. Bernard could not accept this proposition, which was at odds with his entire thesis. He wrote back at once:

> I am aware of the position you set out but I find it completely
> unacceptable. In short I have no patience with those theologians
> who plug their ears and blindfold themselves in the face of science.
> I have made an attempt at the reconciliation and integration of the
> theological and scientific aspects of this problem. My effort will be
> pointless if I am to accept the particular doctrine that at no point
> do theology and science conflict or interact. The idea that scientific
> cosmology can have no influence on theology I find quite
> untenable.

Within a few days Bernard was informed that Kenneth Brown was unwell
and that production would be taken over by John Weltman. He got on well
with his new producer. There were many arguments about style and
organisation and a strong editorial control over the programmes, but the
themes of the lectures were Bernard's alone. They were broadcast each
Sunday evening from 9th November to 14th December 1958. Each one
had to be precisely half an hour in length and, as many Reith Lecturers
have found, both before and since, it was a daunting prospect.

The first three talks ranged over the history and development of
stargazing from Aristotle to the radio telescope. He contrasted the
unshakeable beliefs of the ancients with the extraordinary changes of the
past forty years. In the static universe of the Middle Ages and St Thomas
Aquinas, the Earth was a motionless body, situated at the centre of "the
spacious Firmament on high and all the blue ethereal sky".[261] Resistance
to changing ideas and the doctrines of the Church led to the persecution
of Giordano Bruno, who was burnt at the stake in 1600, the trial of Galileo,
and the demonisation of Copernicus. Kepler's laws of planetary motion
and Newton's theory of universal gravitation transformed man's
understanding of the relationship between the Sun, the Earth and the
planets; but even at the beginning of the twentieth century, the true extent
of the universe was unknown; Bernard was brought up on the idea that the
Sun was near the centre of a system of stars that extended no more than
twenty thousand light years.

The growth of knowledge during his lifetime revealed the
unimaginable scale of the cosmos. We see the Sun as it existed a mere eight
minutes ago, but the light from the nearest star has taken four years to
reach us; when we look at the most distant objects, we are seeing them not
as they are now but as they appeared billions of years ago, when the light
that we can see left them. We know that so far from being at the centre of

a solitary array of stars we are but a pinpoint on the edge of one galaxy among billions of others like it, in the midst of a vast and expanding universe. But for all the enormous growth in our knowledge there was still no final answer to the ultimate problem of the conditions which existed at or before the dawn of time; in this respect we are no more advanced than the astronomers of old; however much our understanding may increase, we reach a point at which science can tell us no more and we are left with the questions of metaphysics, philosophical speculation and belief.

The formation of the solar system from the primeval material, the motion of the planets round the Sun and the question of alternative life forms within the universe were considered during the second lecture; in the third he turned to the great opportunities offered by the discoveries of Jansky and Reber and the evolution of the science of radio astronomy out of the cataclysm of world war. The detection of radio emissions from interstellar hydrogen was soon followed by the discovery of localised sources in regions where there were no visible objects. Initially it was thought that these might be emissions from dark stars in the galaxy, but it was soon realised that they were coming from distant regions beyond the range of optical telescopes.

There was much speculation about the cause of the radio waves emanating from our own galaxy and Bernard contended that they did not originate from its individual stars. Radio telescopy had revealed that the Milky Way is surrounded by a corona and measurements at Jodrell Bank provided evidence of similar features around extragalactic nebulae. There was no final interpretation about these emissions, although Fred Hoyle was convinced that they were emanating from high energy particles in large magnetic fields.

Some of the strong localised sources were identified with unusual visible objects such as the Crab Nebula, the gaseous remains of the supernova, 4,000 light years from Earth, which was observed by Chinese astronomers in 1054AD. The gas from the exploding star moves through 70 million miles of space every day and it was believed that the turmoil caused by the high temperatures produced the radio emissions. Similar reactions had been found in the rather faint remnants of the supernova explosions observed by Tycho Brahe in 1572 and Kepler in 1604. Several thousand radio sources had been identified, evenly distributed across space in the same way as the millions of galaxies within the field of optical telescopes.

At Jodrell Bank Hanbury Brown and Hazard had been able to study the great spiral nebula in Andromeda, two million light years from Earth. Their detailed work in identifying several dozen similar nebulae had established that: "Amongst all the confusion that exists we can say that the spiral nebulae in the universe emit radio waves in the same way as our own Milky Way system." At Cambridge, Martin Ryle had identified a strong source in Cygnus and took very accurate measurements of its position. This enabled American astronomers, using the 200-inch optical telescope at Mount Palomar, to make a precise search of the region. They found that the signal coincided precisely with two great extragalactic nebulae which had collided; they lay at a distance of seven hundred million light years, the very limit of observation even with the Mount Palomar telescope; in spite of that distance the radio signal was very powerful. This had led to the idea that the majority of the signals being received from invisible sources might be from galaxies in collision with one another. The strength and size of the sources observed at Jodrell implied that they lay at a distance from Earth of many billions of light years; this opened up the possibility of probing the ultimate depths of time and space.

The fourth lecture examined state involvement in astronomical research, in the emergence of the new science and in the exploration of space. Many of these developments were motivated by political conflict and the fear of the military might of hostile regimes. They had resulted in massive investment by the United States and the Soviet Union which was justified to the people of each country as the unavoidable consequence of the growth of military power and the requirements of defence. The Sputnik programme had provided the Soviet Union with a major triumph and, although the Americans had not yet achieved such success, the proclaimed purpose of the enterprises was for geophysical and astronomical observation. However, the cost was enormous and it was well known that the launching rockets were military weapons with devastating potential. He concluded by observing that the fate of human civilisation would depend on whether the rockets of the future carried the astronomer's telescope or a hydrogen bomb.

In the last two lectures Bernard turned his attention to the origins of the universe and the problem of achieving a solution to the mysteries of existence. He dealt with the rival theories as to the evolution of the universe. On one side were those who contended that an infinitely dense and infinitely small concentration of matter, described by Abbé Lemaitre in 1927 as the primeval atom, exploded into the vast expansion that produced the cosmos as we know it. On the other were scientists such as Fred Hoyle, who believed in an infinite steady state of continuous creation and replenishment. Seven years later the discovery of microwave background radiation was to provide conclusive proof for the Big Bang; but at the time of the lectures the protagonists furiously raged together.

Both theories accepted that the universe consisted of at least several hundred million galaxies and that their reddened light, the redshift, proved that the universe is in a state of expansion. The galaxies in Hydra, for example, were moving away from us at a rate of 37,000 miles per second; in the space of one minute they would be nearly two and a quarter million miles further from Earth than they were sixty seconds before. An observer on Earth in the present day would be seeing the cluster as it was 2,000 million years earlier. But whether the universe was expanding from a primeval atom or doing so in a state of continuous creation from an infinite time in the past, we reach a stage where physical laws have nothing further to say. "At this point we pass from physics to metaphysics, from astronomy to theology, where the corporate views of science merge into the beliefs of the individual."

For those who associate the universe with God, the creation of the primeval atom is a divine act beyond the scope of scientific investigation and is consistent with the belief in a divine command: "Let there be light". Those who do not believe in a supreme being are left to ponder their inability to explain how the primeval atom came into existence; they can only speculate about a scientific explanation and argue that, in the fullness of time, science would find the answer; in doing so, they rely on faith and believe in the ultimate power of science just as surely as the religious rely on faith and believe in the ultimate power of God.

The conflict between the steady state and evolutionary theories of existence were likely to be resolved within a few years. Whether the universe began in a sudden explosion or had simply existed for all eternity, it seemed unlikely that there could ever be a final explanation for the origin of matter and cosmology must eventually give way to metaphysics. He believed that some of his scientific colleagues would agree with the concept of metaphysical thought; others would not contemplate any limit to the growth of scientific knowledge; some would be aghast at his temerity in discussing such issues. "As far as this group is concerned all I can say is that I sometimes envy their ability to evade by neglect such a problem which can tear the individual's mind asunder."

His lyrical finale to the last of the lectures has a poetic quality which deserves to be repeated in its entirety:

On the question of the validity of combining a metaphysical and physical process as a description of creation, this, as I said earlier, is the individual's problem. In my own case, I have lived my days as a scientist, but science has never claimed the whole of my existence. Some at least of the influence of my upbringing and environment has survived the conflict, so that I find no difficulty in accepting this conclusion. I am certainly not competent to discuss this problem of knowledge outside that acquired by my scientific tools and my outlook is essentially a simple one. Simple in the sense that I am no more surprised or distressed at the limitation of science when faced with the great problem of creation than I am at the limitation of the spectroscope in describing the radiance of a sunset or at the theory of counterpoint in describing the beauty of a fugue.

When I began my talks I mentioned the mixture of fear and humility with which I approached the task. Now you see the irony of the modern astronomer's life in its entirety. The devices of a world war have been forged, with the help of the fear of another, into a system of scientific experiments which take us back through time and space to deal with the origin of the universe.

The lectures provoked a huge response. There were articles in all the leading newspapers, which were full of praise for the series. He received letters from all over the world including such unlikely places as Delhi and Nyasaland. The vast majority were full of admiration. Philip Barford, a music tutor from Liverpool University, found the concluding paragraphs as deeply moving as a great poem or the second movement of Beethoven's last piano sonata; a schoolmaster, Kenneth Proctor, enclosed a donation to the telescope; the taciturn A.P. Rowe sent warm congratulations. There were cranky communications from the usual suspects; in a letter dated 12th November he was asked about "the suppression of discoveries of unknown flying objects, flying saucers and little green men of which I have ample evidence". Bernard replied politely but said that there was not a shred of evidence in support of flying saucers or messages from intelligent beings elsewhere in the universe. There were invitations to speak, more donations to the telescope fund, carefully thought out papers with suggestions and elaborate diagrams and one letterwriter who thanked him for brightening up Sunday nights and stimulating lengthy discussions at work on Monday mornings.

There were also a number of letters which bristled with religious fervour. Several of these were from creationists who expressed amazement at modern ideas of evolution. One anonymous correspondent took him to task severely for daring to depart from absolute adherence to biblical text:

No one can interfere with God's world. The Bible stands unshaken by so-called advancing knowledge. Its divine wisdom is a rock foundation. Man's opposing wisdom is shifting sand. Build your life here on rock so that you, Professor Lovell, will endure through perilous times. The truth of the Bible will free you from the pagan myth of evolution. Heed God's advice. Men like you are to be pitied.

Bernard seems to have retained his equanimity in the face of this diatribe. There was also a lively correspondence in *The Listener* magazine, provoked by a long letter from Arthur Koestler, which was published on 20th November 1958. Koestler accused Bernard of a "series of inaccuracies producing a distorted picture" about the persecution of Galileo. He claimed that the Church of Rome had accepted Galileo's conclusions and the theories of Copernicus and was not concerned that they undermined ancient doctrinal shibboleths. In the first of four letters to the editor, he claimed that, so far from persecuting astronomical research, the Renaissance Church actively encouraged it. He also disputed Bernard's assertion that Galileo had proved that the Earth and the planets were orbiting the Sun. A number of correspondents took up the cudgels over the succeeding weeks. Most were hostile to Koestler's views and were full of praise for the lectures. In one of the last letters, published on 18th December, Lord Brabazon of Tara wrote: "It is indeed sad that Professor Lovell's lectures are over for they have been fascinating."

Bernard maintained a dignified silence in the face of Koestler's criticism and just got on with the lectures but he did not have to wait long to get his own back. On 25th January 1959, the *Sunday Times* carried a review of Koestler's new book *The Sleepwalkers*. The book was a history of the development of cosmology from the Babylonians to Newton with lengthy sections on the lives of Kepler, Copernicus, Tycho Brahe and Galileo himself. The *Sunday Times* reviewer was none other than Bernard Lovell and he made the most of his opportunity. He began by describing *The Sleepwalkers* as "a valuable and provocative book, with a noble aim which is undermined by the author's process of double-think." He criticised the Koestler's hypothesis that the personality of scientists determines the direction of scientific advance; he suggested, as a useful tip, that he should examine the tortuous process through which scientific papers must pass before they are accepted by learned journals; and he recommended that Koestler would do well to study the life of Max Planck, whose quantum theory had ushered in a revolution in physics as great as that of Galileo in cosmology. He finished by congratulating the author for a remarkable piece of historical rebuilding and charged him with intellectual deceit. Koestler wrote a furious letter to the editor of the *Sunday Times*,[262] asserting that Bernard's assessment of Galileo was "flatly untrue" and accusing him of dismissing his arguments in a cavalier fashion. There the dispute ended. The last word on the Reith Lectures properly belongs to the Astronomer Royal, Richard Wooley. In his review of the full texts which were published in February he wrote:

> The Reith Lectures were an undoubted success and were heard and discussed by a large public. Throughout, Professor Lovell suffuses his text with a spirit of adventure and a belief in progress which it is impossible not to admire. All astronomers will salute the lectures and hope that they will serve to augment the stock of public interest in astronomy.[263]

CHAPTER TWENTY-ONE

Space Wars

The telescope was conceived as an instrument dedicated to scientific research. The quest for cosmic rays, which had brought Bernard to Jodrell Bank in 1945, had evolved into a much wider investigation probing the depths of space and the origin of the universe. The first operational use coincided with the launching of the Russian Sputnik and public enthusiasm was immediately aroused by Jodrell's astounding achievement in identifying the carrier rocket and its involvement in the unfolding rivalry between the Soviet Union and the United States. For the next ten years, the role of the establishment in the exploration of space was intimately involved in the space race. This did much to make up for the disappointing decision of the government not to participate and to restore pride in the exploits of British scientists.

Reports of the activities at Jodrell Bank gave the impression that the work of the telescope was concentrated on the tracking of satellites and rockets. In reality this took up very little of the time, ninety-nine per cent of which was filled with important research into the cosmos. In the early years the work had been based entirely on radar, but with the building of the transit telescope and the arrival of Hazard and Hanbury Brown there was a shift of emphasis towards radio astronomy. This research produced the first great discovery of extragalactic radio emissions from the Andromeda Nebula. Radar work continued with the old equipment, however, and the enormous power of the new instrument was used in conjunction with radar devices to track the Sputnik rockets and to send radar signals to the Moon.

In September 1959 Venus was at a close approach to the Earth. This provided the opportunity to transmit radar pulses to the surface and to retrieve the echoes as they returned after five or six minutes. The exact distance to the planet could be calculated by multiplying the speed of light by the time it took the signals to travel there and back. The attempt to obtain this data was carried out over five days but the signals were very weak and the exercise was inconclusive. The figures obtained did not match existing calculations with optical telescopes and although they were published in *Nature* they were widely regarded as unreliable.

The planet's next close approach was in April 1961. By this time the sensitivity of the equipment had been greatly improved and strong signals were obtained. The distance between Earth and Venus was calculated at 93.5 million miles and, although this still produced a discrepancy of 60,000 miles when compared with optical calculations, the figure was accepted internationally as being accurate. Throughout his years as director, Bernard scrutinised every one of the many hundred scientific papers which were submitted for publication. The 1959 paper on the distance to Venus was the only one he approved when he was less than confident in the results. It was a salutary lesson about the wisdom of releasing unreliable data.

Venus is entirely covered in cloud which made it impossible for optical telescopes to ascertain the direction and speed of its rotation. Using radar at Jodrell, in collaboration with the Russian astronomer Chugainov, and the tracking station on the Black Sea, it was eventually established that the planet is in retrograde motion; as it spins the sun rises in the west and sets in the east; the rate of rotation was found to be exceedingly slow; Venus rotates on its axis only once in every 243 Earth days. By the time these results were confirmed, on 9th January 1966, the Americans had beaten them to it using their extremely powerful military radar equipment. This led to the conclusion that the use of radar at Jodrell was now surplus to requirements. With much sadness on Bernard's part, the decision was taken to concentrate on radio astronomy rather than radar research. The equipment was finally switched off in 1966 and it was removed from the site by a scrap metal dealer; some of it had been there for over twenty years.

And Bernard never did find those elusive cosmic ray showers. The nearest that anyone came to doing so was when Francis Graham-Smith, who joined the staff at Jodrell as a Professor of Radio Astronomy in 1964, managed to pick up a radio signal from within a cosmic ray shower. He had a colleague working at the Atomic Research Establishment at Harwell, who was interested in radiation from charged particles, which were moving close to the velocity of light. Graham-Smith takes up the story: "In some circumstances, especially when they are travelling through the air, they can radiate a signal so that with a whole cloud of them, hundreds of thousands of them all radiating, you can actually pick up the pulse as the shower comes in. And we did that. So, I felt one up on Bernard; he had never detected a cosmic ray shower with his radar and I picked up its radiation."

The discovery of the extragalactic radio emissions led directly to the development of techniques designed to increase the resolving power of radio telescopes; they are able to plumb the very depths of space and time but cannot achieve the precise resolution, or definition, attainable with optical telescopes or even the naked eye. Operating on its own, the resolving power of the Jodrell telescope, when working on a wavelength of 1 metre, was about 1 degree of arc,[264] which is twenty times less efficient than the unaided eye. To match the resolving power of the biggest optical telescopes would require a paraboloid with a diameter of 140 miles; quite apart from the expense, the good people of Knutsford, Macclesfield and even Buxton would have some objections to such an instrument blocking out their sky.

The solution to this problem was first developed at Cambridge by Martin Ryle and Francis Graham-Smith using an idea suggested by their wartime experience. The air-interception radar on Beaufighters involved the use of two antennae, one on each wing, connected to the same receiver; this had the effect of narrowing down the precision with which it was possible to locate an object. A single aerial pointed at the sun will pick up radio activity but will not be able to pinpoint its exact location. Using two or more aerials set at some distance apart, it becomes possible to pick out small angular details: when the signals from the two aerials are combined they give a clearer view of the size and position of the source. Such a system is known as an interferometer. At Jodrell the enormous power of the main telescope used in combination with remote aerials led to a massive improvement in precision; the further apart the aerials were positioned, the better the resolution obtained. If they were close to one another they could be connected to the control room; by using cable and, later, radio links it was possible to locate the portable aerial many miles away and to increase the accuracy of the observations even more.

In the early 1950s, Graham-Smith improved the interferometer techniques and was able to establish the positions of radio sources with far greater accuracy than had previously been possible. At that time it was generally believed that these sources were dark stars within the Milky Way, commonly called radio stars. At Jodrell a number of these sources were found by Hanbury Brown and Hazard using the transit telescope. With the detailed measurements taken by radio astronomers, Walter Baader and Rudolf Minkowski at Mount Palomar were able to make precise searches and obtained visual contact with these radio sources; using the 200-inch telescope, they found both the supernova remnant in Cassiopeia and the distant extragalactic nebula in Cygnus. The discovery of this nebula led to the realisation that some at least of the apparently invisible dark stars were, in fact, extragalactic phenomena in the depths of space. Over the next few years many more such radio sources were discovered.

The first thing that had to be measured was the size of the particular source. As the interferometers were refined at Jodrell it became possible to pinpoint the boundaries of an object; by making large numbers of observations, a picture could be built up and the data could be stored and analysed to deduce its structure. Measuring the precise characteristics of these remote objects became a preoccupation and was a major contribution to the exploration of the cosmos. Of prime importance were the strength and frequency of the radio signals and how they changed with time. Different elements project signals at different wavelengths; neutral hydrogen, for example, emits signals on a wavelength of 21 centimetres; in 1963 wavelengths of 18 centimetres indicated the presence of the hydroxyl molecule in interstellar gas clouds; formaldehyde was found on a wavelength of 6 centimetres and the emissions from water molecules on a wavelength of 1.35 centimetres showed them to be among the most prominent constituents of matter in space.

The new telescope at Jodrell was used in conjunction with increasingly remote portable instruments and increasingly distant radio sources were found, some with angular diameters as small as 3 seconds of arc.[265] The precision with which these sources had been identified provided further opportunities for the Mount Palomar 200-inch telescope to attempt visual observation. In 1960 Minkowski photographed a cluster of galaxies in the vicinity of a strong radio emitter in the constellation of Boötes. The photograph extended to 3 minutes of arc; this is just a small fraction of the amount of the sky covered by the moon, which is half of 1 degree of arc. In this microscopic area he found no fewer than sixty previously unseen galaxies, of which one of the brightest was in the exact position of the radio source that had been identified. The redshift of this object suggested that it was receding at nearly half the velocity of light and was 4.5 billion light years from Earth.

As more of the unseen radio sources were located and measured, the signals from objects of even smaller angular size were identified and by constant examination and measurement their locations were fixed. Some of these extragalactic signals were emitted by very concentrated, point-like sources; by 1963 the spectra of these objects had been determined and it became clear that although they had the appearance of stars they were neither stars nor galaxies. The redshifts indicated that they were extremely remote and that their recessional velocities were in the order of eighty per cent of the speed of light. They were named quasi-stellar objects, or quasars. Although their electromagnetic signals appear to be faint because of their distance from Earth, quasars are strong radio emitters and are amongst the most luminous objects in the universe. It is now known that they are powered by gas which is being drawn into massive black holes at the heart of exceedingly remote galaxies. In the view of Francis Graham-

Smith, the discovery and identification of quasars was one of the most important achievements during Bernard Lovell's twenty-two years as director of the Jodrell Bank Telescope.

Bernard's primary role was that of the driver, pushing forward the development of ideas, encouraging innovative research, shaping policy and dealing with the University and the government. Graham-Smith remembers his energy and enthusiasm as the hallmark of his tenure during these years: "You can't look back on this period and say that Bernard wrote the key paper on quasars. He did not. But he made the place work. And he would oversee everything on the scientific side. All the papers were considered by him before being submitted for publication."

He did develop a special interest in one type of star which was discovered by the Dutch American astronomer Willem Jacob Luyten in 1948. These stars were in the category known as red dwarf stars, which are much cooler than the Sun and only visible with a telescope. They are generally dormant, subject to occasional sudden eruptions of brightness, from which they derive the name flare stars. The nature of these eruptions was of some interest, the question being whether they were similar to solar flares, which are radioactive, or caused by something else. As the nearest red dwarf was 300,000 times further from Earth than the Sun, any eruption would have to be many times more powerful than a solar flare if a radio signal was to be detected.

The demands on the time of the telescope were such that even the director had to book his slots but, when he did obtain access, Bernard set about finding any radio emissions that could be connected with the flares. He had been appointed to the Board of Visitors at Harvard where he renewed links with his old friend Fred Whipple. Whipple suggested that they should coordinate their research; he would photograph the flares in Massachusetts at the same time as Bernard made radio observations at Jodrell. As signals came into the control room they were fed through to charts on which they were automatically recorded in pen and ink. Bernard would lay out these long strips of paper on the table; when he examined them there were few indications of unusual signals but every now and then a bump would appear. There were not many of them; 700 hours of observations produced indications of just twenty-three flares, lasting up to eight minutes each. Comparison with the records from Harvard revealed that they coincided precisely with Fred Whipple's photographs. These findings were confirmed in experiments conducted jointly with Chugainov in Russia;[266] they were put beyond doubt in 1972, when a Greek astronomer, Mavridis, photographed a magnificent flare that also coincided with a radio signal at Jodrell.

This study gave Bernard the idea of exploring similar powerful emissions from K-stars, otherwise known as orange dwarfs. That this exercise never got under way was a source of some regret to him in his later years. K-stars have been stable for a very long time and they are of interest to those who are seeking evidence for intelligent extraterrestrial life. Bernard realised that if the emissions from these stars were as powerful as he believed, such a search would have proved fruitless; the strength of the flares would extinguish any chance of life, intelligent or otherwise.

As the search for quasars, remote radio galaxies and other objects deep in space continued, new areas of investigation were constantly opening up. Pulsating radio sources, which pumped out a regular signal and came to be known as pulsars, were discovered in 1967.[267] They also became a fertile subject for speculation about extraterrestrial life. In due course they were recognised as neutron stars, the exceedingly condensed remains of stars that have been destroyed in supernova explosions. It was believed that the regular signals they emitted were caused by the high speed of their rotation and they presented Jodrell with a huge field of further exploration for many years. Methodical search and measurement of the heavens revealed more and more radio sources in every area; they were carefully identified and catalogued before their positions were passed on to the great optical telescope operators, who would then attempt to find the visual counterparts of the radio signals.

From time to time experimental work was interrupted to monitor the further exploits of American and Russian spacecraft. The sensational manned space flights of Yuri Gagarin, on 12th April 1961, and John Glenn in Friendship 7 on 20th February 1962, were tracked with great excitement and other diversions from pure science followed. In 1966 the Russians succeeded in landing a space craft on the Moon. The rocket had been tracked from Jodrell Bank and when the module touched down, the telescope began to pick up the signals from its instruments. Bernard and John Davies were in the control room as this fascinating event unfolded, when suddenly, to their intense disappointment, the signals stopped.

"What a pity," said Bernard; "it's failed." As he spoke the words a picture began to appear on the screen.

"Good heavens," exclaimed Davies, "its transmitting a picture." As they watched the screen, an image began to resolve and it became clear that they were looking at a photograph of the surface of the moon. They managed to transmit the picture to a photocopier and the next morning it was published around the world in newspapers and on television. Nothing was heard from the Russians and it was several weeks before they admitted their success and released their own pictures, which looked slightly

17. *Above:* Thanks from Uncle Sam. Bernard Lovell with US President Eisenhower, 7 July 1960.

18. *Below:* In the control room at Jodrell Bank with Professor Alla Massevitch, the 'honey trap', 1961.

19. *Above:* Bernard Lovell with the first man in Space, Yuri Gagarin, 1961.

20. *Below:* Bernard Lovell holding up the first photograph from the surface of the moon, thereby annoying the Russians, 1966.

21. *Above:* Arise, Sir Bernard. Susan, Bernard and Joyce at Buckingham Palace to receive his knighthood, 1961.

22. *Below:* With Joyce, meeting the Queen Mother, 1967.

23. *Left:* From left to right: Vladimir Kurt, Roald Sagdeev and Bernard Lovell at the 250th anniversary of the Russian Academy of Science, 1974.

24. *Left:* Another royal visitor, the Prince of Wales at Jodrell Bank, 2003.

25. *Above:* The Leviathan telescope at Birr Castle, County Offaly.

26. *Below:* Lovell at Birr Castle, County Offaly, with Patrick Moore and the Earl of Rosse (right). *John C. McConnell.*

27. *Above:* The arboretum lake showing the line of poplars planted to commemorate Bernard Lovell's knighthood in 1961.

28. *Below:* Fifty years on and still in love. Bernard with Joyce by their lake.

29. *Above: Illicium Henryi* evergreen shrub from Western China planted in 1992 in the arboretum.

30. *Below:* 86, not out. With Irene Lamb at the Quinta, October 1999. *Courtesy of Andrea Dale.*

31. *Above:* Irene Lamb cooking sausages on the fire at Garinish West after the gas has run out.

32. *Below:* Four generations gather to celebrate ninety eventful years, 31 August 2003. *Courtesy of the Congleton Chronicle.*

different to the first photograph. It turned out that the equipment which produced the first images distorted the aspect ratio and squashed the picture by a factor of two. The Russians were annoyed that their tardy publication was pre-empted by several weeks and used the differences in detail as a reason to complain. Fifty-three years later, Professor Vladimir Kurt of the Lebedev Institute in the Russian Academy of sciences remembers his reaction as one of amusement:

> The first picture of the Moon when Sir Lowell [sic] had this picture before of our Network Station had this image. But is very fanny [sic] that Sir Lowell change X and Y coordinates of the image.[268]

The angry response of some Russian scientists to being scooped by Bernard is revealed in correspondence with Roald Sagdeev, now of the University of Maryland, in the United States:

> I was saddened to witness a rather petty anger among some of my younger colleagues in Soviet Academy after British newspapers published the first Lunik panorama pictures ahead of *Pravda*. Unfortunately it was reflected in many negative votes when Sir Lovell was nominated to become a Foreign Member of USSR Academy. Perhaps because of this incident we did not see much of Bernard Lovell in Russia lately.[269]

A photograph records the meeting of the three men in Moscow celebrating the 250th anniversary of the Russian Academy of Science in 1974.

One consequence of the Russian success was that it became clear, for the first time, that the lunar surface was solid and would be able to support the weight of an astronaut, in the event of a manned flight to the Moon. This was supremely important for the American Apollo missions. If, as some believed, the Moon's surface was made up of fine dust or sand, there was a real danger that astronauts weighed down with heavy equipment would become submerged. Even if they struggled back to the lunar craft, the vehicle itself could have sunk without trace or have become incapable of lift-off, marooning the passengers in the eerie landscape with no chance of escape.

The head of the manned space programme was George Mueller; when Bernard mentioned to him that the Russians were not intending to put a man on the Moon until they were sure of getting him back, Mueller replied that the Americans would do so in 1969, just as John Kennedy had predicted in his speech to Congress in 1961; everything was checked and,

OK, he said, apart from the small matter of lift-off from the Moon; this was the only manoeuvre that could not be tested. Landing men on the surface of the Moon was a huge calculated risk.

The dangers of the space race had become all too apparent in recent years. On 27th January 1967 three American astronauts were killed, when the cockpit of their craft caught fire during a simulated launch of Apollo 1. A few months later the Russians tested a manned prototype for their moon rocket; when it re-entered the atmosphere the parachute failed, the rocket crashed and the astronaut was killed. The Apollo 10 mission came as close as it could to replicating a moon landing without actually making one. The astronauts detached the lunar module and flew down towards the surface, before rejoining the main payload and returning to Earth; but no one knew how the module would perform on landing or whether a successful take-off could be achieved. There was only one way to find out.

On 16th July 1969, the moment the world had been waiting for arrived. Apollo 11 was launched from Cape Kennedy.[270] Neil Armstrong, Buzz Aldrin and Michael Collins set out on their Homeric journey into the history books, via a short stop on the surface of the Moon. It was less than twelve years since Sputnik 1 had burst through the upper atmosphere; these three men embarked on a voyage that would carry them half a million miles before they returned to Earth. The exhilaration of those three days as Apollo 11 sailed through space was unforgettable. Six months before, the hopes and imagination of the civilised world had been inspired by William Anders, Frank Borman and Jim Lovell; they spent Christmas Eve 1968 orbiting the Moon in Apollo 8 and read the first ten verses of the Creation story from the Book of Genesis to an astonished audience, a quarter of a million miles across the void. They then wished everyone a merry Christmas and concluded with the words: "God bless all of you on the good Earth." Three days later they splashed down safely in the Pacific Ocean.

The Apollo 11 expedition attracted a television audience of more than half a billion people across the world. Millions more heard the radio broadcasts and followed the unfolding drama in the newspapers. Unknown to most of them, the Russians had launched an unmanned spacecraft, Lunik 15, on June 13th. Its destination was the Moon. American scientists feared sabotage or at the very least a terrible accident. What were the Russians up to? They had known that Apollo was about to launch so why had they jeopardised the entire mission? Urgent assurances were sought from the Soviet scientists that they would not change the orbit of their spacecraft or interfere with Apollo 11 in any way. At Jodrell it was observed that the Lunik was on a very different lunar orbit from that of its predecessors and Bernard began to suspect that the Russians would attempt to stage a landing and a take-off whilst the American astronauts were on the Moon.

There were some anxious moments as Eagle, the lunar module, negotiated the final stages of the descent before landing in the Sea of Tranquility at 3.17 Eastern Standard Time on 20th July. Soon after landing Aldrin, who was a devout Christian, celebrated Holy Communion; this was not broadcast at the time because of a lawsuit which had been brought against NASA as a result of the earlier readings from Genesis, on the rather eccentric grounds that religion should not be promoted from above. Some hours later Armstrong emerged and climbed down the steps to utter his famous words: "That's one small step for man. One giant leap for mankind." Lest something should go terribly wrong, the television pictures were broadcast from NASA one minute after they arrived from the Moon. At Jodrell they received the direct signals from the Moon as well, so they had them in duplicate; a fact that lays to rest any of the arguments later advanced by moon landing deniers.

Whilst the Eagle was preparing for lift-off, the signal from the Russian rocket suddenly changed and it began to accelerate towards the Moon, where it crashed in the general area of the American module. Within the hour the President of the Soviet Academy of Sciences was on the telephone asking to be supplied with the data for the last few minutes of the flight of Lunik 15. Bernard said that he was quite happy to send it and would ensure that it went into the next diplomatic bag. No, he was told, that would not do. The data must be taken to Manchester airport; a Russian emissary was already on an aeroplane; he would collect it from there and fly straight back to Russia. It was obvious that the Russians had suffered a systems failure for which they could not account. Their real intentions became clear the next year, when another Lunik landed on the Moon, collected some rock samples and returned them to Earth; plainly this is what they had planned to do on 20th July 1969, in an attempt to steal at least part of the Apollo 11 thunder. Secretly they may even have hoped that Armstrong and Aldrin would be unable to escape, thereby giving their own effort an enhanced appearance of success. In the event, the Apollo mission triumphed, the three astronauts returned to a welcome fit for heroes and the Russians kept their heads down about their disastrous attempt to overshadow the American achievement.

It was Bernard's enthusiasm for creating a big dish that had driven him on through all difficulties and against huge odds, to build the telescope; as time went on, and the results proved its great value, it was perhaps inevitable that he should want to build a much bigger one, which could see even further into the universe. His ambition was to construct an instrument with a diameter more than double that of the Jodrell telescope. Husband agreed to consider the idea and prepared preliminary designs during the early 1960s. The plan was to build the new telescope, with a 600-foot aperture, near Welshpool, in the Welsh Marches. Even when the huge price tag dictated a reduction to 400 feet, there was much local opposition to the scheme and a public inquiry was held at which approval in principle was given. Husband built a scale model and everything looked set for the work to begin. In May 1970, the Undersecretary of State at the Department of Education and Science, Alice Bacon, visited Jodrell Bank and was very enthusiastic. The next day, Harold Wilson called a general election and all bets were off. The election was held on Thursday 18th June. To the surprise of everyone and the consternation of Wilson, the Conservative party won and Edward Heath became Prime Minister. Austerity was the order of the day, the axe fell and the whole project came crashing down.

By the time these plans foundered, important modifications had been made to the original telescope. The principle changes were a structural alteration to the supporting framework and the insertion of a more sensitive reflecting surface. The old dish remained in place and the new one was built on top of it. The cavernous space between the two reached a height of 30 feet at the centre and the whole structure was made much stiffer. The scientists were working with increasingly short wavelengths; on a wavelength of 10 centimetres a deviation in the bowl of more than half a centimetre is liable to distort the signal, so the rigidity of the structure was of vital importance. Husband claimed that these changes presented him with the most difficult task he had ever undertaken and Graham-Smith considers that it was a marvel of engineering. The telescope was out of commission for two years whilst the work was done, at a price which matched the cost of the original construction. The money was provided by the Science Research Council, which had taken over the responsibility for university funding from the DSIR. Just before Christmas in 1967 Bernard managed to strike a deal with the Council: he would delay his plans for the 400-foot telescope if they would pay for the modifications at Jodrell.

The use of the portable telescope had been complemented by fixed instruments, one at Jodrell, another 24 miles away and a third at Defford, the aerodrome which Bernard knew so well from his days at TRE. The definition obtained by the conjoined use of remote systems led directly to plans for more telescopes to be positioned across the country, as a massive interferometer. The absence of funding for the Welshpool telescope led Graham-Smith and others to the conclusion that an extended system provided the best way forward. When this idea emerged, Bernard's disappointment at the loss of his 400-foot instrument was quickly dissipated; as Graham-Smith confirms, he was always receptive to the ideas of others if they caught his imagination and he latched onto this one and made it work. As a result of the change of direction, MERLIN, the multi-element radio-linked interferometer, was created during the 1970s and six telescopes were in full operation across the country by 1981, soon after Bernard had retired as director.

As with everything else, his drive and initiative were vital elements in promoting the new array, but the key to his success was that he was a great communicator. Whether on a personal level or making a speech or broadcasting on the radio or television, he had an extraordinary talent for drawing in his audience; his many appearances with Sir Patrick Moore on *The Sky at Night* are a case in point. The warmth of his manner, his natural charm and his instinctive ability to share his thoughts and ideas with whomever he was talking to and to do so on equal terms were assets of incalculable value. Graham-Smith, who succeeded him as director, testifies to his influence and his ability to carry the politicians and paymasters with him: "This was the level at which he operated. Difficulties were overcome largely because he had made Jodrell a household name. He made it all work." The impact of MERLIN was immediately apparent and the array of telescopes enabled the scientists to make virtual maps of some of the most distant objects in the universe. Thirty-three years after Bernard's retirement, MERLIN, now upgraded and called E-MERLIN, based on the Lovell Telescope, remains a valuable resource for astronomers as they probe ever further towards the dawn of time.

The Cold War and the fear of nuclear attack haunted the world throughout this period. To counter the threat and at least provide some early warning, the British and American governments decided to create a system of defence at Fylingdales, on the North Yorkshire moors. This RAF establishment, which was known as the Ballistic Missile Early Warning System (BMEWS), should have been operational in 1960, but there were many delays and an alternative facility was needed to provide cover until BMEWS was ready. The tracking of Soviet rockets had provided a large body of data about radar echoes from ballistic missiles and the Air Ministry turned to Jodrell Bank. On 16th May 1958 Edward Truefitt, Deputy Scientific Adviser to the Air Minister, wrote to Bernard asking for help and a series of meetings were arranged with senior RAF officers and department officials.[271]

The wheels of government ground on slowly, but progress was made and it was agreed that the Air Ministry would supply a powerful Marconi Transmitter and a state-of-the-art receiver manufactured by Racal. Tests were conducted on meteors and the Aurora borealis and arrangements were made for RAF technicians to receive training at Jodrell so that, in the event of emergency, they could be deployed there immediately. It was thought that the facility would also provide back up for the existing radar defence systems and, on 29th December 1958, Air Vice Marshal Weston wrote to suggest that tests should be carried out on tracking a Canberra Bomber flying at 40,000 feet; these too were successful.

The operation was initially given the codename Project Verify. The Ministry was extremely sensitive about secrecy and to explain the presence of RAF staff at Jodrell it was said that they were being given background training in the tracking of spacecraft. The codename was changed somewhat randomly to Lothario and then to Changlin, on the ground that it had been compromised and it was eventually abandoned when the press got wind of the story. An article appeared in the *Daily Express* on 5th September 1961 and a full account of what was happening was revealed by Chapman Pincher on 21st September under the headline: "Jodrell is ready for Khrushchev". Pincher wrote that the system would give four minutes warning of nuclear attack, a report which provided some good lines for Peter Cook in the satirical review *Beyond the Fringe*. In Cook's impression of a speech by Harold Macmillan, the Prime Minister answers the suggestion that four minutes warning of nuclear attack is inadequate by reminding his audience that some people in our great country can run a mile in four minutes.

The story of Jodrell's involvement in defence was denied on all sides. Bernard, relaxing in the garden of his "large country house" was quoted: "I have absolutely no comment. As far as I am concerned, the telescope is engaged on astronomical research." The DSIR spokesman said: "It is probably only a rumour. Try the Air Ministry." When tried, the man from the Air Ministry came up with: "We don't know anything about it, but we would be prepared to cooperate with Sir Bernard in any way as we are very interested in space." It seems unlikely that the denials were believed by the reading public.

Peter Cook's view of the real value of early warning systems was shared by Bernard in later years. He recalled one of his meetings with Sir Maurice Dean, the Permanent Undersecretary of State for Air, at which Sir Maurice drew him to one side and said: "The Soviets have one thousand missiles targeted on London. I hope everything is in place so you can warn us of an attack."

"If you can tell us where they are," replied Bernard, "we will tell you when they lift off. But there is nothing you could do about it in seven minutes." (Pincher had got the time wrong.)

"On the contrary," said Dean. "In that time we could save one million people and scramble our bomber force to retaliate." What sort of nuclear desert would have greeted the one million saved when they emerged from their shelters was unclear.

Whatever its true value, the West was entirely reliant on Jodrell Bank during these years for an early warning system against nuclear attack. For most of the time this entailed being ready to use the radar facility at short notice, but during the Cuban missile crisis Jodrell was put onto red alert. Talks between Khrushchev and Fidel Castro during 1962 led to a secret agreement that Soviet missiles could be deployed from a base in Cuba. The work of constructing the launch sites proceeded with extraordinary speed and, on 15th October, an American U-2 spy plane took photographs, which clearly revealed what was happening. The Americans were appalled. They issued an ultimatum that the bases must be dismantled with immediate effect and announced a blockade of Cuba. Any vessels containing missiles or equipment would be intercepted and either impounded or destroyed.

The Russians responded to these threats with contemptuous fury. On 24th October Khrushchev proclaimed that a blockade on the high seas was an act of aggression which would propel the world into nuclear war. The antagonists had boxed each other into a corner and there appeared to be no escape from a plunge into Mutual Assured Destruction, or MAD, as it was appropriately called. For four long days, the world held its breath in thrall at the prospect of imminent annihilation. At Jodrell Bank the telescope remained steadfastly focused on the eastern horizon. On 28th October, Khrushchev blinked. The Russian ships turned back, the Soviets agreed to remove their bases and the threat of World War III was averted.

Eleven months later, on 15th September 1963, the establishment at RAF Fylingdales was finally opened. In August Bernard was invited on an official visit to inspect the premises; he was suitably impressed but felt relieved that his involvement in the defence of the realm was, once again, at an end. Some months later he entertained the officers and technicians from Fylingdales on a reciprocal visit to Jodrell. The Air Ministry decided that they no longer needed the equipment they had provided for the telescope. In one of his last acts before he left to take up a new post at the Treasury, a grateful Sir Maurice Dean assigned it to Jodrell Bank, where it remained on permanent loan for the peaceful pursuit of scientific knowledge.

CHAPTER TWENTY-TWO

The Incidental Spy

The work in which Bernard became involved during World War II and the Cold War was highly secret. This caused him no anxiety and he was always able to maintain the strictest confidence, even with those who were closest to him. His secretary, Anthea Hollinshead, who worked for him at Jodrell Bank from 1959 until 1968, testifies to his absolute discretion in all matters of security; the Air Ministry files for those years contain numerous letters from Bernard to government officials and members of the armed forces, many of which she typed; but he was scrupulous never to discuss with her any of the secret matters dealt with in the correspondence and she remained as discreet as her boss about such matters. Maintaining strict secrecy was one thing; but a somewhat bizarre series of events occasioned an apparent brush with the world of espionage, which caused Bernard a great deal of largely unnecessary anxiety.

On 30th October 1952 there was a report in the *Manchester Guardian* that a group of scientists at the University had sent a telegram to President Truman asking for a reprieve for Julius and Ethel Rosenberg who had been sentenced to death, in New York, for passing atomic secrets to the USSR during the Second World War. The case had attracted publicity across the world. There were many people who felt greatly troubled by the safety of the convictions and the extreme nature of the penalties and an international campaign for clemency began. Much of the support for the Rosenbergs came from well known communists and left-wing agitators, but the campaigners also included such eminent figures as the Pope, Picasso, Albert Einstein and Jean-Paul Sartre. The *Manchester Guardian* claimed that one of the signatories to the letter, Peter Astbury, was engaged in cosmic ray research at Jodrell Bank; the report continued that Astbury had been the British delegate at a Hungarian congress, where he made a strong attack on the British government's attitude to the Soviet-inspired World Peace Conference in Sheffield.[272] The suggested connection between Astbury and Jodrell provoked a furious response from a certain Professor A.C.B. Lovell, whose letter refuting the story with some vigour was published in the *Manchester Guardian* on 1st November.

As it happened, the newspaper was also wrong on a second front, having failed to pick up the fact that two of the signatories, Tom Kaiser and William Alexander Scott Murray, did indeed work at Jodrell. Tom Kaiser was a well known communist sympathiser, who had left his native Australia in disgrace, in 1949; he was a brilliant scientist and had been given his job in line with the University's enlightened policy towards discrimination on the grounds of creed or political views. Murray's background could hardly have been more different. His father, Leonard Warren Murray, was a rear admiral in the Royal Canadian Navy who had served with distinction in the Battle of the Atlantic. The Admiral and his wife moved to England after the War and lived at Chapel-en-le-Frith, near Buxton, where the Lovells had dined with them only a few weeks before the Truman telegram.

William Murray had joined the Royal Navy and served on convoy duties during the war. His name appears in the Navy list as a sub-lieutenant between 1943 and 1946, and when he was demobilised he went to Manchester University to study physics. After his graduation he was one of a number of students who joined the staff at Jodrell Bank. Bernard could not understand how such a fine young man came to be mixed up with the likes of Kaiser. He was extremely concerned about the reputation of his relatively new Department of Radio Astronomy and he was worried about the effect bad publicity might have on future funding. It was in this frame of mind that, on 31st October, he wrote to the Vice Chancellor, Stopford, in strong terms, expressing great concern that the link between Jodrell and the telegram might have serious consequences for his work; he asked Stopford to insist on a public apology from the miscrants. The Vice Chancellor agreed that it was a disgraceful episode and said that he had received letters of apology. That might have been the end of the matter, had there not been further adverse comment in the press as a result of the leaking of a telegram, which was addressed to Kaiser at Jodrell. The telegram was from the Rosenbergs' lawyer and requested Kaiser to testify on their behalf at the appeal hearing in the United States, with all expenses paid. This was the last straw for Bernard and he summoned Kaiser and Murray to his office.

"I am exceedingly displeased with your connection in this episode," he told them. "If you wish to take part in politics you will not involve Jodrell Bank. As for you, Murray, I know your parents. With your background, I am amazed at your involvement." After which the two young men left the office with, their tails, it was presumed, firmly between their legs. Not so Murray. A couple of minutes later he returned and spoke to Bernard as if he were the recalcitrant student and Murray the professor:

"Lovell!" he said. "If you talk to me like that, you can expect a visitor from London." A day or two later Bernard was handed a note on War Office writing paper, announcing the arrival of a Major K who wished to speak to him about Mr. Murray. The Major, who was wearing military uniform, was admitted.

"You had better take care with Murray," he barked. "He is one of our top agents. He has penetrated a communist cell in north-west England and must be left alone to carry on his work without interference from you." That was the end of the conversation; the Major nodded and walked out, leaving Bernard with his jaw dropping in amazement. There is no doubt that he took this story at face value and believed what he had been told, no matter how improbable it appeared; he included it in his autobiography with every indication that it was true, even to the extent of protecting the identities of Kaiser and Murray by calling them X and A.[273] It troubled him that he had become embroiled on the periphery of a murky world and he was relieved when Kaiser left the staff six months after the event; Murray followed two years later.

Bernard was involved in highly sensitive work during the war but he had not been in the secret service and if Murray really was a valued agent, it is unlikely in the extreme that MI5 would blow his cover, merely because he had been hauled over the coals by his boss. Could it be that the 'Major' was a stooge sent by Murray, as a practical joke, to get his own back for the dressing down Bernard had given him? The answer to this question is a resounding 'Yes'. Declassified documents in the National Archive show that William Murray was a communist, as were Kaiser, Astbury and a number of other people closely connected with the University. We have already seen that inside the brilliant mind of the scientist there lurked a rather charming naivety and a tendency to take people at face value unless and until the contrary was proved. This characteristic helps to explain some of the anxieties Bernard was to experience in later years.

It was the era of McCarthy; in America and even in Britain there was a feeling of suspicion towards anything out of the ordinary; the constant anxiety was encapsulated in the phrase "Reds under the bed". There was certainly a belief held by some in the local community that the strange activities at Jodrell Bank were being organised by a lot of communists; there was no logical reason for such a view but it certainly existed, as Joyce witnessed late one evening, when she arrived at the local train station with no means of getting home. A kindly gentleman, possibly Colonel Sir John Dixon of Astle Park, near Chelford, saw her plight and offered her a lift. Joyce said that she did not want to take him out of his way, to which he retorted: "I don't care who I give a lift to except those bloody communists at Jodrell." She accepted his offer, in spite of his opinions, and was much amused at his embarrassment when he recognised her as she got into the car.

As it happens, the Colonel's reservations were not as wide of the mark as at first appeared. There was indeed an active communist presence within the physics faculty of Manchester University and MI5 had strong suspicions about activities in the department and at Jodrell. Peter Astbury, the man whom the *Manchester Guardian* wrongly identified as a researcher at Jodrell Bank, joined the Communist Party whilst he was at Cambridge and the Security Service began to take notice of him in 1936 when his name cropped up in connection with other suspected communists.[274] He was a member of the Apostles and a close associate of Guy Burgess; when Burgess defected in 1951, a handwritten note from Astbury, written on Manchester University writing paper, was found amongst his papers at 10 New Bond Street; he was under surveillance for over twenty years.[275] During the War, Astbury managed to duck under the MI5 radar, obtained a commission, and achieved the rank of captain; he was captured at Arnhem and courted publicity after his release, claiming that he had been involved in phantom communications systems during the invasion. In 1947 he joined the staff of Manchester University as part of the cosmic ray team, and although not directly employed at Jodrell Bank, his work was connected with Bernard's original area of research and this connection brought suspicion to bear on the Jodrell activities and upon Bernard himself.

In a secret report dated 11th February 1952, "a reliable source" confirmed a decision by the Communist Party to form two cells at Manchester University.[276] One cell included Joseph Peter Astbury, Thomas Kaiser, William Alexander Scott Murray and other signatories to the Rosenberg letter, all of whom were physicists; the other, it was said, consisted of thirteen students and members of the teaching staff. Astbury's telephone was tapped for several years and the transcripts reveal that he had communist associates with close connections to senior members of the Faculty: these included Brian and Roger Simon, the sons of Lord Simon, the Chairman of the Council, and Brian's wife, Joan, who was an assistant editor of the *Times Literary Supplement*. All three were dedicated communists. Blackett himself was a committed socialist, and the activities of his cosmic ray group were of considerable interest to MI5; this is noted in an undated memo which named Lovell as a member of the group; it is clear that they were all regarded with grave suspicion:

> The relationship of Blackett to this cosmic ray team is very close
> indeed. It is a matter of considerable jealousy in the [physics]

department that Blackett's team is so extraordinarily favoured. Astbury has no more contact with Blackett than the others. One has, and that is Lovell. They all meet frequently in the laboratory or workshop or Professor Blackett's rooms and have private discussions from which all others are excluded. It is felt in the department that this is noticeably a clique.

Blackett has another team entirely outside the department at a place called Jodrell, near Chelford, which is near Knutsford. A team of four people work there, on top secret work, allegedly on the development of radar. These four are never seen in the college, but they are entirely supported and even fed from Manchester. There is a daily service by which food and materials which they require are transported to them. They live there. The only contact is through Lovell, who travels to and fro frequently.

All this gang are notoriously left, active members of the ASSOCIATION OF SCIENTIFIC WORKERS and talk left politics very freely.[277]

The febrile nature of these comments is matched by a number of inaccuracies. Bernard is named at one point as "Cyril Lovell (formerly of Bristol)" and there was nothing secret about what was going on at Jodrell at this stage; the suggestion of a gang of four being supplied from Manchester and of a Svengali, in the shape of Lovell, moving mysteriously between them and the communist sympathisers in the physics department, is nothing short of ludicrous. Bernard had welcomed the election of the Labour government after the war,[278] but he was not, essentially, a political animal, and he was certainly never a communist, by inclination or by membership of the party. His life was dominated by the pursuit of science and, his troubles with the PAC aside, he enjoyed good relationships with governments of all persuasions, something which could not always be said of Patrick Blackett. There can be no doubt of his allegiance to Queen and Country and he had served with honour and distinction during the war.

But the suspicion under which he and the department came in the early 1950s may well have had an impact upon events in later years. The William Murray incident, which he took entirely at face value, worried him greatly at the time, and continued to puzzle him for many years afterwards. It was easy enough to work out that Kaiser was one of the two, but Bernard did not confirm the names of the two people involved in the incident until a few weeks before his death, when I asked him who they were. At the age of ninety-eight his mind was as sharp as ever and he instantly replied: "Kaiser and Murray." National Archive papers and Manchester University records at the John Ryland's Library have established beyond doubt that, sixty years after the events, the accuracy of his remarkable memory was unimpaired. But he still believed that Murray was a spy.

In February 1953 President Eisenhower rejected the Rosenbergs' appeal for clemency and they were executed in the electric chair on June 19th 1953. Papers released by the United States in 1995 strongly suggested that Julius was guilty but that his wife may have been the victim of a terrible miscarriage of justice. Their story remains a fertile ground for controversy in the United States.[279]

As we have seen, the tracking of Sputnik was the catalyst for a close association over the next six years between Bernard and the ministries responsible for defence. During this period he was in regular contact with the Ministry of Defence and the Air Ministry and, in particular with Sir Maurice Dean. This produced a substantial body of highly secret communication discussing the details of the defence systems which were required, the plans for a permanent establishment at Fylingdales, the problems and delays in setting it up, and the threat posed by the Soviet Union.[280] The expansion of Project Verify ran in parallel with Bernard's growing cooperation with Russian scientists, and the rival interests of Russia and Britain placed him in a somewhat invidious position. Not that he ever fully appreciated the conflict. His mind remained focused on the science; for him, international cooperation was a vital ingredient and the secret world of defence and surveillance was a distracting sideline.

His first direct contact with Soviet scientists occurred in 1955, when a group of them arrived at Jodrell Bank for a visit, on their way to a meeting of the International Astronomical Union, which was held in Dublin, because the American scientists, who did not share Bernard's interest in cooperating with the Russians, refused to go to Moscow. Following the help he had given with the Sputnik programme, he was made very welcome in Moscow when the next AIU conference was held there in August 1958. On this first visit to the Soviet Union he went to a number of scientific establishments and was particularly struck by the contrast between the lavish hotels where they were entertained and the neighbouring hovels in which the ordinary people of the Soviet Union lived.

In February 1961 the Russians launched a space probe to Venus. Soon after its departure they lost track of it and several months later they turned to Jodrell Bank for help. Professor Alla Massevitch, who was in charge of Soviet space tracking, had been to Jodrell Bank in 1960 and she led the Russian delegation, which arrived in June and spent several weeks with Bernard, looking for their lost spaceship. They evidently enjoyed themselves and were well looked after during their stay. Alla Massevitch went on several outings with Bernard's secretary, Anthea Hollinshead. One day she drove Alla Massevitch over to Haddon Hall and Bakewell in Derbyshire; she describes the Russian scientist as a lovely woman, who enjoyed the local delicacy, a Bakewell tart, and was much amused by a display of Morris dancing.

One Saturday morning, Bernard told the Russians that they were more than welcome to continue looking for their rocket all afternoon, but that he was going to play cricket. Alla Massevitch said she would come with him. Quite what she made of our national game remains a mystery; all that she saw of it was a group of twenty-two grown men in white flannels and two more in long white coats, who spent the whole afternoon in the pavilion casting gloomy looks at the lowering clouds and complaining about the rain. The search for the Venus rocket was rather more successful, although it never reached its objective; they discovered that it had gone into orbit round the Earth; but at least they traced it and the help they had received from Bernard and his team was much appreciated, in spite of the cricket.

On 25th June 1963, Bernard set off on a three-week visit to the Soviet Union, at the invitation of the President of the Russian Academy of Sciences, Mstislav Keldysh. The Cold War was at its height, it was only eight months since the humiliation of the Russians during the Cuban crisis and Bernard had been involved in the surveillance of Russian missile sites for several years. Under these circumstances a three-week visit to the heart of the enemy camp posed obvious risks for his safety. The dangers never occurred to Bernard, nor were they pointed out to him by the Security and Intelligence Service, or the government, which encouraged him to go. The British establishment was eager to find out all it could about the Soviet facilities, which were shrouded in secrecy.

He was met at the airport in Moscow by Alla Massevitch, who expressed surprise that Joyce was not with him. He said that she had not been invited but Massevitch insisted that she must join him at the first opportunity and arrangements were made for her to fly out towards the end of the trip. The meetings, conferences, lectures and dinners of the first two days heralded a punishing programme, which continued unabated until the middle of July. On 28th June he was flown down to the Crimea, but had time before he left to take a telephone call from home, bringing the news of an extraordinary finish to the second Test Match, at Lords, when Colin Cowdrey saved the day by coming out to face the mighty West Indian fast bowlers with his broken arm in plaster.

Two days touring the facilities in the Crimea culminated in a visit to the most secret installation of all, at Yevpatoria. He was the first foreigner to have been allowed access to the Soviet Union's newest space-tracking station. That he had been invited at all was a surprise to the scientists in charge of the establishment, who made arrangements which were clearly designed to reduce contact between their foreign guest and staff at the establishment to a minimum. The visit was closely controlled. The radio astronomer in charge of the Deep Space Network at Yevpatoria, Leonid Matveenko, recalls the day:

> I received an order from the Academy of Sciences of the USSR to organise coming of Director of JB Radio Observatory Prof. B. Lovell. It was very surprise. DSN was top secret territory. But B. Lovell had special status – guest of Pres. of AS USSR academician M.V. Keldysh, Head of Space Program, which invited of Prof. Lovell for participation in the Lunnic program. We had a problem with visit of Prof B. Lovell. We decided organised holyday and sent all staffs at a beach. DSN entrance was opened and we waited a car with three passenger. I was very surprised when two cars moved to DSN. I met the first car with our guests (Lovell, Shlovsky and Khromov) and we came to special office for discussion. Passengers of the second car (A. Massevich, N. Kardashev, V. Slish) were waiting outside.[281]

He was given the freedom to observe every part of the establishment. Matveenko would not allow him to take photographs and he had to leave his camera in the office; but the Russian had not bargained for his guest's incredible memory for the details he observed during the course of an unbearably hot day, relieved only by a bathe in the cooling waters of the Black Sea.

In the evening, Alla Massevitch told him that he was to be the guest of honour at a midsummer banquet. This was the last thing Bernard wanted, but he had to go. There was much drinking of vodka and numerous toasts before the dancing started at eleven and he was dragged onto the dance floor by several Russian ladies, none of whom spoke a word of English. Then:

> With Khodarev rather merry and no chance of conversation I betook myself to bed having noticed the absence of M and the rest. But in the morning she said, oh no, they had gone...to see a film of the Berkley IUA meeting and had returned to continue the dance at midnight. What a woman![282]

Massevitch was one of a number of distinguished scientists who accompanied Bernard during his tour of the Soviet Union. He had got to know her well during her visits to Britain and suggestions have been made that her presence throughout the visit was a deliberate plot designed to entice him to remain in Russia. He undoubtedly admired her, as the above diary entry indicates; but if she was cast, by her masters, in the role of a Mata Hari, the honey trap was ineffective and he resisted the temptation to succumb to her charms.

They flew back to Moscow and, on 5th July, to his great delight, he was joined by Joyce; but there was no let up in the itinerary. They travelled by night-train to Leningrad, went to the Hermitage and were conducted on a tour of the city during which they were made Honorary Citizens by the Mayor. They visited Peterhof and were taken to the ballet; everything possible was done to make them feel welcome. The next day they flew down to Armenia. There followed a terrifying drive through the mountains with a crazy official driver; the observatory at Byurakan was of great interest and, once again, Bernard was given full access and was able to discuss the latest advances in Russian knowledge with complete freedom. The last two days of their visit were spent back in Moscow, with further talks and lectures and a farewell lunch hosted by Keldysh.

It was during this lunch that a conversation occurred which may give a clue to the openness and warmth of Bernard's reception in the Soviet Union. In discussing his ambition to build an even larger telescope than the one at Jodrell, he mentioned the difficulty of funding such a project, which would cost, he said, 50 million roubles.[283] Pyotr Kapitza told him that such a sum was only a small percentage of the annual budget available to Keldysh. At this point, the President turned to him and said that, if he would remain in Russia, they would build the instrument for him. Bernard's response was that, as an Englishman, he had no desire to do so and wanted to return home; he then asked that Kapitza might be allowed to visit him at Jodrell.

This invitation was afforded a distinctly frosty reception by Keldysh, who said that it might be possible to arrange once Kapitza had finished his work in Russia. Kapitza had spent ten years in Cambridge working under Rutherford, but when he visited his homeland in 1934 he had not been permitted to return to Britain and was forced to continue his research in Russia. He was one of very few men who quarrelled with the head of Stalin's NKVD, Beria, and lived to tell the tale. The reaction of Keldysh to Bernard's request was a sinister reminder that the freedom enjoyed by scientists in the West was not universal; It was clear to him that Keldysh wanted him to remain in Russia and the thought even crossed his mind that, as the authorities had held onto their passports when they entered the country, he and Joyce might be refused permission to leave. They were relieved to get on the aeroplane which took them back to London and even happier to arrive safely back at The Quinta the following evening.

When he returned from this arduous expedition, Bernard was in a state of exhaustion and, within a few days, he became extremely ill. That he was very unwell for several weeks after his return from Russia is beyond question. Bryan Lovell and other members of his family attest to this, as do a number of other people, including his secretary, Anthea Hollinshead. He managed to keep going for a time in spite of his illness. He sent a detailed account of his observations to Lord Hailsham at the Ministry of Science,[284] in which he expressed his enthusiasm for developing international cooperation between radio astronomers. These thoughts included plans discussed with Matveenko for using the telescopes in the Crimea in conjunction with Jodrell Bank as a Very Long Baseline Interferometer (VLBI) to obtain the greatest possible angular resolution of remote radio sources. He also outlined Russian suggestions for cooperation with Britain and America in the space programme, the tracking of lunar and deep space probes and the landing of manned spacecraft on the Moon.

Hailsham discussed these ideas when he went to Washington in August, but the Americans were not interested and said that, if the Russians wanted them to cooperate, they should approach them directly. Hailsham thought that the American plans to put a man on the Moon by 1970 would be best carried forward on an international basis; but he felt that he could go no further in the light of the American attitude:

> I think we shall get more kicks than ha'pence if we try to act as an honest broker in this matter. I suggest that you tell Sir Bernard Lovell that we have taken the matter up with the United States authorities and that they are disinclined to pursue the suggestion unless the Russians are prepared to make the first move and that we sympathise with their point of view.[285]

So, although Jodrell Bank and the Crimean facilities were used in conjunction to create a VLBI, wider international cooperation was shelved. The visit to Fylingdales took place on 9th August, as planned, but it was not until Bernard went to Ireland later in the month, to join Susan and her husband, John Driver, for a holiday, that he began to feel better. Until then, he had felt totally disorientated and he considered giving up his work completely. At one moment he felt so depressed that he wrote to the bursar to tender his resignation and announced, rather bizarrely, that he was thinking of taking holy orders. Fortunately for Science and the Church, his resignation was not accepted and the effect of the holiday, the sea air and several rounds of golf in the bracing winds restored him to health.

The cause of his illness was never diagnosed. Bernard firmly believed that it was the result of an attempt by the Russian authorities to poison him with radioactive material, perhaps to remove his memory of the things he had seen in the Soviet Union or even to kill him – dead men tell no tales. This possible cause for his malaise was suggested to him by the Joint Intelligence Agents who debriefed him, once he had recovered, and the view he arrived at was that, during the visit to Yevpatoria, they had subjected him to powerful radiation.

The Russians must have known that Bernard had been involved in monitoring the potential threat of attacks from their missiles, and the part he played in the defence of the west during the Cuban crisis, not least because the story had been blown in the British press by Chapman Pincher. They had a motive, therefore, to do away with him, if it suited their purposes. From Tsarist Russia to the Kremlin of today, the Russian secret services have never scrupled to harm or murder those whom it chooses. The poisoning of Alexander Litvinenko provides a recent illustration of their ruthless methods. No doubt they would have valued Bernard's defection both to prevent his usefulness to the West and to harness his knowledge and experience to their own endeavours. As for harbouring expectations that he might defect, it seems likely that they will have known of the suspicions under which he and the Manchester Physics Faculty had fallen in the 1950s, not least because of the connection between Peter Astbury and Guy Burgess. Such knowledge may have fostered hopes that he was indeed a communist sympathiser.

Bernard was debriefed on his visit to Russia by the Joint Intelligence Bureau. The debriefing papers, which are dated October 1963,[286] show that he was working closely with the Intelligence Service and that the Department had no doubts about the potential danger into which the visit had put him. The secret report on 'The Visit of Professor Sir Bernard Lovell to the Soviet Union' was to be given limited circulation on a need to know basis only:

> The reason is obvious since he is cooperating with the Russians
> on a scientific programme not connected with intelligence and
> his connection with intelligence must be safeguarded.

These documents were classified until after his death in August 2012, on the grounds that their disclosure would endanger his life. Even then they were only released after an application under the Freedom of Information Act. There is no doubt that his trips to Russia and his contacts with Russian scientists were used by the security services to obtain all the information they could about Soviet installations. They encouraged him to go, regardless of the dangers; when he returned, they interviewed him at length to learn everything he could tell them about the enemy. Whether he knew it or not, he was used as a spy.

The debriefing in October 1963 was very thorough and Bernard described all he had seen. It confirms that the Russians removed his camera, returning it to him solely for sightseeing, so he was unable to take photographs; but he was able to retain the detail in his mind until he could note them in his carefully concealed diary; he later used the notes when he reported back to British security. The location and even the existence of the Yevpatoria base had been a closely guarded secret but Bernard worked out the distances they travelled from the instruments in the car and was able to provide the exact location, including a grid reference; he also prepared a sketch map showing the various installations they took him to close to the Black Sea. He gave detailed explanations of all the apparatus he saw and of its capability; this included "the most powerful interplanetary radar system in the world", as well as paraphernalia used for radio astronomy. There was an underground hall with a magnificent array of equipment, including the master frequency drive; no one without special authority was allowed into this room, which contained a quartz crystal. The power of the transmitter dishes was so great that they were never operated at an elevation below 10 degrees, because of the danger of radiation. The precise specifications of everything he was shown are set out in minute detail in the debriefing documents. The entire establishment had been constructed and put into operation within one year, demonstrating just what can be done when money is no object.

As for the Russian plans for the future, there was to be particular concentration on radar rather than radio astronomy and a push for more powerful transmitters and receivers. The implications of these applications for systems of defence are obvious. They were much more interested in plans to rendezvous in space than in attempts to put a man on the Moon; their primary objective was to establish a large orbiting space station. This would be manned and would circle the Earth at the lowest height possible, consistent with remaining in orbit. The ostensible purpose was improved astronomical observations, but the uses of such a platform for observation of the enemy on Earth were also quite apparent. The report concludes with biographical notes of the most important people he had met in Russia; these included radio, radar and signals experts as well as astronomers.

Had the KGB known the full extent of the information which the British Professor was to pass on to their counterparts back in London, they would no doubt have made sure that he did not get home at all. It is evident that the British authorities gave the quest for information a higher priority than the welfare of one of their greatest scientists, who had, by this time, become a national treasure. As it is, we shall never know for sure whether the illness he suffered on his return was spontaneous or induced. On one hand, his diary records that he was not feeling very well when he arrived in Russia and was suffering from an eye infection at the time of the visit to the Crimea. On the other, when Joyce joined him in Moscow she was so shocked by his appearance that she hardly recognised the husband who had left her at home only two weeks earlier. When he returned to England he became very ill and the nature of his malady was never diagnosed.

There is evidence of a motive and of the opportunity to harm him. At least one senior Russian scientist, Matveenko, regarded his visit with surprise or even suspicion; others, including Roald Sagdeev, thought him "courageous" to become involved with the ruthless Soviet Union at the height of the Cold War. The Russians must have been aware that he was engaged in anti-missile surveillance, especially at the time of the Cuban crisis. He recalled that, during the visit to Yevpatoria, he was left on his own in the transmission room for a few minutes, which could have provided an opportunity to harm him, using dangerous radiation from the powerful transmitter; motive and opportunity have long been regarded as strong evidence of guilt in our criminal courts. Towards the end of his life he spoke of these matters to the press on several occasions and was clear in his own mind that he had been poisoned with radiation. Some people, including Bryan Lovell, incline to the view that he was suffering from extreme exhaustion; others feel that the coincidence of the onset of illness and what we know today of Russian methods indicate the dark hand of the KGB.

The diary of these events, which was released by the John Ryland's Library soon after Bernard's death, contains very little information that was not already in the public domain and offers no clues to the mystery. On the question of a Russian plot, the jury is still out and is likely to remain there. But the documents, which were held for so long in the secret files of the Ministry of Defence, leave no room for reasonable doubt that, during his visit to Russia, Bernard Lovell did his duty as a patriotic Englishman: his dedication to Allied victory during the War had never wavered; in the Cold War he did not hesitate to put the instrument he had created at the disposal of the West; and the MOD papers show that when his expertise was needed once again, he did not pause for a moment in answering the call to act as a spy in the service of his Queen and his country.

CHAPTER TWENTY-THREE

Renaissance Man

In Ancient Greece, the accomplishments of a man or woman were measured by the extent to which he or she approached a condition of intellectual and physical excellence known as *arete*;[287] this indicated a wholeness and nobility of conduct and thought that transcended the ordinary run of experience. In Homer, Odysseus and Penelope illustrate this perfection of human endeavour, which has never been better described than in Robert Whittington's representation of Henry VIII's chancellor, Sir Thomas More:

> A man of an angel's wit and singular learning. I know not his fellow. For where is the man of that gentleness, lowliness and affability? And, as time requireth, a man of marvelous mirth and pastimes, and sometime of as sad gravity. A man for all seasons.[288]

That Bernard Lovell possessed those qualities in abundance is beyond question. He was the personification of *arete* and epitomised the concept of the Renaissance man or, in rather less attractive twenty-first-century speak, the polymath.

It was impossible to meet him without being struck by his easy, self-effacing charm. He could be very direct and his clarity of thought drove him to pursue his aims with a relentless persistence and energy throughout his life. But on a personal level he had a natural respect for other people, which enabled him to relate to them on any level and never to impart any sense of his superior intellect or talk down to them at all. My clearest experience of this quality arose one winter evening in 1995, when my wife and I went to a dinner party given by Michael and Zoe Ashbrook at Arley Hall. After the ladies retired to the drawing room I found myself sitting next to Bernard. The fire blazed in the grate and candles flickered down the long table. As the port went round I asked him some more or less inane question about the speed of light. For the next fifteen minutes I was treated to an extraordinary exposition about Einstein's theory of relativity, the properties of light, the redshift and expansion of the universe. I listened entranced as he unfolded these difficult concepts in terms which even I could readily understand; yet he did so in a way that did not for a moment leave me feeling like the ignorant layman I undoubtedly was. It was an unforgettable experience; I was sorry when it ended and we had to join the ladies.

Three days later a package arrived for me in the post. Inside it was a copy of Bernard's book *In the Centre of Immensities*, and a short note:

> I hope you will find the enclosed helpful. When these subjects arise in the future, I shall always remember our candlelit conversation at Arley.
> Yours ever,
> Bernard.

To make such a thoughtful gesture and to send such a note was second nature to Bernard; but to the recipient it was an act of great kindness and remarkable charm. The book[289] is by far the best and most accessible history of the cosmos that has ever been written, even today. Its foundation was the presidential address that Bernard gave to the British Association for the Advancement of Science in 1975, but for the title the credit must go to Joyce. Bernard had written the lecture and read it out for her approval. "But what shall I call it?" he mused.

"'In the Centre of Immensities', of course," was her immediate response, referring to Thomas Carlyle's *Sartor Resartus*:

> What is Man? Who sees and fashions for himself a Universe, with starry spaces and long thousands of years...skywoven and worthy of a God. Stands he not, thereby in the centre of Immensities, in the conflux of Eternities?

Written nearly twenty years after the Reith Lectures, the book deals with the history of the universe from the perspective of 1977. There was no longer any doubt that it was expanding from a hot Big Bang, the existence of the microwave background radiation had been established and a great deal had been learned about the nature of the expansion and the conditions under which it occurred. What had not changed was Bernard's belief that science would never fathom the ultimate mysteries, but he was no more troubled by this in 1977 than he had been in 1958. He was still convinced that the conflict between science and religion was an illusion and that the search for a scientific solution to the meaning of existence must always revert to metaphysical ideas and to questions of faith. In his conclusion he cites the view of the Swiss physicist, Markus Fierz,[290] that: "the scientific insights of our age shed such glaring light on certain aspects of the experience that they leave the rest in even greater darkness." The last words of the book echo the finale of his Reith Lectures:

> We can apply the spectroscope to gain an understanding of the sunset; we can send a space probe to Venus; but we may never apprehend the ethos of the evening star.

Many people attest to the instinctive charm which was a key ingredient in Bernard's make-up and there are numerous examples of his kindness and generosity. Anthea Hollinshead, who was his secretary during the 1960s, describes him as a wonderful boss who was a pleasure to work for and both indulgent and considerate as the need arose; at one stage he gave her ten months leave of absence, to visit her family in New Zealand and go round the world – a secretary's sabbatical, as she describes it. Some years later, whilst Bernard was in America, she slipped on the highly polished floor in the office and broke her ankle; this was long before the compensation culture of today, but on his return Bernard was so concerned at what had happened that he immediately gave orders for all floors to be sanded.

Janet Eaton worked at Jodrell for many years and became his personal secretary in 2003, working every day at The Quinta. She was devoted to Bernard and describes him as "a perfect gentleman – a lost breed! It was a great privilege to work for him so closely in his later years. You always knew where you were with him and he knew what he wanted. He had such a brilliant memory, that even if it took a bit of time to remember something, you got there eventually." And the magic of the spell he cast affected people of all ages.

Alex Wilbraham remembers growing up in the shadow of Jodrell Bank and wondering whether the man who had built it might be acquainted with God. These thoughts were confirmed when his parents mentioned his name in conjunction with the moon and the stars, and were put beyond a peradventure in Church, when, as the last echoes of the organ died away, Bernard would emerged from behind it. Alex was invited to Jodrell Bank with his father at the time of the Apollo 11 landings and was thrilled to see a tractor on the surface of the Moon. As he grew older Bernard was always ready to organise visits to the telescope for him and his brothers, and to help them unravel the complexity of schoolboy physics.

This ability to relate to all sorts and conditions of people was important to many aspects of his life. In the difficult years of the construction of the telescope he was able to maintain good relationships even with those who were critical of his management of the project. His relationship with Russian scientists was recalled with great affection by many of them. Roald Sagdeev has paid tribute to the way in which he pioneered international cooperation. Leonid Matveenko praises him as one of the first pioneers of radio astronomy and speaks of pleasant memories of the time he spent with Bernard; when he visited Jodrell some years later he was pleased to be presented with two of his books, although it is interesting to note that Bernard was not present during this visit. He did, however, entertain another Russian scientist, Pyotr Kapitza, who was finally allowed to leave Russia and to visit Jodrell Bank as a winner of the 1978 Nobel Prize for Physics.

After Sputnik Bernard never faltered in his dealings with the press and did a great deal to raise the profile of the telescope and keep it in the forefront of public attention. Even in old age his influence continued to hold sway and there were frequent reports and articles and regular television appearances on programmes such as *The Sky at Night*, hosted by Patrick Moore, who admired him greatly and described him as the Isaac Newton of radio astronomy. In 2008 BBC television featured a report on the Lovell Telescope. Once the filming was over, Tim O'Brien, the associate director in charge of communications, was taking the interviewer to her car when she caught sight of a venerable figure, with a walking stick, coming out of the control centre.

"Is that Sir Bernard?" she asked. "Do you think he would say a few words?"

"We had better ask him," replied O'Brien. They did and he would, without any hesitation.

Janet Eaton talks of the astonishment of many interviewers from the newspapers or television at his instant recall of events which occurred before they were born. In 2010, as part of the celebrations to commemorate the 70th anniversary of the Battle of Britain, he was interviewed for a feature on the television news. He was ninety-seven at the time and the young lady who was conducting the interview agreed with Raymond Lowe's suggestion to film it by the lake. Bernard was wheeled out, everything was set up and the camera began to roll. The interviewer asked her first question and Bernard started to talk. Twenty minutes later the interview ended and, as they made their way back to the house, she turned to Ray and said:

"I only asked him one question. He answered the rest without me asking them – we shall have to dub them in. What a brilliant man!"

The exposure gained by the success of the telescope soon led to public requests to visit Jodrell Bank. Bernard was very enthusiastic about broadening participation and acceded to these whenever he could; unfortunately, the demands of research and teaching restricted the time and space available for visitors. In 1964 Bernard persuaded the University to erect a marquee and to allow visitors for a period of two weeks, by way of experiment. It was a huge success. The entrance fee was half a crown,[291] long queues formed in each direction and over 35,000 people came. The experiment was repeated in 1965 and did so well that the University agreed to create a permanent centre, which was opened on 3rd May 1966. In 1971, a planetarium was added and a thirty-acre arboretum was planted by the department of botany. For the next three decades, to Bernard's great joy, more than 100,000 people visited every year. He was always ready to greet them and impart his enthusiasm and knowledge to the armies of visitors. By the time these visitor facilities were pulled down in 2003, much to Bernard's disappointment, many of those who were bringing their children to Jodrell had first been taken there by their own parents or on school trips.

At the centre of his life was the family, with Joyce at its heart. During all the years of difficulties she supported and sustained him and her loyalty to him never wavered. Through the turmoil of war and in the trials of peace she was the foundation stone of his existence and he relied on her sound judgement and took her advice, which invariably proved to be right. She had firm views about the things that mattered and a sure and decisive mind; this was tempered by a wonderful sense of humour and a calm approach to solving the most intractable problems. That their family life was so happy and untroubled was due in large measure to the warmth and love with which she surrounded them all; and he was a wonderful father; as Bryan Lovell says: "He was absolutely straight with you and you always knew where you were; anyone you talk to will tell you that; I am very proud of him." It was a cause of great joy and pride to Bernard and Joyce that each of their five children should follow the example of their parents' long and happy marriage, faithful to the last, as they had promised on their wedding day in 1937.

Holidays in Ireland were a great release from the scientific treadmill. Bernard had recuperated there in 1963, after his trip to Russia and fell in love with the country and its people. In 1966, he bought the island of Garinish West in Bantry Bay as a present for Joyce on the occasion of her fiftieth birthday. There he built a house for her, ferrying everything over by boat from the mainland nearby. A telephone cable was laid across the seabed, but for many years they relied on portable gas cylinders for energy. It became and remains a haven for the whole family. Visitors would be introduced into the delights of island life by being required to swim round it on their arrival; if it was safe enough for the short crossing it was, presumably, safe enough to bathe, even if the waters were on the chilly side of cold. The Earl of Rosse, whose family had become great friends of the Lovells, remembers his initiation with something less than sheer delight, but once it was over, the welcome was all that he could wish for.

The connection with the Rosse family and their home at Birr Castle originated with the father of the present Earl and continued when his son Brendan inherited. It was a friendship which was sustained by mutual interests in both gardening and astronomy. The great optical telescope at Birr Castle, known as the Leviathan, was built by the third Earl in the 1840s and was the largest telescope in the world for more than seventy years. It fell into disrepair early in the twentieth century when the mirror was removed to the Science Museum in London, where it remains to this day; but it was still an instrument of great historical interest and the archives remained an important resource. The castle and telescope lie within extensive and beautiful grounds and gardens, which contain an arboretum planted during the last hundred years. Brendon Rosse and Bernard shared a love of trees and shrubs which created a natural bond that endured even beyond death, when Brendan brought a tree from Birr and planted it in the arboretum after Bernard's funeral on 23rd August 2012. Their friendship was characterised by a spirit of stimulating competition, laced with generosity and Brendan "was able to discuss gardens with his father's old friend on equal terms".

Cricket remained an abiding passion. Soon after the war, Mrs. Evans of Chelford, whose husband was the local doctor, decided to resuscitate the local cricket club, which needed a new ground. She managed to obtain a picturesque field near the village but needed earth-moving machinery to flatten it out. She telephoned Bernard and asked if he would lend her a digging machine from Jodrell. Naturally he was more than happy to oblige and a long association began. He played for Chelford for many years, turning out in his Bristol University cricket cap; when he became captain, he often displayed the relaxed attitude to funding which was evident in other aspects of his life, as Roy Merchant was fond of recounting: "If new mowers or a roller were required he would encourage the committee to buy them, regardless of the lack of funds, on the basis that the ladies would raise the money," as they invariably did. John Evans, the good doctor's son, remembers Bernard as a useful all-rounder and extremely keen. He recalls one match with particular pleasure, in which he and Bernard were the last men in and secured a famous victory over their local rivals, Alderley Edge. John had a date that evening and the young lady was not very pleased when he turned up late. He was forgiven the next week when she saw the headlines in the local newspapers: "Lovell and Evans Save the Day". Another local derby, against Over Peover was written up by the distinguished journalist, Norman Shrapnel, in the *Manchester Guardian*, on 27th June 1955:

> A Chauffeur led the home side (Peover). The visitors, aiming fantastically higher in distance and speed, were captained by a distinguished radio astronomer. The home flag might have been thought to droop at the sight of this lithe expert in cosmic rays looking, in his striped cap, like a senior member of the science sixth, thoroughly capable of hitting scientific sixes.

The visitors elected to bat and the distinguished radio astronomer serenely predicted that he would regard 120 to be a good score. A wicket fell as he spoke and he added, rather less serenely, that it would be possible to win with as few as 80 runs on the board. Five more wickets fell for very few runs:

> The radio astronomer assumed a cosmic expression and strode off to put on his pads. But then there was a stand that carried the afternoon to tea and a declaration, so that he did not bat after all and Chelford won by a mere 46 runs.

Bernard continued to support the village side and to follow its fortunes into his old age.

He had become a member of Lancashire County Cricket Club soon after he arrived in Manchester in 1936 and visits to Old Trafford were eagerly anticipated and much enjoyed, whatever the weather. As time went on he was elected to the committee and became a Vice President and in 1996 he had the great honour to serve as President, in one of the club's most successful years. On one occasion, during this presidential year, Bernard invited John Wilbraham to Old Trafford for the first day of the Test Match. In his enthusiasm for the cricket he had forgotten that John Major, a keen supporter of cricket, was imminently expected and he went down to meet the teams before the start of play, leaving his guest to entertain the Prime Minister. Fortunately Wilbraham was well up to the task of pouring a drink for Major whilst he took an important telephone call from the Foreign Secretary.

Fascinated by every aspect of the game, he loved to talk to the officials, the administrators and especially the cricketers; Michael Atherton was a particular favourite as was Marcus Trescothick, who was educated at the

Sir Bernard Lovell School in Oldland. Bernard brought his scientific expertise to bear at Old Trafford by devising light meters, which were positioned at either end of the ground to help the umpires decide whether play should continue. His belief in the need for electronic aids to assist the umpires was shared by the great cricket commentator, Brian Johnston, who interviewed him 'On the Boundary' for the BBC's Test Match Special on 6th June 1987, during the match between England and Pakistan at Old Trafford. He explained to Johnston that his light meters contained a photosensitive element, which could drive a dial indicating the intensity of the light. If the umpires concluded that the light was too poor for play, they would "offer the light" to the batsmen, who could then chose whether to continue or retreat to the safety of the pavilion. They had kept records which established that the umpires were remarkably consistent in deciding when the light should be offered to the batsman but that, once they had left the field, play was often suspended for much longer than was necessary, as the conditions improved.

The light meters were very reliable and remained in use for several years. Meanwhile Bernard turned his attention to another perennial umpiring problem, leg before wicket or lbw. The improvements in the quality of televised broadcasting had put great pressure on umpires, whose decisions were subjected to scrutiny and criticism by armchair experts in the commentary box and at home. The umpire has to make immediate decisions; the ball, travelling at up to 100 mph has struck the batsman on the pad; the umpire must decide whether it hit the edge of the bat before the pad, in which case the batsman would be given not out; if he judges that it did not hit the bat first he must decide whether it would have hit the stumps if the pad had not been in the way. In reaching his decision he must make judgements about the trajectory of the ball, the height of the projected bounce, whether it had been swinging in the air and any movement off the pitch caused by spin applied by the bowler or by the seam of the ball as it hit the ground; all this is based on a split second observation of the event.

Bernard spoke to two very experienced international umpires, David Constant and Don Oslear about this difficulty and the Test and County Cricket Board agreed to finance a feasibility study. He told Brian Johnston that his system required the use of four extremely sensitive cameras connected to a computer system which would make an instant calculation of whether the ball would have hit the stumps. The computer would then inform the umpire of the result through a system of lights on the scoreboard. The drawback was the cost, which would exceed £100,000 for each installation. The TCCB decided that the expense was prohibitive and the idea was shelved.

Another tricky question for umpires is whether the ball has struck the bat before being caught by a fielder; the slightest contact between leather and willow is enough to seal the batsman's fate, but was that snick the sound of bat on ball or did the bat flick the batsman's pad or the ground as he played his stroke? Once again, these are fine judgements which depend on the skill of the umpire, whose decisions are the subject of endless analysis in television replays which can be slowed down and examined at leisure. The solution Bernard came up with was to insert a small device in the handle of the bat which would be activated by the slightest degree of contact, sending a radio signal to the umpire who would be equipped with an earphone. Initial tests were subject to interference from local taxis and other extraneous signals; but once a discrete signal was achieved Bernard tested it out in the nets. The result was disappointing; the first time he hit the ball with the bat, the sensitive device disintegrated and his only prototype was destroyed. A great deal more work and much expense would be required to perfect these appliances and no further progress was made for many years. Cricket lovers of today are familiar with the successors of Bernard's early attempts, appropriately named Hotspot, Snicko and Hawkeye; but, as Bernard said to Johnston, there is no suggestion that the final decision should be taken away from the umpire and the modern devices frequently cause as many arguments as they solve.

But it was the game itself that he loved; the history of cricket and the records of the great players were never ending topics of conversation. Tales would flow of Jack Hobbs at the Oval or scoring his hundredth hundred at Bath in 1923, Hammond's wonderful cover drive, Fiery Fred Truman's lightning speed and Laker's nineteen Australian wickets at Old Trafford in 1956. When he could no longer travel to the ground and lost his sight, he reverted to listening to the commentaries on the radio, just as he had done with his homemade crystal set eighty-five years earlier at Oldland Common.

Music became a family passion just as much as it was his own. He had been nurtured by musicians, been taught to play the piano and the organ and had honed his abilities to a considerable degree long before he became a scientist, let alone an astronomer. His typically self-effacing assessment of his own ability was expressed as a wish that he had devoted more attention to music and become more of a musician than he did. But his contribution to music was substantial. As with many aspects of his life, he loved to communicate his delight and enthusiasm to others and especially to the young. He formed close links with the Royal Northern College of Music and Chetham's School, and frequently held concerts in the planetarium at Jodrell, where young musicians were given an opportunity to display their talents. He encouraged them to test and stretch their abilities, and when Rose Cholmondeley was asked to select something obscure, she chose to add Schumann's *Variations on an Original Theme* to her repertoire; in subsequent years, other less well known pieces were also included.

Wherever he was in the world Bernard would take every opportunity to attend concerts and he heard most of the great pianists of the twentieth century, from Schnabel and Rachmaninov to Horowitz and Alfred Brendel. He always regarded Schnabel as the master, especially for his playing of Beethoven's late sonatas, but he greatly admired Horowitz and recalled his incredible fingering. In the early days he wrote occasional reviews, for music magazines, including one of a concert given by Rachmaninov in Bristol, which he showed to Rose Cholmondeley.

Geoffrey Lockett and Rose both speak of his wide appreciation and knowledge of the classical repertoire. Bach was his first love, but he had a catholic taste which embraced composers from Beethoven and Mozart to Mahler and Shostakovich. His love of both music and astronomy gave him a great affinity with William Herschel, who had played the organ at the Octagon Chapel at Bath. In 1981, Bernard and Rose Cholmondeley gave a series of concerts in which he talked about Herschel and she played some of his compositions and those of his contemporaries. One of these performances was given at Bath University to celebrate the 200th anniversary of Herschel's discovery of the planet Uranus.

In 2003, a concert was held at Chetham's School of Music in honour of his ninetieth birthday, at which a specially commissioned piece, *Jodrell Suite*, was played. It was composed by five of the students, who had been inspired by a visit to Jodrell Bank and The Quinta and it was comprised of five movements: *The Earth and Far Beyond*, *Le Temps Profond*, *Fanfare of Clouds*, *Journey to Quinters* and *Dance to a Thousand Stars*. The evening was a fitting tribute to a man who had been President of the Chopin Society and of the Guild of Church Musicians, Master of the Worshipful Company of Musicians and much more besides.

Throughout his life, music was an enormous release in times of trouble and a great diversion, which stopped him devoting all his time to astronomy. After a particularly bad day a colleague told him that he could do with a good gin and tonic when he got home. "No," he replied. "I shall sit down at the piano and play a little Bach." His granddaughter, Lucy Driver, describes the whole family being stunned into silence and moved to tears by the power and beauty of the *Leningrad* Symphony of Shostakovich. He adored church music from his earliest youth. For forty years he was the organist in the village church at Swettenham, until he could no longer see the music. He played well, with sensitivity and variation, even if his concentration was sometimes so focused on the music that he forgot to count the verses; then, either he would stop before the end, leaving the congregation to carry on unaccompanied or he would keep playing after they had finished; but no one seemed to mind.

When his playing days were over he used to listen to broadcast and recorded music and he went to concerts until he was too frail to do so and loved nothing more than hearing the old Bechstein in the library being played by visitors such as Rose Cholmondeley or by one of his grandchildren. With the latter he took great pleasure in their success, but was also a demanding task master. Lucy Driver recalls his delight when she passed her grade eight clarinet exam; the praise was immediately followed up by the question: "So, my dear, when do you start your diploma?" How proud he would have been at his funeral to hear another granddaughter, Clementine Lovell, give a stunning performance of the *Pie Jesu* from the Requiem by Gabriel Fauré.

And then there was the garden.

CHAPTER TWENTY-FOUR

The Glory of the Garden

Bernard's love for and interest in trees and plants can be traced back to his earliest years when he roamed the fields and woods that surrounded his childhood home at Oldland Common. When he and Joyce got married and moved into their first house in Manchester, it was Johnny Burrow, the glass blower who encouraged them to start a garden. After the war Fred Sansome and Bernard formed an immediate rapport because of their mutual interests in botany and radar. So when the Lovells moved to Swettenham it was natural that a shared love of gardening should grow into ambitious plans to create something on a much larger canvas. The Quinta was surrounded by rough lawns and some rather neglected trees and shrubs; when they bought the house they also acquired four acres of paddocks, where schemes for planting and extending the gardens soon began to produce exciting results.

As the years passed they managed to buy another thirty acres of pasture, which lay between the house and the edge of the Dane Valley, a few hundred yards away. The usual Lovell enthusiasm took over and developed a programme for turning the bare pastures into an arboretum. Trees and shrubs were planted in abundance, laid out in an expanding network of groves, specimen trees and avenues that soon covered the whole area. Several of the avenues were planted to commemorate great national and family occasions such as the Queen's Silver Jubilee, the Reith Lectures, Bernard's knighthood and their golden wedding anniversary in 1987. Paths were kept mown between the carefully planned groups of trees, most of the work being done by Bernard and Joyce and their children, as they became old enough to be pressed service. Everyone was expected to do their bit, however, visiting friends and family included. A lake was dug out; when it failed to hold water Bernard, Joyce and all the children derived much amusement from the messy process of puddling clay into the bottom to create an impervious lining. As time went on, the arboretum was opened to the public; its growing reputation brought people flocking from near and far and did no harm at all to trade at the Swettenham Arms.

The avenue of native trees planted in the arboretum
with the help of local schoolchildren.

The arboretum now extends to forty acres and contains a huge number of species collected from many parts of the world. There are national collections of pine, ash and oak and many examples of rare, non-native plants, plants which Bernard brought back from the countries he visited, often transporting them in his sponge bag; the seeds or cuttings would then be propagated in the little conservatory attached to the house until they were ready for planting out. By 1990 the collection contained more than two and a half thousand trees and shrubs, many of which were winter flowering varieties such as the Rhododendron Sutchuenense, a native of Sezchuan, which, even in the coldest of winters, flowers in profusion from late January. Over the years Bernard wrote regularly to *The Times* to report the number of different shrubs and trees in flower on Christmas Day; the figure often exceeded one hundred varieties. The plans for the arboretum were meticulously drawn up in a series of notebooks, which included details such as the date of planting and the aspect of the site. The provenance of every seed and plant was recorded in a card index, which also set out the country of origin, the date and method of acquisition and propagation and the progress of each one over the years.

After Joyce died, in 1993, the arboretum began to look a bit run down and tired. Her work and dedication to the gardens had been as great as Bernard's but the years of her illness had severely curtailed her activities and the devotion with which Bernard had cared for her gave him less time to carry on with the work. His grief following her death also played a part in the decline, as did his finances, which, inevitably, had been affected by the cost of nursing care. He decided that, in order to secure the future of the arboretum, he would sell it to the Cheshire Wildlife Trust, who managed to obtain Lottery funding for the purchase of nearly forty acres. Soon afterwards a chance visit led to a renewed enthusiasm, which was of profound importance for his rehabilitation following the loss of his beloved wife.

One afternoon in 1994, Rhod Taylor, a lecturer at the Rease Heath Agricultural College near Nantwich, came to look round the arboretum. He happened to come across two of his former students who were busy putting up some rabbit fencing. They told him that they were working for the Cheshire Wildlife Trust and he asked them who was supposed to be looking after the place. He was not surprised when they answered that no one was doing so but he was sufficiently impressed by what he had seen to telephone the Wildlife Trust and ask whether they were interested in employing him. They said they would be pleased to do so but that he would have to speak to Sir Bernard, who was still in charge, and a meeting was arranged.

Taylor recalls that Bernard was rather suspicious of him when he told him that his subject was arboriculture. It seems that the Prof associated this discipline with forestry and his immediate worry was that Taylor was what he referred to as a chainsaw merchant. A few days later, he agreed to visit the arboretum at Rease Heath, which was not particularly impressive and then went to Taylor's home, where Mrs. Taylor made them a cup of tea. Rhod and his wife were keen seedsmen and propagators and Bernard was very impressed by their cottage garden, every inch of which was occupied by a veritable nursery of plants. He immediately realised that this was just the man he needed to help him, and Rhod Taylor was taken on. It was a partnership that was to last for eighteen years, although Bernard had very decided views and there was never any doubt about the identity of the senior partner.

Rhod Taylor was very entertained by the Prof's disapproval of pruning and his antipathy to chainsaws. Bernard considered that his trees and shrubs should be allowed to grow freely and reach their full potential without being hacked about. The moment Rhod pulled the starter rope of his chainsaw, to do a bit of judicious pruning or to cut down a shrub that was past its best, he knew it would not be long before Bernard heard it and came out to check up on him. By the time he arrived at The Quinta, some of the shrubs were nearly fifty years old and were no longer viable; one disadvantage of a specimen garden is that when an old plant dies there is no substitute readily available. Rhod decided to deal with this problem and embarked on a programme of propagation whereby old specimens could be replaced with new ones as the need arose. As time went on the trust of the senior partner in his junior increased and the complementary methods of the two men were of great benefit to continued development.

Bernard's ambition was to have one example of every genus and species listed in the four volumes of W.J. Bean's *Trees and Shrubs of the British Isles*. He never quite achieved this objective, falling short by some fifty plants, partly because he was perennially optimistic about the hardy nature of the specimens he imported from more temperate climates in Cornwall and Ireland. Rhod would argue that purchasing plants which were not sufficiently hardy was a waste. Bernard would have none of it:

"It's my money," he would say, "I'll do what I like with it." On one occasion he spent about £500 on a large number of plants, all of which Rhod considered to be too tender.

"You'll lose half of them," he said, "they'll never grow in Cheshire."

"It's my money," Bernard insisted, "let's get them planted." Within six months, half of them were dead, as Rhod had predicted; but Bernard would no doubt have considered that the experiment was a success, bearing in mind the survival of the other half. For all their occasional disagreements, Rhod confirms the view of Michael Ashbrook of Arley Hall that Bernard was a superb plantsman, whose reputation as a gardener deserves to live alongside those of his great Cheshire friends, Michael's mother, Elizabeth Ashbrook, and Lavinia Cholmondeley at Cholmondeley Castle.

After a couple of years, it became obvious that the Cheshire Wildlife Trust was not ideally qualified to managing an arboretum. The Tatton Garden Society had been running the old walled garden at Tatton Park for a number of years. Victorian kitchen gardens were becoming all the rage in the mid-nineties; the National Trust, which administered Tatton Park in conjunction with Cheshire County Council, decided to take it over and the Garden Society was evicted. Tatton's loss proved to be Jodrell's gain when the Wildlife Trust sold its freehold interest in twenty-eight acres of the arboretum to the Society, whose members were happy to take it on for £1; twelve acres were retained, as a woodland area and a wildlife sanctuary. Elizabeth Ashbrook was President of the Society at that time and took great delight in emphasising: "I am the President and Bernard is only the Vice." After her death he took over her role, but even when she was President, it was Bernard who was in charge.

The members of the Tatton GS committee knew a great deal about smaller gardens but much less about managing thirty acres of trees and shrubs, which was the Prof's area of expertise. Colonel Geoffrey Sparrow was co-opted onto the committee and recalls that meetings went very well,

The beautiful Heptacodium Miconioides *in the arboretum.*

as long as everyone agreed with Bernard; those who stepped out of line would sometimes get a sharp response, followed by a kindly apology as soon as they resumed singing off his hymn sheet. Bernard was the perfect gentleman in his dealings with people, but the arboretum was his baby and he knew what he wanted to do with it. Under this regime it was restored to its full glory and it is run by the Tatton Garden Society to this day.

For nearly sixty-five years, the garden and arboretum which Bernard and Joyce created gave him enormous pleasure and were a great source of comfort in times of trouble. As long as he was able to do so he played a full and active part in the upkeep, working in the gardens in the morning and at Jodrell in the afternoon. Gardening was a huge relief from the cares that often beset him. One reviewer of the Reith Lectures, who must have known of his interest, wrote that the lectures had been written over a spade. He himself was on record as saying: "when walking and planting in the garden one solves many problems without thinking about them." Guests would be greeted by the sight of the great astronomer on a mowing machine, from which he would issue instructions and put them to work. Irene Lamb, the great companion of his later years, would arrive after a tiring drive from Gloucestershire, wanting nothing more than to put her feet up with a cup of tea.

"Lovely to see you," the Prof would say as he carried her suitcase into the house. "Now I'll take the big mower and you can have the small one. Shall we get going?"

Even when he was almost blind and barely capable of walking, he would be taken out in his electric buggy and his enjoyment of the garden would be complete. Raymond and Anne Lowe worked at The Quinta for the last twelve years of Bernard's life. One winter morning they were at home near Congleton, when Ray received a call from the social services. The panic button that Sir Bernard had finally been persuaded to wear round his neck had gone off but they could get no answer from him on the telephone. Would Ray drive over to The Quinta to check that all was well? He was there in ten minutes and scoured the house for his master without success; then he went into the hut at the back and saw that the buggy was missing. By this time he was in a state of panic himself and ran out into the garden. There had been a heavy frost and, as soon as he reached the lawn, he was relieved to see the tracks of the vehicle going across the grass towards the arboretum. Thank goodness for that, he thought, I'll soon find him. He followed the tracks for two or three hundred yards down the paths until suddenly, to his consternation, they stopped; but there was still no sign of Bernard or Buggy; what could possibly have happened to them? What if he had driven into the lake? Ray rushed back to the house to get help, using his mobile telephone to call Janet Eaton as he did so. Just as he reached the drive he heard a noise behind him and turned. There was Sir Bernard, mounted on the buggy, covered in leaves, twigs and branches looking for all the world like a commando in full camouflage.

"Sir Bernard," he cried, "Are you all right?"

"Of course I am" replied Bernard, "what's the matter with you? You're not due here till lunchtime."

"No, but we were worried about you when you pressed your panic button."

"Panic button? I never pressed it."

"We had a call from social services, Sir Bernard. They said it had gone off."

"Well I never pressed it," said Bernard. "Mind you, I've been through a few bushes this morning."

The enthusiasm for his arboretum never waned and he loved to hear about the garden and to share his encyclopaedic knowledge of the plants; he would never tire of taking people round and giving the Latin name of every plant, explaining their history and origin, even when he could no longer see them. On 31st January 2011, I went to visit him at The Quinta. It was one of the coldest winters on record but, to my untutored amazement, as I drove up to the house I saw a rhododendron in full bloom. Frail though he was, Bernard was his usual sparkling self and as I listened to him talk I was entranced by his stories and dazzled by the brilliance of his memory. Names, dates and incidents were reeled off with the utmost facility and barely a pause for thought. When I got up to leave I asked him the variety of the wonderful rhododendron I had seen on my arrival. For a moment he paused; then he slapped his hand across his forehead and groaned with disappointment:

"Oh Lord! I can't remember anything these days."

"Well that's the only thing you have forgotten in the last hour and a half," I retorted.

"I suppose it is," he said with a merry chuckle, "but at my age I can't expect to remember everything."

CHAPTER TWENTY-FIVE

Forty Years Onward

In 1946 Bernard was appointed an OBE for his wartime service and this recognition was followed by many others. He became a fellow of the Royal Society in 1955; in 1960 he was one of the ten members chosen to present a lecture as part of the Society's Tercentenary celebrations and he received the Royal Society Medal. In 1961, he and Joyce went to Buckingham Palace where he was knighted by the Queen, for services to astronomy. Further awards and appointments flooded in over the years; they included the Gold Medal of the Royal Astronomical Society, of which he was President from 1969-1971, and honorary degrees and appointments from around the world; but he was especially proud that the city he had so despised on his first visit in 1936 should honour him forty-one years later when he became a Freeman of the City of Manchester.

He retired as Professor of Astronomy on 30th September 1981 and was accorded the title of Emeritus Professor by the university he had served so well and for so long. He remained as director of Jodrell until his successor, Francis Graham-Smith, took up his duties the following year. Amidst great celebrations on the thirtieth anniversary of its completion, the instrument was officially renamed the Lovell Telescope. Bernard now had a unique distinction: in the 1950s the writer Nigel Neale had honoured him by giving his Christian name to the fictional television scientist Bernard Quatermass; and in 1987, the University gave his surname to the very real telescope he had created for them.

After his retirement he retained an office at Jodrell and went there almost every day until ill health prevented him from doing so nearly thirty years later. But although he was frequently on the site, taking a great interest in what was going on, always ready to help and advise when asked to do so and being especially supportive of students and young scientists, he never tried to interfere. Francis Graham-Smith had no anxieties that his predecessor was regarding him with a critical eye or looking over his shoulder as he took over the controls. Bernard spent a great deal of time writing and sorting out his voluminous papers. Most of these are now deposited at the John Ryland's Library, the Royal Society and the Imperial War Museum; those in the John Ryland's are listed in a catalogue which is itself over three hundred and fifty pages in length. As Bernard used to say, there is enough paper there to cover several cricket grounds.

Throughout his life he was a prolific writer and published a vast number of books, papers and articles. The books include *Echoes of War*, *The Jodrell Bank Story*, *Astronomer by Chance*, *A Life of Patrick Blackett*, which he wrote for the Royal Society, *Out of the Zenith*, and another book on astronomy, *Pathways to the Universe*, written with Francis Graham-Smith. He and Joyce much enjoyed their collaboration in writing a guide to radio astronomy called *Discovering the Universe*; but his masterpiece is *In the Centre of Immensities*, with his dazzling exposition of the history and nature of the universe, his examination of man's relationship with the cosmos and his penetrating analysis of human purpose and the progress of civilisation.

Freedom from the constant work of administration as director gave much more time for travel, lecture tours and meetings of the Royal Society, the Royal Astronomical Society and other institutions with which he was involved. He also took part in many events organised at Jodrell, some of which are recorded on the Jodrell Bank podcast; there was a series of interviews with Tim O'Brien before live audiences; in 2009 he gave a talk as part of the fortieth anniversary celebrations of Apollo 11; and he continued to promote the work of the telescope through every avenue and with his many influential contacts throughout the world.

Jodrell Bank and the fate of the telescope remained an important preoccupation. MERLIN had been set up as a direct alternative to the plans for a huge telescope and had been a great success over many years. Used in conjunction with the European VLBI system, a resolution of 0.001 seconds of arc had been achieved, a precision which would have been considered impossible only a few years earlier. This led to the production of high definition maps and was an important aspect of research at Jodrell and elsewhere.

Problems of interference from terrestrial fields still exist and are increased with the growth of mobile telephones, satellite navigation and other electronic accoutrements of the modern age; but the scientists have learned to work round these difficulties. Many of the signals are temporary and on the move; in the control room the technicians' objective is to ensure that all the telescopes from around the country are operating; the signals are passed on to the scientific staff who retrieve and interpret the ones they need, disregarding the extraneous material when it appears. The days when Bernard could pick up a telephone and complain about a power line or lobby the authorities and object to a proposed development are long gone.

In 2001, work began on e-MERLIN, upgrading the original system over a number of years, using optical fibre connections instead of landlines. By 2007 the first signals began to come through, but in March 2008 the Science and Technology Facilities Council was faced with a deficit of £80 million and announced that, among other projects, MERLIN was being considered for the axe. The funding of MERLIN, which stood at £2.5 million per annum, was crucial to Jodrell. The press got hold of the story and printed dramatic headlines such as "Jodrell Bank to Close". The director of the new visitor centre, Theresa Anderson MBE, remembers the shock which this somewhat premature prediction caused. Bernard went into battle on the airwaves and in the newspapers, which quoted him as saying: "This will be a disaster for Jodrell Bank. The fate of the telescope is bound up with the fate of e-MERLIN. The establishment cannot survive if the funding is cut." It was the start of a vigorous campaign supported, among others by Silk FM, Macclesfield's local radio station, which produced a rather jolly Jodrell Bank song performed by a group variously named the Radio Astronomers and the Rocketeers. Jodrell Bank had become a household name, largely as a result of Bernard's work over the years in raising its profile. On 9th July, it was announced that funding of £2.5 million would be guaranteed after all and Jodrell was saved. But there was better news to come.

At the end of the decade, plans emerged to create a Square Kilometre Array of telescopes, the SKA, using the vast and open ground provided by the deserts of Australia and South Africa. The idea was to have thousands of small dishes, spread over many square miles; the combined surface area of the dishes would amount to a square kilometre. This would give an entirely new dimension to radio astronomy by virtue of the power and precision of the facility which would enable it to search even further back in time than had previously been possible. An international selection process was announced to choose the establishment that would coordinate this great enterprise and Jodrell Bank defeated all the competition both at home and abroad. When the announcement was made, in April 2011, there was great celebration among all those at Jodrell who had worked so hard to achieve the appointment and it gave Bernard enormous pleasure, as he approached his ninety-eighth birthday. The future of his beloved telescope had been secured. In the autumn of 2010 he had been taken to Jodrell, where he cut the first sod in preparation for the building of the new visitor centre. His last visit to the telescope on 8th April 2011 coincided with the SKA announcement and the opening of the centre, under the directorship of Theresa Anderson.

Over the years there were visits from scientists, politicians, astronauts and veterans of World War II, but one encounter in particular is worthy of special mention. Lala Wilbraham's Polish uncle came to stay with her during the 1980s. His name was Jan Jurjewicz, otherwise known as

'Skippy', and Bernard and Joyce were invited to dinner to meet him. Skippy had managed to escape from Poland after the invasion in 1939 and made his way to England, where he became one of many Poles who gave valiant and distinguished service to the Royal Air Force. Naturally he and Bernard struck up an immediate rapport and it transpired that Skippy had flown aircraft fitted with H2S. The two elderly gentlemen were like a couple of schoolboys in their excitement at this strange coincidence. While Bernard, with typical modesty, was at great pains to insist that it was he who was lucky and privileged to meet Skippy, the Polish ace was equally adamant that the honour was all his.

The Family had been at the centre of his existence. Whatever anxieties and pressures life threw at him, Joyce and the children were a source great joy and constant support. The Quinta was a haven and as grandchildren and great-grandchildren arrived, the fun and laughter provided a relief from the cares of the World. Great events were celebrated there and the huge billiard room which Bernard created in the stable block was the scene of riotous parties, weddings, Christmas plays, charades and family games. During the 1980s the first indications appeared of a problem which was eventually to result in a devastating blow to the equilibrium of the happy family life which the Lovells had enjoyed for so long. Joyce, who had always been incredibly active and had never suffered from ill health, became inflicted with asthma. At first the symptoms did not seem too serious and although she had to cut back to some extent, she was able to continue her former activities. When the problem increased it seems that her medication had side-effects that caused or perhaps accelerated the onset of osteoporosis and she became increasingly debilitated. It was a source of great sadness and anxiety to Bernard and all her family and friends that Joyce, who had been so tall and lithe and energetic all her life, should be reduced to a condition which left her very incapacitated.

By 1991 she was virtually bedridden, and for the next two years Bernard looked after her with great devotion; he was determined that she should remain at home, as she herself wished, and all the necessary home nursing was brought in. Bernard did everything he could to care for her and ensure that she remained as happy and comfortable as her illness permitted. There were many visitors and she was brave and cheerful throughout. She had trained as an English teacher and her love of language and literature never deserted her; Alex Wilbraham recalls that he felt deeply moved when she asked him to read the poems of Keats to her and felt that she derived great comfort from the poetry during her last days. She died on the eighth day of December 1993. They had been married for fifty-six years.

Joyce's death was a terrible blow to Bernard, from which it took him several years to recover. She had been the great companion, support and love of his life for so long that, without her, he was a lost soul. There was consolation in knowing that her suffering was at an end and he had the great comfort of family and friends around him; but the empty house when they had gone and the knowledge that he was alone was hard to bear and for many months he was inconsolable. There were three things which eventually saved him from despair and helped him to get over his grief and continue his life as she would have wanted him to do. The first, as we have seen, was the regeneration of the arboretum; the second was his love of Ireland and the restoration of great optical telescope at Birr Castle.

In the early 1990s, Brendan Rosse decided to return the Leviathan, as the telescope was called, to full working order. The original mirror was still in the Science Museum in London and a replacement had to be found. As Brendan concedes, he knew a great deal more about plants than about pulsars and although he was the owner of the greatest telescope in Ireland his knowledge of astronomy and scientific instruments was minimal. On the way back from one of his trips to Garinish West, Bernard stayed at Birr Castle for a few days and Brendan realised that the answer to his problem was at hand. He suggested that Bernard might like to help with the restoration and the idea was seized upon with alacrity. The first consideration was a replacement for the mirror and it was decided to arrange the manufacture of a much lighter one than the original, using aluminium. The woodwork of the structure was in very poor condition and had to be fully rebuilt to support the new mirror and the system of hydraulic motors which required complete replacement. Much of this work was done by the workshops on the estate and Bernard was just the person to help drive the project forward; his encouragement was a key ingredient in the restoration, he visited Birr at least twice every year between 1994 and 2000, and his contacts with experts at the Royal Society were invaluable. Work began in 1996 and the new mirror was finally fitted in 1999. The fully restored telescope is now a major tourist attraction and educational facility. The science centre demonstrates how the historic instrument was originally built and then restored by the people of Birr.

Bernard's children and grandchildren came to stay with him whenever they could and his many local friends, including the Wilbrahams, the Sparrows, and Geoffrey and Anita Lockett rallied round to help him in his grief; but his final salvation from the slough of despond was Irene. When Bernard and Joyce moved to The Quinta in 1948, Clive and Irene Lamb were their nearest neighbours, apart from the Swettenham Arms. There were very few people in the tiny village and it was not long before Joyce had met them all, making every effort to ensure that as newcomers they should play a full part in village life. She met Irene and the two families formed a friendship which continued after Clive Lamb's business took them away from Cheshire in 1961 and eventually to Tetbury in Gloucestershire, where they were living at the time of his death in 1995.

Bernard's daughter, Judy Spence, also lived in Gloucestershire. She went to see Irene, who was her godmother, and asked if she could be of any help. Irene said that everything was under control except that the church in which Clive's funeral was to take place had no organist.

"You could ask Father to play," suggested Judy. Irene thought this was a marvellous idea and a few days later, Bernard came down to discuss the service. She picked him up at Cheltenham station and drove him to the church. He took one look at the organ and exclaimed: "Good God!" It was not quite what he was used to, but it would have to do. He suggested playing the Overture to Tannhauser, in honour of Clive's mother who was German, saying that Siegfried's March was too long.

"But I hope you're not going to have Crimond,"[292] he added. Irene replied that Crimond was exactly what she was going to have, so Bernard had to overcome his antipathy to the hymn and played it quite beautifully at the funeral.

Some time later, Irene needed some advice about her wood, which had been planted by Clive when they moved to Gloucestershire. She consulted Bernard who offered to strip out the undergrowth and put things in order. This visit marked the start of a deep friendship which helped him, at last, to recover from his grief and which endured for the rest of his life. They visited one another regularly, celebrated birthdays and family events together, and shared their mutual love of music. There were frequent trips to Devon and Cornwall to look at the gardens and, every summer, they would go to Ireland, catching the ferry from Holyhead and staying at Garinish West, where Irene admired the house and the collection of pines and subtropical plants which Bernard and Joyce had planted round the island. They visited Birr Castle to stay with the Rosses and Bernard proudly showed her the work that was being done to restore the telescope. Holidays abroad included trips to Gargellen in Austria, where they stayed with Irene's daughter Patricia and her family, who were there for a skiing holiday. Bernard had never seen the Alps and was enchanted; he and Irene would take the lift to the top of the mountain and join the skiers for lunch. The love and companionship they derived from all this was a great delight to them both and they were completely devoted to one another.

Irene sustained him through old age. Without her he would have given up and, he used to tell her every night, when he telephoned on the stroke of six o'clock: "These calls are the only thing that keeps me going. I look forward to this moment all through the day." When they first got together, Bernard told Irene how lost and alone he had felt going to concerts at the Bridgewater Hall in Manchester and seeing so many couples enjoying the music together; now, once again, he had someone to share it with. He often asked her to marry him, but she was far too sensible to upset the balance of their loving and beautiful friendship.

"Why should we complicate things by getting married?" she would say. The closeness had given a new lease of life to them both. They could spend as much time with each other as they wished, but he would not want to leave Cheshire and she was happy in Gloucestershire, so there was no point in rocking the boat and, possibly, upsetting both their families in doing so.

Like many men parted by death from an adored and loving wife after a long and happy marriage, Bernard was not very good at managing the domestic chores. His mind had always been concentrated on the higher world of science and the practicalities of life had never troubled him; Joyce was responsible for running things but she was no longer there to do so. Irene soon turned her attention to teaching him how to look after himself when he was on his own. She showed him how to use the washing machine and explained that a tumble dryer meant that you did not have to wait for a dry day before you did the washing. One evening they went to have a cosy dinner with Betts and Geoffrey Sparrow. There were only four of them at the table and Betts asked Bernard how he managed when he was on his own. He told her that Irene was teaching him domestic science. She had taken him shopping and bought him a tin of baked beans, conveniently equipped with a key attached to the lid; all he had to do was to pull back on the key to open the tin and pour the beans into a small saucepan; once they were hot he tipped them onto a piece of well buttered toast; his enjoyment of a tasty supper was much enhanced by the satisfaction of having prepared it with his own hands.

"Well that's marvellous, Bernard," said Betts. "Now you can look after yourself."

"That's what I thought," he replied. "But the next time I went to the shop and bought a tin it had no key and I couldn't open it." The conversation moved on and some minutes passed before Betts noticed that Bernard was deep in thought; he seemed almost to be in a trance; it put her in mind of Rembrandt's *Aristotle Contemplating the Bust of Homer*, what amazing ideas were revolving in that wonderful brain? She did not like to interrupt his reverie; after all he might be on the point of solving the mystery of the universe. When he came down to earth again she turned to him:

"Do tell us what you've been thinking about, Bernard."

"I'm still trying to work out how to open that tin!" he replied.

Lala Wilbraham had a regular date at The Quinta for supper and a game of Scrabble. He treated her like a benevolent grandfather and she loved his company and the intensity of the games. Every time they sat down for supper, she was much amused by his announcement that as she was a vegetarian he had arranged for them to have roast chicken. She did not have the heart to tell him that a chicken was not a vegetable.

In December 2001, it became essential to engage someone to look after him on a regular basis; word was put about and an advertisement was placed in the local newspaper, *The Chronicle*. Ann Winterton, who was the Member of Parliament for Congleton, heard that Bernard was looking for someone suitable to cook for him and she telephoned the former mayor of the borough, Raymond Lowe. Would Ray's wife, Anne, be interested in applying for the job? An appointment was arranged and Ray drove her over to The Quinta. Sir Bernard was alone and the interview was a short one. He only asked one question: "When can you start?" The answer was equally to the point: "When do you want me?" The deal was done, Anne started that evening and she cooked for him for the next eleven years. She did not drive, so Ray used to bring her and he too began to do a few jobs about the place, becoming a cross between handyman, butler and gentleman's gentleman.

The Lowes adored looking after Bernard and he grew very fond of them. When they started he was still planting and walking in the arboretum in the mornings and he would go to Jodrell in the afternoons. Anne prepared his lunch and left something for supper; if he gave a dinner party she would cook and Ray would serve and act as butler. Although his eyesight deteriorated his physical strength was remarkable until his ninety-eighth year. One evening in March 2010 he returned from a concert in a state of exhaustion; he ordered his usual late night treat of smoked salmon sandwiches and brandy but then Ray and Anne had the greatest difficulty in getting him up the stairs and into bed. The following morning he was taken to hospital in Macclesfield and then a few days later to a nursing home where he recuperated for several weeks and had physiotherapy which improved his mobility. He was determined to return home and did so as soon as he could. There was now a stair-lift and he had overnight care. He continued to receive many visitors and, although he had become extremely frail, his spirits never flagged and his mind remained as keen as ever until the very end of his life.

It was at this time that Bernard suffered the last great sorrow of his long life. His eldest daughter Susan, who was married to John Driver, died very suddenly and unexpectedly. Susan and her husband with grandchildren and great-grandchildren were frequent visitors to The Quinta over the years.

John was a cricket lover and had spent many happy hours with his father-in-law at Old Trafford. Even in old age, the loss of a child is very hard to bear and Susan's death was a severe blow to the entire family.

To visit Bernard was to be transported back through ninety-eight eventful years to the green pastures of his boyhood, the majestic Wills Physics Laboratory at Bristol, Manchester before the war, the privations of the winter at St. Athan, TRE, and the muddy fields in Cheshire where he created his mighty telescope. We meet once again the men and women who have featured in his life: his father paces the garden at Oldland Common rehearsing his sermon; we encounter Tyndall and his famous lecture; here are Johnny Burrow the glassblower, Taffy Bowen and Charles Husband restored to life; we meet Churchill standing before the fireplace in the cabinet room demanding his squadrons, Eisenhower in the White House expressing the gratitude of the people of America, and the Russian scientists and astronauts in Moscow, trying to tempt him to defect. The shadows of the war and the Cuban crisis are brought graphically before us; a dark February afternoon and the terrible message of Sir Raymond Streat live in the memory, and the soothing balm of Joyce and family life is always a very present help in time of trouble; amongst all these memories, the anguish of the crash of the Halifax V9977 is never forgotten.

During his later years, the fate of Alan Blumlein, Geoffrey Hensby, C.E. Vincent and the crew of the aircraft seemed to weigh ever more heavily upon him. Because of the secrecy which surrounded the operations at TRE Churchill ordered that news of the accident must be suppressed. As a result, the crash was not reported at the time and sixty years later Bernard was at the forefront of a campaign to provide a fitting tribute to those who had died. The money was raised and Bernard unveiled the Defford Memorial on 8th September 2002. But the pain of the loss of the brilliant Blumlein and the young men who accompanied him never faded. He could not help but recall that he had been on the aircraft the evening before and it preyed on his conscience that it was he who had asked Hensby to take Blumlein and his party on the fatal flight. He often spoke of these feelings of guilt to Canon Peter Hunt, who was a frequent visitor. Peter tried to reassure him that he had nothing to reproach himself for; it had been a tragic accident and he was not responsible; but the anxiety remained. Ray and Anne Lowe were requested to fetch his copy of Milton from the library and almost every day he asked them to read to him; the poem he chose was *Lycidas*, Milton's lament on the death of his young friend Edward King, who was drowned whilst sailing to Ireland. There was particular comfort perhaps, in the following passage and in the last four lines, when the contemplative shepherd ends the poem on a note of hope:

For Lycidas is dead, dead ere his prime
Young Lycidas, and hath not left his peer:
Who would not sing for Lycidas? He knew
Himself to sing and build the lofty rhyme.
He must not float upon his watery beer
Unwept, and welter to the parching wind
Without the mead of some melodious tear.
And now the sun had stretched out all the hills
And now was dropped into the western bay,
At last he rose and twitched his mantle blew:
Tomorrow to fresh fields and pastures new.

As he became older and less mobile, Bernard thought a great deal about the philosophical and religious problems he had considered in the Reith Lectures and in his writing. He remained convinced that it was inevitable that the solution to one scientific problem invariably raises another. As he told Naim Attallah in an interview for *The Oldie* magazine in 1992, when they started to use the telescope they believed that they would solve all the major questions about the universe and its origins. The more they discovered the more there remained to investigate. In his old age, he remained firmly of the view that science can never provide a final answer; the scientist, like the religious person, relies on faith, his belief that science is the solution to every question, but cannot prove it. The religious person also relies on faith but is equally unable to prove the foundation of belief. People who absolutely deny the existence of God or some spiritual background to existence are fundamentalist just as much as those creationists who absolutely deny the existence or importance of science. Bernard had no more time for the fundamentalism of scientists such as Richard Dawkins than he had for the fundamentalism of the ardent creationist; on the one hand the creationist is in a state of denial about the science that governs our lives; on the other the scientist denies the validity of faith whilst relying on his faith that science will find the answers.

Faith, as Bernard saw it, is encapsulated in the words of the first three verses of Chapter 11 of St Paul's Epistle to the Hebrews:

Now faith is the substance of things hoped for, the evidence of things not seen. For by it the elders obtained a good report. Through faith we understand that the worlds were framed by the word of God, so that things which are seen were not made of things which do appear.

For many years he carried this text with him and he must have known it by heart; but during Peter Hunt's visits towards the end he invariably asked that it should be recited to him and he found great comfort in the words. He had been brought up in a religious household by parents who believed implicitly that a transcendent being had created the universe and is capable of manifesting himself on earth as a prophet or, in the case of Jesus, in the person of his son. As a young man he was greatly influenced by the writing of Alfred North Whitehead and his lectures, *Science and the Modern World*, published in 1925. Whitehead was concerned to unite the conflicts between religion and science into a coherent view of the reality of existence. There was a strong spiritual element in Bernard's thinking on these matters and as he got older he increasingly agreed with Paul Tilic, the American theologian and philosopher, that faith and belief in God is the condition of becoming overwhelmed by the state of being itself.

When we are deeply moved by wonderful music, the beauty of language, the wonders of nature, or the joys and sorrows of life, we are transported by feelings and emotions that take us beyond the reach of scientific analysis and into the unexplained world of the spirit. In this state we are in the presence of God, in the same way that Whitehead explained the hand of God in creation as being with creation but not before it. Mahler's Ninth Symphony illustrates Bernard's thinking; it was written when the composer knew that he was dying: "The last movement is transcendent and just disappears into nothing; those few moments are like the peace of God, which passes all understanding." He did not share his father's belief in a physical state of life beyond our earthly existence; rather he inclined to the idea of an all embracing cosmic ethic and a spiritual condition that may have existed before our universe and may be eternal.

He had never been confirmed into the Anglican Communion and did not take the sacrament but his love of the music of the Church and the language of the King James Bible and the Book of Common Prayer was always with him. He went to church regularly, sometimes attending both matins and evensong on the same day; and Sunday remained a very important day, even when he could no longer play the organ. All his life he regarded Sunday as a day of rest and he never played cricket or attended a match on the Sabbath. He broke this rule only once, when he was President of Lancashire and the Test Match was continued on the Sunday:

"I had to go," he said, "but I entertained two bishops and an archbishop to lunch, so I was in good company."

As to the existence of life elsewhere in the universe he was open-minded. He did not think it likely that it would be found; if it was it would be purely by chance; but with billions of galaxies, many of them containing billions of stars, the possibility could not be discounted completely. Finding other life would be a miraculous chance but statistically it might be out there.

Late in 2012 Bernard suffered a stroke, after which he rarely left his bed, although he continued to receive visitors until the very end. His mind remained clear, his memory rarely let him down and the sadness at seeing him so very frail was always tempered by his cheerful resignation at his condition. With Peter Hunt he spoke about the worries that preoccupied him and particularly of the crash of V9977. The canon reassured him, talking of the great events of his life and reminding him of the days when he had "walked with kings and presidents".

Peter spoke to him about the Cuban crisis, the threat of nuclear war and the fear it had created. "Who would want to run to a bunker when there was only ten minutes to live?" he asked.

"Don't worry, Peter," replied Bernard, "we get fifteen minutes warning at Jodrell and I will ring you." They would talk and pray together. Hunt often uses an Episcopal cross in his ministry; it was given to him by the bishop who ordained him and he uses it when visiting the sick or the dying; he gets them to hold the symbol of salvation in their hands while he prays. When visiting Bernard, he would place it in Bernard's hand before leaving him and recite the passage from Hebrews that gave the old man such comfort. "To share the spirituality of such a great person was a humbling experience."

On the morning of 6th August 2012 Peter Hunt went to see Bernard. The family had gathered and it was clear that his long life was finally ebbing to a close. The canon sat alone with him for a few minutes. One of the grandchildren was playing the piano in the library, as he talked quietly and placed the Episcopal cross in the hands of the dying man. He recited the passage from Hebrews and said a prayer and Bernard smiled at him; he was semi-conscious, but his face was imbued with an extraordinary sense of peace. Three hours later, surrounded by his devoted family, he died.

The funeral took place at Swettenham on 23rd August. The church was packed and the service was relayed to several hundred people in a tent set up outside the Swettenham Arms. The service was followed by a private burial, witnessed by his four surviving children, the grandchildren and many of his thirteen great-grandchildren. He was buried with his beloved Joyce, in the little graveyard near the church, overlooking the Dane Valley. The grave is just the throw of a cricket ball from the house where he had lived for sixty-four years.

Notes

CHAPTER ONE – THE AGES OF MAN
[1] 'Letter to Mr. D', 1738, quoted in *Journal of John Wesley*, 27th November 1739
[2] *Journal of John Wesley*, 27th November 1739

CHAPTER TWO – UNWILLINGLY TO SCHOOL
[3] The 1921 Education Act had raised the minimum school leaving age to fourteen.
[4] Tyndall gave his Children's Christmas Lecture in 1930. In 1965 Lovell himself gave one of the Christmas Lectures on 'The Exploration of the Universe'.

CHAPTER THREE – BRISTOL
[5] Tuition fees for 1931-32 were £6.13 shillings – fee note in Lovell Archive at Royal Society.
[6] *In Search of England*, H.V. Morton, Methuen, 1925, page 154
[7] *Student Memories of Bristol*, Bernard Lovell
[8] The diary is in the Lovell archive at the Royal Society.
[9] A sealed container which controls electric currents in a vacuum.
[10] Pelham (Plum) Warner, one of the English tour managers.
[11] In the event, Hobbs did not retire until 1934.
[12] *Student Memories of Bristol*, Bernard Lovell
[13] Lovell papers, Royal Society, MS/870

CHAPTER FOUR – THE GRADUATE
[14] Diary, July 1934, Lovell papers, Royal Society, MS/870
[15] *The Astrophysical Journal*, December 1925
[16] *Proceedings of the Royal Society* A, Bernard Lovell, 1936, 157, page 311-330
[17] *Nature*, Bernard Lovell, Vol. 137, 1936, page 493
[18] Diary, June/July 1936, Royal Society, MS/870

CHAPTER FIVE – MANCHESTER
[19] Diary, 6th May 1938, Bernard Lovell papers, Royal Society, MS/870
[20] *Proceedings of the Royal Society*, Vol. 172, 1939
[21] Diary, May 12th 1938, Lovell Papers, Royal Society, MS/870
[22] Diary, May 1st 1938, Lovell Papers, Royal Society, MS/870
[23] Diary, August 1938, Lovell Papers, Royal Society, MS/870
[24] Diary, 20th May 1938, Lovell Papers, Royal Society, MS/870
[25] The President of Czechoslovakia.
[26] Diary, 19th October 1938, Lovell Papers, Royal Society, MS/870
[27] Diary, 22nd October 1938, Lovell Papers, Royal Society, MS/870

CHAPTER SIX – AUGUST 1939
[28] The setting up of the Tizard Committee is documented in the National Archives, File AIR/4481
[29] *One Story of Radar*, A.P. Rowe, Cambridge University Press, 1948, page 6
[30] *Three Steps to Victory*, R.A. Watson-Watt, Odhams, 1957
[31] Report to the Tizard Committee, A.P. Rowe, February 1935
[32] *Radar Days*, E.G. Bowen, Adam Hilger, Bristol, 1987

CHAPTER SEVEN – RADAR
[33] Correspondence contained in the Blackett Archives, Royal Society, D7
[34] *Radar Days*, E.G. Bowen, Adam Hilger, Bristol, 1987
[35] *Radar Days*, E.G. Bowen, Adam Hilger, Bristol, 1987, page 140
[36] The name was changed to 'Telecommunications Research Establishment' in November 1940.
[37] Diary, 21st October 1940, Lovell papers, Royal Society, MS/870
[38] The Fairey Battle, an obsolete aircraft which was still in service.
[39] The letters are contained in File 32 of the Tizard papers at the Imperial War Museum
[40] *Radar Days*, E.G. Bowen, Adam Hilger, Bristol, 1987, page 93
[41] Diary, 21st December 1939, Lovell papers, Royal Society, MS/870
[42] *Radar Days*, E.G. Bowen, Adam Hilger, Bristol, 1987, page 92
[43] *The Gathering Storm*, Winston Churchill, Cassell, 1948, page 406
[44] *Radar Days*, E.G. Bowen, Adam Hilger, Bristol, 1987, page 135
[45] 'Radio Echoes and Cosmic Ray Showers', Patrick Blackett and Bernard Lovell, *Proceedings of the Royal Society*, Vol. 177, 1941, page 183-186

CHAPTER EIGHT – RETURN TO RESEARCH
[46] *Radar Days*, E.G. Bowen, Adam Hilger, Bristol, 1987, page 97

[47] *Radar Days*, E.G. Bowen, Adam Hilger, Bristol, 1987, page 138

[48] *A Scientists War, The War Diary of Sir Clifford Paterson*, R.J. Clayton & J. Algar, 1991

[49] *Radar Days*, E.G. Bowen, Adam Hilger, Bristol, 1987, page 143

[50] *One Story of Radar*, A.P. Rowe, Cambridge University Press, 1948, page 78

[51] 'A Personal History of the Development of CM Technique', Philip Dee, Lovell papers, the Imperial War Museum, BL 1/2

[52] An electronic device for generating microwaves.

[53] Ibid

[54] Diary, 12th June 1940, Lovell Papers, Royal Society, MS/870

[55] 'A Personal History of the Development of CM Technique', Philip Dee, Lovell papers, the Imperial War Museum, BL 1/2

[56] *Radar Days*, E.G. Bowen, Adam Hilger, Bristol, 1987, page 142

[57] 'The Cavity Magnetron', J.T. Randall, 1946, *Proceedings of the Physical Society*, 58, 247. *Fifty Years of the Cavity Magnetron*, W.E. Burcham & E.D.R. Shearman, 1990 (Birmingham University)

[58] 'Robert Watson-Watt, The Father of Radar', Hanbury-Brown, *Engineering Science and Educational Journal*, Vol. 3, Number 1, 1994

[59] *Echoes of War*, Bernard Lovell, Taylor and Francis, 1991, page 56

[60] Ministry of Information leaflet, 1940

[61] *Echoes of War*, Bernard Lovell, Taylor and Francis, 1991, page 53

[62] Report and photographs, Lovell papers, Imperial War Museum, 4/10

CHAPTER NINE – H2S

[63] Air to Surface Vessel.

[64] *One Story of Radar*, A.P. Rowe, Cambridge University Press, 1948, page 119

[65] *Most Secret War*, R.V. Jones, Hamish Hamilton, 1978, page 318-319

[66] *One Story of Radar*, A.P. Rowe, Cambridge University Press, 1948, page 116-117

[67] *The Hinge of Fate*, Winston Churchill, Cassell, 1951, page 250

[68] *Prof, the Life of Frederick Lindemann*, Adrian Fort, Jonathon Cape, 2003, page 236

[69] Butt Report to Bomber Command, 18 August 1941

[70] *The Hinge of Fate*, Winston Churchill, Cassell, 1951, page 250

[71] Ibid, page 250

[72] Ibid, page 250

[73] *One Story of Radar*, A.P. Rowe, Cambridge University Press, 1948, page 116

[74] Ibid, page 117

[75] *Echoes of War*, Bernard Lovell, Taylor and Francis, 1991, page 95
[76] Handley Page was knighted later that year.
[77] Report 12/106 (File D1738) Lovell TRE record, page 4
[78] Burcham Diary, 20th April, 1942, correspondence between Burcham and Lovell, Lovell Papers, John Ryland's Library, Manchester
[79] A full account of this important raid is given in Chapter 27 of *Most Secret War* by R.V. Jones, Hamish Hamilton, 1978
[80] *One Story of Radar*, A.P. Rowe, Cambridge University Press, 1948, page 136
[81] Ibid, page 131
[82] *The Hinge of Fate*, Winston Churchill, Cassell, 1951, page 251-253

CHAPTER TEN – DISASTER AND TRIUMPH
[83] *Echoes of War*, Bernard Lovell, Taylor and Francis, 1991, page 127
[84] Diary, June 8th 1942, Lovell Papers, Royal Society, MS/870
[85] *Echoes of War*, Bernard Lovell, Taylor and Francis, 1991, page 127
[86] *Astronomer by Chance*, Bernard Lovell, Macmillan, 1990, page 75
[87] Annexe 4 to *Aircraft for airborne radar development*, W.H. Sleigh, RSRE Malvern Malvern
[88] Diary, 10th July 1942, Lovell papers, Royal Society, M/S 870
[89] Lovell Papers, Imperial War Museum BL 1/2
[90] 'The Strategic Air Offensive against Germany 1939-1945', Webster and Frankland, *HMSO*, 1961, Vol. 3, page 229
[91] *The Hinge of Fate*, Winston Churchill, Cassell, 1951, page 253
[92] *Echoes of War*, Bernard Lovell, Taylor and Francis, 1991, page 141
[93] Ibid, page 143
[94] Ibid, page 146
[95] *Astronomer by Chance*, Bernard Lovell, Macmillan, 1990, page 84
[96] Both telegrams are in the Lovell papers at the Imperial War Museum BL 1/2
[97] Lovell papers, Imperial War Museum BL 1/2
[98] *Operational Use of H2S*, 9th February 1943, full report in Lovell Papers, Imperial War Museum BL 1/2
[99] 'The Cavity Magnetron in World War II: was the secrecy justified?', Bernard Lovell, Notes Rec. R. Soc. London, 58 (3), 283–294 (2004)
[100] Hachenberg Hachenberg ENGLISHERS RADAR-GERÄT Report, May 1943, Lovell papers, Imperial War Museum BL 1/2
[101] 'The Cavity Magnetron in World War II: was the secrecy justified?', Bernard Lovell, Notes Rec. R. Soc. Lond. 58 (3), 283–294 (2004)
[102] *Closing the Ring*, Winston Churchill, Cassell, 1951, page 6

CHAPTER ELEVEN – U-BOATS AND ROCKETS

[103] *Most Secret War*, R.V.Jones, Hamish Hamilton, 1978, Chapter 37

[104] Air to Surface Vessel radar.

[105] 'The War at Sea', S.W. Roskill, *HMSO*, 1970, Vol. 2, page 112

[106] *Echoes of War*, Bernard Lovell, Taylor and Francis, 1991, page 157

[107] *The U-boat*, Eberhard Rossler, Arms and Armour Press, 1981

[108] *Closing the Ring*, Winston Churchill, Cassell, 1951, page 10

[109] *Echoes of War*, Bernard Lovell, Taylor and Francis, 1991, page 158

[110] *Prof, the Life of Frederick Lindemann*, Adrian Fort, Jonathon Cape, 2003, page 275

[111] *Echoes of War*, Bernard Lovell, Taylor and Francis, 1991, page 161

[112] *The Radar Battle for the Bay of Biscay*, Lovell Papers, 1944, Imperial War Museum BL 4/15

[113] Ibid

[114] *Closing the Ring*, Winston Churchill, Cassell, 1951, page 10

[115] *The U-Boat*, Eberhard Rössler, Arms and Armour Press, 1981

[116] *The Battle of the Atlantic*, Costello and Hughes, Collins, 1997, page 281

[117] *Inside the Third Reich*, Albert Speer, Weidenfeld and Nicholson, page 292

[118] *Most Secret War*, R.V. Jones, Hamish Hamilton, 1978, Chapter 37

[119] *Echoes of War*, Bernard Lovell, Taylor and Francis, 1991, page 166

[120] *Inside the Third Reich*, Albert Speer, Weidenfeld and Nicholson, page 228, footnote

[121] *Closing the Ring*, Winston Churchill, Cassell, 1951, page 8

[122] *Prof, the Life of Frederick Lindemann*, Adrian Fort, Jonathan Cape, 2003, page 273, quote from the Donitz memoirs

[123] 'The War at Sea', S.W. Roskill, *HMSO*, 1970, Vol. 3, page 15

[124] *The Radar Battle for the Bay of Biscay*, Lovell Papers, 1944, Imperial War Museum BL 4/15

[125] Ibid

[126] *Most Secret War*, R.V. Jones, Hamish Hamilton, 1978, Chapter 37

[127] Ibid, Chapter 38

[128] *The Turn of the Tide*, Arthur Bryant, Collins, 1957, page 651

[129] *Inside the Third Reich*, Albert Speer, Weidenfeld and Nicholson

[130] *Closing the Ring*, Winston Churchill, Cassell, 1951, page 205

[131] Ibid, 207

[132] 'The Strategic Air Offensive Against Germany 1939-45', Webster and Frankland, *HMSO*, 1961, Vol. 2, page 284-287

[133] Ibid, page 284

[134] *Winston Churchill*, Elizabeth Longford, Sidgwick and Jackson, 1974, page 114

[135] *Crusade in Europe*, Dwight Eisenhower, Doubleday, 1948

CHAPTER TWELVE – THE ROAD TO VICTORY
[136] Imperial War Museum, Lovell Papers, BL/2
[137] Churchill gives a full description of Window in *The Hinge of Fate*, Cassell, 1951, page 257-259
[138] 'The Strategic Air Offensive Against Germany 1939-45', Webster and Frankland, *HMSO*, 1961, Vol. 2, page 197
[139] Diary, 7th June 1943, Lovell papers, Royal Society, MS/870
[140] *Echoes of War*, Bernard Lovell, Taylor and Francis, 1991, page 195
[141] Imperial War Museum, Air Marshal Sir John Slessor, letter to Bernard Lovell, BL/2
[142] Diary, 27th October 1943, Lovell papers, Royal Society, M/S 870
[143] Imperial War Museum, Lovell TRE record, page 30
[144] Ibid, page 36
[145] *Bernard Lovell: a Biography*, Dudley Saward, Robert Hale, 1984, page 115
[146] *In the Centre of Immensities*, Bernard Lovell, Hutchinson, 1979, page 6
[147] Ground Controlled Interception.
[148] 'The Strategic Air Offensive Against Germany 1939-45', Webster and Frankland, *HMSO*, 1961, Vol. 4, page 315
[149] The Oldie interview, 1992, Naim Attallah, *The Oldie* Magazine
[150] *Astronomer by Chance*, Bernard Lovell, Macmillan, 1990, page 104
[151] *Echoes of War*, Bernard Lovell, Taylor and Francis, 1991, page 145
[152] 'The Strategic Air Offensive Against Germany 1939-1945', Webster and Frankland, *HMSO*, 1961, Vol. 4, page 4
[153] Ibid, page 15
[154] Ibid, page 17
[155] 'Third Report of The Royal Commission on Awards to Inventors', *HMSO*, 1953
[156] Letter from Tait, Imperial War Museum, BL 1/2, page 83

CHAPTER THIRTEEN – COSMIC METEORS
[157] *The Ionizing Effects of Meteors*, A.M. Skellett, 1931
[158] Later published as 'Derivation of Meteor Stream Radiants by Radio Reflection Methods', *Nature*, 158, 5th October 1946
[159] A massive explosion in a white dwarf star, caused by the sudden ignition of hydrogen accumulated on the surface, followed by a violent nuclear fusion. Not to be confused with a supernova.
[160] *The Times*, 14th and 17th December 1934
[161] The closest approach of the comet to the Sun.
[162] Obituary of J.P.M. Prentice, Bernard Lovell, *Royal Astronomical Society*

Quarterly Journal, 1982, Vol. 23, page 452

[163] 'Radio Echo Observations of Meteors', Prentice Lovell and Banwell, *Royal Astronomical Society,* 1947, Vol. 107, page 155

[164] The names are derived from the constellation in which each shower appears.

[165] *The Observatory Magazine,* February 1947, Vol. 67

CHAPTER FOURTEEN – RADIO ASTRONOMER

[166] Diary, Lovell papers, Royal Society, MS/870

[167] Diary, 24th June 1946, Lovell papers, Royal Society, MS/870

[168] 'Radio Echoes and Cosmic Ray Showers', *Proceedings of the Royal Society,* 194, Vol. 177, page 183-186. The conclusion to the paper is set out at the end of Chapter 7

[169] 'Solar Radiations in the 4–6 Metre Radio Wave-Length Band', J.S. Hey, 1946, *Nature,* Vol. 157

[170] 'Radio Echoes from the Aurora Borealis', Lovell, Clegg and Ellyett, 1947, *Nature,* Vol. 160, page 372

[171] An antenna for transmitting or receiving of radio waves.

[172] The distance light will travel in one year at the speed of 186,000 miles per second.

[173] We now know that the galaxy contains between 200 and 400 billion stars.

[174] *The New York Times,* 5th May 1933

[175] The correspondence is in the John Ryland's Library, Lovell papers, JBA/CS7, Box 27 /3

[176] *Royal Astronomical Society Monthly Notices,* Vol. 111-113, 1951-1953

[177] Highly sensitive and precise electronic cable.

[178] 'Radio Emission From the Andromeda Nebula', R. Hanbury Brown and C. Hazard (communicated by A.C.B. Lovell), *Notices of the Royal Astronomical Society,* 1955, No 4

[179] The first account of these experiments can be found in *Nature,* Vol. 166, November 1950, 'Radio Frequency Radiation from the Great Nebula in Andromeda', Hanbury Brown and Hazard

CHAPTER FIFTEEN – A STEERABLE PARABOLOID

[180] 'Brief Notes on the Early Stages of the Paraboloid Negotiations', Bernard Lovell, Royal Society, MS/870

[181] Ibid

[182] *Astronomer by Chance,* Bernard Lovell, Macmillan, 1990, page 200

[183] 'Brief Notes on the Early Stages of the Paraboloid Negotiations', Bernard Lovell, Royal Society, MS/870

[184] Ibid
[185] Ibid
[186] Ibid
[187] Ibid
[188] Lovell Papers, John Ryland's Library, Manchester University, JBA/CS7 29/4
[189] *The Blue Book*, Lovell papers, John Ryland's Library, Manchester University
[190] *Journal of the Royal Society of Arts*, 5th August 1955, page 666
[191] One copy is lodged with the Lovell papers at John Ryland's Library, University of Manchester
[192] Set out on page 149 above .
[193] Diary, 24th May 1952, Lovell papers, Royal Society
[194] Ibid, 26th May 1952
[195] A full transcript fills six foolscap pages in the Diary, Lovell Papers, Royal Society, MS/870

CHAPTER SIXTEEN – HOW TO BUILD A TELESCOPE
[196] Diary, 20th February 1953, Lovell Papers, Royal Society, MS/870
[197] *The Story of Jodrell Bank*, Bernard Lovell, Oxford University Press, 1968, page 50
[198] Diary, 2nd April 1953, Lovell Papers, Royal Society, MS/870
[199] Letter from Husband to Rainford, 31st March 1955, Vice Chancellor's files, 1957-58, John Ryland's Library, Manchester
[200] *The Story of Jodrell Bank*, Bernard Lovell, Oxford University Press, 1968, page 48
[201] *Hansard*, 17th November 1953, Vol. 520, written answers, page 149
[202] Diary, 7th June 1955, Lovell Papers, Royal Society, MS/870
[203] *Hansard*, 12th July 1955, Vol. 548, written answers, page 163
[204] *The Toledo Blade*, Ohio, 9th February 1964
[205] Diary, 21st December 1953, Lovell Papers, Royal Society, MS/870
[206] Diary, 6th & 27th January 1955, Lovell Papers, Royal Society, MS/870
[207] Ibid, 11th September 1953
[208] Ibid, 15th March 1954
[209] Ibid, 28th October 1954
[210] Ibid, 22nd December 1954
[211] Ibid, 31st December 1954
[212] Now Simon Engineering PLC.
[213] Ibid, 10th December 1955
[214] *The Memoirs of the Rt. Hon. The Earl of Woolton Cassell*, 1959
[215] Vice Chancellor's files, August 1957- June 1958, John Ryland's

Library, Manchester University archives

[216] The University agreed to disclose the files to the author on 15th April 2013.

[217] Diary of Raymond Streat, John Ryland's Library, Manchester University Archives, GB 133

[218] *The Story of Jodrell Bank*, Bernard Lovell, Oxford University Press, 1968, page 150

[219] Diary, 9th April 1956, Lovell Papers, Royal Society

[220] Ibid, 6th March 1957

[221] Ibid, 25th March 1957

[222] Ibid, 12th June 1957

CHAPTER SEVENTEEN – CALLED TO ACCOUNT

[223] *Journal of the Royal Society of Arts*, 5th August 1955

[224] Diary, 16th August 1957, Lovell Papers, Royal Society

[225] Minutes of the Committee of Public Accounts, 21st March 1957

[226] Minutes of the Committee of Public Accounts, 21st March 1957

[227] The Report of the Committee of Public Accounts, 13th August 1957

[228] Vice Chancellors file, 1957-8, John Ryland's Library, Manchester University Archives

[229] Mansfield Cooper's note of meeting with Husband and solicitors, 14th February 1958, Vice Chancellor's files, John Ryland's Library, Manchester University Archives

[230] Diary, 19th August 1957, Lovell Papers, Royal Society

[231] Ibid, 23rd August 1957

[232] An international project for scientific cooperation, which was to run from the 1st July 1957 to 31st December 1958.

[233] Ibid, 2nd October 1957

CHAPTER EIGHTEEN – SPUTNIK

[234] *Manchester Guardian*, 7th October 1957

[235] *The Times*, 16th October 1957

[236] National Archive files, 8975596/PREM

[237] *Hansard*, HC Deb, 29th October 1957, Vol. 575, cc30-230

[238] Ministry of Defence document, National Archive Files, 6287280/DEFE

[239] See Chapter Sixteen.

[240] Diary, 1st January 1958, Lovell papers, Royal Society

[241] National Archive files, 442703/PREM

CHAPTER NINETEEN – RESURRECTION

[242] Correspondence in Vice Chancellors files 1957-58, John Ryland's Library, Manchester University Archives

[243] Diary of Raymond Streat, John Ryland's Library, Manchester University Archives, GB 133

[244] Correspondence in Vice Chancellors's files, 1957-8, John Ryland's Library, Manchester University Archives

[245] Minutes of the Committee of Public Accounts, 18th March 1958

[246] Diary of Raymond Streat, John Ryland's Library, Manchester University Archives, GB 133

[247] This is one of the documents placed in the secret 1957-58 Vice Chancellor's files

[248] *The Story of Jodrell Bank*, Bernard Lovell, Oxford University Press, 1968, page 202

[249] Minutes of the Committee of Public Accounts, 18th March 1958

[250] Ibid

[251] Ibid

[252] Note to Armitage dated 10th December 1979, filed in Vice Chancellors files 1957-58, John Ryland's Library, Manchester University Archives

[253] Report of Committee of Public Accounts, 18th March 1958

[254] Vice Chancellor's files 1957-58, John Ryland's Library, Manchester University Archives

[255] National Archives, Kew, 33378889/DEFE

[256] National Archives, Kew, 4097866/DEFE

[257] Pyotr Kapitza was awarded the Nobel Prize for Physics in 1978. He was one of the few Soviet scientists who was not a member of the Communist Party.

[258] *The Big Red Lie* was published by Mallen in 1959

[259] Roald Sagdeev, University of Maryland, USA, correspondence with author, 13th March 2013

CHAPTER TWENTY – REITH LECTURER

[260] The Lovell papers at the Royal Society contain all the Reith lecture correspondence

[261] Joseph Addison's hymn, 1712

[262] *Sunday Times*, 8th February 1959

[263] *Sunday Times*, 22nd February 1959

CHAPTER TWENTY-ONE – SPACE WARS

[264] Arc is a curved line. The Moon and the Sun each cover half a degree of arc, so when the Moon is in front of the Sun it creates a total eclipse.

[265] An arc minute is one sixtieth of a degree and an arc second is one sixtieth of an arc minute.

[266] Lovell and Chugainov, *Nature,* Vol. 203, 1964

[267] The first publication about pulsars was in 1968.

[268] Professor Vladimir Kurt, Lebedev Institute, Russian Academy of Sciences, letter to author February 2013

[269] Roald Sagdeev, University of Maryland, USA, correspondence with author, March 2013

[270] Formerly Cape Canaveral. Renamed in memory of J.F. Kennedy.

[271] The documents relating to this episode are now declassified in the National Archives, Kew, AIR/20/12162

Chapter Twenty-Two – The Incidental Spy

[272] The Sheffield conference on 16th November 1950 was chaired by Dr. Hewlett Johnson, the 'Red Dean', and it broke up in confusion.

[273] *Astronomer by Chance*, Bernard Lovell, Macmillan, 1990, page 187

[274] National Archives, Kew, KV 2/2884-2886, 1936-1958

[275] A copy is in the Astbury file in the National Archive, Kew KV 2/2884-2886 1936-1958

[276] Ibid

[277] Ibid

[278] Diary, following the 1945 election, Lovell Papers, Royal Society, MS/870

[279] 'Remembering the Rosenbergs', New York Times, June 19th 2003

[280] The documents can be found in the National Archives, Kew, DBS KI AIR/20/12162

[281] Professor Leonid Matveenko, Soviet Academy of Sciences, correspondence with author, May 29th 2013

[282] Diary of trip to Russia, Lovell papers, John Ryland's Library, Manchester

[283] About £20 million

[284] National Archive, Kew, DBS KI Archive, PREM/11/5070

[285] Letter from Lord Hailsham to Julian Amery, 4th September 1963

[286] National Archive, Kew, DBS KI, DEFE 44/80D.S.I. Report No. 227

Chapter Twenty-Three – Renaissance Man

[287] Pronounced 'aretay'

[288] Vulgaria, Robert Whittington, 1520

[289] Now out of print but available on the internet, published 1977

[290] Markus Fierz, physicist, 1912-2006

[291] Two shillings and sixpence, in old money, which had twenty shillings to the pound

Chapter Twenty-Five – Forty Years Onward

[292] Jessie Seymour Irvine's setting of the 23rd Psalm

Glossary

With grateful acknowledgement to Francis Graham Smith for permission to raid the glossary of *Pathways to the Universe*, by Francis Graham Smith and Bernard Lovell

AI Air interception radar.

AMRE The Air Ministry Research Establishment.

Andromeda Galaxy Large nearby spiral galaxy. The only one that can be seen with the naked eye.

Angular Diameter The angular dimension of a distant object. The sun and the moon both have an angular diameter of 0.5 degrees, so when the moon is in front of the sun we get a total eclipse. By measuring the angular diameter of remote stars and galaxies and ascertaining their distance from earth, their size can be calculated, even when the angle is only a few thousand seconds of arc. The measurement is a key factor in determining the size and nature of celestial bodies.

Arc Minute Unit used to measure the size of small angles equal to one sixtieth of a degree.

Arc Second Unit used to measure very small angles, equal to one sixtieth of an arc minute or 1/3600 of a degree.

Aurora Luminous curtains or streamers of light seen in the night sky at high northerly or southerly latitudes, caused by electrically charged particles from the sun streaming into the Earth's atmosphere, guided by its magnetic field.

ASV Air to surface vessel radar.

Azimuth The complete horizontal circle of 360 degrees round a given point. The Lovell telescope spins in azimuth like a top at the same time as moving in elevation or declination through the vertical point or zenith. It can thus be pointed at any part of the sky.

Cathode, Cathode Ray Tube A cathode is an electrode through which an electric current can flow. A cathode ray tube is a vacuum tube that generates beams of electrons. The beams are projected onto a fluorescent screen at the end of the tube. Televisions work on this principle.

Cavity Magnetron Invented by J.T. Randall and H.A. Boot, at Birmingham University, it consists of a block of copper drilled through with cylindrical cavities. Magnets on the outer shell of the copper block excite electrons emitted by the cathode within it to a very high level so that they produce powerful microwave signals. The energy created is so great that it can be used to transmit radio waves on a narrow beam through a small aerial for use in airborne radar systems. It is familiar as the power source of the microwave oven.

Centimetre Radar A radar system producing a narrow beam on a short wavelength from a small aerial. Used in the H2S devices created by Lovell for AI, ASV and blind bombing of land targets. The invention of the cavity magnetron (q.v.) enabled sufficient power to be generated for the system to operate.

Chain Home (CH) The network of radar stations which provided the first line of defence from German bombers. It stretched round the coastline from Portsmouth to the Firth of Forth.

Cloud Chamber Invented by C.T.R. Wilson in 1911, a device which can be used to track the ionised trail of charged particles. Moist air is cooled in a chamber and then subjected to high pressure by a system of pistons. The intensity of the cold mist allows the ionised trail of particles to become visible as they enter the chamber. These can be photographed through a glass window in the chamber. Geiger counters instantly detect the entry of a particle and trigger the pistons, a beam of light and the camera.

Cosmic Rays Charged subatomic particles in space emanating from the remnants of supernova explosions and solar flares. When they collide with the earth's atmosphere a variety of particles are created. These highly penetrating particles invade the atmosphere and are present all around us in large numbers. Some, such as muons, constantly fly undetected through our heads and bodies. There goes another one!

Dipole Antenna Simple rod-like aerial for collecting radio waves.

Doppler Effect The change in the observed frequency of sound and electromagnetic waves, when the source of the waves is moving towards or away from the observer. Familiar to us in the sound of a police siren – as it comes towards us the frequency is greater and the sound more high pitched – when it passes us and recedes the frequency is lengthened and the sound trends to basso profundo. Radio waves and light evince similar effects depending on their direction of travel. (See Redshift)

DSIR The Department of Scientific and Industrial Research.

Electromagnetic Spectrum Energy with wave-like properties, consisting of oscillations in linked electric and magnetic fields. The character of the radiation depends on its wavelength. From long to short wavelengths, the different names given to electromagnetic radiation are radio waves, infrared radiation, visible light, ultraviolet light, X-rays and gamma-rays. Under some physical circumstances, the radiation has particle-like properties, as if the energy exists only in discrete 'packets', which are termed photons.

Flare Stars Red dwarf stars whose temperature and mass are lower than the sun. They are subject to sudden bursts of brightness caused by massive flares, much larger than sun flares; these cause strong radio emissions which can be observed in tandem with the optical flares.

GEE Navigation aid used in bombers from March 1942. Groups of three transmitters, some miles apart, sent radar signals which could be picked up in an aircraft. By measuring the distance of each signal at any given moment, the navigator could ascertain the position of the aircraft. The range was limited by the curvature of the earth, but within that range aircraft could be directed accurately over enemy territory.

Ground Returns Airborne radar operating on a waveband of 1.5 metres produces a wide beam which hits the ground ahead of the aircraft at the same distance as the height at which it was flying, so that the echo from a target plane which is more than that distance ahead is obscured by the echoes from the ground. When flying at 10,000 feet, for example, the reflection from any airborne object more than 10,000 feet away becomes muddled by the ground returns from below; as the normal flying height of aircraft deployed during the early years of World War II was no more than 15,000 feet, on board radar contact with enemy aircraft was restricted to a maximum of less than three miles. This problem was solved with the invention of the cavity magnetron which facilitated the use of centimetre radar.

H2S The navigational aid developed by Bernard Lovell to operate in the centimetre waveband. It was of vital importance to the war effort and is fully described in the text.

ICBM An intercontinental ballistic missile.

Interferometer A combination of telescopes, separated by distance and receiving electromagnetic waves that originate from the same source but have travelled through slightly different paths before being collected. The method is used particularly in radio astronomy, where the signals received by pairs or groups of radio telescopes are linked, in order to achieve a high angular resolution.

Klystron A vacuum tube used to generate and amplify microwaves. An American invention, it was used to transmit the signals from radar equipment operating below the 10-centimetre wave band, but was supplanted by the much more powerful cavity magnetron.

Leigh Light A powerful searchlight attached beneath the nose of Coastal Command Wellington bombers. On close approach to a U-boat the light would be switched on, enabling the bomber to make an accurate attack and destroy the enemy vessel. Invented by Commander Leigh of Coastal Command.

Light Year Unit of distance, frequently used in astronomy, equal to the distance light travels in a vacuum in one year, travelling at 183,000 miles per second.

Metox A device fixed to the conning towers of U-boats during the autumn of 1942. It gave the crew early warning of the approach of British aircraft, so that they could surface to recharge their batteries at night but still have time to dive before they were attacked. Bernard Lovell's adaptation of H2S for use as an ASV device emasculated Metox from March 1943. The German Navy never recovered.

Magnitude Measure of brightness of an astronomical object.

Meteors and Meteor Showers The familiar shooting stars, which are caused when the residual particles from comets cross the path of the earth and burn up as they enter the atmosphere. Sporadic meteors occur throughout the year; the meteor showers from certain comets create spectacular firework displays at certain predictable times. The showers occur regularly throughout the year and are identified by the background stars or constellations from which they appear to emanate.

Microwave Background Radiation The residue of the hot dense state of the universe following the expansion from its infinitely small and infinitely dense origin. The discovery of the microwave background radiation by Penzias and Wilson at the Bell Laboratory in America in 1965 settled the dispute between the protagonists of the steady state and big bang theories in favour of the latter.

Nebula The Latin word for cloud, used loosely in astronomy to describe any misty or extended source of light in contrast to the point-like image of a star. In a stricter sense, it is used to describe features of gas and dust rather than clusters of stars or galaxies. The most familiar and easily observed nebula lies in the constellation of Orion, which can be seen during the winter months in the northern hemisphere.

Neutron Star A star composed almost entirely of neutrons, which form as the core of a dying star collapses inwards. Neutron stars have a mass of one or more solar masses contained in a diameter of only a few miles. Pulsars have been identified as being neutron stars.

Oboe First used by the RAF in December 1942 as a bombing aid. Two ground based transmitter stations were used to guide aircraft to the targets. It was very accurate, but the range was limited by the curvature of the earth. Initially only one bomber could be guided every ten minutes, but later the Mosquito aircraft were used to drop marker flares to great effect.

PAC The Public Accounts Committee of the Westminster Parliament which scrutinises public expenditure.

Particles The basic constituents of matter. In the early part of the twentieth century atoms were found to comprise electrons and protons. Further studies and experiments have revealed a large number of particles including neutrons, neutrinos, quarks and muons and theoretical models such as the Higgs Bosun continue to be the subject of research at CERN and elsewhere.

Polar Diagram The nature and shape of radio beams. These depend on the aperture of the aerial and on the wavelength.

Pulsar A cosmic radio source emitting rapid pulses of as they rotate at high speed. Pulsars are the collapsed remnants of supernova explosions. They are very small and extremely dense, being no more than a few miles in diameter and yet containing all the matter from the original star.

Quasar A distant compact object which has the appearance of a star but has a redshift characteristic of a very remote object. Originally called quasi stellar objects, quasars were discovered in 1963 as the optical counterparts of powerful extragalactic radio sources. The redshifts correspond with velocities approaching the speed of light implying that they are billions of light years distant. They are among the most luminous objects in the universe.

Radiant point Meteor showers appear to enter the atmosphere from a particular point in the sky and radiate out as they burn up in the atmosphere. The Showers are named from the part of the sky from which they emerge, usually by reference to the background stars or galaxies.

Radio Direction Finding (RDF) The original name for radar, which operates by transmitting a radio signal, travelling at the speed of light. When the signal hits a solid object it bounces back as an echo, which is picked up by a receiver so that the presence of the solid object and its position can be calculated.

Radio Galaxy A galaxy that is an intense source of radio waves. The radiation comes from two sources, one on each side of the galaxy and is generated by electrons travelling through a magnetic field at close to the speed of light.

Radio Stars Sources of radio activity which did not correspond with visible objects. Originally classified as dark stars within the Milky Way, by the early 1960s it became clear that they are stars and galaxies which are powerful radio transmitters from the depths of space.

RAS The Royal Astronomical Society.

Redshift The displacement of visible light from distant objects towards longer wavelengths at the red end of the spectrum. It indicates that the object is travelling away from the observer as the universe expands.

Supernova The explosion of a star at the end of its life, accompanied by a sudden burst of brightness which increases billions of times and can seen on earth thousands or millions of light years after it has occurred. The crab nebula in the Milky Way is the residue of a supernova observed by Chinese astronomers in 1054.

Transit Telescope A fixed instrument which relies on the passage of the heavens above it to make observations, rather than its own ability to move.

TRE The Telecommunications Research Established, originally AMRE.

Wavelengths Like everything else in the electromagnetic spectrum, including light, radio signals travel in waves. The wavelength of a given signal is the distance from the peak of one wave to the peak of the next. Long wavelengths move in large waves on a wide beam and at a low frequency; shortwave lengths are small, have a high frequency and travel on a narrow beam. For any given wavelength it is possible to obtain a narrower and more precise beam by increasing the size of the aerial; and for any given aerial, the polar diagram narrows as the wavelength is reduced; so for precise radar observation in aircraft, what was required was a small aerial with an output on the lowest possible wavelength, giving the narrowest and most precise possible beam.

Yagi Aerial An aerial invented by the Japanese Hidetsugu Yagi in 1928, which is capable of producing a narrow beam for transmitting or receiving radio waves.

Zenith The point immediately overhead at 90 degrees to the horizon.

Bibliography

Bowen, E.G., *Radar Days*, Adam Hilger, 1987

Bryant, A., *The Turn of the Tide*, Collins, 1957

Clayton, R.J. & Algar, J., *A Scientists War, The War Diary of Sir Clifford Paterson*, IET, 1991

Churchill, W.S., *Closing the Ring*, Cassell, 1951

Churchill, W.S., *The Gathering Storm*, Cassell, 1948

Churchill, W.S., *The Hinge of Fate*, Cassell, 1951

Costello, J. and Hughes, T., *The Battle of the Atlantic*, Collins, 1997

Eisenhower, D., *Crusade in Europe*, Doubleday, 1948

Fort, A.M.S., Prof, *The Life of Frederick Lindemann*, Jonathon Cape, 2003

Graham-Smith F. and Lovell A.C.B., *Pathways to the Universe*, Cambridge University Press, 1988

Jones, R.V., *Most Secret War*, Hamish Hamilton, 1978

Longford, E., *Winston Churchill*, Longford Sidgwick and Jackson, 1974

Lovell, A.C.B., *Astronomer by Chance*, Macmillan, 1990

Lovell, A.C.B., *Echoes of War*, Taylor and Francis, 1991

Lovell, A.C.B., *In the Centre of Immensities*, Hutchinson, 1979

Lovell, A.C.B., *The Story of Jodrell Bank*, Oxford University Press, 1968

Morton, H.V., *In Search of England*, Methuen, 1925

Phillips, D., *Biographical Memoirs of Fellows of the Royal Society*, 1979, 25 74-143, Bragg

Roskill, S.W., *The War at Sea*, HMSO, 1970

Rossler, E., *The U-boat*, Arms and Armour Press, 1981

Rowe, A.P., *One Story of Radar*, Cambridge University Press, 1948

Saward, D., *Bernard Lovell, A Biography*, Robert Hale, 1984

Speer, A., *Inside the Third Reich*, Weidenfeld and Nicholson, 2003

Watson-Watt, R., *Three Steps to Victory*, Odhams, 1957

Webster, C. and Frankland, N., *The Strategic Air Offensive against Germany 1939-1945*, HMSO, 1961

Woolton, the Earl of, *The Memoirs of the Rt. Hon. The Earl of Woolton*, Cassell, 1959

Index